THE PARTY SYSTEM IN GREAT BRITAIN

Party is organized opinion.

Benjamin Disraeli

The Author

Ivor Bulmer-Thomas is well qualified to write a study of the British Party System, not only by virtue of academic attainment—he took a First in " Greats " at Oxford—but by reason of a wide practical experience of its working. He was the Labour MP for Keighley from 1942-49, becoming Parliamentary Secretary, Ministry of Civil Aviation in 1945; and Parliamentary Under-Secretary of State for the Colonies 1946-47; he joined the Conservative Party in 1949 and contested Newport (Mon.) in 1950. He was before the war for seven years on the editorial staff of *The Times*; was chief leader writer for the *News Chronicle* from 1937-39, and now he is Deputy Editor of the *Daily Telegraph*; he has written seven other books. He believes that the British party system, for all its shortcomings, is the best way yet found for settling what the policy of this country shall be. " But for its successful working," he says, " it depends upon a spirit of mutual tolerance which cannot be manufactured but may be found in the Smoking Room of the House of Commons."

THE
PARTY SYSTEM
IN GREAT BRITAIN

by

IVOR BULMER-THOMAS

Formerly M.P. for Keighley and
Parliamentary Under-Secretary of State
for the Colonies

PHOENIX HOUSE LTD
LONDON

To the memory of
THE RT. HON.
WILLIAM EWART GLADSTONE
'the rising hope of those stern and unbending Tories'
four times Prime Minister
in a Liberal administration
for nearly sixty-three years a member of Parliament
this work is dedicated by the author
in gratitude for the year spent at his foundation of
St. Deiniol's Library,
Hawarden

Printed in Great Britain
by Western Printing Services Ltd., of Bristol, for
Phoenix House, Ltd., 38 William IV Street, Charing Cross, W.C.2

First published 1953

Preface

WHEN THE WRITING of this book was suggested to me my first thought was that it would be superfluous. But when I came to examine the published literature of the subject I found that no systematic study of the British party system had been made since *The Government of England*, by A. Lawrence Lowell, president of Harvard University, which was first published in 1908 and went into a new edition in 1912. The section on the party system in that work is, however, only one of eight different subjects treated, and it is hardly an exaggeration to say that no systematic study of the British party system has been made since M. Ostrogorski, a French professor of Russian origin, published *La démocratie et l'organisation des partis politiques*, which was translated into English in 1902 under the title *Democracy and the Organisation of Political Parties*.[1] Fifty years is a long time in itself, and these fifty years have not only been momentous in the history of the country but have seen the collapse of the Liberal party, the rise of the Labour party to the position of one of two chief parties in the state, the disappearance of the southern Irish members from Westminster, attempts to create nationalist parties in Wales and Scotland, the birth of the Communist party and the proliferation of minor parties. Despite all these changes the pattern of British public life maintains an impressive continuity, but it is high time that someone should do for the parties to-day what Ostrogorski did at the turn of the century; and an essay which I have recently contributed to *Parliament: A Survey*, edited by Lord Campion, and a series of essays in the Hansard Society's journal *Parliamentary Affairs* which appeared as this book went to the publishers, and have now been issued as a book under the title *The British Party System*, only emphasize the need.[2] As I look back on what I have written, I am

[1] The select bibliography given in an appendix includes general reflexions on the party system, histories of periods in the life of particular parties, and expositions of the aims of the parties, but no systematic study of the British party system as a whole in recent years.

[2] It must also be admitted that Ostrogorski's book, for all its great merits in dealing with its period, suffers from the defect of seeing British politics from the outside; and it may be doubted whether Ostrogorski fully understood all the influences at work. He was led in consequence to adopt a rather cynical attitude to party politics. Even Bryce, in his preface to the English edition, felt constrained to protest: 'Leniency is indeed the last thing he shows to any party; and it is only in respect to the Rhadamanthine attitude he preserves throughout that I feel bound to utter a note of mild dissent. . . . I cannot but think that M. Ostrogorski exaggerates the power and the poison of what he calls the caucus in England, and that he does not quite sufficiently allow for the healthy influences that are at work to correct whatever dangers its growth may involve.' (*Loc. cit.*, vol. i, pp. xlii–xliii.)

v

conscious of how much more there is to be said, and can regard it only as a first attempt to fill the most conspicuous gap in the literature of British politics; but I could not decline the task as it was impressed upon me that I had one qualification for doing it in that I have seen the two major parties from the inside, both as a candidate and as a member of Parliament.[1] In writing this book I have supplemented my own knowledge by questions put to members of the staff of most of the parties at work to-day, and I am grateful for their help. I am particularly grateful to Mr. James Orr-Ewing, Conservative agent in South Kensington, for reading the proofs and making many valuable suggestions.

This is not intended to be mainly a work of history, and I cannot pretend to have done more than sketch what Dr. Trevelyan in his Romanes lecture called 'this vast, unwritten theme of party history'. As he so truly says, 'the history of party, if it ever came to be fully written, would be a new method of approach to English history as a whole'. It would frustrate the purpose of this book if I were to attempt to rewrite the history of England from a new angle, nor have I the leisure and the competence to do it. But I have given so much of the history of party organization before 1900 as is essential to set the subject in its proper perspective; and I have dealt in somewhat greater detail with the development of parties in the present century. I have not attempted to state the principles and policies for which the various parties stand. This is done in many books, and is done by the parties themselves at each general election. It is best done for each party either by that party officially or by one of its own members. Most of the following pages are devoted to the organization of the parties and to a study of the working of the party system in practice. This is where the existing literature of the subject is most notably defective. I have not shrunk from pointing out tendencies that seem to me undesirable wherever they may arise, but I have attempted to do so impartially, and if I have erred in any matter of fact I shall be glad to be informed.

I.B.-T.

London, *January 1953*

---

[1] When I fought my first election as a Labour candidate in 1935 a woman said to me 'Call yourself a Socialist! Why, you drink, and go to church; you're nothing but a Tory!' This was a refreshing point of view for which, considered historically, there is much to be said. Thirteen years passed before I felt obliged to admit that my Yorkshire interlocutor was right, and that I was 'nobbut a Tory'. I 'crossed the floor' of the House of Commons, and after a short period without party label sat in the remainder of that Parliament as a Conservative; and I fought the next election as a Conservative candidate. But these differences with former colleagues are not reflected in this book, which is not concerned with the substance of policy, but only with the manner of its making.

CONTENTS

Preface   v

PART I: GROWTH OF THE PARTIES

Chap. I. Parties and the Constitution   3
     II. Origin of the Party System   7
    III. Growth of Party Organization   12
     IV. Conservatives and Liberals: and Some
          Others   29
      V. Entry of the Labour Party   38
     VI. Eclipse of the Liberal Party, 1918–1931   47
    VII. Labour's Allies and Rivals, 1918–1931   49
   VIII. The Parties Reshuffled, 1931–1951   57

PART II: THE TWO-PARTY SYSTEM

     IX. Rout of the Lesser Candidates, 1950–1951   83
      X. Demand for Electoral Reform   92

PART III: PARTY ORGANIZATION

     XI. Parliamentary Party Organization   109
    XII. Constituency Party Organization   133
   XIII. Regional, National and International
          Organization   147
    XIV. Parliament and Outside Bodies   188
     XV. Party Conferences   196
    XVI. Selection of Candidates   204

PART IV: THE FRINGE OF PARTIES

   XVII. Ancillary Organizations   213
  XVIII. Non-party Political Organizations   221
    XIX. Parties and the Press   231
     XX. Parties and Religion   247

PART V: SOME CURRENT PROBLEMS

    XXI. Parties and Individuals   259
   XXII. Parties and Local Government   274
  XXIII. Future of the Parties   283
         Epilogue   296
         Select Bibliography   311
         Index   325

Part I

Growth of the Parties

CHAPTERS I–VIII

B

Parties and the Constitution

THE FIRST FACT that needs to be noted about the British party system may seem rather startling. The British party system is unknown to the constitution.[1]

We need not take this too tragically. The office of Prime Minister was also unknown to the constitution until Chequers was presented to the nation and an act of Parliament became necessary in 1917 for its acceptance as 'the official country residence of the British Prime Minister'. No one will deny, however, that from 1714 onwards one of his Majesty's ministers, usually the First Lord of the Treasury in modern times, has also been Prime Minister, or at any rate prime minister, although he did not receive that title in acts of Parliament or other official documents. It is equally true that the British party system has been for several centuries the pivot round which our constitutional processes turn, though the names and even the existence of parties are sedulously ignored in all official documents.

When a man stands for Parliament he does so as John Bull, Esquire, of 1 Gladstone Avenue, Beaconsfield, Barrister-at-law, or whatever his name, address and description may be. The constitution blandly ignores any arrangements he may have with other persons for securing his election. In the eyes of the constitution, he is an individual of a certain address and occupation and the constitution cares nothing—knows nothing—about his membership of a party. All he has to do if he wishes to stand for Parliament in the division of Little Wisdom is to find one elector of Little Wisdom to propose him, another to second him, and eight others to assent to his nomination, and to put down £150 as a deposit which will be returned to him if he gets one-eighth of the votes cast. It is laid down by the Representation of the People Act, 1949,[2] that the nomination paper shall state the full names, place of residence and description of the candidate, but it is hastily added, 'The description shall not refer to the candidate's political activities'. The description usually given is the candidate's occupation, *e.g.* miner, or

---

[1] Some might say, 'To the written constitution'; or that the place of parties in the constitution is governed by custom or convention rather than by law.
[2] Second Schedule, Parliamentary Election Rules, Rule 7.

3

style, *e.g.* Privy Councillor or K.B.E. It is now rare for a candidate to describe himself as 'gentleman'. The fiction that the candidate is a simple individual filled with a desire to serve his country in Parliament is encouraged by the fact that if he is adopted as the candidate of a local party association the very next act of the association is to dissolve itself until the election is over. When polling day comes and the elector enters the polling station, he is given a ballot paper with the surnames of the candidates printed in large capitals, and their other names, place of residence and description printed in ordinary type. Unless he has taken the trouble to inform himself before he enters the polling station —and admittedly the various parties do their best to enlighten him in the preceding weeks—he will get no guidance about Mr. Bull's or any other candidate's party affiliations. When the names of the candidates are similar, as in the contest between Ivor Guest and Haden Guest in Brecon and Radnor in 1935, or between Perkins and Parkins in South Gloucestershire in 1950 and 1951,[1] it is tempting to simplify the voter's task by adding 'Conservative' or 'Labour' as the case may be, but constitutionalists shrink from the suggestion, and rightly as I shall hope to show, even though I should not care to assert that every voter in Brecon and Radnor or in South Gloucestershire in the cases mentioned cast his vote as he had intended. The only guidance offered in such cases under the Representation of the People Act, 1949,[2] is that if a candidate's surname is the same as another candidate's, small capitals may be used for his other names; and if his other names are also the same as the other candidate's, small capitals may be used either for his description or for his residence, unless each of them is the same as that of another candidate with the same names. At this point the draughtsmen throw in their hands.

If Mr. Bull gets more votes than anyone else, it is the duty of the returning officer to say, 'I declare Bull elected'—not 'I declare the Conservative (or Labour) candidate to be successful'. (I have once seen a lady mayor wave her cocked hat from the town hall balcony and call out 'We've won', but this was a momentary lapse in the excitement of victory and is not to be taken as a precedent). When Mr. Bull goes to Westminster he will find that his official position is 'the honourable member for Little Wisdom' and that the House of Commons officially takes no cognisance of his party affiliations. If he makes a speech the

---

[1] An even more remarkable coincidence was reported in the *Daily Express* of 24 December 1951. It was announced that a retiring councillor, William Henry Smith, of Hall Green, Birmingham, was to have as his opponent another William Henry Smith.

[2] Second Schedule, Appendix.

newspapers will describe it as by Mr. J. Bull (Con., Little Wisdom) or
Mr. J. Bull (Lab., Little Wisdom) or in some other appropriate way,
but in *Hansard* it will be reported as by Mr. J. Bull (Little Wisdom), and
every attempt to make the editor of *Hansard* introduce party labels has
been successfully resisted. When there is cross-voting in the lobbies it
is always interesting to see who has strayed from his usual fold, and
the newspapers always give the information, but the official *Votes and
Proceedings* gives no clue; if Mr. Churchill were one day to vote with the
Labour party or Mr. Attlee with the Conservatives it would be front-
page news for the newspapers, but the *Votes and Proceedings* would
take no more notice of it than if they had voted the other way round. It
is too much to expect that this studious avoidance of party labels in the
official publications should be followed by members in their speeches,
but the hand of tradition is heavy, and direct references to members'
party affiliations are rare. When a member wishes to refer to other
members of his own party he will normally say 'My honourable
friends', and occasionally an older phrase will be heard, such as 'Those
with whom I normally associate'.

But Mr. John Bull, M.P., soon finds that although parties are never
mentioned in official publications, and seldom on the floor of the
House, they govern almost every action of his parliamentary life as
they governed his election. No one has a right to any particular place
in the House, unless he puts a card there before prayers and occupies it
during prayers. But in practice members of the same party always tend
to sit together, encouraging each other at appropriate moments with
that curious chant of 'Hear, hear' known as 'Cheers'; and not only do
members of the same party sit together but the gradations within a
party, whether of seniority or of opinion, also tend to get associated
with particular benches, so that sitting in the right place becomes a
high ritual act. The Speaker is absolutely free to call on any member
he pleases to open, continue or close a debate; but John Bull will soon
observe that by a mysterious process the Speaker's choice nearly always
falls on two leading members of opposed parties to open a big debate
and another pair to close it, while in between his eye tends to get caught
by members of opposite parties in turn. Party enters into almost every
action and decision of the House, from the election of a Speaker to
the question whether the House should sit beyond 10.30 p.m.; for the
division lists on these questions will be found to contain almost the
same names as on the nationalization of steel, or on other big issues of
policy. If Mr. John Bull, M.P., deliberately or inadvertently strays into
an unexpected lobby, he will find eyebrows raised next day, and if he

does it often he will be asked for an explanation, not only by his party associates in the House but by those who worked for his return in his constituency. Mr. Bull finds before long that the business of Parliament is ground out between two mighty party machines and, while he may regret that there is not more scope for individual action, he will reflect that if there were no parties the country's business would largely go undone. He will accept the position that he can best do what he wants to do in Parliament through his party, and he will realize that if he wishes to retain his seat in Parliament it is not sufficient to find ten people who will put their names to his nomination paper at the next election; he must have the backing in his constituency of a party organization which will say 'Vote for Bull' and be able to get enough people to do so. The party system may be still unknown to the constitution, but Mr. Bull had better familiarize himself with it if he wants to be useful in Parliament and to reappear there after the next appeal to the country.[1]

[1] It is very common, I am told, for presiding officers at parliamentary as well as local government elections to be asked for the names of the Conservative and Labour candidates. They always decline to give the information. There are usually members of the party just outside the building who will readily supply it.

—— II ——

Origin of the Party System

THE ORIGINS of the British party system go back a long way. Two of the British parties in existence to-day, the Conservatives and Liberals, are generally regarded as having a continuous history from the Tories and Whigs of the reign of Charles II. There are, indeed, some who would go still farther back. Dr. Johnson used to say 'the first Whig was the devil', as being the leader of the heavenly opposition, but we need not take him too literally; and it is only a strong partisan spirit that finds the first Whig in Cain, who slew his Tory brother Abel. But even so sober a historian as Mr. Keith Feiling believes that the first germs of Whig and Tory in England may be dated from the wedding of Henry VIII to Anne Boleyn;[1] and Mr. S. B. Chrimes,[2] while admitting that parties in our sense of the word could not come into existence until quite modern times, is of opinion that the roots of our parties must be sought in the middle ages, inasmuch as 'the struggles for power in the later medieval and early modern era were real, and at times violent, and sometimes resulted in a genuine shift of the balance of political power, and were necessary preludes to modern developments'. The opposition of Whigs and Tories certainly arose out of the strife of Roundheads and Cavaliers in the Civil War; and although we may not call the Roundheads and Cavaliers political parties in the modern sense of the term, the party system had undoubtedly taken shape by 1679 when those members of Parliament who supported the Bill to exclude James, Duke of York, from the Throne were dubbed Whigs and those who opposed it were named Tories. The names were not compliment-ary.[3] 'Whig' is probably a shorter form of whiggamore, and the whiggamores were a body of insurgents from the west of Scotland who in 1648 marched on Edinburgh. The name Whig was properly given to adherents of the Presbyterian cause in Scotland in the latter half of the seventeenth century and was applied to the exclusioners in derision.

[1] *A History of the Tory Party, 1640–1714*, p. 13. It is true, as mentioned below, that he regards the original Tory party as having disappeared in 1714 and a new Tory party as having come into existence with the death of the younger Pitt.
[2] *Parliamentary Affairs*, vol. v, no. 1, winter 1951, p. 1. (*The British Party System*, p. 1.)
[3] See the *Oxford English Dictionary*, from which this information is drawn.

7

The term Tory, an anglicized form of an Irish word meaning a pursuer, was even less polite. In its original sense it was used in the seventeenth century to denote one of the dispossessed Irish who became outlaws and lived by killing and plundering the English settlers and soldiers. It was equivalent to 'bog trotter'. It was applied by the exclusioners to their opponents because they noticed that the Duke of York tended to favour Irishmen for his friends. A delightful example of the way the names Tory and Whig were bandied about may be found in Narcissus Luttrell's *A Brief Historical Relation of State Affairs* for the year 1681: 'The latter party have been called by the former Whigs, fanaticks, covenanteers, bromigham protestants, etc.; and the former are called by the latter, tories, tantivies, Yorkists, high flown church men.' But these nicknames, given in derision, were accepted with pride, and from 1679 onwards they were regularly used to denote the two great parties in Parliament. Mr. Nigel Birch aptly compares the way in which the survivors of the British Expeditionary Force derided by the Kaiser in 1914 as a 'contemptible little army' gloried in the name 'Old Contemptibles'.[1]

The original Tory party was eclipsed in 1714 and the country was ruled by Whig governments for most of the century. According to one view, enjoying the support of Mr. Keith Feiling's great name,[2] the original Tory party disappeared in 1714 and no Tory party existed, in the modern sense of party, perhaps till the death of the younger Pitt. According to another view, which most active Tory politicians like to hold, their party was only in abeyance and 'the essential and permanent character' of Toryism has remained unchanged from Bolingbroke to the present day. It has been equally argued whether the Whigs of 1832 are to be regarded as identified with the cause 'for which Hampden died on the field and Sidney on the scaffold'. According to Mr. R. J. Cruikshank,[3] 'The first politicians to be called Liberals in this country were the immediate heirs of the Whigs of the eighteenth century—or, to put it more truthfully, of Charles James Fox's new Whigs'. The question is of little consequence except for students of history, as the good things achieved in the struggles of the old Tories and Whigs—the safeguarding of the reformation settlement in the Church of England with toleration alike for Roman Catholics and Protestant dissenters, the establishment of the King's position as a constitutional sovereign, the definition of his relations with Parliament, and the development of representative government—have now become

---

[1] *The Conservative Party*, p. 7.   [2] *The Second Tory Party 1714–1832*, p. v.
[3] *The Liberal Party*, p. 11.

the common possession of all parties, while their errors and prejudices have been forgotten. What matters more is that out of the clash of Tory and Whig parties after the Napoleonic wars, whether they are strictly identical or not with the seventeenth-century parties bearing the same name, the Reform Act of 1832 was produced. That act is the first great landmark in the history of the British party system. It is with that act that parties in the modern sense of the term began.

The enlargement of the franchise brought about by the Reform Act, modest though it seems to us to-day, was revolutionary in its effects. The change which it brought about in the parties is reflected in their nomenclature. From that time Tories began to call themselves Conservatives and Whigs began to call themselves Liberals. The names laid emphasis on attitudes of mind on which the respective parties liked to pride themselves—and who will deny that these attitudes both have value and that both ought to find a place not only in every party but in every individual seeking to serve his country? The Conservative emphasizes the value of tradition and his preference for natural growth to artificial creation, holding with one of his early predecessors that 'if it is not necessary to change it is necessary not to change'. The Liberal looks favourably on all changes tending in the direction of free institutions. Though the words had been used as opposites as early as 1801, there is really no incompatibility between them, and whether the one attitude or the other should be emphasized depends on the circumstances of the day. There is a time to innovate and a time to conserve. There was no sudden change in the names of the parties in 1832. The Duke of Wellington did not send out a letter to Tories, saying 'Now you will call yourselves Conservatives', nor did Earl Grey address his fellow-Whigs with the words, 'We are the Liberals now'. It just happened that about that time the term Conservative began to be applied to themselves by Tories. John Wilson Croker, at the time member of Parliament for the University of Dublin, is believed to have been the first person to use the name in this sense, in the *Quarterly Review* of January 1830, though in his mouth it could hardly have had the softer *nuance* than Tory which it bears to-day, for he was the type of Tory generally known as 'crusted', preferring to give up his seat in 1832 rather than sit in a reformed Parliament. When various party organizations were created later in the century the term Conservative was adopted in their names, and the term Tory was not. There was a time, in the sixties, seventies and eighties more particularly, when Conservatives toyed with the idea of calling themselves Constitutionalists. In 1867, as we shall see, the term Constitutional was used along with

Conservative in the title of an official organization; and the Constitutional Club founded in 1883 can be set against the Conservative Club established in 1840. Conservatives still like to think of themselves as defenders of the constitution, and the title 'Constitutional candidate' marked a stage in Mr. Churchill's return to the Tory party as recently as 1924. But the name Conservative has prevailed over the name Constitutional. The word Conservative has, however, never wholly driven out the word Tory. It has always been used by opponents as a term of abuse, perhaps because it can be hissed out more vehemently than the longer word, and it has been as proudly accepted by modern Conservatives as it was by their seventeenth-century ancestors. Lord Randolph Churchill gave it a new currency by calling himself a Tory Democrat in the eighties, and at the present time the declaration 'I am a Tory', either by itself or amplified into 'a good old Tory', 'an old-fashioned Tory', or 'a Tory of the old school', can always be trusted to bring rounds of applause from a Conservative audience. The Conservative defeat in 1945 led, indeed, to a marked revival in the use of the older term, which found official sanction when the party's weekly journal called *The Onlooker* was incorporated in *Tory Challenge*.

The term Whig has long been completely driven out by the name Liberal, though several of my Liberal friends like to think of themselves as 'the last of the Whigs'. There is perhaps a difference from the rise of the name Conservative in that Liberal was never simply an alternative for Whig. There is more than a difference of *nuance* between Whig and Liberal. The truth appears to be that from about 1820 Whigs and Liberals coexisted in the same party; and the Whigs gradually died out or left the party, leaving the Liberals in possession of the field. The last Whig Prime Minister was Earl Russell (formerly Lord John Russell) in 1866; the first Liberal Prime Minister was Gladstone in 1868. Like the terms Whig and Tory, but unlike the name Conservative, the word Liberal was originally a term of abuse accepted as a badge of honour by those to whom it was applied; and just as Whig came from Scotland and Tory from Ireland, so Liberal came from Spain and France. The Spanish *Liberales* were a group of reformers at the beginning of the nineteenth century who were in power from 1820 to 1823 and roused general abhorrence by the violence of their opinions and actions. There was a group of French *Libéraux* with similar aims held in like detestation by men of traditional views. At the beginning of the eighteenth century the term Liberal came to be applied by opponents to the advanced section of the Whigs, often in the Spanish or French form, and no doubt with the implication that their views and conduct were un-English; but as the name was already used in a good sense, these advanced Whigs were not averse from accepting the designation. Southey, for example, wrote in 1816 of the British *Liberales* as opposing the continuance of the Alien Bill. When party organizations came to be created, the Whigs were already on the decline, the Liberals on the ascendant, and so it came about that the term Liberal rather than the name Whig came into official use.

III

Growth of Party Organization

IT IS TO THIS QUESTION of party organization that we must now turn, for this was another, and far more important, change brought about by the Reform Act. Before 1832 there was no organization of parties throughout the country. The political parties before that date were groups of men in Parliament who thought alike on great issues and generally spoke in the same sense and voted together. Their relations and friends in the country would also describe themselves as Tories or Whigs, and every great house in the land was a centre of Tory or Whig social activities, but there was no local party to which they could belong, nor any party organization of any sort outside Parliament; and even inside Parliament there was no organization of members in the modern sense of the word—only groups of members who held the same broad opinions and who would meet from time to time in each other's houses to discuss their course of action. If a man wished to become a candidate for Parliament he made his own arrangements for doing so. The electorate was small, often absurdly small, and very often there was some powerful patron, described as 'the prevailing influence', who was able to determine how a majority of electors would vote. The simplest and least expensive way of becoming a member of Parliament was to win the favour of such a powerful patron. If a Whig landlord were succeeded by a Tory, or a Tory by a Whig, his tenants were expected to change their views to accord with the new 'prevailing influence'; and in cases where the landlord changed his allegiance his tenants were required to change also, on the principle, 'When father turns, we all turn'. Where the electors were not under the control of a landlord they could usually be corrupted, and their votes went to the highest bidder. The first signs of the extension of party activity from Parliament to the country came when the Government, instead of buying the votes of members of Parliament directly—and there was even a place in the House of Commons where members went to claim their price after they had voted—began to bribe the electors to return members who could be trusted to be subservient. An officer of the party with a bag full of money from the public funds would make his presence felt during elections; and the Opposition with its more limited means followed suit to the best of its ability. It is amazing that in such a period of general corruption the standards of parliamentary debate and executive ability should have remained so high. It was against this background that the two Pitts waged war and that Sheridan, Burke and Fox declaimed; and although the methods of the eighteenth century would have been abhorrent to William Ewart Gladstone, he owed his first seat in Parliament to the influence of the Duke of Rutland over the electors of Newark.

REGISTRATION ASSOCIATIONS

The Reform Act, 1832, swept away the 'rotten boroughs' and greatly enlarged the electorate. The duty of preparing lists of electors was given to the overseers of the poor in each parish, and any qualified elector could make a claim to be inscribed or an objection to the name of any person who had in his view been wrongly entered. A 'revising barrister' was appointed to examine claims and objections and in due course to declare the list closed.

Despite the great popular demand behind the Reform Act, there were many qualified electors who did not care to have their names on the list; in many cases they feared it might prejudice their business connexions, and for a long time to come a favourite method of bringing pressure to bear on an elector was to threaten to withdraw business from him. There were also many cases of attempts by unqualified persons to get on the lists, and, of course, there were many doubtful cases. In these circumstances it became a matter of great importance to the parties to ensure that in any constituency all their own qualified supporters were duly registered and that all unqualified supporters of their opponents were removed from the registers. For this purpose 'registration societies' or 'registration associations' were formed in various localities shortly after the Reform Act. They generally had the party notables of the locality for their officers, and the work of scrutinizing the electoral register was usually done by a local solicitor. This was the beginning of constituency party organization.

Sir Robert Peel, who had succeeded to the leadership of the Conservative party, gave the movement a great impetus. This is how he expressed the new problem in a letter to a friend written on 8 November 1838:[1]

'The Reform Bill has made a change in the position of parties, and in the practical working of public affairs, which the author of it did not anticipate.

[1] *Sir Robert Peel*, by C. S. Parker, vol. ii, p. 368.

'There is a perfectly new element of political power—namely, the registration of voters, a more powerful one than either the Sovereign or the House of Commons.

'That party is the strongest in point of fact which has the existing registration in its favour. It is a dormant instrument, but a most powerful one, in its tacit and preventive operation.

'What a check it is at this moment upon the efficiency and influence of the existing Government, backed as it is by all the favour and private goodwill of the Crown, and by a small majority of the House of Commons. It meets them every day, and at every hour. Of what use is the prerogative of dissolution to the Crown, with an unfavourable registry, and the fact of its being unfavourable known to all the world? The menace of dissolution is only laughed at.

'Then it is almost impossible to make any promotion, or vacate any office, for fear of sustaining a defeat.

'The registration will govern the disposal of offices, and determine the policy of party attacks; and the power of this new element will go on increasing as its secret strength becomes better known and is more fully developed. We shall soon have, I have no doubt, a regular systematic organization of it. Where this is to end I know not, but substantial power will be in the Registry Courts, and there the contest will be determined.'

More concisely, in 1841, Peel told his supporters at Tamworth, 'Register, register, register'. With his encouragement 'registration associations' began to be set up in the country to ensure the registration of qualified electors of known Conservative views, and the Whig-Liberals did likewise. This was the modest beginning of the vast party organizations covering the whole country that we know to-day. 'Where this is to end I know not'—nor perhaps do we. Every successive enlargement of the electorate—in 1867, in 1884, in 1918 and in 1929 —increased the necessity for that nation-wide organization of parties which the prescience of Sir Robert Peel had foreseen. The vote was gradually extended to all adult men, and then in two stages to all adult women, but the problem of ensuring that no supporter's name gets omitted from the register of voters, and that he records a vote when the opportunity arises, remain two of the main duties of local party organization; and Peel's 'regular systematic organization' has become far more regular and far more systematic than even he foresaw. As for the watch that he realized Governments would keep on opinion among the electorate, this also has become far more developed than he could have foretold. The rough tests of personal observation and the by-elections have now given place to scientifically conducted polls of public opinion which enable the experts to say with a high degree of accuracy not only how the electorate would vote after dissolution but how many seats the main parties would obtain. The 'secret strength' of parties has become front-page news and politicians are always nervously looking at graphs of their popularity. Sir Robert Peel would not have liked the new world which in rough outline he foresaw; but no doubt he would have adjusted himself to it as to the changing circumstances of his own day.

NEW CONCEPTION OF MEMBERS' DUTIES

Sir Robert Peel also perceived that the enlargement of the electorate involved a change in the conception of the responsibilities of a member of Parliament. Those responsibilities, as conceived before the Reform Bill, had been expressed in classic form by Burke in his speech at the conclusion of the poll at Bristol on 3 November 1774.[1]

'Certainly, gentlemen, it ought to be the happiness and glory of a representative to live in the strictest union, the closest correspondence and the most unreserved communication with his constituents. Their wishes ought to have great weight with him; their opinion high respect; their business unremitted attention. It is his duty to sacrifice his repose, his pleasures, his satisfactions to theirs; and above all, ever and in all cases, to prefer their interest to his own. But his unbiased opinion, his mature judgment, his enlightened conscience, he ought not to sacrifice to you; to any man, or to any set of men living. These he does not derive from your pleasure; no, nor from the law and the constitution. They are a trust from providence, for the abuse of which he is deeply answerable. Your representative owes you, not his industry only, but his judgment; and he betrays, instead of serving you, if he sacrifices it to your opinion.'

Burke's conception of the duty of electors was to choose a good man and let him get on with the job; it would be open to them not to choose him again if he did not come up to their expectations. The successful candidate went to Parliament unfettered by any pledges and his duty there was to speak and vote on each issue according to his best judgment as it arose. This high conception of a member's duty was possible in the days of a narrowly restricted electorate, but after the Reform Act of 1832 the doctrine, though never formally abandoned, and still implicit in the law and constitution, could no longer be held in its original purity. In order to win the suffrages of a large number of electors to whom the candidate was not personally known it became necessary to tell them in rather more detail what he proposed to do if elected to Parliament.

This is what Sir Robert Peel did in his 'Tamworth manifesto' of

[1] *The Works of the Rt. Hon. Edmund Burke*, 1826, vol. iii, pp. 18–19.

1835. He had accepted the King's invitation to form a Government in 1834 and advised the King to dissolve Parliament. He himself had to seek re-election at Tamworth. In a memoir[1] he thus recorded the origin of the Tamworth manifesto:

'Immediately after the completion of the Cabinet I proposed to my colleagues that I should take advantage of the opportunity which the approaching election would afford, and in an address to the constituent body of Tamworth declare the general principles upon which the Government proposed to act. My colleagues entirely approved of this course and of the address which I submitted to their consideration.'

In the address itself, before turning to specific questions of policy, he said:

'My acceptance of the first office in the Government terminates, for the present, my political connexion with you. In seeking the renewal of it, whenever you shall be called upon to perform the duty of electing a representative in Parliament, I feel it incumbent upon me to enter into a declaration of my views of public policy, as full and unreserved as I can make it, consistently with my duty as a minister of the Crown.

'You are entitled to this, from the nature of the trust which I again solicit, from the long habits of friendly intercourse in which we have lived, and from your tried adherence to me in times of difficulty, when the demonstration of unabated confidence was of peculiar value. I gladly avail myself also of this, a legitimate opportunity, of making a more public appeal—of addressing, through you, to that great and intelligent class of society of which you are a portion, and a fair and unexceptionable representative—to that class which is much less interested in the contentions of party, than in the maintenance of order and the cause of good government, that frank exposition of general principles and views which appears to be anxiously expected, and which it ought not to be the inclination, and cannot be the interest, of a minister of this country to withhold.'[2]

Here we have the origin both of the modern election address and of the party leader's election manifesto. Here also we have the beginnings of a process which has led to the dangerous modern doctrine of the mandate—the doctrine that a member of Parliament may not act in the House except in accordance with a mandate he has received from the electors and that, having received such a mandate, he is obliged to carry it out even though altered circumstances may make it undesirable and public opinion may have changed. This is the doctrine that would

[1] *Memoirs by Sir Robert Peel*, edited by Stanhope and Cardwell, vol. ii, p. 58.
[2] *Ibid.*, p. 59.

turn a member of Parliament from being the representative of his constituents into their delegate. Peel's subsequent life shows clearly that he
did not regard this doctrine as implicit in the presentation to the
electors of a 'frank exposition of general principles and views'. He
tells us that he had adopted at an early period of his public life 'the
opinions generally prevalent at the time among men of all parties, as
to the justice and necessity of protection to domestic agriculture',[1] and
this was the policy he presented to the electors in 1841 when he became
for the second time Prime Minister. But circumstances compelled him
in 1842 to acquiesce in a reduction of the amount of protection given
to home-grown corn, and the failure of the potato crop in 1845 led
him to carry through the complete repeal of the Corn Laws. In justifying himself to the electors of Tamworth in 1847 he 'could not admit the
incompetency of the present Parliament to deal with this as with every
other question of public concern,'[2] that is to say he stood upon Burke's
doctrine. But the representative of a newer generation was at hand and
in biting invective Disraeli denounced him as a turncoat and traitor.

FIRST PARTY HEADQUARTERS

The twenty years from 1846 were a period of confusion in British
party politics. Party lines were blurred, men's allegiances were often
uncertain, parliamentary majorities were small, and Parliament was
dominated by the personalities of Palmerston and Russell. At that
time Great Britain might easily have moved into a system of many
parties and *bloc* governments such as many continental countries have
come to know. There were several factors that brought this period of
confusion to an end and made the opposition of the great Liberal and
Tory parties the basis of British public life. The death of Palmerston
removed a powerful personality to whom parties had never been more
than a means to an end; and at his death Disraeli thought it opportune
to announce 'the truce of parties is over'. Under Disraeli's leadership
the Conservative party had recovered from the depths to which it sank
after Peel's defection. The Peelites had themselves failed to form a
permanent group and had dispersed their several ways. These are all
important factors in ending the period of confusion, but due weight
must also be given to certain steps in party organization taken by
Liberals and Conservatives.

The formation of 'registration societies' was the first big step in party
organization throughout the country. It was the Liberals who took the

---

[1] *Memoirs*, vol. ii, pp. 98–99.   [2] *Ibid.*, p. 106.

next big step, in 1861, by setting up in London the Liberal Registration Association, which had among other duties the task of promoting and co-ordinating constituency registration associations composed of 'gentlemen of known Liberal opinions'. Though it was in form an association of the principal Liberal supporters throughout the country, in practice it never met as such, and the control was kept firmly in the hands of the parliamentary whips. It was, in fact, an instrument for enabling the whips to discharge their extra-parliamentary work, and was the first party headquarters in the modern sense of the term. Under its lead a large number of constituency registration associations was quickly brought into being. The name of the body was later changed to the Liberal Association, but it has always been more commonly known, and still is to-day, as the 'whips' office'.

It may appear strange that the formation of national party headquarters should have come so long after the need for a countrywide organization was recognized, and the explanation is in part that the functions of party headquarters had previously been discharged by two political clubs founded about the time of the Reform Bill—the Carlton for the Conservatives, and the Reform for the Liberals.[1] Here the provincial notables of the parties were able to meet the national leaders, and each had its political committee maintaining close relations with the registration societies. The Carlton Club has continued to play a major unofficial rôle in the Conservative party, but with the decline of the Liberal party the Reform has become purely social.

REPRESENTATIVE CONSTITUENCY ASSOCIATIONS

The registration societies set up immediately after the Reform Act of 1832 were not representative bodies. The officers and the election committee were not elected by the whole body of members. They were self-elected and self-perpetuating. It was inevitable that in the course of time the members should claim some control over the selection of officers, and the desirability appears first to have been recognized by the Conservatives. The registration association which had been formed by the Conservatives in Liverpool in 1832 was reorganized in 1848 into a Constitutional Association on a largely representative basis. Among its objects were 'to promote by all legal means the election of members of Parliament for the borough who subscribe to and uphold the principles of the association' and 'to promote by all legal means the election of such candidates for the town council as are members of this associa-

[1] See below, pp. 213–14.

tion'. The association was based upon the wards. The Conservatives in each ward elected a chairman, a secretary and a ward committee. The chairman and secretary from each ward served on the general committee of the association, which included in addition thirty members chosen by the association as a whole.

We may recognize in this Liverpool body the pattern of the modern representative constituency association. But it was a long time before the example was generally followed. A number of other Conservative associations of a representative character had been formed before 1867, but the extension of the franchise brought about by the Reform Act of that year gave a great impetus to the movement. The Reform Act of 1867 is second, indeed, only to the Reform Act of 1832 as a landmark in the development of the British party system. Many new Conservative associations were formed in the next few years, and the newly enfranchised artisans flocked into them in large numbers. In 1876 the total number of Conservative associations of all types in England and Wales was reckoned to be nearly 800. At that date they were still mainly unrepresentative in character, but the size of their membership differentiated them from the old registration societies and made it only a matter of time before a representative character was bound to be conceded. Developments among the Liberals hastened the process. The Liberals had been slower to perceive the desirability of representative associations, and do not appear to have had any before 1867. But when the demand came it was associated with a tightening in party machinery that left a permanent mark on the British party system and has, indeed, been not without its influence far beyond these islands.

Among other changes the act of 1867 provided that Liverpool, Manchester, Birmingham and Leeds were each to send three members to Parliament; but in order, as it was intended, to ensure that the minority should get some representation the Lords had inserted, and the Commons had accepted, a clause that no elector in those towns should vote for more than two candidates. William Harris, the Radical secretary of the Birmingham Liberal Association, reflected that three-fifths of the electors of that town voted Liberal, and that this was sufficient to carry all three seats if the votes were evenly distributed among the candidates. But in default of adequate machinery for ensuring this result, there was a danger that the Liberal votes would be given to the more popular or better-known pair of the Liberal candidates. The secret of getting a judicious distribution of votes, Harris told the electors, was 'vote as you are told'; but it was possible to get electors to vote as they were told only if they had complete confidence in the party machine and the party managers. This would best be achieved, Harris thought, by transforming the association into a representative body with the officers and committee chosen by the members. The new rules were adopted in October 1867 and provided that every Liberal subscribing a shilling should be a member of the association, and that the annual meeting of members should choose the officers and twenty members to serve upon the executive committee. This committee was to include also three members chosen by a ward committee to be elected by the members of the association in each ward; as well as certain other members and co-opted members. There was also a larger body known as the general committee and consisting of not more than twenty-four members from each ward together with the executive committee; from the approximate number of members it was known as 'the Liberal four hundred'. This larger body was to determine the policy of the association and to nominate the three Liberal candidates for Parliament. The number of Liberal voters in each ward was ascertained, and the Liberals in each ward were told for which pair of candidates they should vote. Despite some protests against 'dictation', on the whole they voted as they were told, and three Liberals were returned for Birmingham, in defiance of the intentions behind the act of 1867.

The association was not so successful in getting candidates elected to the school board set up in accordance with the Education Act of 1870, for which the system of voting was 'cumulative', that is, an elector could distribute his votes among the candidates or give them all to one candidate; but in 1873 fresh life was infused into the organization by its new secretary, Francis Schnadhorst, and Joseph Chamberlain, the rising political star of Birmingham. Their object was to gain control of the municipal government of the town, and the association was reconstructed on a ward basis. In each ward all who signified their adherence to the objects of the association met in an annual meeting and elected a chairman, a secretary and a committee for the ward. Each ward annual meeting also chose three persons to serve with the chairman and secretary on the executive committee of the Birmingham Liberal Association and a number of persons, fixed in 1877 at thirty, to serve on the general committee. The central executive committee was comprised of five members from each ward, as indicated above, together with the four officers and thirty co-opted members; the four officers together with seven members elected from its own number formed the management sub-committee. The general committee was composed of thirty members from each of the sixteen wards together with the executive committee. From the approximate number of its members it became known as the 'Liberal six hundred'. The policy of the association was determined, and candidates for Parliament and the school board were nominated, by the 'six hundred'; the candidates for the town council were nominated by the ward committees. The new organization was immediately successful in its object of gaining control of the municipal life of Birmingham. Joseph Chamberlain was chosen mayor of Birmingham in 1873, and the association secured the return of sixty-six out of sixty-eight members elected to the town council in the four years 1873–76. In the same period it won all the parliamentary seats and a majority on the school board. The efficacy of the new Birmingham machinery could not be gainsaid, and the example began to be copied by Liberals in other parts of the country; and the Birmingham Radicals went about the country trying to stimulate such representative bodies. There were many misgivings about public men being diverted from the consideration of policy to the control of machinery, but they were in part allayed by the good use that Joseph Chamberlain and his friends made of their control of the Birmingham town council to set an example of progressive municipal government. The Conservatives could not afford to lag behind, and one by one all the local associations, Conservative and Liberal, were transformed to a representative basis. The power of the party machine has perhaps never since been so great as it was in the Birmingham of Schnadhorst and Chamberlain, but their example led to the universal adoption of a representative form of association and to a general tightening of party discipline.

NATIONAL UNION OF ASSOCIATIONS

The second great development that sprang from the Reform Act of 1867 is the grouping of constituency associations into a national union and the holding of a national party conference. It was again the Conservatives who took the lead in this development. The decision to form the National Union of Conservative and Constitutional Associations was taken at a meeting held on 12 November 1867 at the Freemasons' Tavern, London, which turned out to be the first in a long series of annual Conservative conferences. The decision is worth repeating in the words of a statement made at that conference, as recorded in the minutes, for the relationship between the centre and the constituencies was there defined in terms which could still be used to-day and have influenced other parties:[1]

[1] I owe this quotation from the manuscript minutes to Mr. H. V. Armstrong, secretary of the National Union until 1952.

'The working classes of England some time back commenced forming themselves into associations to support the present Government upon the question of reform, and to maintain the fundamental principles of our ancient constitution. It was felt that their position would be strengthened and their influence augmented by the formation of a central union. Conferences were convened in the early part of the present year to consider the question, which were numerously attended by representatives, especially from the northern districts, and it was there resolved to establish a union for this purpose. On the present occasion it is proposed to finally settle the name, rules, and constitution of this society, and to appoint the first officers. This association will afford a centre of communication and action between local associations supporting constitutional views. There is, of course no intention to interfere in any way with local action; the object of the union is to strengthen the hands of local associations where existing in their respective districts, and to encourage the establishment of associations in districts where they are wanting, and further to organize associations by the holding of meetings for the general expression and diffusion of constitutional principles, and the dissemination of sound information upon topics of general political interest, and to secure the combined action of all constitutional associations.'

The National Union of Conservative and Constitutional Unions then formed retained this name until 1912. On the fusion of the Conservative and Liberal Unionist wings of the party it was then renamed the National Unionist Association of Conservative and Liberal Unionist Organizations, and in 1924 it received its present name of the National Union of Conservative and Unionist Associations. Throughout its long history it has, however, generally been known simply as the National Union. For the first few years of its life it did not attract much attention. At the second, third and fourth conferences, held in 1868, 1869 and 1870, there were present, including the officers, only seven, thirty-six and thirty-five persons. The National Union was put on the political map in 1872, when the conference was accompanied by a banquet at the Crystal Palace where Disraeli made a remarkable speech, putting his faith in the inherent conservatism of the working classes and laying down the main principles that Conservative policy was to follow for the next generation. By 1878 the National Union had so grown that it was decided to form provincial unions to which some of the functions of the central council were delegated. In 1884 Lord Randolph Churchill was elected chairman of the National Union, and it figured prominently in the dispute between him and the parliamentary chiefs of his party.[1] The effect was greatly to increase the

[1] This is related in the next chapter.

prestige of the National Union and to give it a more democratic organization. The central council of the union, whose members were partly elected and partly co-opted, had already roused some criticism of its unrepresentative, self-electing character, and furthermore the real direction in electoral matter was vested in a 'central committee'. This was a body, distinct from the union, which had been set up in 1880 after the Conservative defeat in that year to improve the party organization; it had become permanent and, working under the control of the whips, had exclusive control of the funds subscribed for election campaigns. Lord Randolph Churchill and his friends sought to make the central council more representative and to secure for it some of the funds controlled by the central committee. After much guerrilla warfare, peace was restored and a compromise effected in 1885. The central committee was abolished, and the central council became wholly elected. A thorough reorganization of the National Union was taken in hand, and although Lord Randolph Churchill had no part in it, the reconstruction is due to the campaign that he initiated. A chief feature of the reconstruction was that henceforth every recognized constituency association was given the right by virtue of its existence to join the National Union; previously the right of admission had to be claimed, and was subject to the fulfilment of certain rules. Henceforth the National Union became a truly representative organization covering the whole country. The new rules were adopted at a special conference in 1886, and by 1887 the number of associations taking part in the union was 1,100.

CONSERVATIVE CENTRAL OFFICE

A further step in party organization had been taken by the Conservatives after their defeat in the general election of 1868. Disraeli in opposition then made it his business to improve the party organization, and in particular to see that every 'constituency had a suitable prospective candidate in the field before the dissolution of Parliament'. No doubt with one eye on the Liberal headquarters established in 1861 he caused to be set up in 1870 a Conservative Central Office under the control of the whips with Mr. (later Sir) John E. Gorst, M.P., as the party manager, that is, the head of the office under the general direction of the whips. (From 1871 onwards he was known as the principal agent.) In the National Union and the Central Office the Conservatives obtained a dual organization which has preserved its main outlines to the present time. For several years the National Union and the Central

Office were quite distinct bodies occupying separate premises. In order to avoid overlapping of work, the headquarters of the National Union were in 1872 moved to the premises in Parliament Street occupied by the Central Office, and the two organizations have always since been housed in the same building—at the present time in Abbey House, Victoria Street, Westminster, conveniently close to the Houses of Parliament—but each has maintained a distinct existence. As a further measure of ensuring full harmony and proper intercommunication it was arranged in 1878 that the chief whip in the House of Commons should sit on the central council of the National Union and attend meetings of all committees. By 1911 the work had grown to such an extent that it was decided to create the post of chairman of the party organization to take over the duties at the central office previously performed by the chief whip. The first chairman appointed was Sir Arthur Steel-Maitland, and henceforth the chief whip was freed from all extra-parliamentary duties.

NATIONAL LIBERAL FEDERATION

The Conservative success in the general election of 1874 is largely attributed to the strengthening of the party organization by the creation of the National Union and the Central Office. Out of seventy-four constituencies where seats had been won, sixty-five had Conservative associations affiliated to the National Union. 'Disraeli', as Buckle wrote in his life of that statesman, 'was . . . responsible for starting the first great party machine, and he reaped the harvest in the victory of 1874.'

The lesson was not lost upon the Liberals. Joseph Chamberlain and Francis Schnadhorst took the initiative in 1877 by inviting Liberal associations to send delegates to a conference at Birmingham convened for the purpose of creating a national federation. Delegates from ninety-five associations accepted the invitation, and Chamberlain was asked to preside. In his speech he expressed the hope that through the proposed federation they might see 'a really Liberal Parliament, outside the imperial legislature, and, unlike it, elected by universal suffrage and with some regard for a fair distribution of political power'. William Harris, who had founded the 'Liberal four hundred', also spoke, and with the adoption of the constitution prepared by the organizers of the meeting the National Liberal Federation came into being. Chamberlain was elected president and Schnadhorst was made the secretary. Gladstone, at that time nominally in retirement but everywhere regarded as the real leader of the party, addressed a meeting in Birmingham during the evening of the conference and gave the federation his blessing as holding up 'the banner of a wider and of a holier principle' than the power of the purse.

The constitution set up two bodies. The larger one, known as the council, was composed of delegates from local associations roughly in proportion to the population of the town or district they served. It was to meet in different towns year by year, and was to be in effect the annual conference of the federation. The smaller body, called the general committee, consisted of the officers of the federation together with delegates from the associations and co-opted members. One of the main tasks of the committee was to help form local associations based on popular representation; and only such associations could be admitted to membership of the federation. The general committee was to meet in Birmingham.

The National Liberal Federation resembled the National Union of Conservative Associations in being a national federation of constituency associations holding an annual conference as its chief activity; but there was a marked difference in the aims and methods of the two bodies. The National Union made no claim to determine the policy of the Conservative party, and indeed the first nine conferences passed no political resolutions. H. Cecil Raikes, who was one of the founders of the National Union and its chairman from 1869 to 1874, declared with truth that 'the union had been organized rather as what he might call a handmaid to the party than to usurp the functions of party leadership'.[1] Joseph Chamberlain, Schnadhorst and Harris had a very different conception of the purpose of the National Liberal Federation. In their view its main object was to determine the attitude of the Liberal party in Parliament to the great questions of the day. In the words already quoted, Chamberlain had described it as a 'Liberal Parliament', with the implication that it would not only endorse the policies of the leaders but would formulate those policies by open debate. The function of the party conference in the shaping of policy is a question that is still not settled, but in 1877 it was a revolutionary doctrine that the formulation of policy should be taken out of the hands of the party's front bench and given to the chosen representatives of local associations meeting in a body outside Parliament.

For this reason Disraeli and the press were quick to dub the National Liberal Federation as 'the Birmingham caucus', and this name became very widely adopted. But this purpose was as alien to the

---

[1] Report of the conference of 1873.

minds of the Liberal front bench as to those of the Conservative; and for many years, despite Gladstone's blessing, the parliamentary leaders of the Liberal party looked with faintly concealed disapproval on the new body. Instead of the close harmony that usually prevailed between the Conservative Central Office and the National Union, there was open friction between the Liberal Central Association in London and the National Liberal Federation with headquarters in Birmingham. The former was Whig in its outlook and firmly controlled by the whips; the latter was Radical and, though no less effectively controlled by its officers, was outwardly based on popular representation.

The value of the 'caucus' was proved in the general election of 1880. The Liberal success in that election is commonly attributed to the famous speaking tour throughout the country in which Gladstone denounced with fiery eloquence the atrocities of the Turks in Bulgaria and the eastern policy of Disraeli. It was an innovation that filled Queen Victoria with alarm, for hitherto ministers and ex-ministers had in general confined their political speeches to Westminster and their constituencies; but the example had been set, and the leader's speaking tour has now become an essential part of the machinery of a general election. But though Gladstone's share in the Liberal victory of 1880 can hardly be minimized, the new instrument of the National Liberal Federation made a less spectacular but almost equally notable contribution to it. This was clearly recognized at the time for Chamberlain was given a seat in the Cabinet, in preference to Sir Charles Dilke, though he had been only four years in Parliament, and Schnadhorst came to play a big part in the counsels of the party.

But the whips did not like the National Liberal Federation any the better for providing them with so many members owing an allegiance outside their control, and the possibilities of friction increased when the council, like the general committee, began to pass resolutions urging various reforms upon the Government. Chamberlain had indeed resigned the office of president of the federation, as he could hardly remain at the head of a body having among its objects the bringing of pressure to bear upon the Government, but he continued to make the big evening speech held at the same time as the annual meeting of the council. The deadlock was not resolved until the breach between Chamberlain and Gladstone in 1886 over home rule for Ireland plunged the whole Liberal party into confusion. At a special meeting of the council Chamberlain's Irish proposals were defeated and an amendment supporting Gladstone's policy was carried by a large majority. Chamberlain thereupon withdrew from the federation, and in due course helped to form the Liberal Unionist Association; and the National Liberal Federation came under the control of Gladstone and the parliamentary leaders.

Having obtained control of the federation, the parliamentary leaders had to decide how to deal with it in order to prevent it from again becoming a thorn in their flesh. The headquarters were removed to London—this would in any case have been necessary as Chamberlain's control over the electors of Birmingham remained complete—and it was housed in the same building as the Liberal Central Association. Schnadhorst, the secretary of the federation, had followed Gladstone rather than Chamberlain, and the integration with the whips' office was made more complete by his appointment as honorary secretary of the association. Several changes in the constitution were adopted in 1887, of which the most important was the creation of district federations, The general effect was to remove the suspicion that the federation was an instrument of the Radical wing of the party and to make it acceptable to all Liberals. By 1888 the number of affiliated associations, which was only 255 in 1886 before the split, rose to 716. The council continued to pass resolutions purporting to set forth the policy of the Liberal party, and a statement of policy issued in 1887 repeated the language used when the federation had been formed ten years earlier:

'The essential feature of the federation is the participation of all members of the party in the formation and direction of its policy, and in the selection of those particular measures of reform and progress to which priority shall be given.'

But as the party was destined to remain in opposition until 1892, these policy resolutions were not felt to be an embarrassment until the party returned to office in that year with a precarious majority. The National Liberal Federation retained that name throughout the convulsions that shook the Liberal party in and after the first world war, but in the reconstruction of the Liberal party machinery that was carried out in 1936 its place was taken by the Liberal Party Organization.[1]

By 1890 the foundations of the party system as we know it to-day had been laid. There were constituency associations of a representative character bound together in a national federation and assisted by a national headquarters; there was the party annual conference; there was the party election manifesto; and there was the leader's speaking tour. Since that date there have been few innovations in structure, but

[1] The present organization of the Liberal and Conservative parties is described below in Part III.

there has been a marked increase in the power and influence of the party machines. The major developments since that date are of a different order. They are the rise of the Labour party and the decline of the Liberal party; the extension of party organization to cover women as well as men after the grant of the franchise to women; and the extension of party organization to local government elections. Most of those developments will be covered in later chapters, but as the organization of women does not differ fundamentally from that of men it will not be separately treated. The fair sex played a notable part in politics, of course, long before the franchise was extended to women, certainly since that famous Westminster election of 1784 when the beautiful Duchess of Devonshire (Georgiana Spencer) gained at least one vote for Fox by kissing a shoemaker. This is the kind of bribery that is difficult to control! But naturally the extension of the franchise to women in 1918 and 1929 has been reflected at all levels of party organization; and as there are more female electors than male, the canvassing of women voters has become a particularly important part of electioneering.

─── IV ───

Conservatives and Liberals: and

Some Others

To our Victorian forefathers the opposition of the Conservative and Liberal parties seemed as permanent as the strife of Tories and Whigs had appeared to their own forefathers.

> *I often think it's comical*
> *How Nature always does contrive*
> *That every boy and every gal,*
> *That's born into the world alive,*
> *Is either a little Liberal,*
> *Or else a little Conservative!*

So sang Private Willis of the Grenadier Guards in W. S. Gilbert's *libretto* for *Iolanthe*; and this was sufficiently true when *Iolanthe* was written in 1882. For about sixteen years before that date almost every boy and girl born in Great Britain had indeed been born into a Conservative or a Liberal household. But in the twenty years before 1866 the division of the country into Conservatives and Liberals had by no means been so clear, and if *Iolanthe* had been written four years later than it was the truth of Private Willis's sentiments would not have been so self-evident. Moreover at Westminster there were always the Irish members to confuse the battle between Conservatives and Liberals; and on the wing of the Liberal party the discerning eye could see a substantial body of members, styling themselves Radicals, who frequently behaved as though they were a distinct group.

IRISH NATIONALISTS

The Act of Union brought 100 Irish members to Westminster. The number was increased to 105 by the Irish Reform Act, 1832. This was a big fraction of the House, but the Irish members were not homogeneous. Ulster returned a solid block of Protestant Tories, and even in the southern counties the Whig and Tory landowners were able for a long time to influence the election of members. But the genius of

29

Daniel O'Connell, who was himself returned for Clare in 1828, welded the Roman Catholic members from Ireland into a compact and determined body. The number of his followers never rose above forty, and sometimes fell to twelve. But his early triumph in wresting Roman Catholic emancipation from a hostile Government showed what could be accomplished by a small body of members who knew what they wanted and acted together to get it. Nor was O'Connell's influence based solely on his supporters in the House of Commons. His strength at Westminster was derived from the Catholic Association which he had organized throughout Ireland with the parish priests as his local agents and which maintained a constitutional but ceaseless pressure upon the harassed authorities. Both in the organization of a nation-wide political movement and in the conduct of a parliamentary group O'Connell set an example which has notably influenced the growth of parties in Great Britain.

When O'Connell entered Parliament he supported the Whigs and the cause of reform. There was an estrangement when Grey was obliged to repress the violence that, in default of O'Connell's wishes, broke out in Ireland, but he returned to his Whig allegiance and strongly opposed the Government formed by Peel in 1841. With the help of the Irish priests he convened huge meetings in 1842-3 to demand the repeal of the union as he had previously demanded Roman Catholic emancipation. He had created a monster that he could not control, and before his death in 1847 he saw the cause of repeal backed by revolutionary methods that he abhorred.

The disestablishment of the Irish Church in 1868 gave a new turn to Irish politics, for many churchmen who had previously supported the British connexion now threw in their lot with the Nationalists. Chief among them was Isaac Butt, who in 1870 founded the Home Government Association for Ireland and in a speech demanding an Irish Parliament for local affairs turned the Irish Nationalists into a 'home rule' party. He was himself returned to Parliament and in 1874, when secrecy of the ballot had been established, he found himself at the head of fifty-nine home rule members at Westminster.

Butt died in 1879, but even before his death the leadership had been assumed by Parnell, who initiated the Irish Nationalists into a policy of deliberate obstruction at Westminster. In 1880 Gladstone became Prime Minister for the second time; but although the Irish votes in Great Britain had gone mainly to the Liberals, Parnell persuaded the Nationalists to hold themselves aloof from both the British parties, and henceforth in the House of Commons the Irish Nationalists sat together, and always on the Opposition side. This is perhaps the origin of the saying that the Irish are always 'agin the Government'. From this time forward until the representation of the twenty-six counties of southern Ireland ceased in 1921 there were rather more than eighty Nationalist members at Westminster, and as they were a well-disciplined body the way they voted was a matter of no little concern to the two great British parties. After Gladstone's conversion to home rule in 1886 it was inevitable that the Irish Nationalist influence should in general be used on the Liberal side. The Irish Nationalists were, indeed, usually reckoned as a wing of the Liberals in the computation of majorities by the parliamentary handbooks of the day; but they always maintained a separate existence and on some notable occasions, such as the passage of the Education Act in 1902, they voted with the Conservatives. When they sided with the Conservatives against the Liberals, as in that case, it was usually in support of the interests of their Roman Catholic brethren in Great Britain. Their existence at Westminster was of great value to the Roman Catholic community in England and led one of its prelates to exclaim, when home rule was under discussion, 'We can't afford to lose a man of you'.

RADICALS

The Radicals are less easy to define than the Irish Nationalists. They had no compact organization and no party discipline. But they were recognizable by a common political outlook, which has been thus defined :[1]

'They inherited a jacobin philosophy of the rights of man, and in particular the right of every man to an equally valuable vote (which implied equal constituencies and a secret ballot as well as universal suffrage). They had an egalitarian dislike of all forms of privilege and patronage, whether in Parliament, the services, the Church or in land tenure. They comprised dissenters with a puritan dislike of temporalities and ceremonial; they were inspired with Bentham's utilitarian principles. Had all these doctrines been pressed by a compact party based on a wide franchise, the resultant conflict would indeed have been revolutionary.'

If this judgement is correct, we may indeed be grateful that the Radicals did not form a compact party. They normally voted with the

---

[1] *Parliamentary Affairs*, winter 1951, pp. 94–5. (*The British Party System*, pp. 92–3.) The valuable study *English Radicalism 1832–1852*, by S. Maccoby is based on the belief that 'Of the imposing list of "reforming" acts, drafted in Downing Street and passed at Westminster, a deeper explanation is necessary than one conceived mainly in terms of Cabinet or parliamentary personalities' (*ibid.*, p. 7).

Whigs or Liberals, and are rightly regarded as a wing of the Liberals, but they disliked the Whig domination of the Liberal party almost as much as they disliked the Tories. It is easier to identify the individual Radicals than to say what they stood for as a body. Before the Reform Act of 1832 the House of Commons included only a few Radicals such as Burdett and Lambton (later Lord Durham).[1] The passage of the Reform Act brought many more Radicals into the House, and their usual strength cannot be reckoned at fewer than thirty and perhaps ought to be put as high as fifty. They included such brilliant and persistent members as Grote, Roebuck, Molesworth, Bright and Cobden. The Radical movement may be regarded as having come to an end in 1886[2] when Joseph Chamberlain led his followers into an alliance with the Conservatives on the issue of Irish home rule in circumstances to be described.

Though they never constituted a separate party, the Radicals made a notable contribution to the technique of political organization. The National Political Union which was founded by them in Birmingham to agitate for the Reform Bill set a pattern for the future. The Anti-Corn Law League, in which the leading spirits were Cobden and Bright, and the Chartist movement, with which Radicals were associated, developed the technique of mass meetings and monster petitions, the formation of public opinion, and organized pressure upon the Government to an extent that has not subsequently been improved. No doubt they owed something to the inspiration of O'Connell's Catholic Association, but he had the advantage of a ready-made organization in the Irish priesthood, and theirs is the credit for first applying these techniques to the very different soil of England. Towards the end of the movement, as we have already had occasion to notice, Joseph Chamberlain in association with Schnadhorst was responsible for a further tightening of constituency organization and for developments in national organization. It is interesting that these developments, like earlier ones, should have taken place in Birmingham, which was the spiritual home of the Radicals. They may also be given the credit, if

[1] The origin of English Radicalism may be found, as it is by Maccoby (*loc. cit.*, p. 1) in the election of Wilkes as one of the members for Middlesex on 28 March 1768.
[2] Though the name may still occasionally be heard to-day, as, for example, when Lady Megan Lloyd-George, Mr. Edgar Granville and Mr. Emrys Roberts justified the way they had voted in the House of Commons by saying, 'We believe that by our action we have reasserted the Radical position, which we intend to uphold on every occasion that presents itself.' (*Manchester Guardian*, 11 November 1950.) In the intermediate period, Labouchere was one of those commonly styled Radicals.

credit is the right word, for initiating the practice of extracting pledges from candidates.

The Radicals were responsible, not only for these new techniques in political organization, but for carrying a substantial volume of reform. By the time the movement came to an end, almost all the domestic aims set before themselves by the Radicals in 1832 had been achieved. The secret ballot, household suffrage and many other reforms had all been enacted before Joseph Chamberlain set out on his new course. Cobden and Bright had, indeed, failed in their ambitious campaign to secure universal peace by mobilizing public opinion, but peace was not an ideal that the British nation alone could command; and in preparing the public mind for the repeal of the corn laws they had achieved a political triumph second in that century only to the passage of the Reform Act.

PEELITES

But that skilful advocacy and organized pressure would not have availed so soon if there had not been famine in Ireland and if Peel had not been Prime Minister. It was this combination of circumstances that led to the rise of the most brilliant of all the groups that blurred the opposition of Conservatives and Liberals in the nineteenth century. Peel's recognition in 1846 that repeal of the corn laws had become inevitable compelled him to break with the party which he had led with such distinction from the morrow of the Reform Bill. Some 120 Conservative members of the House of Commons followed him. A great gap was torn in the Conservative party, but the hard core remained under the leadership of Lord Derby, Disraeli and Lord George Bentinck. At the general election of 1847 the Peelites were reduced by more than half, but were still a considerable force in Parliament. If they allied themselves to the Whigs, they put the Tories in a hopeless minority; and if they allied themselves with their former Tory protectionist friends, they left the Whigs with a majority of one. But they did not become a third party, and could never have done so because of their internal differences. 'We have no party', wrote Gladstone to his father in 1849, 'no organization, no whipper-in; and under these circumstances we cannot exercise any degree of permanent influence as a body.'[1]

The death of Peel in 1850 removed the strongest bond of union between them. In 1852 Gladstone discerned four shades of opinion among his friends: Newcastle was almost alone in wishing to form a

[1] *The Life of William Ewart Gladstone,* by John Morley, book iii, chap. 3.

C

new party, Graham was ready to join the Liberals, Goulburn and the great bulk of the group would like to have found a way of returning to the Conservatives without sacrificing their views on free trade, Gladstone himself was for maintaining independence but without forming a new party.[1] The general election of that year left them about forty strong, and there was much discussion about whether they should sit on the Government side with the Tories or the Opposition side with the Whigs. Except for Graham, who took his place on the front Opposition bench, they sat eventually below the gangway on the Opposition side. There was also much discussion about how they should describe themselves. The name, like that of the seat, has an almost mystical significance in Parliament. It was then that Graham declared Paley's maxim about religion to be just as true in politics: men often change their creed but not so often the name of their sect. Not for the last time in the history of British politics the name Liberal-Conservative was proposed; and Lord John Russell caustically observed that Whig expressed in one word what Liberal-Conservative expressed in seven. In the end, protection being no longer an issue, many of the Peelites found their way back to the Tory benches and the Conservative name; while others discovered their true place and name among the Liberals. Gladstone's own transition was completed in 1859 when he took office under the Liberal Palmerston a few days after he had voted to keep the Tory Government of Lord Derby in; and this may be regarded as the end of the Peelites.

'FOURTH PARTY'

During Mr. Gladstone's second Government in the years 1880-5 there was danger that Lord Randolph Churchill might have made another rift in the Conservative ranks. Elected to Parliament in 1874, he began to attract notice about 1878 by the virulence of his attacks on the 'old gang' of Conservatives sitting on the Treasury bench, not only on Sclater-Booth, afterwards Lord Basing, whose County Government Bill he denounced as the 'crowning dishonour to Tory principles' and the 'supreme violation of political honesty', but on the Conservative leader, Sir Stafford Northcote, himself. When the general election of 1880 put the Liberals on the Treasury bench, Lord Randolph Churchill was equally scathing in his denunciation of Gladstone ('the Moloch of Midlothian') and the Opposition chiefs. He and his associates in the House—Sir Henry Drummond Wolff, Sir John Gorst

[1] *The Life of William Ewart Gladstone*, Book iii, chap. 7.

and occasionally Arthur Balfour and a few others—were nicknamed the 'fourth party' and gradually formulated a policy of progressive Conservatism which they described as 'Tory democracy'. He took the campaign for 'Tory democracy' from the House to the country, and in the spirit of a knight errant stormed the Radical citadel of Birmingham itself. In 1883 he helped to found a new nation-wide political organization, the Primrose League, dedicated to 'the maintenance of religion, of the estates of the realm, and of the imperial ascendancy of the British Empire'. The name was suggested by Lord Beaconsfield's 'favourite flowers'.[1] Drummond Wolff suggested to Lord Randolph Churchill the foundation of a Primrose League; the idea was accepted with enthusiasm, and next year there were 747 knights, 153 dames and 57 associates gathered in 46 habitations. The League has shown greater longevity than many auxiliary political organizations, and now has Lord Randolph Churchill's great son as its grand master. In the year after the formation of the League, 1884, Lord Randolph Churchill was nominated chairman of the National Union of Conservative Associations against the resolute opposition of the parliamentary leaders of the party. The struggle between the old Conservatism and Tory democracy had come to a head. If Lord Randolph Churchill had pressed matters at this time, with his parliamentary prestige, his control of the party machine and the new instrument of the Primrose League, he might have broken the Conservative party even more decisively than Peel had done. But there was no great specific issue of policy involved, only general trends, and wiser counsels prevailed on both sides. Lord Randolph Churchill withdrew from the chairmanship of the National Union and the parliamentary leadership accepted a substantial injection of Tory democracy. When Lord Salisbury formed his first Government in 1885 he won the co-operation of Lord Randolph Churchill as Secretary of State for India; and when he came to form his second administration in 1886 he gave the great office of Chancellor of the Exchequer to his brilliant lieutenant, who was still only thirty-seven years of age. Lord Randolph Churchill was not wholly reconciled to his colleagues but the danger of a permanent 'fourth party' was over.

[1] The foundation for this belief is the card affixed to a wreath of primroses at Beaconsfield's funeral in 1881: 'His favourite flowers: from Osborne: a tribute of affectionate regard from Queen Victoria'. It is alleged by some that his liking for primroses was in his salad rather than in his buttonhole. ('They say primroses make a capital salad', said Lord St. Jerome in *Lothair*.)

LIBERAL UNIONISTS

It was the Liberal, not the Conservative, party which was destined to be broken about this time; and by an irony of fate it was Gladstone who was destined to break it as his master Peel had broken the Conservative. The occasion was his conversion to the principle of home rule for Ireland, and ninety-five 'dissentient Liberals', as he called them, led by Lord Hartington and Joseph Chamberlain, voted against him in the House of Commons. He was not surprised nor pained by the vote of the Whig aristocrat, but the action of the Birmingham Radical puzzled and distressed him. 'He never made speeches like that when he was on our side,' he later complained. 'Yes, he did,' said an unusually candid friend, 'but you never listened to them then.'[1] At the ensuing general election seventy-eight Liberal Unionists, as the dissentients called themselves, were returned. This was a serious defection from the Liberals, but not such as to destroy the Liberal party, which was again in office in 1892, with the 'grand old man' as Prime Minister for the fourth time. The Liberal Unionists were faced with the same perplexities as had troubled the Peelites. Were they to hope for reunion with their old Liberal friends when the Irish issue was out of the way? Were they to constitute a new party? Or were they to coalesce with their former political antagonists? The question posed itself at once in 1886, when Lord Salisbury offered to step aside if Lord Hartington would attempt to form a Government, but Lord Hartington declined the honour. The time had not yet come when the Liberal Unionists could contemplate a coalition with the Conservatives. But the way of reconciliation with the Liberals was even harder. Hartington could be forgiven, but the cries of 'Judas' hissed at Chamberlain from the Liberal benches were not easily retracted or forgotten. When Lord Randolph Churchill in a moment of aberration resigned from the Government, Lord Salisbury's offer was renewed, but although Lord Hartington again felt obliged to decline, his lieutenant Goschen, whom Lord Randolph Churchill 'forgot', accepted the vacant Exchequer, and established his reputation there. The course of the Liberal Unionists was becoming clearer and in 1895 the eighth Duke of Devonshire, as Hartington had then become, Chamberlain and other members of their group, accepted office in Salisbury's third administration. At the general election of 1892 only forty-seven Liberal Unionists had been returned,

---

[1] I was told this anecdote by the late Sir George Leveson-Gower, who had previously been one of Gladstone's private secretaries and in 1886 was his colleague in the House of Commons.

but their number rose to seventy after the general election of 1895, and was almost maintained, at sixty-eight, in the general election of 1900. The Liberal Unionists thus constituted a substantial group in the House of Commons, and though in a coalition with the Conservatives they maintained an independent organization. But soon they were to be perplexed by the issue of protection. Chamberlain had moved ever farther from his Radical starting point and in 1903 resigned from the Government to conduct his historic campaign in favour of tariff reform. The Duke of Devonshire, who had hardly veered from the position he held in 1886, resigned a little later for the opposite reason—that the Prime Minister, Balfour, was moving too far from free trade. The Liberal Unionists in general sided with Chamberlain, and the Duke of Devonshire severed his connexion with them. At the general election of 1906 their numbers fell to twenty-three, but rose to thirty-one in the general election of January 1910 and to thirty-four at the general election of December 1910. By this time the Conservative party had accepted Chamberlain's ideas and had become protectionist in its policy once more. Long habit of acting in concert had made the differences between Liberal Unionists and Conservatives a difference in name only; and a formal fusion was effected in 1911 under the name of the Conservative and Unionist party. From that time onwards the normal official designation of a Tory candidate, member or organization, has been 'Conservative and Unionist'. But some candidates, members and organizations have for historical reasons always preferred to call themselves 'Unionists' and others simply 'Conservative'.[1] The term 'Coalition Unionists' was used to denote those Conservative and Unionist candidates who in 1918 supported a continuance of the coalition under Lloyd George. Joseph Chamberlain's sons always described themselves as Unionists, and not until November 1952 did the Birmingham Unionist Association become the Birmingham Conservative and Unionist Association. In Scotland the name Unionist is still officially employed to the exclusion of Conservative.

[1] For example, the South Kensington Conservative Association, the Rossendale Conservative Association, the Carlisle Conservative Association.

V

Entry of the Labour Party

THE RISE OF THE PEELITES and the Liberal Unionists, though of much significance for policy, did not make any great or permanent alteration in the British party system. The two older parties after giving rise to them settled down to an ordered existence as a volcano subsides after eruption; and the products of the eruption flowed in due course to their proper stations. But about the time that the Liberal Unionists first entered into a coalition with the Conservatives a more radical disturbance of the British party system began to make itself felt.

James Keir Hardie had convinced himself that the interests of the labouring classes would be properly looked after only when they had a party of their own independent both of Liberals and of Conservatives. As the delegate from the Ayrshire Miners' Union he had put this point of view before the Trades Union Congress in 1887, without much acceptance, and in the following year he contested a by-election in Mid-Lanark as an Independent Labour candidate. He polled only 712 votes but, nothing daunted, he succeeded in creating a Scottish Labour party with himself as secretary. The Scottish initiative was followed south of the border, especially in the West Riding. A Labour Union was formed in Bradford in 1890 and a similar body was set up in Colne Valley a few months later. In 1892 Hardie secured election to Parliament for West Ham, and his appearance at Westminster in a cloth cap is now seen as a portent, though at the time regarded by most commentators as an oddity. A year later, in 1893, he obtained his immediate objective when in a meeting at Bradford he succeeded in welding the local groups into a national organization under the name of the Independent Labour party. It was a new phenomenon in British politics for two reasons: it was committed to a political creed, the creed of socialism, and it was unashamedly based on class. The older parties had their special outlooks on life and were stronger among some sections of the community than others. But neither of them had any ideological commitments, and each could adopt an empirical attitude to the problems of the day. They came near to being ideologically divided on the issue of free trade *versus* protection, but were never formally committed, as the Independent Labour party was committed to socialism. The older parties also differed in that each of them appealed to the whole nation for support. It was true that until 1885 only a restricted part of the nation enjoyed the vote, but the Queen's government could not be carried on, nor effective opposition organized, without a mass support far beyond the confines of the franchise. The main organization of industrial workers, the trade unions, had on the whole tended to give their support to the Conservatives before 1868, and not unnaturally as the Liberal party was identified in their minds with *laisser-faire*; but from 1868 onwards the leaders of organized labour began to look more towards the Liberal party. Encouraged by the extension of the franchise in 1867, three industrial workers—George Howell, W. R. Cremer and E. O. Greening—fought in the general election of 1868 as Liberals, and although none was successful, this was the beginning of an alliance between 'working-class candidates' and the Liberals which was to last until 1906. An attempt was made about the same time to secure the election of 'working class candidates' distinct from both the Liberal and the Conservative parties, but it came to nothing. A London Working Men's Union had been created in 1866 with this object, but owing to lack of funds it did not sponsor any candidates in the general election of 1868. About that time a Labour Representation League was formed 'to secure the return to Parliament of qualified working men, persons who by character and ability command the confidence of their class' and it promoted the candidature of George Odger, a shoemaker, at a by-election in Southwark in 1870 against both the Liberal and the Conservative candidates; but when the miners Thomas Burt and Alexander MacDonald were returned for Morpeth and Stafford respectively in the general election of 1874 as a result of the League's efforts, they accepted the Liberal whip and were for all practical purposes Liberal members, though described as Labour at the time and often regarded as the first Labour members even in the sense in which the phrase is used to-day. After the general election of 1880 their number was increased by Henry Broadhurst; as a stonemason he had taken part in the rebuilding of the Palace of Westminster after the fire, and a hammer and chisels which he used are still shown in one of the rooms where members may receive visitors. It became the policy of the Liberal party to facilitate the return of a number of such 'working class members', who were dubbed 'Lib-Labs', and who numbered eleven in the eighties. Despite these successes the Labour Representation League died, and in its place the Trades Union Congress created a sub-committee to act in co-operation with its own parliamentary committee set up in 1869 (and now the general council of the T.U.C.); but this sub-committee broke away from the T.U.C. and under the name of the Labour Electoral Association allied itself openly with the Liberal party.

The formation of the Independent Labour Party at Bradford in 1893 thanks to the efforts of Keir Hardie is therefore the first successful example of the creation of a party distinct from the historic British parties of Tories and Liberals. But it was still not the Labour party as we know it to-day. To study the rise of the Labour party we have to move forward to 1899 when the Trades Union Congress instructed its parliamentary committee to call a conference on the question of labour representation in Parliament. This was held on 27 February 1900 at the Memorial Hall, Farringdon Street, London, and was attended by delegates from about 70 trade unions and also by representatives of the Independent Labour party, the Social Democratic Federation and the Fabian Society. The Social Democratic Federation was the name adopted in 1883 by the Democratic Federation founded in 1881 by an old Etonian with a flowing beard, H. M. Hyndman, who was said by his enemies to have become permanently embittered against society because his father had left most of his wealth for the building of churches. Despite its name it was committed to the creed of Karl Marx which Hyndman had espoused. In 1884 Hyndman himself, along with William Morris and Belfort Bax, seceded and founded the Socialist League, but the Social Democratic Federation continued to exist. The Fabian Society was founded in the winter of 1883–4 by Edward R. Pease and others with the lofty aim of 'reconstructing society in accordance with the highest moral possibilities'. Within the next few years it was joined by George Bernard Shaw, Sydney Olivier, Graham Wallas and Annie Besant, who caught the public notice with their contributions to *Fabian Essays* (1889). Though the Fabian essayists were all socialists, and the Fabian Society published tracts advocating socialism almost from the outset, its name was intended to indicate an empirical approach to political problems. The original aim of the society was not to create a new party—though it often urged the trade unions to form their own party—but to 'permeate' the traditional parties with its ideas, working through either party as seemed most opportune to translate its ideas into realities. It was successful in getting a great deal of 'gas and water socialism' on to the statute book before the meeting convened in February 1900. At that date the trade unions were far from committed to socialism, and many trade unionists were actively hostile to it. In this atmosphere the final resolution carried by the conference was inevitably a compromise which did not commit the new party to any specific creed or even policy.

The resolution, for whose drafting James Ramsay MacDonald, a leading light in the Independent Labour party, was mainly responsible, simply pledged the conference 'to establish a distinct Labour group in Parliament, who shall have their own whips, and agree upon their own policy, which must embrace a readiness to co-operate with any party which for the time being may be engaged in promoting legislation in the direct interest of labour'. A committee called the Labour Representation Committee was elected for this purpose, and as this body has a continuous history with the Labour party as we know it to-day, its formation is generally regarded as the origin of the Labour party.

Some enthusiasts like to find the origin of the Labour party in a much earlier age. They see it as continuous with the Chartist movement, and they look on Robert Owen (1771–1858) with special affection as a pioneer. The explanation is to be found in a distinction, which is still valid, between the Labour party and the Labour movement. There was a Labour movement, in the sense of a movement to improve the condition of the labouring masses, long before there was a Labour party, or indeed any parties. John Ball and Wat Tyler have a place in it no less than John Booth and Ernest Bevin. When we come to the Chartists we get nearer to a political party inasmuch as they sought the attainment of their objects through parliamentary reforms, but they had no thought of founding a new party. The labouring masses were wholly unfranchised until Disraeli's Reform Act of 1867, and it can be reasonably argued that they were not represented by the old Tory and Whig parties; but it would be straining the meaning of words to identify them with the yet unborn Labour party. The origins of that party may, however, though the name was not yet employed, be found in the Labour Representatation Committee set up in 1900.

It had one significant structural difference from the older parties and even from the Independent Labour party. Whereas they were composed of individuals, the new party envisaged by the Labour Representation Committee had no provision for individual membership. Membership was open only to Labour and Socialist organizations who applied for affiliation and paid an affiliation fee based on the number of their members. It was not until 1918 that the Labour party constitution was amended to provide for individual membership, and the individual members still constitute a small part of the total membership. This fact will call for fuller consideration in a later chapter.

The Labour Representation Committee began its work with MacDonald as its secretary and its offices in his flat. It was faced almost immediately with a general election, but managed to put in the field fifteen candidates, of whom two were elected; Hardie, who had not secured re-election at West Ham in 1895, was returned for Merthyr Tydfil and Richard Bell, secretary of the Amalgamated Society of Railway Servants, succeeded at Derby. But the trade unionists were still not wholly reconciled to the new party. In particular, strange as it may seem to-day, the Miners' Federation, which found the money to secure the election of a dozen members of Parliament and to maintain them when elected, refused to affiliate to the new party, and its members accepted the Liberal whip in the House of Commons.

But the Labour Representation Committee was steadily winning support and its prestige was increased by three victories at by-elections. In 1903 the fourth annual conference of the committee took a decisive step in the history of the British party system. It was resolved that members elected to Parliament through its efforts should 'abstain strictly from identifying themselves with, or promoting the interests of, any section of the Liberal or Conservative parties'. Endorsed candidates were required to 'accept this pledge or resign', and were directed to 'appear before their constituencies under the title of Labour candidates only'. The sanction for these requirements was provided by another resolution of the same conference, which decided to make a levy of one penny a member annually on all affiliated organizations for the purpose of maintaining its members of Parliament in the House of Commons and meeting their election expenses; no drawings were to be made until £2,500 had been accumulated, after which all M.P.s sponsored by the Labour Representation Committee were to receive £200 a year. (This was, of course, before the statutory payment of members, which began in 1911).

This resolution could not have much effect on the fortunes of the Conservatives, but it rang the death-knell of the Liberal party. In order to maintain its position as one of the two great parties of the state, it was essential for the Liberal party to win a high proportion of the votes cast by the industrial workers to whom the franchise had now been extended. The Liberal hold on this great section of the electorate was now threatened by the rise of a new body describing itself as the workers' own party and at that time unashamedly based on class representation. If the new party continued to gain support at the same rate as in its first three years it would soon make it impossible for the Liberal party to secure a majority in the House of Commons. Year by year Liberals would be bound to ask themselves 'How long halt ye between two opinions?' At each election some who had previously voted Liberal would vote Conservative, others Labour. The conviction would grow that a Liberal vote was a wasted one, and in the end only the hard core of Liberals would be left. There has been much recrimination over the way in which Lloyd George wrested power from Asquith in 1916, and he has been accused of destroying the Liberal party. Beyond doubt his quarrel with Asquith accelerated the process, but the party trends before 1916 are clear evidence that the disintegration of the Liberal party would have come about in any case as an inevitable result of the decision taken by the conference of the Labour Representation Committee in 1903. The history of the new party from that date is not, indeed, one of steady progress year by year. It had its setbacks and failures, its uncertainties of aim and divisions on policy, and was as much the victim of personalities as the older parties had been. But if we neglect the variations from year to year, or even the occasional setbacks at elections, and study the general trend we can see that as far back as 1903 the bell had already tolled for the Liberal party.

But these consequences were concealed by the tremendous victory at the polls gained by the Liberals in 1906 and the brilliance of the Government which then came into office. It was like the flaring up of a star into a *nova* before it finally sinks into a decline. The magnitude of the Liberal victory obscured the fact that the victory was gained against the Conservatives, and that the Labour party—the name was formally adopted in 1906—had sensibly increased its strength. The new portent at Westminster did not pass unnoticed; indeed, it caused some stir, but its full significance could not then be appreciated. Of the fifty-one candidates sponsored by the Labour Representation Committee, no fewer than twenty-nine were returned. The Liberals had their own trade union supporters, and had put up as hitherto a number of 'working class candidates', of whom twenty-five were elected; when the Liberal Cabinet was formed at the end of 1905 Henry Broadhurst had been made Under-Secretary of State for the Home Department and John Burns, who had once been a member of the Social Democratic Federation, entered the Cabinet as President of the Local Government Board. The Liberal chief whip, Herbert Gladstone, had moreover entered into arrangements whereby Liberal and Labour candidates did not oppose each other in certain constituencies. But these concessions were in vain. In June 1908 the Miners' Federation became affiliated to the Labour party and its fifteen members in the House of Commons thenceforth accepted the Labour whip; as Victor Grayson in 1907 had won a by-election in Colne Valley as an independent socialist[1] and also

[1] When I fought the adjoining constituency of Spen Valley in 1935 I found that his meteoric career had left abundant memories, and many people persisted in believing that he was still alive; he had not been heard of after a visit to Australia.

accepted the whip this brought up the number of Labour members to forty-five. The Amalgamated Society of Railway Servants and smaller unions soon followed the example of the miners. In the two general elections of 1910 the party met with a slight setback, and lost three seats on balance. But its relative importance was enhanced by the much greater decline in the Liberal membership and the recovery of the Conservatives, which meant that the Labour party had become a balancing factor in the House. After the general election of 1906 in a House of 670 members there were 157 Conservative and Unionist members (134 Conservatives and 23 Liberal Unionists), 376 Liberals, 25 Liberal and Labour members, 29 Labour members and 83 Irish Nationalists, which gave the Liberals a substantial majority over all others. After the first election in 1910 there were 275 Conservative and Unionist members (242 Conservatives and 23 Liberal Unionists), 275 Liberals, 40 Labour members, and 82 Irish Nationalists. The Liberals could govern only with the support of the Labour and Irish members. This result was confirmed at the second election in 1910, after which there were 274 Conservative and Unionist members (240 Conservatives and 34 Liberal Unionists), 270 Liberals, 42 Labour members and 84 Irish Nationalists. Though only one-sixteenth of the whole House, the Labour members could not be ignored by the Liberals. The Labour party did not meet with much success in the by-elections of the next few years; but in the House of Commons it had already become a power.

Eight momentous years were to pass before another general election could be held, and perhaps it was just as well for the fortunes of the Labour party that no appeal to the country could be made during the first world war, deeply divided as it was on the pacifist issue. One wing of the party led by MacDonald and Snowden was strongly opposed to participation in the war, and another led by Arthur Henderson held that participation was essential. But other developments favoured the growth of the party. When the first coalition Government was formed in 1916 by Asquith, Arthur Henderson was invited to become President of the Board of Education with a seat in the Cabinet. Within sixteen years of its formation the Labour party was already in the highest counsels of the land with all the power, prestige and access to information conveyed thereby. But more was to follow. Lloyd George's rift with Asquith was deepening, and before the year was out a second coalition had been formed under his virile but ruthless leadership. Not only was Henderson in the War Cabinet with two Labour colleagues, John Hodge and George Barnes, also in the ministry, but the Liberal party suffered a cleavage which not even time has been able to heal.

If the view taken in these pages is correct, the Labour party would in any case have come in due course to be one of the two main parties in the state, but the feud in the Liberal ranks hastened the process. Moreover the pacifism in the Labour party, which might have wrecked it if the constitution had required an election to be held in 1915 or 1916, actually helped its fortunes in the end. The revulsion which was felt against the horrible necessities of war when the peace seemed safely established—alas! on illusory foundations—led many people to vote Labour just because it held no responsibility before 1914.

But pacifism was no qualification in the 'khaki election' of 1918. In this election Lloyd George appealed to the country for a continuance of his wartime coalition. The general theme was 'We have won the war, let us win the peace'. but many discordant notes such as 'Hang the Kaiser' and 'Squeeze them till the pips squeak' inserted themselves into it. The Asquithian Liberals were, of course, excluded from the list of coalition candidates by mutual desire; whether a Liberal member in the old Parliament received the 'coupon' or not was made dependent on whether he had voted for or against Lloyd George's supersession of Major-General Sir Frederick Maurice as Director of Military Operations in a celebrated division in 1918. The majority of Conservative and Unionist candidates supported a continuance of the coalition and received the Lloyd George 'coupon', but a substantial minority did not. The parliamentary Labour party wished to stay in the coalition, and four Labour ministers actually did so, but a special party conference held within three days of the armistice decided on immediate withdrawal; a strong speech in favour of withdrawal was made by Bernard Shaw. The four Labour ministers who remained were reinforced at the election by a new body of candidates standing under the name of the National Democratic party and by one seamen's candidate, who may be collectively described as coalition Labour.

In the atmosphere of December 1918 and in the state of the party machines most candidates who received the 'coupon' started with an immense advantage over their opponents, and it is hardly surprising that in a House of 707 members 483 Coalition candidates were returned. This was the fact which had greatest importance and roused most interest at the time. But from the long-term point of view two other results stood out: the Liberal party had been severely weakened and the Labour party was markedly gaining in popular support.

The 483 supporters of the coalition in the new House of Commons included only 136 Liberals. The coalition, though it had a Liberal Prime Minister, rested mainly on 334 Conservative members. There were another fifty non-coalition Conservatives, bringing the total number of Conservatives in the House to 384. There were only twenty-nine non-coalition or Asquithian Liberals, and the new House therefore contained only 165 Liberals divided into two irreconcilable factions. Great as was the decline in the Liberal fortunes since 1906, or even since 1910, there were never to be so many Liberals in the House again.

If they had only to consider the Conservatives, the Liberals might have hoped to recover their fortunes with the turn of the political tide. But there was the new factor of the Labour party.

In February 1918 the Labour party had given itself a new constitution continuing the system of direct affiliation by trade unions and other organizations but providing also for individual members and for the setting-up of constituency parties. This gave it the machinery to fight a general election on a national basis for the first time, and it threw 363 candidates into the field. Of these fifty-seven were elected. This result disappointed enthusiasts, being only fifteen more than the number elected in 1910 out of a much smaller number of candidates. But there had been only a few months in which to improvise the new party machinery, and the electorate in the full flush of victory was disposed to give short shrift to pacifist candidates. In these circumstances fifty-seven members was a significant total and there were four other members who might normally be expected to vote with them. They were numerically twice as strong as the Asquithian Liberals, and therefore the strongest of the Opposition groups. The Labour party had reached another stage on the road to power.

VI

Eclipse of the Liberal Party, 1918-1931

THE STRUGGLE between the Labour and Liberal parties for the rôle of chief opponent to the Conservatives continued for a decade after the first world war and was resolved only in 1929. The first test came in 1922, when the Conservative members of Parliament in a meeting at the Carlton Club decided to withdraw from the coalition. Lloyd George was obliged to resign, and his place was taken by a purely Conservative administration. There were a few leading Conservatives such as Lord Birkenhead and Austen Chamberlain who stuck to Lloyd George, but the great bulk of the Conservatives following the advice of Baldwin favoured a return to party politics. Parliament was dissolved, and at the general election 344 Conservatives were returned, a decline of only forty on the 1918 figure. Those Liberals who sided with Lloyd George called themselves National Liberals, and fifty-three of them were returned. There were sixty-four Liberals 'without prefix or suffix' or 'Wee Frees' following Asquith's leadership. The total number of Liberals in the House was thus 117, divided into two almost equal sections who were not on speaking terms. The Labour party put 414 candidates into the field and 142 of them were successful. There had been seventy-five Labour members at the dissolution; the Labour representation was therefore almost doubled and exceeded both wings of the Liberal party put together.

At that time it seemed impossible that the two wings of the Liberal party could be 'put together', but a temporary reunion was effected in 1923 when Baldwin, who had become Prime Minister on the death of Bonar Law, decided to appeal to the country for a mandate to introduce protection. The old Liberal war-horses smelt the familiar battle and decided to pull together. But even with such a rallying cry they secured only 158 seats whereas the Labour party, putting 428 candidates into the field, increased its representation to 191. The Conservatives returned 258 strong, and though the largest single party in the House were outnumbered by Labour and the Liberals combined. In a fateful decision for the Liberals, Asquith decided to turn the Tories out and give Labour its first chance of office. Though he fully realized that his Government could exist only on the sufferance of the Liberals

MacDonald accepted office, and a Labour Prime Minister was at No. 10 Downing Street within twenty-three years of the formation of the party. He did not show much gratitude to the Liberals, whom he treated as 'patient oxen', and within a year he was turned out of office by them over the withdrawal of the prosecution of J. R. Campbell, editor of the *Workers' Weekly*, a Communist paper. The rout of the Labour party at the general election was completed by publication of the 'Zinoviev letter'. The Conservatives returned 419 strong (including seven 'Constitutionalists') and were given a spell of five years in office, a welcome change after three elections in two years. The Labour party fought on a bigger scale than ever before, contesting 515 seats out of the 615, but it was fighting against heavy odds and its numbers in the House fell to 151. The real losers in the election were, however, the Liberals. In their minority position, they had enjoyed the old sensation of power, first putting Labour in and then turning it out, but the polls brought a heavy retribution. Only forty-two Liberals took their seats in the new Parliament. Their discomfiture was increased during the general strike of 1926, when the old feud between the leaders was reopened, Asquith backing the Government and Lloyd George supporting the strikers.

In 1929 Parliament was dissolved at the end of its statutory lease of life. In five years the political pendulum had swung far and the number of Conservatives returned fell to 260. The Liberals made a supreme effort to regain their supremacy. Asquith's death in 1928 had left Lloyd George in the sole leadership of the party. The political funds accumulated by him, which he had resolutely declined to throw into the common Liberal funds despite the reunion, were lavishly used, and 512 candidates took the field. Furnishing himself with a galaxy of economic talent, Lloyd George stumped the country on the attractive cry, 'We can conquer unemployment'. But only fifty-nine Liberals were returned the increase of seventeen being totally disproportionate to the effort made. The Labour party, also putting 512 candidates into the field, obtained the return of 289 members. Though a minority in the House of 615 members, they were the biggest single party, and when the King's invitation came MacDonald had no hesitation in forming his second administration. The country had made up its mind that it wanted the Labour party, and no longer the Liberals, as the alternative to the Conservatives. Because the Labour Government could not continue in office without their support they again enjoyed the sensation of power, as in 1923, but every subsequent election has confirmed its illusory nature.

──── VII ────

Labour's Allies and Rivals, 1918-1931

IT IS NOW TIME to look back on other developments that had taken place while this contest was being resolved. The Labour Party was never in the position of being the sole challenger to the Liberal party for its place as the opponent of the Conservatives. Its history has been like the course of a whale, which attracts a host of minnows in its wake. Almost from its first days it has had small parties associated with it or goading it into more extreme courses of action or even trying to supplant it.

The Independent Labour party was affiliated to the Labour party, and, as we have seen, was one of the three bodies which called it into being. But it always had an independent existence within the Labour party. It held its own conferences, put up its own candidates for Parliament, had its own policy, and had its own conception of parliamentary tactics, which in the end made further partnership with the Labour party impossible. Early in the century the Social Democratic Federation turned itself into the Social Democratic party; but it is in the nature of left-wing movements to breed secessions, and extreme elements in Scotland broke away from it to form the Socialist Labour party while London malcontents formed the Socialist party of Great Britain. The British Socialist party, the Socialist Labour party and the Socialist party of Great Britain were all Marxist. The Independent Labour party was Socialist but did not necessarily follow the teachings of Karl Marx. Before the first world war the Labour party was not committed to socialism, and it included many in its ranks, especially among the trade unionists, who were not socialists and some who were definitely hostile to socialism. The I.L.P. regarded itself as a 'ginger group' within the Labour party, while the British Socialist party, the Socialist Labour party and the Socialist party of Great Britain denounced the Labour party from outside for its lukewarmness in the Socialist cause. The Labour party, the Independent Labour party, the Fabian Society and the British Socialist party were separately affiliated to the Second or Socialist International, which embarked on a campaign just before the first world war in favour of 'Socialist unity' in each country. The negotiations for a United Socialist Council—there was never any possibility of fusion—broke down because the British Socialist party wanted to allow candidates to stand under the label 'Labour and Socialist', a proposal which the I.L.P. opposed, not because it was unfavourable to socialism, but lest it should open the door to 'Labour and Progressive' or even 'Labour and Liberal' candidatures. But the I.L.P. agreed to support the British Socialist party's application for affiliation to the Labour party, and this was accepted in 1916.

The conversion of the Labour party to socialism went on apace during the war, but even when they were converted to the substance some of the trade union leaders still sought to avoid the name. They realized that although this would rejoice the hearts on their left it might lose them support on their right which in numbers and in influence was far more important. If asked to choose between the disgruntled intellectuals of the British Socialist party and the mass of co-operative consumers throughout the country, Arthur Henderson, who had not belonged to any socialist organization until he joined the Fabian Society in 1912, had no doubt of the answer. A few co-operative societies were already affiliated to the Labour party, and Arthur Henderson would like to have welded the Labour party and co-operators into a single whole; he even played with the name 'People's party' for that purpose. But the co-operative movement was not prepared for such a step. This movement had a long and honourable history from the day in 1844 when twenty-eight cotton operatives opened their shop in Toad Lane, Rochdale. Hitherto, co-operators had kept strictly to their conception of themselves as engaged in a new system of mutual trading. While keeping a watchful eye on legislation affecting consumers, they had preserved a rigid neutrality between parties; and several proposals for supporting the Labour party had been turned down before the first world war. During the war co-operators became irritated with various items of Government policy which they thought bore more harshly on them than on other traders, but the movement was not yet ready to join forces with the Labour party, and in 1917 the Co-operative Congress at Swansea decided to organize a Co-operative party of its own. It ran its first candidate, unsuccessfully, at a by-election early in 1918. At the general election later in the year it put ten candidates in the field, and one of them was elected. A new party had been born, and it survived all the perils of infancy. We shall follow in due course its subsequent history, and we shall see that it became a wing of the Labour party, but in origin it was distinct.

Co-operators having set up their own party in 1917, when the Labour party came to re-write its constitution in February 1918 it was exposed to stronger temptation to identify itself with socialism, but it still shrank from the use of the name. The new constitution included among the party objects,

> 'To secure for the producers by hand or by brain the full fruits of their industry, and the most equitable distribution thereof that may be possible, upon the basis of the common ownership of the means of production and the best obtainable system of popular administration and control of each industry and service',

and the words 'upon the basis of the common ownership of the means of production' may be regarded as a vague acceptance of the socialist aim. The new constitution also included among the party objects,

> 'To co-operate with the Labour and Socialist organizations in the dominions and the dependencies with a view to promoting the purposes of the party',

and

> 'To co-operate with the Labour and Socialist organizations in other countries',

but the Labour party still avoiding saying explicitly that it was the Socialist party. The story of these names is not unlike that of Whig and Tory. The name 'Socialist' was used by opponents to discredit members of the Labour party, but was increasingly accepted by members as a badge of honour. The Labour party in due course began to drop its hesitancy. The party objects were re-defined so that the above-quoted section now runs,

> 'To secure for the *workers* by hand or by brain the full fruits of their industry and the most equitable distribution thereof that may be possible, upon the basis of the common ownership of the means of production, *distribution and exchange*, and the best obtainable system of popular administration and control of each industry or service,'[1]

and in 1945 the party election manifesto flamboyantly declared, 'The Labour party is a socialist party and proud of it', though even then the authors hastened to add, 'But socialism cannot come overnight, as the product of a week-end revolution'.

But this was far off, in 1918 when Lloyd George appealed to the country for a continuance of his wartime coalition. Four of the Labour ministers in that coalition accepted the 'coupon' and were re-elected, but one resigned for reasons of health in 1920, one did not stand again in 1922, one was then defeated, and the fourth, though

---

[1] My italics.

elected in 1922, was defeated in 1923. The National Democratic party, made up of members of the Labour party, had taken the field in 1918 in support of a continuance of the coalition, and ten of its candidates were elected. Of these one went over to the Labour party and the other nine were defeated in 1922. This was the end of the brief history of the National Democratic party, though history, as we shall see, to some extent repeated itself in 1931.

While the Labour party was shedding its more moderate members, a more formidable danger arose in the other direction. The formation of the Third or Communist International in March 1919 with head-quarters in Moscow split the socialists of every country in Europe. International socialist unity had never been more than a dream, and even the dream had been shattered by the outbreak of war in 1914. Now there were two rival bodies claiming to be the centre of inter-national socialist unity; and though they might not differ on the ulti-mate nature of a socialist commonwealth they had very different ideas on how to get there. In 1920 the second congress of the Moscow body laid down twenty-one conditions for membership of the Third Inter-national. Among other conditions it prescribed that all constituent parties must set up 'a parallel illegal machinery', conduct propaganda in the armed forces, rigidly exclude all 'reformists' and 'centrists', and remove all 'unreliable elements'. A minority of the Italian Socialist party, a majority of the French socialist party and a majority of the German Socialist party accepted the conditions. The minority of the Italian Socialists became the Communist party of Italy; the majority of the French Socialists became the Communist party of France; a Communist party had existed in Germany since 1918 and the majority of the Socialists joined it to form the United Communist party of Germany.

In considering the tangled negotiations at this time it must be remem-bered that there was then no clear distinction between socialism and communism. Attempts to set up a Communist party in Great Britain or a Socialist party affiliated to the Third International, had been made soon after the creation of the Moscow body; but the real object-ive was masked under the name of a campaign for 'socialist unity'. The Labour party was wise enough to have nothing to do with this cam-paign and the I.L.P. dropped out of it, but persistent efforts continued to be made to form the British Socialist party, the Socialist Labour party and various local bodies such as the South Wales Socialist Society and the Workers' Socialist Federation (a secession from the militant suffragists under Miss Sylvia Pankhurst's leadership) into a Communist party. These efforts were at first frustrated because the British Socialist party wished to retain its affiliation with the Labour party whereas the other bodies were hostile to the Labour party. The executive committee of the Socialist Labour party soon withdrew from the negotiations, but a majority of the members disagreed with the executive and some of them called a conference which repudiated the executive and ordered negotiations to be resumed. As a result a Communist party unity group was formed and with the British Socialist party it constituted a 'joint provisional committee for the Communist party' which summoned a Communist unity conference for July 1920. At that conference the Communist party of Great Britain was born and it had to take an early decision on its attitude to the Labour party. The joint provisional committee sought guidance in the most authoritative quarter, and from Lenin himself it received a letter saying, 'I am in favour of participation in Parliament, and adhesion to the Labour party on condition of free and independent Communist activity.' At the conference in July a resolution in favour of affiliation was carried, though by only 115 votes to 85; and in August the executive committee of the new party made its first application for affiliation in a truculent letter to which Arthur Henderson replied, 'The basis of affiliation to the Labour party is acceptance of its constitution, principles and programme, with which the objects of the Communist party do not appear to be in accord'. In the name of socialist unity there opened a battle in which no quarter was to be given on either side. In 1921, 1922, 1923 and 1924 the Communist party, enduring all rebuffs at the behest of its Moscow masters, renewed its request for affiliation, and each year the Labour party conference by an overwhelming majority supported the party executive in rejecting it. But Communists were still eligible for membership of the Labour party, and, if selected, could become delegates to conferences and candidates for Parliament. They made the fullest use of the opportunities afforded to them in this way, and in 1923 a well-known member of the Communist party, S. Saklatvala, having pledged himself to accept the Labour party constitution, was endorsed as a Labour candidate and elected to Parliament. The Labour party in self-defence against these fraternal attentions ruled in 1923 that delegates must 'individually accept the constitution and principles of the Labour party'; in 1924 it decided that no member of the Communist party should be eligible as a Labour candidate, and that no member of the Communist party should be eligible for individual membership of the Labour party; and in 1925 it indicated that, in its opinion, trade unions should refrain from nominating delegates belonging to non-affiliated parties, including the Communists, as delegates to Labour Party conferences. The door against Communist penetration of the Labour party was locked, bolted, and barred and in order to get into the Labour party thereafter Communists had to go underground.

The Labour party found it a welcome relief to turn from the attentions of the Communists to relations with the Co-operative party. The one Co-operative member who had been elected to Parliament in 1918 promptly joined the Labour party. There were, indeed, close relations between the Co-operative and Labour parties from the outset, but the Co-operative Congress, representing the great mass of unpolitically minded co-operators as well as many Liberals and some Conservatives, was suspicious, and in 1920 turned down a plan for a 'Labour and Co-operative political alliance'. In the next few years it required all the ability of the Labour party's draughtsmen to find formulae permitting the Labour party to support approved Co-operative candidates while shutting out Communists.

In 1922 four Co-operative members were elected and in 1923 there were six, of whom one was given office in the first Labour administration. Five Co-operative members were returned to Parliament in 1924. As the Labour party stiffened in its attitude to the Communists, the Co-operative movement grew more cordial, and at the Co-operative Congress in 1925 a resolution was at last passed in favour of arrangements with the Labour party over candidates and elections. A joint committee of the two parties in 1926 made an agreement for avoiding contests between Labour and Co-operative candidates and for the conduct of joint electoral campaigns. It also provided that local Co-operative parties were eligible for affiliation to divisional Labour parties; the Labour party constitution already provided that co-operative societies might affiliate directly to the Labour party, and in 1927 one society, the Royal Arsenal, chose to do so rather than to affiliate to the Co-operative party. Fear of further acts of this character may have made the Co-operative Congress more disposed to join arrangements with the Labour party, but the survival of the old hostility is shown by the closeness of the vote in favour of the arrangements—1,960,000 to 1,843,000. From that day the Co-operative party has really been a wing of the Labour party. Under the new pact nine Co-operators were returned in the general election of 1929, and their most prominent member, M. A. V. Alexander (now Lord Alexander), joined the Cabinet as First Lord of the Admiralty.

The Independent Labour party, which ranked in the eyes of the

Labour party as an affiliated 'Socialist society', lost an extreme left-wing to the Communist party within six months of that party's formation, but it continued to press for a much more radical advance to socialism than many of the trade union elements in the Labour party were prepared to accept. Its outlook was expressed in the slogan 'Socialism in our time'. Until this date the driving force in the Labour party had come mainly from the I.L.P. Its leaders carried more intellectual equipment than the trade unionists and it was the main agent of propaganda for socialism. But MacDonald and Snowden, the most gifted and powerful of the I.L.P. leaders, were becoming estranged from it and sought to make the Labour party itself the instrument of their ideas. The estrangement became obvious in 1926–8, after the general strike had opened the minds of constitutionally-minded members of the Labour party to the dangers of 'direct action'. The first open sign of the divergence between the I.L.P. and the trade union section in the Labour party came in 1926, ironically enough over an I.L.P. proposal for a national system of family allowances, which was defeated at the Labour Party conference by 2,242,000 votes to 1,143,000. This was part of an I.L.P. 'Living wage plan', which was put in full before the Labour party conference in 1927 and was defeated after having been described by MacDonald as full of 'flashy futilities'. In revenge the I.L.P. had refused to nominate MacDonald for the post of party treasurer or even as a delegate to the conference; henceforth his membership of the I.L.P. was nominal, and Snowden resigned from it in 1928.

The divergence soon covered almost the whole field of policy from birth control to war. At the I.L.P. conference in 1928 James Maxton, who had become its effective leader, defined its mission as to be 'a Socialist party within the Labour party'; but it was becoming increasingly obvious that it could not much longer remain within the Labour party. After the general election of 1929 there were thirty-seven I.L.P. members, of whom seventeen sat for Scottish seats. The difficulties in which the minority Labour Government became enmeshed made the I.L.P. section increasingly restive. Maxton had tried to ensure that if the Labour party accepted office it would seek to carry out a fully socialist policy, and court defeat, but this was not Mac-Donald's view and in fact the Government drifted without a policy while unemployment reached frightening heights. In 1930 the I.L.P. conference approved a statement declaring the I.L.P. to be 'an independent socialist organization, making its distinctive contribution to Labour party policy and having its distinctive position within the party'; at the same time membership of the I.L.P. parliamentary group was made conditional on full acceptance of I.L.P. policy. In pursuance of this decision a letter was sent to I.L.P. members of Parliament asking them to pledge themselves to accept the policies of 'Socialism in our time' and 'Internationalization in our time' approved by the I.L.P. conference and requiring them to vote against the Parliamentary Labour party if there was a conflict with I.L.P. policy. The Parliamentary Labour party's standing orders required that members should not 'vote for any motion, amendment or prayer contrary to the decision of the party meeting', though members were permitted to abstain on matters about which they had conscientious scruples.[1] There was thus a direct conflict, and the Labour party retaliated by refusing to endorse I.L.P. candidates at by-elections and prospective parliamentary candidates for the next general election. Efforts were made to patch up the differences, but they had not been resolved when the economic crisis of 1931 transformed the British political scene.

[1] See below, p. 125.

——— VIII ———

The Parties Reshuffled, 1931-1951

THE YEAR 1931 is, like 1846 and 1886, an epoch of swift and dramatic change in the British party scene. The first crack in the party structure was made by Sir Oswald Mosley, the most extravagant figure in British politics in recent generations. After entering Parliament in 1918 as a Conservative and sitting for a time as an Independent, he had become a Labour member in 1926 on the nomination of the Independent Labour party. In the Labour Government of 1929 he was made Chancellor of the Duchy of Lancaster, and under the leadership of J. H. Thomas he was given a special responsibility for countering the disturbing rise in unemployment. Failure to get his ideas accepted led him to resign from the Government. A resolution supporting his ideas was defeated at the Labour party conference in 1930 by only 1,251,000 votes to 1,046,000, and Mosley was elected to the national executive of the party in place of J. H. Thomas. It seemed as though the Labour party, even if it did not accept his leadership, must accept his ideas. Sir Oswald Mosley then committed one of those incalculable acts, like Randolph Churchill's resignation, that alter a whole career. He announced that he was forming a new party on the basis of a memorandum, *A National Policy*, which he had written with Mr. Aneurin Bevan, Mr. John Strachey and others who now blush to recall their association with him. Mr. Bevan declined to follow Sir Oswald Mosley into the New party and Mr. Strachey resigned within a few weeks of joining. Sir Oswald Mosley was expelled from the Labour party, and set about the organization of the New party for the next general election, in which he announced that he would field 400 candidates.

The next crack in the party structure was seen among the Liberals. Sir John Simon (now Viscount Simon) and Walter Runciman (later Viscount Runciman) had been forced to the conclusion that in the changing economic pressures upon the country it was no longer possible rigidly to maintain the doctrine of free trade. There were many other Liberals, especially those actively engaged in business, who shared their views. In June 1931, when the economic crisis was mounting, they declined any longer to accept the Liberal whip in Parliament in order that they might hold themselves ready to propose any measures,

57

including tariffs, that were demanded by the economic needs of the country. To distinguish themselves from the other Liberals, they styled themselves Liberal Nationals, choosing that order of the words to avoid confusion with the National Liberal Federation. Some of the Liberal associations in the country followed the lead of Sir John Simon, others remained wedded to the principles of free trade, and others halted between the two opinions. While hoping that a reconciliation might be possible the Liberal Nationals began to prepare an organization for the next general election.

The election came with all the elements of high drama in September 1931. The economic crisis had grown worse since Sir Oswald Mosley's resignation. In July 1931 the number of the unemployed rose above 2,750,000, the country had a mounting deficit on its balance of payments and the Budget was heavily out of balance. The report of the May committee on the British financial position created universal alarm. The Cabinet was obliged to consider severe and unpopular measures of economy in the public expenditure. All the members appear to have agreed, very reluctantly in many cases, to all the proposed economies except one, a cut of 10 per cent in unemployment benefit. On this issue the Labour Government broke up.

The Labour Cabinet met in the morning of Saturday, 22 August 1931, failed to reach agreement, and adjourned till the afternoon. In the meantime Neville Chamberlain and Sir Samuel Hoare (now Viscount Templewood) for the Conservatives, and Sir Herbert Samuel (now Viscount Samuel) and Sir Donald Maclean for the Liberals, arrived at No. 10 Downing Street, by invitation to consult with Snowden and MacDonald. The Conservative leader, Baldwin, was in Paris on his way from Aix-les-Bains; the Liberal leader, Lloyd George, was recovering from an operation. At its afternoon meeting the Cabinet again failed to reach agreement and adjourned till the evening of the following day, Sunday. The King, who had arrived at Balmoral only on Friday, felt it to be his duty to return immediately, took a night train on the Saturday evening and arrived in London on the Sunday morning. MacDonald called on his Majesty at 10.20 a.m., and advised him to consult the leaders of the other parties on the course to be followed. In pursuance of this advice the King saw Sir Herbert Samuel that same morning and Baldwin, who had in the meantime returned from Paris, in the afternoon. Sir Herbert Samuel advised the King that the best prospect of securing a broad-based Government would be if there were no change of Prime Minister; and he has also recorded in his memoirs that Baldwin was of the same opinion. The Labour Cabinet

resumed its meeting at 7 p.m., and in the course of the sitting Mac-
Donald visited the King for twenty minutes and then returned to
Downing Street. After the Cabinet ministers had dispersed, Sir Herbert
Samuel arrived at the Prime Minister's residence by the front door and
Baldwin and Neville Chamberlain, to avoid sightseers, by the garden
entrance.

Labour ministers have recorded that they dispersed that night expect-
ing to be out of office next day and to see Baldwin at the head of a
Conservative administration; and Neville Chamberlain said in a public
speech that he went to bed under the same impression. But the actual
course of events was much more dramatic. At 10 a.m. on Monday the
King received MacDonald, Baldwin and Sir Herbert Samuel, and it was
officially announced that the formation of a National Government was
under consideration. The Labour Cabinet met at noon for the last
time, and the news conveyed by MacDonald led to scenes of bitter
recrimination. According to one who was present, MacDonald told his
colleagues that they were out of office owing to his resignation but that
he had again kissed hands as Prime Minister and proposed to form
a National Government drawn from all parties. It seems more probable, however, that what he told the Cabinet, or should have told it,
was that he proposed to hand in his resignation, which involved the
fall of the whole ministry, and expected before the day was out to
accept a commission to form a National Government. At any rate it
was not till 4.10 p.m. on this fateful Monday afternoon, following another meeting with Baldwin and Sir Herbert Samuel, that he formally
tendered the resignation of his ministry and accepted the King's commission to form a National Government drawn from all the principal
parties.

There is almost universal agreement that King George V, on whom
fell a heavy burden of responsibility at this time, acted with complete
constitutional propriety.[1] The late Lord Passfield, who as Sidney Webb

[1] Sir Harold Nicolson's official life *King George V* has not appeared in time
for me to use it in preparing this chapter, but it will clearly be a main source in
future for the discussion of these events. The formation of the National Government is related in chapter xxvii, pp. 453-69, and the constitutional propriety of
the King's action is justified on p. 466n. Mr. Nicolson relies on the justification
already provided in Lord Samuel's *Memoirs*, pp. 221-2: 'Mr. MacDonald's
resignation was the necessary consequence of an irreconcilable division in his
Cabinet. The King then acted in strict accordance with precedent in following the
advice of the outgoing Premier: that was to bring into consultation the spokesmen
of the two parties which could furnish a majority in the House of Commons able
to sustain a new administration. The invitation to the Prime Minister to return
to office, and to form a new administration on an all-party basis, was the course
advised by them. So far as I was myself concerned, neither directly nor indirectly
did any expression reach me of any personal opinion or wish of his Majesty. In

had been a principal architect of the Labour party, and on whose published account[1] and private conversations I have largely relied for this record of what took place on the Labour side, had no doubt that the King's attitude was wholly correct; in his view MacDonald had estimated that at least half the Labour party would follow him, and on this basis the King was justified in authorizing him to proceed with the formation of a National Government. Moreover, the King had received similar advice from the other party leaders he had consulted; and therefore, as Lord Samuel observes in his memoirs, 'the King acted on the advice unanimously tendered to him.' In his first conversation with Sir Herbert Samuel, MacDonald had expressed much doubt about the course he should pursue, but when the suggestion of heading a National Government was made his mind was receptive. It seems probable that he had, unknown to his colleagues, been turning over such an idea for a long time past; this was, at any rate, the conclusion of his colleague Passfield, who, meditating on these events at a later date, perceived the influence of an article written in the *Observer* early in 1931 by its editor, J. C. Garvin. In the responsibilities of office he had come to find his socialist colleagues increasingly tiresome, and when the suggestion of a National Government headed by himself was made the seed fell on well-prepared ground.

But he had not prepared the ground in his party, and only fifteen Labour members of Parliament followed him. Three of his former Cabinet colleagues—Snowden, Thomas and Sankey—agreed to join the National Government. Snowden had no love of MacDonald, but he was an orthodox and austere financier who considered it his duty to remain at the Exchequer until the country's finances were put right. Thomas had endured much at the hands of his Labour colleagues, and was as sick of them as they of he. Sankey was really only an 'honorary member' of the Labour party in virtue of his chairmanship of the Coal Industry Commission and his report recommending nationalization; he had no deep socialist convictions.

The Labour party was not cleft in twain, as it might have been in

every particular the principles and practice of our democratic constitution were scrupulously observed.' One point brought out by Mr. Nicolson is the important part unexpectedly played by Sir Herbert Samuel. Not only did Lloyd George's convalescence compel him to act for the Liberals, but through the accident that Baldwin 'had strayed off into the streets and could not be located' the King saw him before the Conservative leader; and according to his private secretary, Sir Clive (later Lord) Wigram, he found 'Sir Herbert Samuel the clearest-minded of the three and said that he had put the case for a National Government much clearer than either of the others'. (*Loc. cit.*, p. 461.)

[1] *The Political Quarterly*, January–March 1932, vol. iii, no. 1, pp. 1–17.

those hectic days when men had to take quick decisions. It lost for the time being all influence and such little prestige as it had retained, but the solid core of the party remained intact both in Parliament and in the country. MacDonald's decision in 1931 has many points of similarity with Peel's in 1846, but MacDonald was not able to take with him more than one-eighth of the members who followed Peel. One reason is the energy with which Arthur Henderson threw himself into the task of repairing the damage caused by MacDonald's action. The careers of these two men make an interesting contrast. MacDonald had been the prime spirit in creating the Labour Representation Committee in 1900 and for years had been the darling of the I.L.P. He was bitterly opposed to participation in the first world war and resumed the leadership of the Labour party after the war because the Clydeside extremists preferred him to Clynes. Henderson was in no sense a socialist until 1912, and not only did he favour participation in the first world war but he served in the War Cabinet. The two men disliked each other, and MacDonald took the Foreign Office in 1923 as well as No. 10 Downing Street rather than see Henderson there. But thereafter MacDonald moved steadily away from the extremism of his youth while Henderson moved towards the full socialist position. Their paths crossed in August 1931 for an angry moment and then diverged, never again to meet.

The attitude of the Liberal party illustrates the accidents on which the course of history turns. Its leader, Lloyd George, was ill at the time, and it fell to Sir Herbert Samuel to tender advice to the King. In pursuance of that advice the Liberals in Parliament gave their support to the National Government and two of them—Sir Herbert Samuel himself and Lord Reading—were included in the Cabinet. But Lloyd George's subsequent career makes it clear that if he had been well his advice might have been different; and when he returned to his parliamentary duties he gave no support to the National Government.

The Conservative party generally, like Neville Chamberlain, had no thought until the very day that a National Government was to be formed. But the Conservative party in Parliament and in the country rallied to a man in pursuance of its leader's call for a national policy under a National Government, and Conservatives formed the bulk of the support on which MacDonald relied.

It was inevitable that a general election should be held as soon as the immediate financial crisis had been averted. The parliamentary situation in September 1931 was quite unlike any contemplated by the electors in May 1929, and only a new appeal to the country could ascertain whether members had popular support for their conduct in

Parliament. The Conservative party organization was united under Baldwin's leadership and its whole weight was thrown into support of the National Government. The Liberals, as already explained, were divided over tariffs but they were united on the necessity of sustaining the National Government except for Lloyd George, his son, his daughter and his son-in-law, who described themselves as Independent Liberals to distinguish themselves from the Liberals and the Liberal Nationals. The Labour Party organization had remained under Henderson's control; not one constituency Labour party followed MacDonald and Snowden, and the MacDonaldite candidates styled themselves National Labour and hurriedly improvised an organization for the election. The quarrel between the Labour party and the Independent Labour party was too bitter, however, to be resolved even in face of approaching disaster, and although the I.L.P. was still formally affiliated to the Labour party its candidates in 1931 did not receive the endorsement of the Labour headquarters and for practical purposes it stood as an independent party. For this reason twenty-three of its candidates transferred their allegiance and stood as endorsed Labour candidates. The contest was not a 'coupon' election, and there were sixty cases in which two candidates supporting the National Government fought each other in single-member constituencies and one in which three candidates supporting the National Government fought for two seats. Nevertheless the broad picture of the election was that of a contest between the Labour party on the one side and a united front of Conservative, Liberal and National Labour candidates on the other. There were two intrusions into this simple picture—the Communists and Sir Oswald Mosley's New party.

The election was distinguished by the vituperation with which the Labour party assailed their lost leaders, and by the invective with which Snowden branded his erstwhile colleagues. The National Government, appealing for 'a doctor's mandate', had an overwhelming success. No fewer than 473 Conservatives were returned, compared with 260 in 1929, which gave them a majority of 331 over all others, the biggest majority any single party has ever enjoyed in the history of British politics.[1] There were seventy-two Liberals, including the Lloyd George family group of four, instead of fifty-nine in 1929. Thirteen National Labour members were returned. If we discount the Lloyd George group, there were 554 supporters of the National Government in the

---

[1] The Liberals are commonly said to have had a majority of 356 in 1906, but this figure is obtained only by adding the Irish Nationalist and Labour members to their own.

new House, enjoying a majority of 493 over all others. The Labour party, which had 289 members in 1929, was reduced to a mere forty-six, if we count only successful endorsed candidates; but in addition two others who would not give the required pledges were returned and three I.L.P. members, as well as one Independent, Josiah Wedgwood, who acted with the Labour party. Such slaughter had never been seen on a political battlefield; Lansbury was the only Labour Cabinet minister to keep his seat, and the fact that Mr. C. R. Attlee and Sir Stafford Cripps were returned at a time when Arthur Henderson, J. R. Clynes, Mr. Greenwood, Mr. Herbert Morrison, Mr. Dalton and many other more prominent figures in the Labour movement were sent into the wilderness helps to explain much of the party's subsequent history. The massacred Labour party could find small comfort in the fact that others had fared worse still. Sir Oswald Mosley's vaunted 400 candidates turned out to number twenty-four, and not one was elected. Mr. John Strachey, who had left the New party soon after its formation, was bottom of the poll standing as an Independent. The Communists, with twenty-six candidates in the field, achieved a like distinction; not one was elected.

INDEPENDENT LABOUR PARTY

On the morrow of such a defeat it might have been expected that the Labour party and the Independent Labour party would have patched over their differences. But dissidence seems inherent on the extreme left of the political world. The I.L.P. took the view that the Labour party had fallen because it had compromised with capitalism; but although the new leaders of the Labour party were anxious to clear themselves of any charge of 'MacDonaldism', they realized that they could not hope to regain power except by convincing the electorate of their moderation. A battle between the moderates and the extremists, among whom Sir Stafford Cripps rapidly took the lead, was joined. Some members of the I.L.P. put their hopes in the success of the extremists, but Maxton seemed determined to wash his hands of the Labour party whatever the outcome. At the Easter conference of the I.L.P. in 1932 it was decided to continue affiliation to the Labour party only if the standing orders of the parliamentary party were modified. Many members of the Labour party now admitted that they ought to have voted against the Labour Government, but the standing orders were reaffirmed with the proviso that they might need re-drafting if a Labour Government again took office. This was not good enough for the I.L.P., and at a special conference in July 1932 disaffiliation from the Labour party was carried by 241 votes to 142. The I.L.P. thus broke an association with the Labour party which had lasted for thirty-two years and reverted to the status of an independent party which it had enjoyed from 1893 to 1900. But it did so at the cost of a substantial secession. In Scotland those who seceded formed the Scottish Socialist party, a body of which we shall hear no more. In England Frank Wise set up the Socialist League. Only seventeen I.L.P. candidates took the field in 1935; eleven of them contested Scottish seats, and the only four successes were in Glasgow. By this time the I.L.P. had ceased to be an effective force either in Parliament or outside. I remember Maxton saying to me shortly after I entered the House in 1942, 'You know, Thomas, the trouble with me is that I can't hate anyone any more.'[1] There was much truth in this self-judgement. Maxton had become universally beloved, and the Speaker could always rely on him to dissolve a tense situation by the *mot juste*, but the crusading zeal had gone. Maxton, Mr. John McGovern and Mr. Campbell Stephen were again returned for their Glasgow constituencies in 1945, and when Maxton died in 1946 his place was taken by another I.L.P. member, Mr. J. Carmichael. The chastened I.L.P. applied in that year for re-affiliation to the Labour party. The application was rejected by the national executive of the Labour party, confident of its strength on the morrow of its great electoral victory, and at the annual conference no one even bothered to ask why. In 1947 the three I.L.P. members in Parliament decided to conform and were given the Labour whip. The I.L.P. continues to maintain an organization in the country where it can, and put up candidates against Mr. McGovern and Mr. Carmichael in 1950 and in 1951, but it has not since had a member in Parliament and it is merely a shadow of its former self.

CO-OPERATIVE PARTY

The Labour party's relations with the Co-operative Party, though not free from tensions, were a marked contrast with its relations to the I.L.P. The Labour minority in the 1931–35 Parliament included a single Co-operative member, but in 1935 nine Co-operative candidates were successful out of twenty-one. They continued to behave as an integral part of the Labour party. In 1938 the Co-operative party

---

[1] Among other rich sayings of 'Jimmie' Maxton I remember the following. He told me that when he had asked a taxicab-driver to take him to the House of Commons that morning the driver asked, 'Stage door, sir?'

adopted a written constitution. At the outbreak of war Co-operative representatives were invited to attend meetings of the National Council of Labour, and in 1941 this informal arrangement was made formal, the National Council of Labour being reconstituted so as to include equal representation of the Labour Party, the Trades Union Congress and the Co-operative Union.[1] There was some annoyance and forceful speaking among Co-operative members when the purchase tax was introduced, but it did not lead to any breach with the Labour party.

In April 1945 the Co-operative party conference rejected by an overwhelming majority a proposal that the party should affiliate nationally to the Labour party, and Mr. Alfred Barnes, M.P., said that affiliation would mean political extinction. The conference accepted, however, by 5,488,000 votes to 1,247,000 an amendment in favour of negotiations for a new agreement with the Labour party designed to promote effective co-operation between the two parties. In due course an agreement, superseding that of 1926, was ratified in 1946 by the Labour party conference and the Co-operative congress. The general object of the new agreement was to encourage local co-operative society parties to affiliate to constituency Labour parties without severing their ties with the Co-operative party, and in this way to bring about a more intimate connexion between the two bodies. The agreement provided that where a local Co-operative party was unable to affiliate to the constituency Labour party the relationship might be governed by a special agreement. Arrangements were made for running joint candidates both for parliamentary and for council elections. It was laid down that Co-operative candidates for Parliament would need to be selected by the constituency Labour party also and would run under the designation 'Co-operative and Labour.' They would be required, like Labour candidates, to sign a form binding them, if elected, to join the parliamentary Labour party and to act in harmony with its standing orders. At the general election of 1945 the Co-operative party put up thirty-three candidates and contributed twenty-three members to Labour's great majority as compared with nine in the previous Parliament; Mr. A. V. Alexander (now Viscount Alexander of Hillsborough) became First Lord of the Admiralty with a seat in the Cabinet and Mr. Alfred Barnes Minister of Transport. Thirty-three candidates were again put up at the general election of 1950, but the number of members returned fell to eighteen. In the general election of 1951 sixteen candidates were successful out of thirty-eight candidates. A new constitution, covering both national organization and society parties,

[1] See below, pp. 181–182.

D

was adopted by the Co-operative party conference and approved by the Co-operative Union congress in 1951. The most important alteration was the addition of the following words to the declaration required to be made by individual members of the Co-operative party and members of the national committee:

'I am not a member of any organization which sponsors or supports parliamentary or local government candidates in opposition to the candidates either of the Co-operative party or of any other party with which it has an electoral agreement.'

As the Labour party is the only body with which the Co-operative party has an electoral agreement, this ensures that the representatives of the retail societies on the national committee shall not be opponents of the Labour party.

NEW PARTY

The New party did not recover from its obliteration in the general election of 1931. By 1932 Sir Oswald Mosley had convinced himself of the virtues of the corporative state, and was well on the way to founding the British Union of Fascists with which, on account of its contempt for parliamentary institutions, we need no longer concern ourselves. The New party was wound up.

COMMUNIST PARTY

When 'MacDonaldism' had been exorcized, the Communist party renewed its attempts to secure affiliation to the Labour party. Just as Hitler declared that he had no need of a navy and colonies because he could find them in Paris, so the Communists argued that they had no need of a nation-wide political and industrial organization because they could find it in the Labour party—if only they could get control of Transport House. For several years the main energies of the Labour leaders were spent in rebuffing these unwanted attentions. They knew well that the Communists wished to embrace the Labour party only in order to strangle it.

The Communist party made a formal request for affiliation in November 1935, which was rejected by the national executive of the Labour party because 'the fundamental difference between the democratic policy and practice of the Labour party and the policy of dictatorship which the Communist party had been created to promote was irreconcilable'. In January 1937 the campaign took a new form when the Communist party, the I.L.P. and the Socialist League issued a manifesto calling for 'unity in the struggle against Fascism, reaction and war and against the National Government'. The Socialist League, in which the leadership had been assumed by Sir Stafford Cripps after Frank Wise's death, was the only one of the three bodies affiliated to the Labour party and was promptly expelled. When Sir Stafford Cripps, Harold Laski and Mr. G. R. Strauss challenged the executive's action at the annual conference they were heavily defeated. The United Front was normally understood to be confined to 'working class forces', but later in the year a campaign was opened for a Popular Front to embrace Liberals also, and indeed anyone who was prepared to turn out the National Government. This was done in the name of resistance to Fascism, but I do not remember any occasion on which Popular Front speakers pointed out that their hearers could best resist Fascism by joining the armed forces. The national executive of the Labour party liked the Popular Front no more than the United Front, though it took no disciplinary action in 1939 when the Oxford City Labour party withdrew its candidate in favour of the Master of Balliol, Dr. A. D. Lindsay, fighting on a Popular Front programme. In 1939 it was forced to take such action by the renewed activities of Sir Stafford Cripps, who was expelled for circulating a memorandum advocating the Popular Front and written for the executive. His associates, Mr. Aneurin Bevan and Mr. G. R. Strauss, were also expelled for persisting in the campaign, and the annual conference upheld the expulsion by a large majority. Mr. Bevan and Mr. Strauss soon made their peace, but Sir Stafford Cripps was out of the Labour Party until 1945.

This, and still more the outbreak of war, with its exposure of the ter-giversations of the Communists, brought the Popular Front campaign to an end, but in 1943, when the alliance with the Soviet Union created a new atmosphere, the Mineworkers' Federation asked the Labour party conference to permit affiliation provided that the Communist Party agreed 'to accept and abide by the constitution of the Labour Party'. Despite this powerful support the proposal was defeated, and so was a fresh application by the Communist Party itself in 1946. A new rule was then adopted to debar these tiresome affiliations in future.

Unable to burrow into the Labour ranks, the Communists met with no success at the polls. They had only one candidate, Mr. William Gallacher, elected in 1935 and only two in 1945, when he was joined by Mr. Philip Piratin. In 1950 the Communists made their biggest electoral bid so far and put up 100 candidates; not one was elected, and only Mr. Gallacher, Mr. Piratin and Mr. Pollitt avoided the forfeiture of their deposits. The party fought on a more modest front in 1951 concentrating partly on favourable areas and partly on Labour leaders' seats, but once more not a single candidate was returned.

NATIONAL LABOUR PARTY

The National Labour party had been called into being by the exigencies of 1931 and it never had any deep roots in the country. At the general election of 1935 only eight National Labour members were returned, compared with thirteen in 1931, and it is fair to say that none would have been returned but for Conservative support. J. H. Thomas was the only Labour minister in the National Government of 1931 to be returned, and he resigned his seat in 1936 after a Budget leakage. MacDonald was defeated in a bitter fight at Seaham by Mr. Shinwell, but returned a year later in a by-election for the Scottish Universities; he died at sea in 1937. The National Labour organization did not long survive and its members went their several ways. There was much opposition in the Labour Party to the return of any who had left it or been expelled from it in 1931, but the Edinburgh conference in 1936 decided that such persons could be readmitted with the consent of the local parties concerned and the approval of the national executive. Sir William Jowitt (now Earl Jowitt) was the most prominent of those who did so, and at a later date Mr. (now Sir) Harold Nicolson, who had joined the National Labour party without having previously been a member of the Labour party, stood as a Labour candidate. Mr. Malcolm MacDonald, after serving with distinction as a minister, left the parliamentary field in 1941 for the services of the Crown overseas.

LIBERALS AND NATIONAL LIBERALS

The divergence between the Liberals and Liberal Nationals, which had opened over the tariff question in June 1931, deepened after the election. The Conservatives would like to have gone to the country on this issue, and the fact that the Liberals and Snowden were inflexibly opposed to protection was one reason why MacDonald sought 'a doctor's mandate' instead of placing specific proposals before the country. But the size of the Conservative element in the new House of Commons made it inevitable that the demand for protection should be renewed. When a general tariff of 10 per cent *ad valorem* was decreed, Sir John Simon and his followers accepted it on its merits, but the other Liberals and Snowden could not stomach it. The National Government as formed in August 1931 was able to remain in existence only by the partial abrogation of the doctrine of Cabinet solidarity which had been rigidly observed since the Duke of Wellington's last administration a hundred years earlier. The division became more acute after the Ottawa conference in 1932. Sir John Simon and that section of the Liberals which looked to his leadership accepted the Ottawa duties on their merits, but Sir Herbert Samuel and his followers, as well as Snowden, left the National Government on this issue. This withdrawal killed any hope of reconciliation between the 'Samuelites' and the 'Simonites', and the division has become permanent, although efforts were made to avoid setting up rival organizations in the same constituency or one Liberal candidate against another.

The Liberals and Liberal Nationals contested the general election of 1935 as separate parties. The Liberal Nationals put forty-four candidates into the field and had thirty-three of them elected; the Liberals threw 161 candidates into the fight and saw twenty-one of them emerge successful. Sir Herbert Samuel was among the defeated candidates, and the leadership of the reduced party in the House of Commons fell to Sir Archibald Sinclair (now Viscount Thurso), whence the 'Samuelites' became the 'Sinclairites'. The National Liberal claim that to fight as an independent party meant extinction, and that the only way to preserve the Liberal name and Liberal principles was in association with the Conservatives seemed on the way to justification. When the next general election came, in 1945, the Liberal Nationals entered fifty-one candidates, and, under conditions extremely unfavourable to their cause, thirteen were returned. The Liberals put 304 candidates into the field, and had the mortification of seeing only eleven of them elected. Among the defeated were Sir Archibald Sinclair. The leadership of the little band devolved on Mr. Clement Davies, once a Liberal National, but it has never become customary to call them the 'Daviesites'. Major Gwilym Lloyd George also secured election as an Independent Liberal, associated with the Conservatives though not a member of the Liberal National organization.

In 1936 the National Liberal Federation was dissolved and its place was taken by the Liberal Party Organization. This removed the objection to the name National Liberal, and after the war the Liberal National party became the National Liberal Party. Lloyd George's followers in 1922 had also called themselves National Liberals in contra-distinction to the Liberals 'without prefix or suffix', but there is no continuity between the two schisms in the Liberal body; some of the contemporary National Liberals, such as Lord Simon, were Asquithian

Liberals in 1922 and others, such as Sir Geoffrey Shakespeare, were Lloyd Georgian Liberals.

In the light of its experience in 1945 the Liberal party decided that it must make a supreme effort to recover its place at the general election of 1950. Otherwise it would inevitably be squeezed out of Parliament within a short time. The party felt that it must put into the fray enough candidates to command a majority in Parliament if sufficient were elected, and so remove the reproach that it could not provide an alternative Government. In fact, it put 475 candidates into the field—more than at any election since 1929. The result was a shattering disappointment to its hopes; only nine were elected, two of them with Conservative support. The party had devised a novel scheme for insuring at Lloyd's against the loss of deposits—wisely, as it turned out, for 319 out of 475 candidates forfeited £150 for not securing one-eighth of the total votes polled.

By 1950 twenty years of working together had brought the National Liberals very close to the Conservatives. In the summer of 1946 the National Liberals approached the Liberals with a view to the reunion of all Liberals on the basis of co-operation with all who were opposed to socialism. The chairman of the Liberal party executive insisted, however, that reunion could be only on the basis of opposition to both Conservatives and Labour. This was not a condition acceptable to the National Liberals, who thereupon opened negotiations with the Conservatives for a closer relationship. In May 1947 an agreement was signed by Lord Woolton, chairman of the Conservative party organization, and Lord Teviot, chairman of the National Liberal organization, and for that reason usually known as the Woolton–Teviot agreement. In accordance with it recommendations were issued over their joint signatures with the suggestion that Conservatives and Liberals should form combined constituency associations under a mutually agreed title indicating their community of effort and purpose. The united associations, it was added, would be eligible for affiliation both to the National Union of Conservative and Unionist Associations and to the National Liberal Council. By the general election of 1950 united associations or combined committees had been formed in sixty-two constituencies, and each of these had adopted a candidate of either Conservative or Liberal origin. Seventeen of them were elected, and of these two had stood as Conservative and Liberal candidates, four as Conservative and National Liberal, two as National Liberals, seven as National Liberal and Conservative, and two as Liberal and Conservative. On 4 May 1950 it was announced that these seventeen members had formed a Liberal Unionist group, thus reviving an honoured name in a different meaning. The group, it was stated, had its own chairman and whip, and held weekly meetings with particular reference to the Liberal point of view, but all the members of the group accepted Mr. Churchill's leadership, and the members of the group were eligible to attend Conservative committees. In February 1951 a conference at Hastings arranged by the National Liberal Council was attended by over 250 Liberal and Conservative representatives from combined organizations.

The general election of 1951 confirmed the verdict of 1950. The Liberal party decided to concentrate its strength on the most favourable seats, and put 109 candidates into the field; only six were elected. Once more about sixty Liberal Unionist candidates took the field under various designations, and twenty of them were elected—one as a National Liberal, seven as National Liberal and Conservative, two as Conservative and National Liberal, seven as Liberal and Conservative, and three as Conservative and Liberal. It seems clear that if the Liberal party continues to fight as an independent body taking on all comers it is doomed to extinction; and also that the National Liberals are becoming more and more closely identified with the Conservative party. They have, indeed, brought to the Conservative party reinforcements second only in quality and in numbers to those brought by Hartington and Joseph Chamberlain in 1886.

COMMON WEALTH

When the Labour and Liberal parties agreed to enter the war-time coalition under Mr. Churchill's leadership in 1940 an 'electoral truce' was negotiated. Under this truce the parties in the coalition agreed that when a seat fell vacant they would not put up a candidate against the person nominated by the party that held the seat before the vacancy. This was obviously essential as the coalition could not long have survived a series of party skirmishes in the constituencies; it was also fair as the party organizations could not be maintained at full strength during the war. It was expected that under the electoral truce there would not normally be a contest to fill a vacancy. This was galling to Sir Richard Acland, the bearer of a famous Liberal name, and himself a Liberal member, who had become converted to Christian socialism and preached it with an evangelical fervour. He did not at first join the Labour party, which in truth found the new gospel and the manner of its preaching rather strange, but in 1942 he founded a new party which was named Common Wealth. The new party, not being bound by the electoral truce, made no small splash in the political waters for a few years. It declared its aim of fighting every constituency where a 'reactionary' Government candidate was in the field and not opposed by Labour or some other 'progressive' candidate. Labour voters throughout the country, realizing that their fortunes were on the upgrade, were restive under the electoral truce, and voted in large numbers for Common Wealth candidates, of whom two were elected in 1943 and 1944, making with Sir Richard Acland himself a new compact party of three in the House of Commons.[1] The open support of the Labour rank and file for Common Wealth candidates was embarrassing to the Labour leaders, pledged as they were to observe the electoral truce and benefiting by it from time to time. In 1943 the National Executive put Common Wealth on its list of proscribed organizations, membership of which was incompatible with membership of the Labour party. (The Communist habit of giving fancy names to their organizations had compelled the Labour party to draw up such a 'Black list' for the guidance of the faithful.)[2] When the war came to an end and the electoral truce collapsed, it was seen how artificial the support for Common Wealth had been. At the general election of 1945 Common Wealth put up twenty-three candidates, but retained only one of its three seats. Sir Richard Acland was defeated, and when he returned to the House it was as a Labour member. Common Wealth continues to exist, but it did not contest the general elections of 1950 or 1951.

WELSH NATIONALISM

The Welsh and Scottish Nationalist parties, not being elements in the coalition, were also not bound by the electoral truce and the Scottish party at any rate benefited from the fact to the extent of securing its one, and so far only, representative in Parliament.

The Welsh Nationalist party was first in the field, having been founded in 1925. Its official name is *Plaid Cymru*, which means simply the 'party of Wales' or 'the Welsh party'. Welsh nationalism is based in the first place on the existence of Welsh as a living language, though the rapid decline in the number of Welsh-speaking Welshmen was one of the factors that led to the formation of the party. Its principal founder, and first president, was Mr. John Saunders Lewis, of the

---

[1] One of the best pieces of *repartee* I remember in the House of Commons took the following form. In the debates on the Education Bill, 1944, Sir Richard Acland in an interchange with Mr. Chuter Ede asked, 'Does the Parliamentary Secretary believe that the age of miracles is still here?', to which Mr. Ede instantly retorted, 'Well, I haven't tried to create a new party'.

[2] See below, p. 219.

University College, Swansea, lecturer in Welsh language and literature in the University of Wales. The party contested its first parliamentary election in 1929, but it did not attract much attention and the candidate lost his deposit. In April 1934 Mr. Saunders Lewis resigned from the presidency 'lest the party become involved in his religious views'—he is a Roman Catholic, and it is indeed curious that the founder of the Welsh Nationalist party should have been a Roman Catholic rather than a Nonconformist—but he was unanimously re-elected. The party first drew public attention upon itself to any marked extent on 9 September 1936, when three men walked into Pwllheli police station to announce that they had set fire to buildings at the new R.A.F. camp at Penyberth. They were Mr. Saunders Lewis, the Rev. Lewis Edward Valentine, a Baptist minister of Llandudno, and Mr. J. D. Williams, senior master at Fishguard county school. After the hearing before the magistrates it is significant for the cause of the Welsh Nationalist party that the defendants were greeted with hoots from a crowd of some thousands, some of whom had been thrown out of work by the damage, and that one of the sureties was molested. In the trial at the Caernarvon assizes on 13 October 1936 the jury failed to agree and in due course the unusual step of ordering a new trial to be held at the Central Criminal Court in London was taken. There were protests from the Welsh nationalists, and even a deputation from Welsh members of Parliament to the Prime Minister, but the trial duly took place in what the Welsh nationalists regarded as an alien court, and each of the defendants was sentenced to imprisonment for nine months.

The incident is thus referred to in a work by one of Mr. Saunders Lewis's successors in the presidency of the party:[1] 'The misery that drives nations to rebellion made her (Wales) cringe like a frightened cur, and the one act of heroism that illuminated the scene at Penyberth in September 1936 showed how deep the shadows were.' This is magnificent rhetoric, but despite the severe unemployment, which drove many Welshmen to seek work in England, very few Welsh people put their faith in Welsh nationalism, and most Welshmen would have preferred to see more armament work in Wales, even if provided by 'England'. Since this one act of arson, the Welsh Nationalist party has addressed itself to the peaceful persuasion of the Welsh people rather than to deeds of 'heroism'. It has sought, in particular, to inculcate the following principles laid down in its constitution:

'1. To secure for Wales the same status and constitution within

[1] Gwynfor Evans, *Plaid Cymru and Wales*, p. 15.

the British Commonwealth of Nations as is now possessed by Canada, Australia, South Africa, Eire, etc.[1]

To secure for Wales a Parliament having full power to make laws for the good of Wales, with a government responsible to that Parliament.

'2. To safeguard the culture, language and traditions of Wales by giving them the official recognition and support of the Government.

'3. To secure for Wales the right to become a member of the League of Nations.'

The party's official language is Welsh, but it issues publications in Welsh and in English. *Y Ddraig Goch* has been published since 1927, monthly in Welsh, and *The Welsh Nation* is published monthly in English. Most of the party's pamphlets are published in both languages. Most of the branches use the Welsh language exclusively, but some use English only and some use both languages. In the party's annual conference it is the practice to interpret all English speeches into Welsh and all Welsh speeches into English. The party has a number of English men and women as members—sympathizers who wish to revive or strengthen Welsh nationality.

More recently a Welsh Republican Movement (*Mudiad Gweriniaethol Cymru*) has been started. It has no connexion with the Welsh Nationalist party, and the chief executive authority in it is its council. The first two of the twelve points in the Welsh Republican manifesto are:[2]

'1. That Wales must be a sovereign, democratic republic, subject only to such authority as it may accept or subscribe to as a member of the community of free nations.

'2. That the King of England, whether in person as liege lord or through any constitutional agency as monarch, shall have no jurisdiction in or dominion over Wales or any person in Wales.'

A further point in the manifesto states that 'ownership shall be by and for use only', which presumably would commit a Welsh republic to an extreme form of socialism. The movement does not call itself a party, but as there was a Welsh Republican candidate—who polled 631 votes—at Ogmore in the general election of 1950 it behaves in some respects as a party. It issues a paper, *The Welsh Republican*,[3] every two months from an address in Cardiff. The paper is written mainly in English, and it is noteworthy that one of the points in the manifesto, while stipulating that Welsh shall be 'the first and official language of the republic of Wales', adds that 'in the circumstances which have resulted in Wales through English rule the English language shall be

---

[1] This was drawn up before Eire severed her connexion with the Commonwealth. It is rather hard on New Zealand to be dismissed as 'etc.'

[2] Published in *The Welsh Republic*, by C. Bere.   [3] *Y Gweriniaethwr*.

used as a second language and as such shall be officially recognized'. The movement has few members and little standing. So far as Welsh nationalism has been roused, the Welsh Nationalist party has been a more potent influence, and has attracted some of the leaders of Welsh cultural life.

One of the difficulties in the way of rousing Welsh national feeling is that the mountains of central Wales create a barrier between north and south. Parodying one of Julius Caesar's best known lines, we may say: *Gwalia est omnis divisa in partes tres.* In consequence there is no natural capital for Wales; in order to get from one part of Wales to another it is often most convenient to go into England first;[1] and when north Walians and south Walians meet they often find it easiest to do so in Shrewsbury, Hereford, or even London. The Welsh Nationalist party has made its headquarters in Cardiff, with branch offices in Caernarvon and Aberystwyth, but few north Walians would regard Cardiff as the capital of Wales, although it is much the largest town in the principality. In August 1952 the party had 210 branches—a few of them in England— and the total membership is distributed fairly evenly among the Welsh population. If we judge by the fate of the party in parliamentary elections, it has not as yet made much impact on Welsh consciousness. Not a single Welsh Nationalist has yet been sent to Westminster. The number of Welsh Nationalist party candidates was eight in 1945, three in 1950 and two in 1951; nearly all lost their deposits. The party has had more success in local elections. In April 1952 seventeen of its candidates contested county council seats, and twelve were elected. But in Parliament the people of Wales obstinately prefer to be represented by the older parties, in the main by the Labour party; and no doubt the leading Welshmen in the older parties—a David Lloyd George in the past, a James Griffiths or an Aneurin Bevan in the present —reflect that the Parliament of the United Kingdom provides them with a bigger stage for their activities than a Welsh dominion could ever do.

But this is not the whole story. The determined agitation of the Welsh Nationalists has not been without its effects. It has not won them seats at Westminster, but it has been a factor in compelling the older parties to recognize Wales as a nation and to propose political machinery appropriate to that recognition. The Liberals, for whom Wales has proved a last stronghold, have gone farthest in this recognition,

---

[1] Welsh nationalists say that this is because Welsh communications have been devised by Englishmen for the benefit of England, but this is hardly convincing and ignores the natural barriers.

and would give Wales, on the analogy of Northern Ireland, a Parliament of its own for local affairs while continuing to send members to the United Kingdom Parliament at Westminster. Several prominent Welsh members of the Labour party had pledged themselves, before the general election of 1945, to a Secretary of State for Wales on the analogy of Scotland; but when their party was called upon to form a Government, the only change it made was to create a Council for Wales which no one wanted and which has satisfied no one. Before the general election of 1950 the Conservatives undertook that, if returned, they would see that the oversight of Welsh affairs was made the responsibility of a Cabinet minister; this pledge was repeated in 1951 and carried out by giving the Home Secretary, Sir David Maxwell Fyfe, this responsibility. Himself of pure Scots descent, he was given an additional Welsh under-secretary in his department to help him with this unfamiliar addition to his duties when the Ministers of the Crown (Parliamentary Under-Secretaries) Act, 1952 made this possible.

SCOTTISH NATIONALISM

The Scottish National party, as an organized party, was founded in 1928; but national political aspirations in Scotland have a longer history.[1] The Young Scots' Society that existed before the first world war was an adjunct of the Liberal party. After the first world war the Scottish Home Rule Association and the Scots National League canalized those political aspirations. The association believed in trying to persuade the existing United Kingdom parties to come out in favour of home rule, and it pinned its faith in particular on the Labour party. The League sought full Scottish statehood and did not believe that this would ever be conceded by the United Kingdom parties. It came to consider itself as a national party, and wished to put up parliamentary candidates of its own, though events outran this decision. On personal grounds rather than on grounds of policy there was a breakaway from the league and the Scottish National Movement was founded. Attempts by members of the Home Rule Association to amalgamate the three bodies broke down over the attitude to be adopted to the existing United Kingdom parties. Members of the league and the movement persisted in their efforts, and decided to create a national party. Some of the members of the association accepted the basis proposed, and the

---

[1] See *The Scottish National Party: What it is and what it stands for*. An address by the President of the Scottish National Party (T. H. Gibson) at Glasgow on 1 February 1951.

'National Party of Scotland'—as it was at first called—came into being. The three old bodies in due course disappeared, and the Glasgow University Nationalist Association, whose formation had been influenced by the league, associated itself with the formation of the new party. Later a body calling itself 'the Scottish party' came into existence, but it was ultimately amalgamated with 'the Scottish National party', to use the name eventually adopted by the body created in 1928.

The National party has made its headquarters in Glasgow. This seems curious at first sight, as Edinburgh is the indubitable capital of Scotland, and the Scottish character of Glasgow has been greatly diluted by Irish immigration. But the new party had taken root in Glasgow, which happens also to be the leading centre of Celtic studies. Gaelic is not a living language as Welsh is, and there has never been any question of attempting to revive it as an official language. The party is content in its literature to use the English language, though there are many expressions—such as the demand that members shall pay their subscriptions 'timeously'—that sound strange to southern ears.

The aims of the Scottish National party are thus defined in its *Constitution and Rules*:

'A. Self-government for Scotland—that is, the restoration of Scottish national sovereignty by the establishment of a democratic Scottish government, freely elected by the Scottish people, and whose authority will be limited only by such agreements as will be freely entered into with other nations or states for the purpose of furthering international co-operation and world peace.
'B. The furtherance of all Scottish interests.'

The party first contested a parliamentary election—a by-election in North Midlothian—in 1929, when the candidate gained some 900 votes. It had no success, however, until the electoral truce brought it some adventitious support at the by-elections in the second world war. Dr. D. R. McIntyre, standing as a Scottish Nationalist, actually won Motherwell against a Conservative candidate in April 1945. There was a great stir and no little resentment among all members—for the House likes its ancient traditions—when Dr. McIntyre at the Speaker's call marched from the bar of the House to the clerk's table without sponsors for the purpose of taking his seat and proceeded to make a speech at the table. He did not, however, sit in the House long enough to make much impact upon it—he was a member for only thirty-two days—and his crushing defeat at the general election of July 1945 showed that he had been elected by the votes of Labour electors chafing under the electoral truce. Neither Dr. McIntyre nor any other Scottish Nationalist candidate has secured election at any subsequent date. Eight Scottish Nationalist candidates fought in 1945, four in 1950 and two in 1951; in addition two candidates stood in 1950 under the label Scottish Home Rule, one under the label Scottish Self-Government, and one as an Independent Scottish Nationalist, but with equally little success.

The party has so far not entered candidates for local government elections to any great extent, but it has recorded a number of successes in such elections, notably at Motherwell, Alva and Doune.

In recent years a serious threat to the Scottish Nationalist party has developed within Scotland. Mr. John MacCormack, a Glasgow solicitor, revived the idea of a movement that should be outside parties and should seek to permeate the existing parties with Scottish national aspirations. He hit on the name of the Scottish Convention for his movement, and the choice of the name helps to explain its success. But no doubt the chief reason for its success is a realization by most Scotsmen that a complete severance from England would be a disaster for Scotland and would deny Scotsmen many openings for their abilities and energies. In 1947 the Convention summoned the first Scottish National Assembly, an unofficial Scottish Parliament in embryo, and the assembly has since been held annually. Another decisive stroke was taken in 1949, when the Convention drew up a 'covenant'; the name was again happily chosen, for 'covenant' is a word that sets Scottish hearts stirring. The aims of the movement can be seen from the extract from the covenant:

'We solemnly enter into this covenant whereby we pledge ourselves, in all loyalty to the Crown and within the framework of the United Kingdom, to do everything in our power to secure for Scotland a Parliament with adequate legislative authority in Scottish affairs.'

As the covenant was taken round the towns and villages of Scotland, signatures were collected with amazing speed. Observers spoke of a 'prairie fire'. By June 1951 it was claimed that two million signatures had been obtained, and even if some of them appeared several times this is still a remarkable proportion of a population that totals—men, women and children—only a little over five millions.

Early in 1951 the covenant movement seemed on the point of converting itself into a party. The covenant committee announced in April of that year that it would seek pledges from parliamentary candidates with regard to its aims, and that where the answers were unsatisfactory it would sponsor candidates of its own. This announcement created much division of opinion, for a great deal of the support received by the

movement was given on the understanding that it was not a party; and
in September 1951 the committee announced that it would not put up
candidates in the ensuing general election. In place of putting up
parliamentary candidates it came out in favour of a plebiscite.

Though the covenant movement has not contested elections, and the
Scottish Nationalist party has had no success in so doing, the Scottish
nationalist movements, like the Welsh, have not been without their
influence on the policy of successive governments. The more ebullient
expressions of Scottish nationalism, such as the temporary theft of the
coronation stone from Westminster Abbey, may be ignored, nor need
the protests against the proclamation of her Majesty as Queen Elizabeth
II be taken too seriously. But the covenant movement has provided
ample evidence, if evidence were needed, that Scotland feels herself a
nation and wishes to be treated as such. The Liberal party, as in the
case of Wales, has gone farthest in its readiness to make concessions to
Scottish nationalism. The Liberal election manifesto for 1950 contained this pledge, repeated in a different form in 1951:

> 'A Liberal government would give the Scottish and Welsh people
> the right to manage their own affairs by setting up a Scottish and a
> Welsh Parliament to deal with matters of particular concern to Scot-
> land and Wales respectively, while matters concerning the whole king-
> dom would be decided in Westminster.'

The Scottish Liberal party claims to have played 'its full share' in the
first Scottish National Assembly that met in 1947, and later in the
committee set up to prepare specific proposals for self-government, and
it has adopted as its own the statement of policy issued by that committee.[1] The Labour party when in office initiated certain changes in
parliamentary procedure whereby the second reading of Scottish bills
of a non-controversial character might be taken in the Scottish grand
committee provided that ten or more members did not object; they
also accepted the Conservative resolution extending the powers of the
Scottish grand committee to discuss the Scottish estimates. Mr.
Hector McNeil, when Secretary of State for Scotland in the Labour
Government, appointed a committee under the chairmanship of Lord
Catto to inquire into the possibility of separating the financial and
trading statistics of Scotland from those of England, and so providing
a firm basis for discussion of the consequences of self-government. The
committee eventually reported, on 24 July 1952, that the fiscal statistics
could be separated, but would have no meaning, whereas the trade

---

[1] *Scottish Self Government*, issued by the Scottish Liberal party.

statistics could not be separated short of setting up a customs barrier. In the meantime the Conservative party had come into office, and on the same day that the Catto report was issued the Government announced the appointment of a Royal Commission under the chairmanship of the Earl of Balfour 'to review, with reference to the financial, economic, administrative and other considerations involved, the arrangements for exercising the functions of her Majesty's Government in Scotland, and to report'. A Minister of State for Scotland and an additional under-Secretary for Scotland had already been appointed. These steps need not be attributed entirely to the influence of the Scottish Nationalist movements, but no doubt the agitation of these movements played their part; and they are worth recording as showing that parties and movements which fail to secure, or do not aim at securing, parliamentary representation may nevertheless achieve their aims, in whole or part, by their indirect influence on the existing major parties.

If there is less to record about the Conservative party in these years than its importance in the state would appear to warrant, it is because it has not suffered the internal convulsions of the other parties. 'Happy is the party that has no history.' There have been major differences of opinion among Conservatives on policy—notably over India in 1931–35 and over foreign policy in 1935–39—but these differences have been conducted within the framework of the party organization, and even at the height of the differences no question of secession has ever arisen. The Conservative party in these years has received accretions from many quarters; it has lost only a few individuals.

There have been startling changes to record in the twenty years under review, but at the end the picture left is that of two major parties and their associates, highly organized and well entrenched in the country, and they alone able to provide the Queen with a Government. To this aspect of the British party system we must now turn.

Part II

The Two-Party System

CHAPTERS IX–X

——— IX ———

Rout of the Lesser Candidates,

1950-1951

WHEN WE BEGAN this brief historical sketch we found the House of Commons divided into two parties, Tories and Whigs, and as we come to our own time we find the House of Commons again divided into two parties, Conservatives and Labour. The composition of the House of Commons immediately after the general election of 1951 was:

Conservatives	321
Labour	295
Liberal	6
Irish Nationalists	3
Total	625

In a House of 625 members there were only nine who had not definitely associated themselves with the two major parties. In fact, the figures are even more striking, for five of the successful Liberals (Mr. D. W. Wade in Huddersfield West, Mr. A. F. Holt in Bolton West, Mr. E. R. Bowen in Cardigan, Mr. R. Hopkin Morris in Carmarthen, and Mr. Clement Davies in Montgomery) were not opposed by Conservative candidates, the first two under constituency arrangements between Conservatives and Liberals and the last three by a self-denying ordinance on the part of Conservatives; and although no one can say whether they would have been defeated if so opposed they undoubtedly received many thousands of Conservative votes in their contests with Labour candidates; Mr. J. Grimond in Orkney and Zetland was the only Liberal candidate to win in a three-cornered fight. Furthermore, the figure of three Irish Nationalists given above includes one Irish Labour member (Mr. J. Beattie, Belfast West), who was formerly leader of the Northern Ireland Labour party but resigned in 1934 and joined the Irish Labour party with headquarters in Dublin; for voting purposes he may be counted with the Labour members. We shall not greatly err in saying that after the general election of 1951 in

83

a House of 625 members there were only three members who did not owe their election to one or other of the two major parties.

As we have already seen, there have been many changes and not a few convulsions in the British party system between the reigns of Charles II and Elizabeth II, but throughout there have always tended to be two main parties. They have not always been the same parties, but after each convulsion there is a tendency for two main parties to emerge again. There is therefore nothing surprising in the return of the British people after a period of confusion to a two-party system in which the Labour Party has taken the place of the Liberal as the chief opponent of the Conservatives. But the outlines of the two-party system have never been so stark as they are to-day, and it is worth examining the recent general election results to see how this has come about.

The transformation in the House of Commons brought about by the general election of February 1950 is shown in the following table, which gives the membership of each party in the House of Commons at the dissolution and immediately after the general election:

House of Commons, 1950

	At dissolution	After general election
Labour	391[1]	315
Conservatives and associates	216	298
National	2	0
Liberals	10	9
Communists	2	0
Irish Nationalists	2	2
Independents	16	0
Speaker	1	1
Total	640	625

There were sixteen Independents in the House at the dissolution, none after the general election. The Representation of the People Act, 1948, abolished the twelve University seats which, even in the conditions of 1950, might have returned some Independent members; there were six Independents representing the Universities at the dissolution and one (Sir John Anderson, National) unattached to any party. Thirteen Independents went to the poll in the territorial constituencies, but not one was returned. A comparison of the results in Cheltenham, Rugby and Bridgwater shows clearly that many electors who had given a vote for an Independent in 1945 decided in 1950 that

[1] Including seven vacant seats formerly held by Labour.

they must transfer their allegiance to an official party candidate. In Cheltenham and Rugby the same persons who had been top of the poll in 1945 were bottom in 1950; in Bridgwater the candidates were different, but it is again the case that whereas an Independent headed the poll in 1945, five years later the Independent was at the bottom of the poll. All three defeated Independents were men with national reputations generally reckoned to have given good service in Parliament. The constituency of Bridgwater was unaltered, and that of Cheltenham only slightly altered, whereas the changes at Rugby were not such as to invalidate the conclusion that in 1950 Independents were not wanted.

Cheltenham

1945: Electorate 49,173		1950: Electorate 48,784	
D. L. Lipson (Ind. Con.)	16,081	W. W. Hicks-Beach (Con.)	18,009
Miss P. Warner (Lab.)	11,095	A. G. James (Lab.)	13,027
W.W. Hicks-Beach (Con.)	9,972	D. L. Lipson (Ind.)	10,449

Rugby

1945: Electorate 66,696		1950: Electorate 44,228	
W. J. Brown (Ind.)	18,615	J. Johnson (Lab.)	15,983
J. Lakin (Con.)	17,049	J. Dance (Con.)	14,947
R. H. Lewis (Lab.)	10,470	W. J. Brown (Ind.)	8,080

Bridgwater

1945: Electorate 53,896		1950: Electorate 51,884	
V. Bartlett (Ind.)	17,937	G. Wills (Con.)	21,732
G. Wills (Con.)	15,625	N.E.Carr (Co-op. & Lab.)	16,053
N. Corkhill (Lab.)	5,613	S. King-Hall	6,708

A particularly good illustration of the strength of the party tie and the dependence of a candidate on it is provided by Southampton. Standing for this two-member constituency as a Conservative in 1945 Mr. W. Craven-Ellis, who had sat for the division since 1931, obtained 24,367 votes; standing as an Independent in 1950 for the Itchen division, one of the two divisions into which the borough was divided, he obtained 1,380 votes. It was obviously not Mr. Craven-Ellis but the Conservative party for whom 23,000 of his supporters in 1945 had voted.

The lesson is reinforced by the fate of the five Labour Independents, all members of the last House, who had been expelled from the Labour party and were opposed by official Labour candidates. In all cases they polled fewer votes than both their Labour and Conservative opponents. The case of Mr. D. N. Pritt in North Hammersmith, a constituency almost unchanged by redistribution, is specially instructive. In 1945 his official Labour opponent lost his deposit; in 1950 Mr. Pritt polled 10,388 fewer votes and the official Labour candidate polled 10,181 more. Owing to changes in the electorate caused by death and coming-of-age over a period of five years it would be fallacious to regard this as a straight transfer of 10,000 votes from one candidate to the other, but a general impression of that character is certainly not erroneous. The detailed figures are:

North Hammersmith

1945: Electorate 40,350		1950: Electorate 41,472	
D. N. Pritt (Lab. Ind.)	18,845	F. Tomney (Lab.)	13,346
L. Caplan (Con.)	7,516	T. Gee (Con.)	10,406
W. H. Church (Lab.)	3,165	D. N. Pritt (Lab. Ind.)	8,457
		M. Pick (Lib.)	1,402

Except for two Irish Nationalists in Northern Ireland, candidates from the smaller parties were wiped out as completely as the Independents. The 1,868 candidates who contested the 625 seats stood under thirty-three different labels,[1] but not every label indicated a party. Some of the labels indicate candidates put forward jointly by two parties, and others were adopted by candidates, who might have described themselves as Independents, to indicate the particular item of policy which interested them. Nevertheless, as many as sixteen organized parties (or eighteen if we count the Ulster Unionists and the Northern Ireland Labour party separately) put forward candidates. They are: the Conservative and Unionist party (including the Ulster Unionist party); the National Liberal party; the Liberal party; the Labour party (including the Northern Ireland Labour party); the Co-operative party; the Independent Labour party; the Socialist party of Great Britain; the Communist party; the Social Credit party; the Scottish Nationalist party; the Welsh Nationalist party; the Welsh Republican movement; the Irish Nationalist party; Sinn Fein; the Anti-Partition of Ireland League; the Irish Labour party. Picturesque as this list is, it does not exhaust the British political scene, for Common Wealth, did not put up any candidates in 1950; but its organization is kept in being, and it contested local government elections as recently as 1949. If

---

[1] Conservative, Unionist, Conservative and Unionist, Ulster Unionist; Independent Conservative; National Liberal; Conservative and Liberal, Conservative and National Liberal, National Liberal and Conservative, Liberal and Conservative; Liberal; Independent Liberal; Labour, Co-operative and Labour, Northern Ireland Labour; Independent Labour, Labour Independent, Independent Socialist, Socialist Party of Great Britain; Irish Labour; Communist; Social Credit; Scottish Nationalist, Welsh Nationalist, Irish Nationalist, Scottish Self-Government, Scottish Home Rule, Independent Welsh Nationalist, Welsh Republican, Irish Anti-Partition, Sinn Fein; Christian Democrat; Independent. In addition the Speaker stood without any label.

Common Wealth is added to the above list of parties contesting the 1950 general election the British political scene may be regarded as made up of a Conservative party; two Liberal parties, of which one is allied to the Conservatives and the other has no outside affiliations, six Socialist parties, among which the Co-operative is allied to Labour, and seven Nationalist parties. Naturally they vary greatly in strength, some having the most rudimentary organization and being little more than a name on an office door. If we link together the allied parties (that is, parties which supported each other's candidates), the number of candidates put forward by the several parties at the general election of 1950 and the number elected are as follows:

General Election, 1950

Party	Candidates	Candidates Elected
Labour and associates	617	315
Conservative and associates	621	298
Liberal	475	9
Communist	100	0
Independent Labour	2	0
Socialist Party of Great Britain	2	0
Common Wealth	0	0
Social Credit	1	0
Scottish Nationalist	4	0
Welsh Nationalist	7	0
Welsh Republican	1	0
Irish Nationalist	2	2
Sinn Fein	2	0
Anti-Partition	1	0
Irish Labour	2	0
	1837	624

This gives us a total of 1,837 candidates put forward by organized parties and 624 members elected. The addition of the Speaker, who was successful in securing re-election against an Independent Liberal, brings the total number of members to the full complement of 625. There were 31 candidates not put forward by organized parties, 13 standing as Independents and 18 under 'fancy' names, which brings the total number of candidates to 1,868, the largest number of candidates ever to present themselves at a British election.

Although fourteen organized parties put up candidates, only four were successful in getting any elected. We may leave the two Irish Nationalists out of account as they decided not to take their seats; and if we do we can well see the complete rout of all the minor parties.

A minor party may be defined for this purpose as one which put up fewer than 100 candidates; in fact, none of the minor parties put up more than seven candidates, and the Nationalist parties are, of course, organized only on a regional basis. But if we turn to those parties organized over the whole country which put up 100 or more candidates we see just as vividly the return to the two-party system.

Apart from the Conservatives and Labour, there were two such parties. The Communists put up 100 candidates and did not get a single one elected. The Liberals put up 475 candidates, and had nine of them elected. Out of the 100 Communist candidates 97 lost their deposits; only Mr. Gallacher and Mr. Piratin, the two Communist members in the previous House, together with Mr. Pollitt, the secretary of the party, escaped this ignominy. Out of the 475 Liberal candidates 319 lost their deposits; and the underwriters at Lloyd's took a sourer view of the Liberal party.

Within twelve months a general election was held again. Chastened by their previous experience, and unable to make a similar effort after such a short interval, the Liberal, Communist and minor parties put up fewer candidates. The results are therefore not so instructive for our purpose, but they are sufficiently conclusive and confirm the lessons drawn from the 1950 contest.

Not a single Independent was elected. Mr. W. J. Brown, who had decided not to contest Rugby again, put up a gallant fight in Fulham West as an Independent, but he did so with Conservative support. If we omit him, seven candidates stood as Independents, and all lost their deposits. An Independent Socialist candidate in Glasgow and a British Empire party candidate in Ogmore (who ought to be reckoned an Independent because I am not aware that there is a British Empire party apart from this candidate) also lost their deposits. A split in the Conservative organization in Newcastle Central led to an Independent Conservative standing there in opposition both to the Liberal and Conservative candidate (Major Gwilym Lloyd-George) and to the Labour candidate, and he polled 5,904 votes, much the highest vote secured by any Independent, but was bottom of the poll.

The Socialist party of Great Britain, Social Credit, the Welsh Republican party and Sinn Fein, like Common Wealth, refrained on this occasion from putting up candidates, preferring to lick their old wounds rather than expose themselves to fresh blows. Of the minor parties the Independent Labour party, the Scottish Nationalist party, the Welsh Nationalist party, the Irish Republican party, the Irish Labour party and the Anti-Partition of Ireland League entered a few candidates. The Liberals and Communists decided to concentrate their forces on the divisions where they had most support. The Liberal band was less than a quarter of what it was in 1950, the Communist only one-tenth. The candidates and members elected were as follows:

General Election, 1951

Party	Candidates	Candidates Elected
Conservative and associates	617	321
Labour and associates	617	295
Liberal	109	6
Communist	10	0
Independent Labour	3	0
Scottish Nationalist	2	0
Welsh Nationalist	4	0
Irish Republican	2	1
Anti-Partition of Ireland	2	1
Irish Labour	1	1
	1367	625

If we add the nine Independents not covered by the above list, we get a total of 1,376 candidates compared with 1,868 in 1950.

It will be seen that in Great Britain, the minor parties and the Communists were routed as completely as the Independents; not one of them was elected, and most of them received negligible support. The three I.L.P. candidates, the four Welsh Nationalist aspirants, one of the two Scottish Nationalists, and the one Anti-Partition candidate standing for an English constituency (Bootle) lost their deposits. All the ten Communists lost their deposits. Out of the Liberal 109, only six were sent to Westminster, and in addition to losing 66 deposits the Liberals had the mortification of knowing that five of their number owed their success in all probability to Conservative support.

We must now ask if there were any special factors operating in 1950 and 1951 to bring about these results. In the case of the Communists at both elections and in the case of the Independent Labour candidates in 1950 the hardening of opinion against the Communists and their fellow-travellers is undoubtedly such a factor. After their experience of the Soviet Union's imperialist expansion and the fomenting of industrial unrest by British Communists men who had looked with indulgence on Mr. Gallacher's presence in the House from 1935 and even on Mr. Piratin's from 1945 hardened their hearts in 1950. This intensification of anti-Communist feeling would suffice to explain the rout of the Communists.

But no such explanation will account for the Independents or the Liberals. The standing of Independent members of Parliament in general was higher than ever before and the qualities of the individual candidates were widely appreciated. There was no antipathy to Liberalism; on the contrary, it had become fashionable in most political circles to say, 'We are all Liberals now'. The Liberal attitude to individual freedom and the redistribution of wealth had become the common possession of all parties; and Liberals themselves were no longer disposed to press as formerly they were wont their specific doctrine of free trade.

The fact that Liberalism had penetrated other parties so extensively was one reason, of course, why fewer electors felt it necessary to vote Liberal. The Liberal party now had nothing specific to offer. But this is not the whole explanation. It had already become clear before polling day both in 1950 and in 1951 that little would separate the Labour and Conservative parties; and we can understand the results only if we give a high place to this fact. By 1950 the technique of taking a public opinion poll had been so improved that an accurate assessment of the way the electors would vote could be given each week. This was something very different from the personal observations and newspaper reports, all subjectively coloured, on which earlier estimates had been based. In 1950 it became clear at an early stage that the contest between the Conservative and Labour parties was going to be, in the Duke of Wellington's words about Waterloo, 'a close-run thing, the damned closest-run thing you ever saw in your life'. In these circumstances every vote counted, and electors who might otherwise have been disposed, knowing that their own party was assured of a big majority, to 'give the Liberal a chance' or to 'let the Independent have a run for his money', felt inhibited from such electoral luxuries. Moreover the issues in 1950 were felt by most of the nation to be too grave for such experiments. In 1945, after six years of war in which there had been little domestic legislation, the time was obviously ripe for big changes, and electors were disposed to give their votes freely. In 1950, after five years of Labour rule, Conservatives felt that the safety of the national economy was at stake and Labour thought that its work was being challenged. Among persons of Conservatives and of Labour sympathies alike word went round, 'Now is the time for all good men to come to the aid of the party'. Those who would not describe themselves as Conservatives or Labour, but who shared the general outlook of Conservatives or Labour, felt obliged perhaps for the first time in their lives to give a Tory or Socialist vote. 'I'm absolutely neutral in this election,' I heard one lifelong Liberal declare, 'I don't care who gets them out.' He voted Conservative, but no doubt he had his counterpart who said, 'I'm not going to let the Tories in,' and voted Labour. It was in this tense atmosphere that the Liberals, Communists, minor party candidates and Independents went down, leaving behind them a trail of forfeited deposits.

The election of 1951 was really the same contest over again, and with much the same result except for the difference that the Conservative party henceforth provided the Government and not Labour. Once more the public opinion polls made it clear that only a small percentage of the total vote would separate the Conservatives and Labour; and by this time the statisticians had produced their 'cube law'[1] deducing from the total votes cast the seats that each of the major parties would win, and thus bringing the facts home to the simplest intelligence. Once more it was obvious that every vote counted; indeed, it was even more obvious, for electors now had before them the knowledge of the small margins that had separated victors and vanquished in so many constituencies in 1950—a mere twenty-eight votes in Stroud and Thornbury, thirty-one in Spelthorne, and so on, forty-five candidates getting in by fewer than 1,000 votes. The electors now had fewer Liberals, Communists, minor party candidates and Independents on whom they could bestow their favours, but they were in any case in no mood for such experiments. The rout of 1950 was completed in 1951.

These are the peculiar factors of the 1950 and 1951 elections tending to eliminate the Independents and smaller parties, but we must also concede that there are more permanent factors tending to promote the emergence of two strong parties. The first is that the British people on the whole instinctively prefer it to a many-party system, and the second is that our electoral arrangements favour it. Naturally the Liberals emphasize the latter rather than the former, and indeed are disposed hotly to deny that the British people have any such preference; but neither can be doubted on a close examination of the facts, to which we must now turn.

[1] See below, p. 98.

X

Demand for Electoral Reform

OUR ELECTORAL SYSTEM certainly discourages small parties and tends to their elimination. Since 1950 it has been strictly uninominal, that is to say, each constituency returns one member to the House of Commons. Until 1950 there were a few university and territorial constituencies returning two members, but this was discontinued under the Representation of the People Act, 1948[1]; and even before 1950 the British system was to all intents and purposes uninominal. In each constituency the candidate who gets more votes than any other candidate is declared elected.

It is easy to see that under this system the candidates of small parties have slender chances of election. The big parties put up candidates in almost every constituency, and only on rare occasions is the candidate of a small party able to muster sufficient votes to defeat both of them. He may amass a creditable total of votes, but unless it exceeds that of any other candidate he will not be elected. This does not mean that his candidature may be neglected; he may have considerable 'nuisance' value, even though he has not the remotest chance of election, and his candidature, by its diversion of votes, may have the effect of causing one rather than another of the candidates of major parties to be elected. It is more than probable that in the general election of 1950 Mr. A. Creech Jones, then Secretary of State for the Colonies, lost his seat at Shipley through the intervention of a Communist who polled only 237 votes; for the Conservative victor's majority was only 81, and in the absence of a Communist most of those 237 votes would probably have gone to the Labour candidate. On the other side it is more than likely that Mr. T. E. Watkins (Lab.) owed his election for Brecon and Radnor to the intervention of a Liberal, with the approval of his headquarters but against the decision of the local Liberal association; for his majority was 2,829, whereas the Liberal polled 3,903, most of which in those counties would probably have otherwise gone to the Conservative.[2]

[1] Now embodied in the consolidating measure, the Representation of the People Act, 1949.

[2] This cannot be certain, for in 1951, when there was no Liberal candidate, the Labour vote increased by 2,053 to 24,572 and the Conservative vote increased by 2,799 to 22,489. The Labour candidate was therefore again returned, but it is not certain how far this was due to new votes or in what manner the Liberal poll of 3,903 was split up.

The intervention of the candidates of small parties may therefore not be without significant results; but their own chance of taking their seats at Westminster are small.

Most of the British parties named in previous chapters have such small support that they would not secure representation under any conceivable system, and are therefore not interested in alternative arrangements; they are satisfied with the value of contesting an election for propaganda. But the Liberals, since they ceased themselves to be one of the two major parties, have become acutely conscious that under different electoral systems they could secure a much larger representation. They point out that under the present British system it is possible for a candidate to be returned on a minority of the votes cast and for a candidate to be unsuccessful though he obtains nearly 50 per cent of the poll. This is quite true, and two illustrations may be given, even though they are not perhaps the illustrations that the Liberal party would itself choose. In the general election of 1950 Mr. Edgar Granville, standing as a Liberal against three opponents, was returned for the Eye division of Suffolk although he obtained only 37 per cent of the votes cast, whereas in Pembrokeshire Major G. Lloyd-George, standing as a Liberal and Conservative against a Labour opponent, was defeated although he secured nearly 49.9 per cent of the recorded votes. At that election Mr. Granville re-entered Parliament though his poll was fewer by 12,131 than the combined votes cast for his opponents, and Major G. Lloyd-George was kept out of Parliament by a margin of 129 votes separating him from the winner. No fewer than 187 members were returned on minority votes, the excess of their combined opponents' polls over their own ranging from Mr. P. H. Collick's 76 at Birkenhead to Mr. Granville's 12,131 in the Eye division; in as many as 151 cases the winner's poll was exceeded by more than 1,000 by the combined totals of his opponents, whereas in straight fights forty-five candidates lost by fewer than 1,000 votes. The 187 minority winners were thus distributed among the parties: Conservatives and associates 106 (Conservatives 102, Conservative and National Liberals 2, Liberal and Conservative 1, National Liberal 1), Labour 76, Liberal 5.

In 1951 only thirty-seven seats were won on minority votes. This was due to the much smaller number of Liberal and minor party candidatures, which is another way of saying that there were many more straight fights. The distribution among the parties was as follows: Conservatives 23, Labour 13, National Liberal 1. The amount by which the winner's poll fell short of the combined total of his opponents ranged from Mr. Ian Harvey's 158 in East Harrow to Mr. J. H.

Harrison's 9,151 in the Eye division; and in twenty-eight cases the winner's poll was exceeded by more than 1,000 votes, whereas in forty-four cases candidates were defeated by fewer than 1,000 votes. But though the total of minority wins is not so spectacular as in 1950, the individual cases are just as instructive. In the Eye division Mr. Harwood Harrison, turning the tables on Mr. Granville, was elected although he obtained only 40.6 per cent of the votes cast in a three-cornered fight, whereas Mr. N. L. D. McLean, losing by 16 votes to Mr. E. A. A. Shackleton in a straight fight, was beaten although he gained 49.98 per cent of the votes cast.

To point out these facts is no more than to point out that a sprinter may win the 100 yards in 11 seconds and lose in 10 seconds. In order to win he has to produce the right speed in the right place at the right time. It is of no more avail for the defeated candidate to say 'I should have won if I had been fighting in Eatanswill' than it is for the defeated runner to say 'I should have been first if I had been running at the White City'. It just happens to be our electoral system. But it is not the only possible electoral system, and the Liberals especially are convinced that our electoral system ought to be changed. Long before the Liberal decline gave one of our political parties a practical interest in this question there was also an influential body of opinion convinced on abstract grounds that our electoral system is unjust and ought to be modified in favour of some system of proportional representation; John Stuart Mill gave it his powerful support.

The argument is put in its most cogent form by looking at the total number of seats won by a party's candidates in proportion to the total number of votes cast for them in the country. At many points in the previous narrative Liberal readers have no doubt protested to themselves that the strength of the Liberal party cannot be measured by the number of its seats in the House of Commons. At the general election of 1929, when only 59 Liberals were returned, 5,208,510 votes were cast for Liberal candidates; and when the Liberal party reached the nadir of its fortunes in 1950, with only nine successful candidates, the total Liberal poll was still 2,621,489. (It was only 730,551 in 1951, but the main reason was that only 109 Liberal candidates were nominated, and the 1950 figure is a better indication of Liberal votes in the country.) This is true enough, but I have so far deliberately avoided reference to it because the British constitution and the British electoral system know nothing about the total vote given for a party in the country. There are many countries in which the electors do vote for a party list—and in some there is only one party list for which they can vote—but it has never been the British system. It is, of course, a fiction that we vote for candidates rather than for parties, though personally I believe it to be a valuable fiction—one of Plato's 'medicinal lies'—and the fiction has been wearing ever thinner. The practice of counting the total number of votes cast for a party's candidates sprang up in the eighties. In *Dod's Parliamentary Companion* it appears to have been first done in 1886. It marked the increasing subordination of the individual to the party machine. At many elections the value of the computation was lowered by the large number of uncontested returns, but in more recent years, when few seats have been left uncontested, the figures for the total party polls have given a more accurate indication of party strength in the country. These total party polls are now watched with almost as keen an interest as the number of seats obtained in the House of Commons, and become a basis for policy. After the 1950 general election Mr. Churchill, by adding together the Conservative and Liberal votes, was able to argue that the Labour Government had no mandate for going ahead with the nationalization of steel; and after the general election of 1951, from the Opposition front bench Mr. Attlee was able to pride himself on representing the largest number of votes cast for any one party. (There were 13,948,385 votes for Labour and Co-operative candidates, of whom 295 were returned, and 13,724,418 votes for Conservatives and associates, of whom 321 were returned.)

When the total number of votes cast for a party's candidates are matched against the number of seats won, some curious results are observed. All parties have suffered or benefited in their turn. It is now the turn of the Liberals to suffer, but in 1906 they benefited greatly; in that year Conservative candidates polled 2,463,608 votes but only 157 of them were elected, whereas 3,111,929 votes secured the return of 430 Liberal and Labour members. In 1929 the Conservatives polled 8,656,473 votes and obtained 260 seats, whereas Labour polled 8,389,512 votes and obtained 288 seats—fewer votes and more seats; the Liberals polled about five-eighths as many votes but obtained only a fifth as many seats—5,308,510 votes and 59 seats. But whereas the Conservatives had suffered in 1929 and Labour benefited, in 1931 the rôles were reversed. With a poll of 11,905,925 the Conservatives obtained 470 seats, whereas Labour with a poll of 6,649,630 gained only forty-six seats—over half as many votes but only a tenth as many seats. In 1935 the Labour poll recovered to 8,250,000, almost identical with the 1929 figure, but only 154 Labour members were returned, a little more than half the 1929 figure. It is perhaps not surprising that James

Middleton, the secretary of the Labour party, observed, 'There is no bigger gamble on earth than a British general election.'

Even more curious results can be found by dividing the party poll by the number of candidates returned, and saying, for example, that in 1951 it took 42,630 votes to elect a Conservative, 47,282 to elect a Labour candidate, and 121,758 to elect a Liberal candidate. Except as mathematical exercises, these calculations have no value, because that is not the way our votes are used and never would be under any conceivable system. It is inherent in this conception that a vote is wasted unless it is a vote given to a winning candidate, but it is easy to see that a vote may have value even though given to a loser. Let us turn from these mathematical trivialities. It is, however, legitimate and pertinent to consider the relation between the total poll and the seats gained, and to consider whether changes in the electoral law should be sought to bring them into a closer relationship. Before we can settle this question we must, however, dispose of another. We have shown that the British system tends to discourage and eliminate small parties, but we have not shown that it favours the emergence of precisely *two* strong parties.

If there were three large parties of equal strength the British electoral arrangements would not discriminate between them. But this state of affairs has never been more than momentary. It is what the physicists call a state of unstable equilibrium; and as soon as one of the parties drops below the strength of the other two to an appreciable extent the voters tend to turn away from it. Cynics may connect this with a desire to back the winning side.[1] But although a fair proportion of the population may regard a general election as the political version of the Grand National, the tendency of electors to turn away from the smaller parties is based on more solid reasons and seems to be the result of deliberate choice on the part of the electors reinforcing the mechanical working of our electoral arrangements. There is at least one piece of evidence to support this view. The Liberal party claims to have ascertained as the result of a public opinion poll that 38 per cent of the electors would have voted Liberal in February 1950 if they had thought that the Liberal party could form a government.[2] Even if we doubt the figure, it is a fact within the personal knowledge of all candidates that many Liberals voted Conservative or Labour because they knew the Liberal candidate had no chance of success. The slogan, 'A Liberal

---

[1] I well remember how, in my first election campaign, an elector whose vote I was canvassing looked me in the face and said, 'I've voted in nine elections and I haven't backed a loser yet.'

[2] See the letter from Sir Andrew McFadyean in *The Times*, 26 November 1951.

vote is a wasted vote' has had a devastating effect on the fortunes of the Liberal party because it coincides with the inclinations of electors to put themselves, in a phrase used by Mr. Arthur Greenwood in 1934, 'under one umbrella or the other'.

This tendency in the minds of electors is reinforced by a physical peculiarity of the chamber in which the House of Commons meets. The way in which the rectangular shape of the chamber discourages the system of small parliamentary groups shading insensibly one into the other and encourages the opposition of large organized parties has been stated in classic form by Mr. Winston Churchill in the happiest of his minor speeches; and although Mr. Churchill, no doubt out of courtesy to his Liberal allies in the wartime coalition, did not specifically say that it favoured the *two*-party system, that is the only implication that can be drawn from his words. In moving on 28 October 1943 that a select committee be appointed to consider and report upon plans for the rebuilding of the House of Commons Mr. Churchill said :[1]

> 'There are two main characteristics of the House of Commons which will command the approval and support of reflective and experienced members. They will, I have no doubt, sound odd to foreign ears. The first is that its shape should be oblong and not semi-circular. Here is a very potent factor in our political life. The semi-circular assembly, which appeals to political theorists, enables every individual or every group to move round the centre, adopting various shades of pink according as the weather changes. I am a convinced supporter of the party system in preference to the group system. I have seen many earnest and ardent Parliaments destroyed by the group system. The party system is much favoured by the oblong form of chamber. It is easy for an individual to move through those insensible gradations from left to right but the act of crossing the floor is one which requires serious consideration. I am well informed on this matter, for I have accomplished that difficult process, not only once but twice.'

For historical reasons Parliament will always be the focus of British political life, and our political arrangements outside tend to be a reflection of those inside the chamber of the House of Commons. The physical shape of the chamber may therefore, as Mr. Churchill suggests, have had not a little to do with our party organizations. It would be interesting to reflect what might have happened if the House of Commons had gone on sitting in the octagonal chapter house of Westminster Abbey instead of moving in 1547 to the rectangular chapel of St. Stephen!

[1] H. C. 393 Deb. 5s., cols. 403–4.

B

If the British people have a deliberate preference fostered by tradition and reinforced by our electoral arrangements for the two-party system, is their instinct sound? Are there good reasons for maintaining our present system? Or ought we to seek some new system?

One general principle behind the British system is *Vae victis!* The winner scoops the pool, and the losers are penalized; the more heavily they lose, the more severely they are penalized. It is so difficult for the minor parties to get any seats that they tend to be eliminated. As between two major parties, an empirical law has now been enunciated showing a mathematical connexion between the number of votes they obtain in the country and the number of seats they win in Parliament.[1] If only two parties contest the election, the law states that the ratio of the seats they obtain in the House will be the cube of the ratio of the votes they obtain in the country. To put it in an extreme form, if one party obtains twice as many votes in the country as the other, it will have eight times as many seats in the House of Commons (because the cube of two is eight). It is not claimed that there is or can be any proof of this law, only that it is exemplified in practice. It omits, of course, consideration of the minor parties; and a subsequent refinement has been made to allow for those seats held by a party with very large majorities. (The point is that, where a party wins a seat by the super-fluously large majority of 30,000 or so, the votes would be better spread over constituencies which it loses by small margins; large majorities are heartening to the rank and file, but the party headquarters wish that they could move many of the voters to other registers!) With these allowances it fits the facts reasonably closely. We need not examine it in detail for our purpose, but it brings out the fact that under the existing system the winning party is generally advantaged and the losing party penalized.

On the surface this seems unfair, and in order to remedy the unfairness various schemes of electoral reform have been suggested. Before we can decide between them, we must ask ourselves what is the object of a general election. The decision between our present electoral system and others cannot be made on the basis of such facts as we have already enumerated. They are often recited as though they were the end of the matter, whereas really they are only the beginning. They are admittedly consequences of our present system, and some of them are paradoxical, but they may be necessary consequences of some desired end. There are fundamental objections to all schemes of electoral reform yet proposed.

[1] See the *British Journal of Sociology*, vol. i, no. 3, 1950.

(a) The assumption behind schemes of electoral reform is that the object of a general election is to secure a Parliament reflecting the state of opinion in the country. This sounds plausible, but a Parliament which accurately reflects the views of electors on polling day may soon cease to do so on account of changes in public opinion. As a new general election cannot be held every day, we must accept the fact that this primary object of electoral reform cannot be secured for very long.

(b) A second objection to electoral reform is that there are several different forms of it, differing greatly in their effects; and there is no one of them that is self-evidently better suited than the others to achieve the object of securing an accurate reflexion of public opinion. The British system of voting was called by the Royal Commission on Electoral Systems in 1910[1] the 'relative majority' system, and is described by M. Duverger[2] as the 'simple majority vote with only one ballot', but it is more commonly and more graphically known as the 'first-past-the-post' system. This system may have its defects, but it has one clear merit that when a candidate is declared elected everybody can see the reason. When the returning officer declares John Bull to be elected, everyone understands that it is because he has received more votes than anyone else. All schemes of electoral reform call for the application of some degree of mathematical treatment to the voting, and even though the theory behind this treatment may be academically convincing, the connexion between the results and the voting will not be very obvious to the public, and confidence in the system may be weakened.

The advocates of one type of electoral reform do not propose to disturb the arrangement by which the country is divided into constituencies each returning one member. They propose, however, that no candidate shall be elected unless he has an absolute majority of the valid votes cast, and two ways of ensuring this result are suggested. One is the *second ballot*. If no candidate obtains an absolute majority of the votes cast, all the candidates except the two who obtained most votes are eliminated from the contest, and a second ballot is held to decide between those two candidates, of whom one is naturally bound to get an absolute majority. The other system is the *alternative vote*. The voter is asked, not simply to put a cross opposite the name of the candidate he wishes to see elected, but to express his order of preference among the candidates by putting the figures 1, 2, 3 and so on (so far as

[1] Cmd. 5163, p. 3. The Royal Commission was told that there were 300 systems of proportional representation in existence but many of these are only variants of the main types.
[2] *L'Influence des systèmes électoraux sur la vie politique.*

necessary or so far as he desires) by the side of their names. When the papers are first examined only first preferences are counted; if a candidate has received an absolute majority of the first preferences cast, he is declared elected, but if no candidate has received such a majority, the candidate who has received the lowest number of first preferences is eliminated, and his papers are distributed among the candidates, if any, marked with a 2 on them. If this still does not result in a candidate getting an absolute majority of the votes cast, the process is repeated until it does. It is easy to see that the alternative vote is a method of achieving the same result as a second ballot without the trouble of going through a second poll; the elector indicates in advance how he would vote if it became necessary to hold a second ballot.

Both the above systems are sometimes included in the term proportional representation, but this term is properly reserved for those systems of electoral reform based on constituencies returning more than one member. The constituency may be small, returning only two members; or large, returning many members; or indeed the whole country may be treated as a single constituency. There are two main systems of proportional representation in use. Under the system of the *single transferable vote* relatively small constituencies return several members (say four to six) and the voter indicates his order of preference among them. A 'quota' of votes has first to be determined. According to the Royal Commission, the quota is 'so fixed that it can be obtained by a number of candidates equal to the number of seats to be filled, but by no more', and in practice it is determined by dividing the number of valid votes cast by the number of seats to be filled increased by one, and adding one to the quotient so obtained; if, for example, there are six seats to be filled, the quota is obtained by dividing the total number of votes by seven, neglecting the remainder, and adding one to the quotient. The reasons for so doing may be valid but are hardly obvious to the average voter.

When the ballot boxes are opened, the first preferences are counted, and those candidates who have obtained the 'quota' or more are declared to be elected. If all the seats are not filled by this means, the excess of votes over the 'quota' obtained by the successful candidates are given to the names marked 2; and if this does not fill all the seats, the process is continued until it does. The second main system of proportional representation is that of the *party list*. Under this system the constituencies are large, and the electors vote for lists of candidates drawn up by the parties. Each party is entitled to a certain number of seats in proportion to the number of votes it has received in the constituency, and if the party is entitled to n seats the bearers of the first n names on the party list are declared to be elected.

In the text-books two other methods of obtaining direct representation for minorities are usually noted. We have already encountered them in Chapter III. There is firstly the *limited vote*, by which the elector is allowed to vote for a number of candidates less than that of the seats to be filled; and we have seen how the Birmingham Radicals managed to defeat this provision for the representation of their city in the Reform Act, 1867.[1] There is secondly the *cumulative vote*, under which the voter is given as many votes as there are seats to be filled, but is allowed to spread them over several candidates or to put them all on one candidate as he pleases; the Birmingham Radicals were not so successful in overcoming this provision for elections to the Birmingham school board. We need not, however, concern ourselves with these proposals as a matter of current politics. The party list system is that which prevails in Italy and France, with some modifications, and is the system which the term 'P.R.' probably suggests to the average man interested in these matters. But in this country the system of the single transferable vote now holds the field among advocates of electoral reform. The Liberal party formerly supported the alternative vote, but in its declining fortunes the alternative vote would not to-day give it many seats and to-day it favours the single transferable vote based on constituencies returning several members. This system, which would ensure for it the return of a number of members proportionate to its voting strength, is also favoured by the Proportional Representation Society; and when the subject of electoral reform is broached in Great Britain, it is usually this system that the advocate has in mind.

From this description it is clear that there is no system of electoral reform that can be claimed as inherently just and natural. It is unlikely that anyone will claim that the consequences of the various systems are the same—that the single transferable vote will give the same results as the party list system, for example—and yet they are all put forward in the name of securing a fairer system of representation for different points of view. Moreover in all these systems, it is not easy for the elector to see the connexion between the vote he casts and the result.

(*c*) Another objection to electoral reform would not apply to those systems retaining single-member constituencies, but it applies to all forms of proportional representation based on constituencies returning several or many members. In all such cases the bonds between a mem-

[1] See above, pp. 19–20.

ber and his constituents are weakened, and those who are familiar with the British system at his best cannot fail to regret such a weakening. Under the British system there is no doubt who is the parliamentary representative of the constituency and the channel of communication with the Government; and he is rightly a person of standing in his constituency. Once he is elected, though he has almost certainly been elected on a party programme, he regards himself, and is treated, as the member for the whole constituency; and those who voted against him are just as much entitled to his services as those who voted for him. His position is weakened and made ambiguous when shared with half a dozen—or perhaps fifty—others, nor are his constituency burdens eased thereby but rather increased. I once asked a French deputy how his constituents chose between him and his five colleagues to be the recipient of their grievances, and he replied with a wry smile, 'They write to us all'. The manner in which constituents take their least grievance to their member instead of seeking redress through the appointed channels now imposes a very serious burden on members and, unless checked, can destroy our parliamentary system by diverting the minds of members from affairs of state to personal problems and discouraging able men from standing for Parliament; the right to take a 'case' to the member of Parliament ought to be regarded as an ultimate sanction and not the normal procedure. The member represents his constituents, but it is even more important that he is a legislator and 'watch-dog' for the country as a whole. These criticisms of our present system are justified, but it must not be supposed that the remedy lies in proportional representation; this would only aggravate the evils.

(d) The greatest of all the evils that flows from schemes of electoral reform has yet to be mentioned, and it applies not only to proportional representation but also to proposals based on single-member constituencies. All the schemes of electoral reform yet proposed would tend to create a state of affairs in which it would be difficult for any single party to obtain a majority. Advocates of electoral reform can point to cases, most notably Italy since 1948, where it has not prevented the accession of a party to power with a big majority in the legislature, but there are nearly always special circumstances to explain such phenomena, and they are in the nature of *tours de force*. The difficulty in obtaining a parliamentary majority is indeed a necessary consequence of trying to ensure that all shades of opinion in the country are represented in Parliament according to their voting strength. Whereas our present system tends to eliminate minor parties, electoral reform tends to encourage them; and not only would old parties be kept in being, but new parties would proliferate. In consequence it would be unlikely that any party would gain sufficient seats to be able to form a Government by itself. It would be obliged to enter into a coalition with one or more parties, or would depend on their favour for continuance in office. Party programmes at elections would become meaningless because they could not be carried out; and policy would in fact be determined by secret negotiation between the parties in Parliament. This state of affairs can, of course, come about under our present system, and did come about in 1923 and 1929, and none of those who took part in the Government of those days desired to repeat the experiment; but it is more likely to happen under proportional representation. The parliamentary situations created by the elections of 1950 and 1951 were not ideal, but they would have been worse under proportional representation. Whereas in 1950 Labour had 315 seats, the Conservatives and their associates 298 and the Liberals 9, under a system in which seats are distributed according to total votes Labour would have had 288, Conservatives and associates 271 and Liberals 57. In such a situation effective government would have rested in the hands of the Liberals; and the paradox would have arisen that, in the name of securing an accurate reflexion of public opinion, the country would have been governed by a party which secured only 9.1 per cent of the votes cast. Whereas in 1951 the Conservatives and their associates had 321 seats, Labour 294, Liberals 6, and others 3, if the seats had been distributed according to total votes the Conservatives and their associates would have had 302 seats, Labour 303, Liberals 15 and others 4.[1] Only one seat would have separated the major parties, and effective power would have rested in the hands of the 15 Liberals, sent to Parliament by only 2.5 per cent of those who voted.

Though these consequences are not intended by its advocates proportional representation therefore weakens the link between a member and his constituents, makes for weak government, and tends to substitute backstairs intrigue for open parliamentary debate. But is it right in its fundamental assumption?

Those who defend our present system admit frankly that the object is not to secure a Parliament mathematically reflecting all the shades of opinion in the country. The primary object of a general election, they say, is to ensure that the Queen's Government is carried on effectively.

[1] Figures issued by the Proportional Representation Society. The figures do not include Barnsley, where polling took place later owing to the death of a candidate, but cover the four unopposed returns.

The Queen's Government will not be carried on effectively unless it is based on public opinion, but this need only mean a broad correspondence; and in any case her Majesty's ministers must be responsive to public opinion not only on polling day but every day. If this broad correspondence is secured, as it is, by limiting her Majesty's ministers to the party which has fared best at the polls, the object of effective governance will be secured by giving the Government party rather more seats in the House of Commons than it would secure on the basis of votes cast. This result is achieved in a rough and ready way by our present electoral system. It is foolish to make extravagant claims for it. The system is not ideal, and can be harsh, but it works, and works better than any system that has been proposed to take its place. It deals harshly with minority party organizations, but not, be it noticed, with minority party opinions. It is probable that minority opinions are more considerately treated under our two-party system than they would be under any system of separate representation. Under our system there are few candidates whose seats are so secure that they can ignore any substantial minority in their constituencies; on the contrary, they have to be solicitous for minorities.

Taking our system by and large, we should be ill advised to change it radically. It is significant that France and Italy, two countries whose elections are conducted by proportional representation, should recently have introduced changes, known in France as *apparentement des listes* and in Italy as *apparantamento delle liste*, designed to ensure that successful parties get more seats than they would be entitled to hold on a strict representation according to votes; and this has been done to avoid the evils of weak government mentioned above. Very often foreign deputies have deplored to me the defects of their systems as compared with our own. Proportional representation has only one obvious advantage, which is that a leading figure in a party can always be sure of election. In the United Kingdom no statesman, however eminent, is exempt from defeat merely by virtue of his position, and among the names of defeated candidates have been Gladstone, Balfour, MacDonald and Churchill. But is this necessarily evil? Perhaps it is good for them that they, like ordinary mortals, have to fight for their seats.

There seems no case, therefore, for a radical alteration in our present electoral system, but this does not mean that a few experiments in proportional representation might not be attempted in particular constituencies. One of the reasons for regretting the abolition of the university seats is that they were decided by a form of proportional representation; and this could have been introduced also into the two-member constituencies if they had not been abolished. It would be possible, even now, if it were desired for other reasons, to introduce a form of proportional representation into cities such as Cardiff or Bradford returning three or four members. This would be the British way—to make a cautious experiment, proceed further if successful, abandon it if not.

But on the whole the evidence suggests that our present system is better than any alternative yet devised. The two-party system is not only favoured by our electoral system but corresponds to the instincts of the British people; and those instincts are sound. Let us now look at the working of the system.

Part III

Party Organization

CHAPTERS XI–XVI

XI

Parliamentary Party Organization

THE BRITISH PARTIES began as groups of members of Parliament holding divergent views on the great questions of the day, and in studying party organization let us therefore begin with the parties in Parliament.

THE PARTY WHIPS

A member of Parliament becomes a member of a parliamentary party by taking its 'whip'. This term contains an age of history in a syllable. It reminds us of the time when members of Parliament were mainly country gentlemen who rode to hounds in the recess and when Parliament always adjourned for the Derby. A 'whipper-in' is defined by the Oxford English Dictionary as 'A huntsman's assistant who keeps the hounds from straying by driving them back into the pack with a whip', and the same authority notes than in 1828 the word was used for 'the action of "whipping up" the members of a party for a parliamentary division, or any body of persons for some united action'. The term 'whipper in' was originally used in Parliament as in the hunting field for a member who discharged this duty for his party, but in course of time it became reduced to 'whip'. In this sense the Oxford English Dictionary defines a 'whip' as 'a member of a particular party in Parliament whose duty it is to secure the attendance of members of that party on the occasion of an important division', giving the first instance in 1853. Later the term was applied to the call or appeal made by such a person, and is defined by the dictionary as 'The written appeal issued by a Parliament "whip" to summon the members of his party', the first use being noted in 1879. Though members of Parliament are now more likely to spend their recesses in factories than in the hunting field, the term 'whip' is still in general use in these two senses.

The whips in the first sense of the word come under the direction of the chief whip. Each party has a chief whip and assistant whips in the House of Commons and in the House of Lords. The chief whip is a person of great authority in the party, and on his efficiency the smooth working of the parliamentary system depends. The chief whip and his fellow whips have rooms near to the chamber. In the chamber the chief whip normally sits a place or two away from the party leader, ready to give him counsel at any moment about the business of the House. But in the chamber the whips rarely speak a word except 'I move that this House do now adjourn', or as tellers to announce the figures of a division. Their work is done behind the scenes.[1] It is their task to arrange with the whips of other parties on what days the business of Parliament shall be taken, and it is in this context that they are referred to as 'the usual channels'; to 'keep a house', that is to ensure that there is always a sufficient attendance of members to form a quorum and more particularly to give support to their own chosen speakers; and above all to ensure that the members of their party are in the right division lobby at the right time. The whips are given the oversight of members from regions—Scottish whip, Yorkshire whip, and so on—and they keep careful lists of what members are in the House and how they vote. When a bill goes into committee, a whip is assigned to the committee to watch his party's interests in the proceedings, and he carries out in the committee in a more informal manner the same type of work that the whole body of whips does in the House. It is work that calls for much self-effacement, patience, tact and restraint, and not every member of Parliament is temperamentally suited for it. As they cannot make speeches in the House, the whips do not have the same opportunities as other members of 'keeping themselves in the public eye', and if they represent marginal constituencies this may handicap them in their electoral contests—though not necessarily, for there are many members of Parliament whose speeches do them far more harm than their silence could possibly do. It is therefore an advantage for a whip to sit for a safe seat. The chief whip whose instructions to his fellow whips usually took the form, 'Find out what that member is doing, and tell him not to do it', is no doubt apocryphal; but it illustrates the tactful nature of the work that the whips are required to do.

Owing to the need to supervise the public business and to ensure that a House is kept, the whips have to spend long hours on the bench, and they arrange a rota among themselves to ensure that there is always one whip at least on the front bench. The whips are thus doubly penalized, unable to speak themselves and compelled to listen to the speeches of

---

[1] The circumstances in which Lord Ammon resigned his post as chief Government whip in the House of Lords in July 1949 are without precedent. Lord Ammon was also chairman of the Dock Labour Board, and observed in reply to questioning by the press over the telephone that the Government had 'gone crazy' in their attitude to a statement issued by the board with reference to the strike of dock workers troubling London at the time. His dual position put him in a difficulty, of course, and his resignation as chief whip followed within twenty-four hours.

others. It may be asked, what are the compensations that make men willing to accept this rôle. There is the satisfaction on both sides of the House of being 'in the know' and of taking part in the preliminary arrangements of the public business; and an appointment as a whip is often the first stage in a ministerial career—and a very good training.

When their party is in office the whips are ministers. The chief whip is then known as the Parliamentary Secretary to the Treasury. He has nothing to do with financial matters, nor does he have an office in the Treasury buildings, but as the Treasury is the senior home department it adds to his and to the department's standing to reckon him a Treasury minister. (The Prime Minister is similarly reckoned to be First Lord of the Treasury). The Parliamentary Secretary to the Treasury is also commonly known as the Patronage Secretary. This is another term that contains an age of history. The office was created, and the name given, in 1714 at a time when ministers had in their disposition many jobs in the customs, the posts and the public service generally, and it was the duty of the Patronage Secretary, as conceived in those days, to use their power to influence the votes of members of Parliament. Electors demanded jobs from their members in return for their votes; the Government wanted the members' votes; and it was the task of the Patronage Secretary to see that everyone was satisfied. 'It is rather a roguish office' as Wilberforce said to Steele when this latter was appointed to it by Pitt. This open corruption of members and electors ceased even before, and long before, appointments to the public service were taken out of the hands of ministers and regulated by the Civil Service Commission. But the term Patronage Secretary is still not inappropriate to-day as the chief whip's advice is sought on a large number of appointments and honours. In promoting back-benchers to be junior ministers, or in moving junior ministers around, the Prime Minister of the day would almost certainly consult his chief whip, for he has the best opportunities of knowing how the persons concerned stand with Parliament, and it is in Parliament that ministers are made and destroyed. In the case of his senior colleagues the Prime Minister of the day naturally has better opportunities of forming his own judgement, but he will often consult the chief whip on the question whether a particular minister will be acceptable to the House of Commons in a particular job.

It is more than likely that the chief whip is consulted over the conferment of political honours, and certainly if they involve the elevation of a member of the House of Commons to the Upper House. Though himself not in the Cabinet, nor usually reckoned in the modern phrase to be of 'Cabinet rank', the Parliamentary Secretary to the Treasury is in fact one of the most influential members of the Government. Five of his whips are also Treasury ministers and are known as Lords Commissioners of the Treasury. Another three are ministers of her Majesty's Household (Treasurer, Comptroller and Vice-Chamberlain). These have certain duties to perform in connexion with the Household—one of them has, for example, to send a daily report of the proceedings in Parliament to the Queen—but most of their time is occupied in assisting the chief whip to expedite the business of Parliament.

In addition to these eight ministers, or nine with the chief whip, it is customary to appoint two or three members as assistant whips (unpaid); they are not ministers but are officers of the party. The main Opposition party has a similar number of whips, but they are, of course, all unpaid.

We must now turn to the second parliamentary meaning of the word 'whip'. During the session the business for the following week is announced each Thursday in the chamber by the leader of the House, and the whips then send to all members of their party a message setting out the business each day, underlining any items that call for emphasis, and drawing attention to times when divisions are expected. Such a message is also known as a whip. The weekly whip is sent by post to arrive each week-end at an address given by the member, and other whips may be sent as occasion demands, for example, if there is a last-minute change in the business. If an item of business is of ordinary importance it is underlined once; if it is of more than ordinary importance, it is underlined twice; if it is of extraordinary importance it is underlined three times. These are called 'one-line whips', 'two-line whips', and 'three-line whips'. It is not usual for more than three underlinings to be employed nowadays, though as many as five have been used on occasion in the past. A debate or a vote of censure would always be regarded as three-line business. If a member receives a three-line whip, he understands that he must either be present for that item of business or must give a satisfactory explanation for his absence. The only explanation that will be accepted as satisfactory is that he is so ill as to be unable to attend or that he is 'paired' with a member of the opposite party. Members are said to be 'paired' when they agree not to vote, knowing that if they did they would vote in opposite lobbies. In former days 'pairing' was common even for social reasons, but in recent years 'pairing' has been frowned upon, and is now recognized as allowable only when one member of the pair must be unavoidably absent. It is recognized, for example, that members of the Government, especially those in the oversea departments, must occasionally be absent from the country on the public business, and in the Parliament elected in February 1950, in which the Labour Government held a slender majority, the Conservative opposition conceded that it was desirable to provide pairs in such cases. If members of Parliament have speaking engagements at a time when a three-line whip requires their attendance in the House, they are normally expected to cancel the engagement, and 'pairing' would be regarded as allowable only when a minister, or some leading figure on the other side, has arranged to make a speech of great importance which in the public interest should not be cancelled or even postponed.

Before a big division takes place the whips can nearly always account for all their flocks. Members present in the House are noted as they arrive; those who have 'paired' or are ill are expected to inform the whips' office; if there is anyone not thus accounted for the telephones are set ringing to his home, office, club or any other place of likely resort; by the time the bells ring for an important division the whips on either side can generally say what the figures will be; and if there is anyone who has been avoidably absent unpaired, he will get some black looks when he next appears. In these recent Parliaments of small majorities one of the most heinous offences a member can commit is to forget that he has agreed to 'pair' and to appear in the division lobby; for him also there will be black looks next day, and perhaps an entry in a 'black book'. The standard of whipping has been extremely high in all recent Parliaments.

The receipt of the whip is the outward and visible sign that a member of Parliament belongs to the parliamentary party whose whips have issued it. The whip is normally given automatically to all those members whose candidature at the preceding election was approved by the party's national headquarters. It is not the case in modern times that John Bull, Esquire, arrives at the House of Commons and says to himself, 'Which party shall I join?' In almost every case the new member is already committed to membership of a party—or, if an independent, is committed to not joining a party. But sometimes there are peculiar cases which justify the withholding of, or a delay in granting, the whip. Occasionally there is a split in the local organization in a safe division, and an unofficial candidate defeats the official candidate standing on the same programme. In such cases the whip may be withheld until a local reconciliation is effected; or it may not be sought.

The whip may also be withdrawn if the member's activities are deemed to be incompatible with membership of the party; or the member may himself intimate that he no longer wishes to receive it, which is tantamount to resignation from the party. In neither case is the person's membership of the House affected thereby, only his membership of the party. As was said at the outset, the constitution ignores parties, and membership of a party is regarded as a private arrangement, like membership of a club.

But who has the power to withdraw the whip? In the Labour party such a decision is taken at a meeting of the parliamentary party; in the Conservative party the power is vested in the leader. This introduces two new conceptions.

THE LEADER OF THE PARTY

The term 'leader of the party' is an ancient and honourable British title, and we are rightly not influenced by the way in which it has been misused in certain countries in recent times. Every parliamentary party has its leader. The practical need for such a leader is felt most acutely on the floor of the House, where decisions frequently have to be taken on the spur of the moment, often without the opportunity of consulting even with those immediately around. There must on these occasions be someone who can answer for the party as a whole.

The practical need is also felt acutely when the Sovereign is obliged to look for someone to commission to form a Government. On such occasions it is desirable that there should be one person, known to enjoy the confidence of his fellows, on whom the Sovereign's choice can fall. Otherwise the Sovereign would have to fill each post individually, and there would be no guarantee that the persons so chosen would work together as a team. The practice of designating a Prime Minister, and asking him to choose his colleagues, is the most effective way of ensuring that Cabinet solidarity which has, with rare exceptions, prevailed since the reign of William and Mary.

Apart from these exceptional occasions, the smooth working of the party is helped by having one trusted person in the position of leader. There may be other feasible methods—an oligarchy, for example—but none is so satisfactory, The leader is not, of course, a dictator; it is his duty to lead, not to dictate. He depends for his authority on maintaining the confidence of the great body of his party, and if that confidence is withdrawn, or even sensibly diminished, he has no option but to resign.

The leadership of the party is primarily a parliamentary conception, but it has come to be accepted that the leader of the parliamentary party is also leader of the party in the country. (The Communist party is an exception in that when Mr. Gallacher was in Parliament he was never recognized as the Communist leader in the country, that rôle, though not the title, probably belonging to Mr. Pollitt; but Communist members have been so rare that the exception is not really worth noticing.) In the constitutional parties it would hardly be possible to have a different leader in the country from the parliamentary leader.

In the nineteenth century the members of the party in the House of Commons and the party peers in the House of Lords used to meet separately to choose their leaders, and of these two parliamentary leaders one usually stood out by general acclaim and the acknowledgement of the other as the party leader in the country. The only exception followed the death of Beaconsfield in 1881, from which date Lord Salisbury and Sir Stafford Northcote shared the leadership of the Conservative party until 1885, when Salisbury became Prime Minister and Northcote went to the Upper House as Lord Iddesleigh. By that date Northcote's treatment at the hands of the 'Fourth party' had ruled him out of consideration as a Conservative Prime Minister. In th se days it was common, of course, for the party leader in the country to be a peer, but it would hardly be possible to-day. Lord Salisbury, who retired at the beginning of the century, was the last peer to be so recognized and the last to be Prime Minister.

The leader of the Liberal party is still chosen exclusively by Liberal members of the House of Commons; they are now a very attenuated band but the principle remains the same. The Conservative leader in the House of Commons was originally chosen exclusively by his Conservative colleagues in that House, but in view of his wider responsibilities and the growing importance of party organization in the country there have been successive enlargements of the electoral college. In 1922 Bonar Law was elected leader of the party by a meeting which included Conservative peers and parliamentary candidates as well as Conservative members of the House of Commons; and in 1937 the executive committee of the National Union of Conservative and Unionist Associations was invited to take part in the meeting which elected Neville Chamberlain as leader. It remains the position that the leader of the Conservative party is chosen by the Conservative and Unionist members of the House of Commons and the House of Lords, all prospective Conservative and Unionist parliamentary candidates in the United Kingdom, and the executive committee of the National Union of Conservative and Unionist Associations. It is open for consideration whether it would not be more constitutionally proper, and more in keeping with the traditions of the Conservative party, to revert to the practice whereby the leader is chosen solely by his colleagues in the House of Commons. The enlargement of the electoral college has made no practical difference, as will soon be seen, for the electors have always been called upon to ratify a *fait accompli*; but the enlargement of the college appears to have come about through chance as much as through deliberate intention.

The leader of the parliamentary Labour party becomes *ipso facto* leader of the Labour party. The Labour peers share in his election, and also elect their own leader in the House of Lords. At first they were *rarae aves*, but by the conversion of some and the ennoblement of others they have now risen to the not inconsiderable total of sixty-one.[1] What was once known as 'the thin red line' now fills several benches.

The formal machinery for electing the several party leaders is as described above, but in practice history has often dictated the choice of the electoral colleges. When a Prime Minister dies in office or retires, especially if he dies or retires without tendering any advice on the question of his successor, it becomes necessary to have a new Prime Minister before a new party leader can be chosen, for 'the Queen's government must be carried on'. In such circumstances the responsibility resting on the Sovereign is great. It is perhaps the only case where real power remains, in theory at any rate, in the hands of the Sovereign. But in practice there is often only one possible successor, even though not formally chosen leader of the party. If the Sovereign's choice were to fall on anyone else, he would soon be obliged to report that he was unable to form an administration. But the Sovereign is likely to be well informed about such a situation and in modern times it is improbable that a person who could not secure the confidence of his party would be so commissioned. The only real difficulty would arise if there were no obvious successor, and two or three candidates had equal merits in the eyes of the party. But this has rarely happened.

When Lord Salisbury retired in 1902, King Edward VII sent for Arthur Balfour, who kissed hands as Prime Minister before he was elected leader of the Conservative party; his election as leader duly followed, and it would have been unthinkable to have chosen anyone except the person on whom the Sovereign's choice had fallen. In this case the King had no difficulty in deciding that his choice should fall on Balfour, who would have been the selection of the party even if he had not already become Prime Minister. When Balfour retired in 1911, the party was in opposition, and Bonar Law succeeded him by the election

[1] January 1953.

of his fellow-members of the House of Commons; when Bonar Law retired in 1921 through ill-health, Austen Chamberlain succeeded him, again by the election of Conservative members of the House of Commons. On all subsequent occasions when a leader of the Conservative party has had to be chosen, there was already a Conservative Prime Minister at No. 10 Downing Street, and no one else would have thought of accepting nomination. In 1922 Austen Chamberlain wished the Conservative party to remain in the coalition, but his point of view did not prevail in the party meeting, and after the general election King George V in full accordance with constitutional propriety sent once more for Bonar Law, who was elected leader on this occasion after he had become Prime Minister. When illness compelled his retirement in 1923, the King sent for Stanley Baldwin, who also was subsequently elected leader. When Baldwin himself retired in 1937 King George VI sent for Neville Chamberlain, who was likewise chosen leader after kissing hands as Prime Minister. When Chamberlain resigned as Prime Minister in 1940, Mr. Churchill was commissioned to succeed him in that office, but Chamberlain remained leader of the party until his death, and therefore Mr. Churchill was already Prime Minister when elected leader. In most of these cases there was no doubt on whom the King's choice should fall for the office of Prime Minister, and in some he had the benefit of the outgoing Prime Minister's advice. Mr. Churchill has related in a tense narrative the interview with himself and Lord Halifax at which Chamberlain decided 'whom he should advise the King to send for after his own resignation had been accepted'.[1] 'I have had many important interviews in my public life, and this was certainly the most important.' The only occasion on which a constitutional problem presented itself, that is, the only occasion on which there might be any doubt about whom the Conservative party would choose as its leader, was in 1923, when the King had to fill the gap left by Bonar Law's retirement. Lord Curzon coveted and expected the succession, and the shattering of his dreams has now become part of English literature.[2] It was, indeed, at first intended to invite him to succeed Bonar Law, but the King received representations, both from the Labour party as the official Opposition and also from leading Conservatives, that made him change his mind and send for a commoner. The King's decision to send for Baldwin was not only constitutionally proper but correctly interpreted the mind of the party, as subsequent events showed. The time had gone by when a Prime

[1] *The Second World War*, vol. i, *The Gathering Storm*, p. 523.
[2] See Harold Nicolson, *Curzon: The Last Phase*, pp. 353–56.

Minister could be a peer, and Lord Halifax disqualified himself on this ground with equal propriety and public spirit at the momentous interview seventeen years later.

In the Liberal party the Sovereign's choice of a Prime Minister has come before the formal election to the party's leadership on several occasions. The most notable was in 1880, but on this occasion it was popular acclaim that pressed Gladstone on the Queen despite her preference for Hartington, who had been titular leader of the party in the House of Commons for the past six years. There was some doubt for whom the Queen should send when Gladstone finally resigned in 1894, but when her choice fell on Lord Rosebery he was accepted as the leader of the party. In 1908 when Campbell-Bannerman resigned, Asquith had already kissed hands as Prime Minister—at Biarritz, of all unlikely places—before becoming leader of the party, but in this instance there was no ambiguity about the party's desire.

There does not appear to be in the history of the Conservative or Liberal parties any instance of a contest for the leadership in the sense of a taking of a formal vote. As already shown, the choice has been obvious, or the formal meeting has merely ratified what the course of events had already decided. In the Labour party there was a notable contest for the leadership in 1935. When Lansbury resigned the leadership on the pacifist issue, Mr. Attlee, who had been the deputy leader since 1931, was elected to succeed him. The general election later in the year brought back many new faces to Parliament, and Mr. Attlee's position as leader was challenged by Mr. Herbert Morrison and Mr. Arthur Greenwood. When the vote was taken, Mr. Attlee won by a substantial majority. There were later attempts to displace him, but none came to a vote. Even in 1945, on the morrow of the party's sweeping victory in the general election, 'a group of the so-called intellectual wing', according to a writer in *The Times Literary Supplement* of 10 July 1948,[1] 'sought to argue that he should not accept the King's invitation to form a government until there had been a meeting of the parliamentary Labour party to consider an alternative leadership'. But on the morrow of the greatest victory in Labour's history Mr. Attlee could afford to ignore such representations, and his position as leader was confirmed then and in the two subsequent Parliaments without a contest.

The fact that to-day Mr. Churchill and Mr. Attlee are respectively leaders of the Conservative and Labour parties shows that there can be a wide range of leadership. No greater contrast in personalities could

[1] Reviewing *Mr. Attlee*, by Mr. Roy Jenkins, M.P.

be imagined; yet each is now the unchallenged leader of one of the great bodies of organized political opinion.

THE PARTY MEETING

The party meeting is now an essential element in the party machinery in Parliament. From earliest days, no doubt, members of the same party met in their houses or clubs to formulate a common policy or common course of action, but in modern times the party meeting has become more formal and stereotyped, though there is still a big difference in the practice of the several parties.

One structural difference is that the Conservative members in the House of Commons and Conservative peers in the House of Lords meet separately, but the 'parliamentary Labour party' is a single entity covering Labour members in either House. Labour peers hold their own meetings as occasion demands, but they also attend the regular meetings of the parliamentary Labour party along with Labour members of the House of Commons. The practice no doubt grew up because the number of Labour peers was originally very small, and has continued although they are now a more substantial element in the parliamentary party.

An even more important difference is that the organization of the parliamentary Labour party is closely defined, whereas the Conservative organization is loose and informal. The Conservative arrangements are partly governed by usage and partly settled empirically by the needs of the time. In 1945 there were relatively few Conservative members who had been in the House when the Conservative party was last in opposition, and in 1951, when the Conservatives returned to power, there were not many who could recall what their practice had been before 1939.

The Conservative and Unionist Members' Committee in the House of Commons is essentially a back-benchers' organization. It is commonly known as the 1922 Committee from the meeting of Conservative members at the Carlton Club which decided in 1922 to bring the coalition to an end. It normally meets every Thursday evening when Parliament is sitting, the time being chosen as the business for the following week can then be announced. When the party is in office, ministers do not attend meetings, but if it should be desirable for the sense of the meeting to be conveyed to ministers the chairman would see that this was done. When the party is out of office, ex-ministers may attend the meetings, but this is largely a matter of time and personal inclination, and some ex-ministers would attend only when invited. Whether ex-ministers attend or not, the feeling that the meeting is a body of back-benchers is preserved. A well-liked back-bencher is chosen at the beginning of the session to be chairman of the committee. Two vice-chairmen, a treasurer, and two secretaries are also chosen, and twelve members are elected to constitute with the officers an executive committee. The executive committee normally meets weekly just before the full committee. The meeting of the full committee discusses the forthcoming business in the House, but no attempt is made to define the policy of the party. In the Conservative party it is the prerogative of the leader to formulate policy. But the discussions in the party meetings are naturally one of the factors that help him in his formulation.

The meeting of the parliamentary Labour party differs in important respects. Not only are the party chiefs eligible to attend, but they normally do so; and even when the party was in office, the Prime Minister and other leading members of the Government frequently put aside pressing cares of state to attend its deliberations. There was a move at one time to convert it into a back-benchers' organization, but this was suspected to be a device to separate the leaders from the rank and file, and no more came of it. The tradition of the older parties has usually been followed in having a popular back-bencher as chairman, at any rate when the party chiefs are in the Government, but in the present Parliament the leader of the party, Mr. Attlee, has assumed also the chairmanship of the party meeting. The executive body of the parliamentary Labour party is not called the executive committee[1] to avoid confusion with the national executive committee of the Labour party outside Parliament. It was called the administrative committee until 1945; when the Labour Government was formed in 1945, a liaison committee was substituted for it; and since Labour went into opposition in 1951 the executive body has been known as the parliamentary committee. The party chiefs, whether in office or out of office, have been eligible for membership of this executive body. When Labour served in the wartime coalition, there was a certain amount of restiveness among the back-benchers at the domination of the administrative committee by ministers, and it was agreed that apart from the leader, the deputy leader and the chief whip, who were members *ex officio*, only three ministers could be elected to serve on the committee; the chairman and vice-chairman of the party were also *ex officio* mem-

---

[1] Except in the constitution of the National Council of Labour, which has presumably not been revised to take account of the change.

bers, and thirteen non-ministerial members were elected. When the party was called upon to provide the government in 1945 it was no doubt felt that such an administrative committee might appear to compromise the responsibility of ministers, and in its stead there was created a liaison committee—presumably for liaison between the Government and back-benchers—consisting of the chairman and vice-chairman of the parliamentary party, the Lord President of the Council, the chief whip, a representative of the Labour peers and the secretary of the parliamentary party;[1] in 1950 in order to increase back-bench representation on the liaison committee an additional vice-chairman of the parliamentary party was chosen. When Labour returned to opposition in 1951, there was no further need of a liaison committee, and a parliamentary committee consisting of the leader (who was also, as we have seen, chairman of the parliamentary party), the deputy leader, the chief whip and twelve elected members was constituted.

In favour of having the party chiefs present at the party meeting it can be argued that otherwise they tend to get too remote from the back-benchers, and there is loss on both sides; in favour of their absence, it can be argued that back-benchers will speak their mind with greater freedom. But the reason why the Labour chiefs are so assiduous in their attendance at the meetings of the parliamentary Labour party is that binding decisions on policy are there taken. For this reason the debates are often pungent and do not lack an element of the dramatic. In 1943, for example, the party meeting decided to table an amendment expressing its dissatisfaction with the Government's intentions with respect to the Beveridge plan and to take it to a division, even though its own chiefs were ministers in the Government; after the unedifying spectacle of ministers and back-benchers walking into different lobbies the amendment was defeated by 335 votes to 119. On two other occasions, concerned with policy in Greece and compensation for land values, the party meeting decided to abstain from supporting its ministers in the division lobby. Because such important decisions are taken, there is normally a much larger attendance of members at the Labour party meeting than at the Conservative. Meetings have sometimes been held weekly, sometimes fortnightly; and special meetings are convened when necessary. It is only natural that interest tends to languish when ministers feel it necessary to give economic dissertations to the members, and reaches its heights when questions of a member's

[1] The secretary of the parliamentary Labour party is not a member of Parliament but a salaried official.

personal conduct are under discussion. Such questions arise fairly often and in some cases take a serious turn because the decision to withdraw the whip from a member is vested in the party meeting, and not, as among the Conservatives, in the leader.

In view of these differences it is not surprising that the press has followed the meetings of the parliamentary Labour party with a keener interest than those of the Conservative, nor that lobby correspondents and reporters have sought to gather from those present rather more information than is conveyed by the bare official announcement. The whole House, and indeed the country, were, however, shocked to learn in 1947 that two Labour members of Parliament had been receiving money from newspapers for supplying them with news about what took place at meetings of the parliamentary Labour party.[1] The unfortunate business need not here be recalled if it were not that the action of the House with regard to the reports of the Committee of Privileges thereon raises a constitutional issue of some importance. On 30 October 1947 the reports were taken into consideration and the two members named therein were given the opportunity of making personal explanations. One of them was, without a division, found guilty of 'gross contempt' of the House for unfounded imputations against unnamed members of insobriety in the precincts of the House, and guilty of 'grave contempt' in persistently misleading the Committee of Privileges in his evidence. These findings raise no new constitutional principle. It was then further resolved, by 198 votes to 101, that the same member was 'guilty of dishonourable conduct which deserves to be severely punished' in 'corruptly accepting payment for the disclosure of information about matters to be proceeded with in Parliament obtained from other members under the obligation of secrecy'. A motion providing that this member should be suspended from the service of the House for six months was amended to read that he be expelled 'for his gross contempt of the House and for his misconduct', and in this amended form was carried by 187 votes to 75. By 152 votes to 92 the other member was found 'guilty of dishonourable conduct which deserves to be severely punished' in 'corruptly accepting payment for the disclosure of information about matters to be proceeded with in Parliament'. Without a division it was then resolved that he be reprimanded by Mr. Speaker for his misconduct, and, standing in his place uncovered, he was so reprimanded. A few weeks later, on 10 December 1947, the leader of the House moved:

[1] See *Report from the Committee of Privileges*, 23 July 1947, House of Commons Sessional Paper no. 138, and *Report from the Committee of Privileges*, 4 August 1947, House of Commons Sessional Paper no. 142.

'That, if in any case hereafter a member shall have been found guilty by this House of corruptly accepting payment for the disclosure and publication of confidential information about matters to be proceeded with in Parliament, any person responsible for offering such payment shall incur the grave displeasure of this House; and this House will take such action as it may, in the circumstances, think fit.'

On a division the motion was carried by 287 votes to 123.[1]

No one is likely to defend either the members who took payment for disclosing confidential information or those who offered it to them. The action of the members was undoubtedly a grave offence against the parliamentary Labour party. But was it an offence against the House of Commons? These party meetings are not part of the machinery of the House. No reference to them will be found in the standing orders or elsewhere. The constitution ignores parties, and *a fortiori* it ignores party meetings. How then could it be maintained that the members had committed an offence against the House? This was the question that troubled many members when asked to vote for the motions described above. They urged that it was proper for the parliamentary Labour party to expel them from its membership, or to take any other action that it deemed fit, but that the House of Commons could not properly proceed against them. By a majority with a large number of members not voting—the House decided otherwise. The motions then passed come near to elevating party meetings to the status of part of the constitutional machinery of the House. But it is important to notice that they do not actually do so. In studying their constitutional significance we must ignore their context, and the speeches made, and the motives of those who voted, and confine ourselves to the actual words of the motions; and in these motions there is no specific mention of party meetings. Such meetings are indeed essential to the working of Parliament, but their value lies in the fact that they are outside the constitutional machinery.[2]

This leads to another question of some interest. It is sometimes asked whether the caucus system as developed in Australia and New Zealand has any parallel here. In those two countries the meeting of the parliamentary party, or caucus, has exceptional importance. Both on the Government and on the Opposition side, the caucus decides policy and the action to be taken with regard to parliamentary business. Moreover

---

[1] The debates will be found in 443 H.C. Deb. 5s., cols. 1094–1239, and 445 H.C. Deb. 5s., cols. 1091–1154.
[2] Those who wish to pursue this question should particularly study the evidence given by the Clerk of the House, Sir Gilbert (now Lord) Campion, before the Committee of Privileges in 1947 (Sessional Paper no. 138, pp. 1–7, 106–17, 123–7).

the caucus of the dominant party chooses the persons to fill the various ministerial offices. Not only does the caucus choose the Prime Minister, but it also assigns him his colleagues, and decides their policy for them during the session. Though the system began with the Labour party in both countries, the Liberals in Australia and the Nationalists in New Zealand have followed suit. The advantages of the system from the point of view of party discipline and cohesion are obvious; no dirty linen is washed in public, all differences are settled behind closed doors, and to the outside world the party presents a united front. But it has equally obvious dangers, which have been stated after a study on the spot by Lord Campion with all the authenticity attaching to a former Clerk of the House of Commons:

'The logical end of the process seems to be the transfer of power without individual responsibility to the caucus, with the reduction of Cabinet ministers to the status of its spokesmen in Parliament . . . Democracy should think again before it ties itself to a system under which free and open debate in Parliament, the cutting edge of political progress during three centuries, will be reduced to a pretentious and expensive formality.'[1]

From what has been said above it will be clear that no such reproach can be made against the Conservative party in our own Parliament. The party meeting is essentially a meeting of back-benchers at which the party chiefs are not normally present, and it makes no attempt to take decisions on policy; that is the task of the leader of the party, guided no doubt by any representations made to him by the party meeting or from other quarters, but free in the last resort to follow his own judgement. No Conservative meeting would seek to suggest the names of ministers, and the administrations that have been formed by Conservative Prime Ministers always show the impress of their own personalities. The Liberal party in Parliament is now reduced to six members, but this also has been the Liberal practice; and it is obvious from the divergent ways in which Liberals have voted in recent years that no attempt can have been made to take binding decisions on policy at their party meetings.

As far as the Labour party is concerned, the party meeting has never made any attempt to select the ministers when in office. Groups of members have from time to time attempted to get ministers removed and others substituted, but this has not been unknown in the older parties; the party meeting as such has never made any claim to this

---

[1] *Sunday Times,* 27 March 1949.

power, and a Labour Prime Minister's right to choose his colleagues is as undisputed as a Conservative's.

It is not, however, possible to exonerate the Labour party so completely from the charge in respect of policy-making. There is, indeed, one big and welcome difference from the Australian and New Zealand practice. In those countries there is no attempt to preserve collective ministerial responsibility in the caucus; ministers speak and vote according to their personal opinions and may take opposite sides. In the United Kingdom, however, when the Labour party has been in office ministers have always presented a united front in the party meeting—even on those difficult questions during the wartime coalition, such as the Beveridge report, compensation for land values, and policy in Greece, when the personal opinions of many might have inclined them to speak and vote in a different sense.

Though this difference may be conceded, it cannot be denied that the parliamentary Labour party at its meetings does attempt to take decisions which are binding on its members and to limit that 'free and open debate in Parliament' which has been 'the cutting edge of political progress during three centuries'. The best proof of this fact is contained in the standing orders of the parliamentary Labour party.

Clause IX of the Labour party constitution lays down:

'7. No person may be selected as a parliamentary Labour candidate by a constituency Labour party, and no candidate may be endorsed by the national executive committee, if the person concerned:

.   .   .   .   .

(d) does not undertake to accept and act in harmony with the standing orders of the parliamentary Labour party.'

The standing orders themselves were in the following form in 1945:

'1. For the purpose of securing concerted action in the House, members shall consult the officers of the parliamentary party before tabling any motion, amendment or prayer, or other proposal which may involve party policies or decisions, and shall not vote for any motion, amendment or prayer contrary to the decision of the party meeting.

'2. Where there is persistent refusal to observe the decisions of the parliamentary party, it shall be the duty of the liaison committee[1] to bring a recommendation to the party meeting to report the member to the national executive committee, who shall consider the matter in its constituency and other aspects with which the national executive committee is concerned. The member concerned shall have the right

---

[1] Now the parliamentary committee.

to be heard both by the parliamentary party and the national executive committee.

'3. It is recognized that on certain matters, for example religion and temperance, members may have good grounds for conscientious scruples, and in such cases they may abstain from voting.

'(The above standing orders may be amended, rescinded, altered, added to or suspended for such period and under such conditions as may be determined upon by a duly constituted meeting of the parliamentary Labour party.)

'Note.—Members should take advantage of party meetings in suitable instances to raise questions of party policy concerning which they may have doubts.'

After the general election of 1945, when Labour members were returned to Parliament in numbers far beyond their expectations, there was a widespread desire in the party to get rid of these standing orders, and the party leadership was not averse. The standing orders had been necessary to restrain the I.L.P., but they had been a source of constant friction, and the I.L.P. was moribund, whereas the new body of Labour members was animated, for the time being at any rate, by the enthusiasm of a great victory; moreover, the Labour majority was so great that a few extravagances could be safely tolerated. In January 1946 a resolution was passed by the parliamentary Labour party suspending the standing orders.

They remained suspended, thanks to resolutions moved at the beginning of each session, until March 1952. The Parliaments that followed the general elections of 1950 and 1951 found the Labour party in a very different spirit from that of 1945—its numbers reduced, its purpose uncertain, its leadership challenged. Mr. Aneurin Bevan, Mr. Harold Wilson and Mr. John Freeman had resigned from the Labour Government in April 1951 on a disagreement over the amount of the country's resources that should be allocated to rearmament, and the dissensions that then opened grew deeper, until it appeared to many that Mr. Bevan was challenging Mr. Attlee for the leadership of the party. Matters came to a head in February 1952, when a division took place in the House of Commons on rearmament, and fifty-seven Labour members sided with Mr. Bevan against the official leadership of the party. This scandal led the party leadership to seek the re-imposition of standing orders. The resolution suspending the standing orders as they stood in 1945 was first carried, which meant that the standing orders as quoted above again came into force. But the opportunity was taken to make certain revisions, and the standing orders as they were finally adopted in March 1952 and as they now stand are as follows:

'1. The privilege of membership of the parliamentary Labour party involves the acceptance of the decisions of the party meeting. The party recognizes the right of individual members to abstain from voting on matters of deeply held personal conscientious conviction.

'2. The parliamentary party have the right to withdraw the whip on account of things said or done by members of the party in the House. The member or members concerned shall have the right to be heard at the party meeting before the whip is withdrawn.

'3. The national executive committee shall be informed of any decision to withdraw the whip.

'4. It is the duty of the parliamentary committee to bring before the party meeting cases of serious or persistent breaches of party discipline, and in appropriate cases to recommend to the party meeting that the member or members concerned shall be reported to the national executive committee. The member or members concerned shall have the right to be heard by the parliamentary committee and the parliamentary party.

'5. For the purpose of securing concerted action in the House, members shall consult the officers of the parliamentary party before tabling any motion, amendment or prayer, or other proposal which may involve party policies or decisions.

'6. These standing orders may be amended, rescinded, altered, added to, suspended or reinstated for such period and under such conditions as may be determined, after due notice, by a duly constituted meeting of the parliamentary Labour party.'

There are two main differences from the older version. The 'conscience clause' is now extended so as to cover any 'deeply held personal conscientious convictions', and no attempt is made to restrict it to religion and temperance. It is rather surprising that the revision did not take the opportunity of adding the word 'known' before 'conscientious conviction', as was generally expected at the time, for this would help to prevent the sudden discovery of conscientious objections; but it is easy to see that in the empirical course of politics decisions involving conscientious scruples may have to be taken although they have not arisen before. The second big difference arises in the third clause of the new orders. As it is drafted, this would appear to give the parliamentary committee the right to bring before the party meeting persistent breaches of party discipline outside Parliament. This extension of the clause may not have been intended, and it remains to be seen whether this wider interpretation will be invoked in practice.

If a Labour member of Parliament acts strictly in accordance with these standing orders, he cannot take any parliamentary action without consulting the officers of the party except to put down questions and perhaps to raise matters 'on the adjournment' when he gets the opportunity. There is not much comfort to the constitutionalist in the note at the end of the older version—there is presumably no significance in its omission—for the effect is to transfer the real debate from the floor of the House to the private meeting of the party upstairs, and this is precisely what the constitutionalist objects to. It is true that at such a meeting the member who has 'doubts' is able to put his point of view, but the occasions on which he can make it prevail are rare, for the officers of the party are generally able to assure themselves of a majority, and thereafter he is expected for ever to hold his peace. An outstanding exception occurred just before the war when Mr. Hugh Dalton, defeated in committee, took the issue to the party meeting and persuaded it to give up the practice of voting against the Service estimates. The dissatisfied member may not in any circumstances vote against his party; the utmost licence accorded to him is that he may abstain from voting when a matter of deeply held, personal, conscientious conviction is at stake.

This is hardly the 'cutting edge of political progress'. It may produce an outward appearance of uniformity, but it will lead to inward death. Clearly members of a party have an obligation of loyalty to it, and if they venture to differ publicly from it they must do so only for grave public reasons and not simply to air their own views. But when there are differences within a party on great public issues, no ultimate good can come from stifling the fact. It would not have been in the interests of the country that Joseph Chamberlain should have been told to raise his doubts about free trade at the party meeting, or that more recently Mr. Churchill should have been told to abstain silently from voting on the Munich agreement. It is sufficient check that statesmen who venture to differ publicly from their colleagues on such issues are taking grave risks with their political future.

With this much said, it needs to be added that in practice Labour members have not taken their standing orders *au pied de la lettre*, and this has saved their party from the worse consequence of its theory. Their attitude has been rather like that of Benjamin Jowett when asked if he could still sign the Thirty-nine Articles—'Forty, if you please'. There has not been any noticeable difference in practice between the years when the standing orders were in operation and those in which they have been suspended; the knowledge that the standing orders could not be enforced was, in fact, a main reason for their suspension. If pressed to justify their licence, the recalcitrant members have stretched the conscience clause, which led Mr. Attlee to complain on one occasion that 'conscience is a still, small voice, not a loud-speaker'.

We are bound to feel some sympathy with the Labour party in framing these standing orders, for it has had to meet persistent attempts by Communists and their sympathizers to destroy it from within; and although the Independent Labour Party in its long quarrel with the Labour party over the standing orders may appear at first sight to have been protecting the traditional rights of members, in reality this was not so for it would have subjected them to the control of a body outside Parliament altogether, the I.L.P. conference.[1]

PARTY COMMITTEES

The full meeting of Conservative or Labour members is too large for a detailed discussion of policy, nor can all the issues that may arise in Parliament be adequately discussed at a single weekly meeting. In order that specialists may give more attention to particular aspects of policy than is possible for the full party meeting, each of the two main parties has a number of committees or groups for their consideration, and these in turn may be divided into sub-committees or sub-groups. A chairman, one or more vice-chairmen and one or more secretaries are elected or appointed for each of these committees, but there is normally no fixed membership. The elections may be made at the party meeting or by a meeting of members summoned for the purpose. Notice of the meetings is given with the weekly whip, and members may usually attend any meeting that interests them. In practice there is nearly always a small body of members keenly interested in the subject who attend every meeting, and when some topic of current interest is under discussion a larger number of members attend, especially if it is likely to be debated in the House. The present list of committees or groups is as follows:

Conservative Committees

Agriculture and Food
Civil aviation
Commonwealth Affairs
Defence
Education
Finance, trade and industry
Foreign affairs
Fuel and power
Health and social security
Home Affairs
Housing, local government and
Labour   [works
Transport

In addition to these 'functional' committees, corresponding to the several ministries or groups of ministries, there is a Scottish Unionist members' committee with its own officers. The Ulster Unionist mem-

[1] See above, p. 55. The charge that the Labour party also subjects members to the control of a body outside Parliament, namely the party's national executive committee, is examined below, p. 191.

F

bers also meet from time to time to consider their special problems, and no doubt if there were a larger Conservative representation from Wales the Welsh members would also constitute themselves into a committee.

Labour Groups

Administration of the
   nationalized industries
Agriculture and food
Arts and amenities
Blitzed areas
Colonies
Commonwealth
Defence and services
Education
European co-operation

Films
Finance
Fisheries
Foreign affairs
Housing and town planning
Local government
Public information
Social services
Trade and industry
Civil defence

The Labour members of the House of Commons are also divided into area groups, of which the following exist:

Scottish Labour
Welsh Labour
London
Northern
Yorkshire
Lancashire and Cheshire

East Midlands
West Midlands
Eastern
South-western
Southern

These groups do not meet so often as the 'functional' groups.

All such groups, functional or regional, may be looked upon as committees of the party meeting and responsible to it. Frequently they report to it, and their reports are helpful in deciding the attitude of the party to forthcoming business in the House. In addition various sections of members may meet from time to time to consider their attitude. In the Labour party the trade union members constitute a section of special importance, and the co-operative members, though less important, are a far from negligible group. Furthermore, *ad hoc* committees are set up from time to time by members on their own initiative as particular problems call for discussion. Wherever two or three Englishmen are gathered together they form themselves into a committee, and for good or ill our British habit of addressing ourselves to a political problem is to resolve that a committee be appointed to consider it. Our system of government is committee government, the Cabinet being the apex of a vast pyramid of official and unofficial committees. During any sitting of the House of Commons in the late afternoon it may be taken for granted that while the public business is being discussed on the floor of the House at least a dozen committee meetings are being held privately upstairs. A very large part of a conscientious member's time is spent in attending such meetings, and it is through them that the attitude of the parties to the great issues under debate is crystallized.

These party committees are not, of course, to be confused with the standing committees of the House. These are part of the official machinery of the House and the committee stages of most bills is taken in them instead of on the floor of the House. Their members are nominated by a selection committee appointed by the House, and the selection committee is directed to have regard to the composition of the House, which means that the standing committees must reflect the party strengths in the House.

The value of the party committees naturally depends on the individual worth of their members, and especially of the chairman and secretary. Committees which can call on a great deal of experience and dis-interested service can be of great value to the party, and to ministers when the party is in office. But when committees get under the control of the personally ambitious or the 'cranky' they may become a serious nuisance. The Foreign Affairs group of the Labour party was a thorn in the flesh of Ernest Bevin as Foreign Secretary, and Lord Winster and I found its Civil Aviation group in 1945–46 no less troublesome. The system has to be accepted with its defects as well as its merits, but on the whole it plays a valuable part in shaping policy, in ensuring in-formed debate on the floor of the House and in the standing com-mittees, and in training future ministers.

The organization of a parliamentary party as described above requires a small, salaried secretariat. It would be possible for each parliament-ary party to finance its own secretariat out of the contributions of members, but their salaries are subject to many calls, and in practice the secretariat is provided both in the Conservative party and in the Labour party by the national headquarters. This is one of the points of inter-action between the party organizations inside and outside the House to which attention will need to be given later; and apart from the financial aspect, it has the advantage of ensuring that the parliamentary and national parties do not get out of step.

If in the above pages the organization of only the Conservative and Labour parties has been described, it is because these are now the only fully articulated parties in Parliament. The Liberal members, now reduced to six, can settle their day-to-day problems without elaborate machinery. The National Liberals, as already noted, no longer describe themselves as a parliamentary party but, along with associated members, constitute the Liberal Unionist group within the Conservative and Unionist party. The Co-operative members inside the House do not constitute a separate group but are a group within the Labour party; they have their own chairman and their separate meetings, but they do not receive a separate whip and they attend the meetings of the parliamentary Labour party.

—— XII ——

Constituency Party Organization

THE UNIT OF PARTY ORGANIZATION in the country is normally the parliamentary constituency. This has come about for historical reasons in that the original purpose of party organization in the country was the registration of voters of known political views with the object of securing the return of like-minded members; and it has continued because the main object of party organization in the country is still to secure the return of candidates to Parliament. Constituencies are of two kinds—parliamentary boroughs, or divisions of parliamentary boroughs, and divisions of parliamentary counties. In some parties this introduces slight differences into the local organization.

The Conservative, Liberal and Labour parties are organized in this manner on a constituency basis. The Co-operative party is based upon retail societies whose trading areas frequently do not coincide with parliamentary constituencies, and the party has tried to reconcile this fact with the need to contest elections on a constituency basis. Its constitution provides for society co-operative parties formed by a single society operating in one or a number of constituencies; district society parties formed by a number of societies operating in one or more constituencies; and county constituency parties formed by a number of societies operating within only one parliamentary division. The Communist party is not usually organized on a constituency basis, but has branches in towns and factories; and when a constituency election is fought an *ad hoc* organization is set up for the purpose. The minor parties also are frequently not organized on a constituency basis, but have branches in towns or districts. In their case this does not seem to spring from a political philosophy. The branches of these parties usually revolve round one zealot, and it is for purely empirical reasons that where he lives there is a branch of the party; if they had greater resources, no doubt they also would organize themselves on a constituency basis. But in the Communist party it may be possible to see the influence of a different theory. The separate organization of factory branches is reminiscent of the 'soviets of toilers' deputies', and it suggests that if the Communists had their way Parliament would not be based, or at any rate not exclusively based, on the representation of geographical areas.

In the Conservative and Liberal parties the name usually given to the constituency organization is 'association', for example, the South Hammersmith Conservative and Unionist Association and the Newport Liberal Association. In the Labour party the name given to the constituency organization is 'constituency Labour party', for example, the Keighley Constituency Labour party. As already indicated, the unit of Co-operative party organization is also called a party; and in the Communist and other minor parties the name given to the local unit of organization is 'branch'. This suggests another difference in outlook, for whereas the older parties are built up from below, the Communist party is organized from above. The Conservative, Liberal and Labour parties are all built out of autonomous local units, but in the Communist party the local units are the creations and servants of the Communist party of Great Britain.

We have spoken hitherto of local units of the Conservative party, but in fact the name used locally may be the Oxbridge Conservative Association, the Oxbridge Conservative and Unionist Association, or the Oxbridge Unionist Association.[1] In England and Wales the term normally used is Conservative and Unionist Association, but there are a few local bodies with the title Conservative Association. As already noted, in Scotland the term used is Unionist Association, and in Northern Ireland the term used is Ulster Unionist. Where the context requires, the term Conservative in these pages must be understood as implying those local variations. Furthermore, in recent years there have come into existence several united organizations of Conservatives and Liberals, the local body being known in some cases as the Conservative and Liberal Association, in others as the Liberal and Conservative Association. The order of the names probably indicates a local *nuance*.

CONSERVATIVE ASSOCIATIONS

A Conservative constituency association is composed of individual members who reside in or are 'connected with' the division. The great bulk of members are always residents in the division, but membership is open also to persons who have business interests in the constituency, or formerly lived in it, or in some other way feel a connexion with it. Each constituency association makes its own rules, with guidance from headquarters if desired. The Conservative party issues model rules, but

[1] See above, p. 37.

as these are meant only for guidance there are many local variations. It is, however, always the case that the rules lay down the objects of the association, and that persons are eligible for membership if they declare their support of those objects and contribute a minimum sum annually to its funds. The objects always include support for Conservative principles and policy. In all cases the minimum subscription is low, and in many cases it was fixed at a shilling a year a long time ago. With the fall in the value of money, this has now become a merely nominal sum, but most associations are reluctant to increase it. Most members pay more of their own free will, and a large part of the funds of the association comes, not from subscriptions, but from whist drives, sales of work, fêtes and similar social activities.

The rules may provide for men and women to be members of the association on the same footing, or they may provide for women to be organized in a women's branch, and if so desired for men to be organized in a men's branch. There is nearly always provision for a Young Conservative organization in the constituency. This is usually open to all young men and women between the ages of 15 and 30; all members automatically become members of the constituency association, but do not have a vote at association meetings until the age of twenty-one.

Branches of the association are set up in each ward (in a borough constituency) or polling district (in a county constituency). Some form of devolution is desirable for conducting normal constituency work, and is essential in the busy three weeks preceding a parliamentary election; and it is convenient to base the devolution on the units of local government, as the contesting of local government elections has now become second in importance only to parliamentary elections in the work of a constituency organization.

The rules must provide for the election of officers of the constituency association, who are normally a president, a chairman, three vice-chairmen (one man, one woman and one Young Conservative), and an honorary treasurer. The president is a distinguished local figure, but is not normally expected to play an active part in the affairs of the association; the chairman is the officer on whom the bulk of the work and responsibility falls. The rules must also provide for an executive committee, which usually consists of the officers of the association, the chairman of each committee set up, two elected representatives (one man and one woman), or more in boroughs, from each ward or polling district branch, one representative from each ward or polling district branch of the Young Conservative association, one representative from each Conservative club, and up to six co-opted members. A number of committees of the executive council are set up. A finance and general purposes committee is essential, a women's advisory committee and a Young Conservative committee desirable, and other committees for such matters as political education, publicity, local government and trade union affairs are optional.

Each branch of the association in a ward or polling district has its own officers (usually a chairman, one or more vice-chairmen, an honorary treasurer and an honorary secretary), and a committee consisting of the branch officers and such other members as are deemed by the branch annual meeting to be necessary.

The ultimate authority in a Conservative association rests in the whole body of members assembled in a general meeting. Such general meetings may be annual or special. The annual general meeting elects the officers, receives the audited accounts of the association and the report of the executive council, and in general declares itself satisfied or dissatisfied with the way the business of the association is being conducted. A special general meeting may be called for any good reason, such as the approval of a prospective parliamentary candidate put forward by the executive committee.

CONSTITUENCY LABOUR PARTIES

The organization of a Conservative association as described above could be applied with only a change of name to a Liberal or National Liberal association. But when we turn to the Labour party we come to a different conception. At the time the Labour party was set up it had no provision for individual members, but consisted of a number of affiliated bodies; and although provision has been made since 1918 for the enrolment of individual members, the affiliated membership is still by far the greater part of its whole membership.

Constituency Labour parties do not have quite the same freedom in drafting their rules as a Conservative or Liberal association. Clause III. 2, of the party constitution lays down that 'each constituency Labour party . . . must . . . adopt the rules laid down by the party conference'. Among the rules are these, based on Clause II of the constitution and here taken from the Labour party's 'Constitution and rules for constituency Labour parties and local Labour parties in county constituencies.'

'(1) There shall be two classes of members, namely—
(a) affiliated organizations,
(b) individual members.

'(2) Affiliated organizations shall consist of—

(a) Trade unions and branches thereof affiliated to the Trades Union Congress or recognized by the general council of the Trades Union Congress as *bona fide* trade unions.

(b) Co-operative societies, branches of the Co-operative party and other Co-operative organizations.

(c) Branches of those socialist societies affiliated to the Labour party nationally.

(d) Branches of those professional organizations which, in the opinion of the national executive committee, have interests consistent with those of other affiliated organizations and which are affiliated to the Labour party nationally.

(e) Trades councils.

(f) Any other organization or branch thereof which the national executive committee deems eligible for affiliation.

(3) Individual members shall be persons of not less than sixteen years of age who subscribe to the conditions of membership.'

Among the conditions of membership are that each individual member must 'either reside in the division, or be registered therein as a parliamentary or local government elector.' It is laid down that an individual member must, 'if eligible, be a member of a trade union affiliated to the Trades Union Congress or recognized by the general council of the Trades Union Congress as a *bona fide* trade union'; and that 'a person who does not contribute to the political fund of his or her trade union may not be an individual member of and may not take part in the work of the party as a member of an affiliated organization'. There is also a rule that 'a person who is a member of a political party or organizations ancillary or subsidiary thereto declared by the annual party conference or national executive committee in pursuance of conference decisions to be ineligible for affiliation to the Labour party may not be an individual member of and may not take part in the work of this party as a member of an affiliated organization'. This condition is, of course, primarily aimed at Communists.

In a county constituency it is provided that there shall be in each municipal borough or urban district therein a local Labour party formed in the same way as the constituency Labour party out of affiliated organizations and individual members; this refinement does not exist in boroughs which are parliamentary constituencies, and there we can pass straight from the constituency to the ward organization. In boroughs and in county divisions alike it is laid down that 'individual members of this party shall be attached to ward committees'; that 'individual women members of the party shall in addition be organized in women's sections and that women's sections may be established on a ward basis'; and that 'individual members of the party aged between sixteen and twenty-five years may be organized in branches of the Labour party League of Youth'.

The Labour party does not carry the practice of having affiliated bodies down to the ward level. The general picture of Labour party organization is therefore as follows: In each ward of a borough or polling district of a county should be found a ward committee consisting of individual members (including women as well as men) and a separate women's section, and there may be a branch of the Labour League of Youth. Each constituency Labour party consists of the individual members' section (constituted by those ward committees and women's sections) and affiliated bodies. In the main the affiliated bodies are the local branches of trade unions, together with the local trades council in a borough or trades councils in a county, but they may include a co-operative society or the local branch of the Fabian Society.

Final authority in a constituency Labour party is vested in a general committee. It is provided in the rules that 'the management of this party shall be in the hands of a general committee consisting of delegates elected by affiliated organizations . . . and the following party organizations: ward committees, women's sections and Leagues of Youth, together with the secretaries of ward committees who shall be *ex officio* members with voting power.' The basis of representation is left to be decided by the constituency party subject to the approval of the national executive committee; but the general principle adopted is that every delegate has one vote and that the number of delegates to which an affiliated organization, ward committee or other body is entitled is based on the number of paying members.

The individual members do not meet as a body, as they do in the Conservative or Liberal parties, but send delegates to join with the delegates from trade unions and other affiliated organizations. Such delegates are usually instructed beforehand by their organizations how they shall vote, and this is an important difference from Conservative and Liberal practice to which it will be necessary to revert.

The affiliation fees payable by affiliated organizations are left to be arranged by the constituency Labour party with those organizations, and the whole sum is retained by the constituency party; the trade unions, as we shall see later, are directly affiliated to the Labour party nationally and pay substantial affiliation fees to it directly. The affiliation fees should correspond with the number of members of a trade union who contribute to its political fund, that is to say, who have not 'contracted out' from the political levy which is collected at the same time as their ordinary trade union dues. It is laid down that the contribution of individual members is to be at least 6d. a month, and of this 6d. a year is paid by the constituency party to the party head-quarters; otherwise these members would make no financial contribution to the national work of the party. The method by which this is done is ingenious: membership cards are sold by the head office to the constituency Labour party at 6d. each, and the secretary has to judge rather nicely how many he will need or risk having cards on his hands that he cannot sell. It follows that the published figures of the individual membership of the Labour party, based on cards issued and not returned, is a maximum and perhaps ought to be somewhat diminished to get the true membership.

The general committee holds an annual meeting and may be convened for special purposes, such as the selection of a prospective parliamentary candidate. At the annual meeting there are elected the officers, an executive committee and two auditors. The officers are a president, two vice-presidents, a treasurer, a financial secretary and a secretary; where there is a paid agent, he is usually the secretary also. The executive committee consists of the officers and a number of other members bearing such proportion to the whole membership as is approved by the national executive committee; officers and members of the executive committee must be duly appointed delegates to the general committee.

CO-OPERATIVE PARTIES

The rules of local co-operative parties make provision for individual members, who have to pay a minimum subscription fixed by the rules and to make a declaration, already noted, which guarantees that they are not opposed to the party's association with the Labour party. But such individual members are incidental to the existence of the co-operative party, and it is believed that the total number of such individual members is only about 16,000 out of more than 10,000,000 members of Co-operative societies. A co-operative party could exist without a single individual member. A local co-operative party comes into being by the decision of one or more co-operative societies to form it; and this decision is taken by a majority vote. The party is governed by a council; in the case of a society co-operative party the council may consist of representatives elected by the members of the society as a whole, or it may be composed of representatives from the management committee, representatives from the educational committee, representatives from auxiliary organizations, members elected by and from the general meeting of the society, and members elected by and from the society's staff; in the case of district and constituency parties, provision is made for all the participating bodies to be represented. The officers are a chairman, vice-chairman, treasurer and secretary, and the council may elect annually from its number an executive committee. Where the party covers more than one constituency, the council may set up constituency parties; and branches composed of individual members may also be set up. The funds of the party are provided by (a) such sums as may be provided by the society or its management committee; (b) affiliation fees from other co-operative bodies; (c) individual membership subscriptions; and (d) money-raising efforts approved by the council. The party is required to register with the national Co-operative party, and to operate such regulations as may be made by the national committee.

Members of co-operative societies which have not affiliated to the Co-operative party may form themselves into a 'voluntary party'. The constitution adds that 'the voluntary party shall have for its main object the political education of the members of the society and the securing of a decision in favour of affiliation to the party, or the creation of a local co-operative political organization as the case may be.'

COMMUNIST BRANCHES

The Communist party resembles the traditional parties rather than the Labour party in being based solely upon individual membership. But this may be from necessity rather than from choice, as all the organizations whose affiliations it would like to secure are attached to the Labour party.

Membership of the Communist party, according to the party rules as revised in 1952, is open to persons of eighteen years and upwards who accept the aims of the party, pay their dues regularly, and work in a party organization. Members are required to belong to and assist in the work of their appropriate trade union or professional organization and their co-operative society. They have also the duty, 'with the assistance of the party, to improve their political knowledge and understanding of Marxist-Leninist theory, to take part in discussion of party policy, to equip themselves to take an active and helpful part in the working-class movement, to read, study and popularize the *Daily Worker* and party literature, to win new members to its ranks, and to take part in the activities of their party organization'. A considerable section of the rules is occupied, nevertheless, with the procedure for suspending or expelling members who are guilty of breaches of the party rules or any other conduct detrimental to the party; and for dealing with lapses in subscriptions. As befits a zealous minority the Communist party has a much higher subscription than any other. Membership dues are 6d. a week. In each quarter of thirteen weeks the total subscription is thus allocated: 2s. 3d. to the (national) executive committee, 2s. 3d. to the district committee, 1s. 6d. to the branch, and 6d. to the central election fund. Membership dues for unemployed members, housewives and old-age pensioners are reduced to 2d. a week, allocated in the same proportions as the full subscription.[1] The 'organizational structure' of the Communist party is declared to be 'based on the principles of democratic centralism'. This is defined as meaning: (a) the election of all leading party committees; (b) the responsibility of all such leading party committees to submit reports at regular intervals to the party organizations which have elected them; (c) minorities shall accept the decision of the majority; (d) the lower party organizations shall accept the decisions of the higher party organizations'. In practice this fourth illustration is predominant and in 'democratic centralism' it is easy to see the centralism but not so easy to discern the democracy.

The rules state that 'the basic unit of the party is the party branch', and such units are organized 'on the authority of the district committee'; the district committees in their turn are constituted by the (national) executive committee. There are two types of branches. A 'factory branch' comprises 'all party members employed in a particular factory, pit or other place of work'; a 'local branch' comprises 'members living or employed in a defined area, with the exception of those members organized in a factory branch'. Every party branch is required to hold an annual general meeting, at which a branch committee is elected; the branch committee elects the officers of the branch. All members are required to produce their party card at business meetings, and loss of a party card is 'regarded as a serious breach of responsibility'.

NATIONALIST PARTY BRANCHES

The Welsh Nationalist party is also composed of individual members. The unit of organization is the branch (cangen). A branch may be

---

[1] By an amendment to its constitution accepted in 1950 the Labour party gives individual membership for a shilling a year, instead of six shillings, to old-age pensioners who have retired from work.

established in any district with the sanction of the executive committee, and the branches are not normally co-terminous with parliamentary constituencies; many are in villages. Naturally most branches are within the borders of the principality, but some have been sanctioned in English towns where there is a Welsh population; for example, a branch was established at Coventry on 5 December 1951. A member of a branch must accept the principles of the party and subscribe a minimum sum of half a crown a year. The branch is required to transmit this minimum subscription to the party headquarters, but is allowed to retain half its other receipts. Persons living in places where there is no branch may be enrolled by the district committee or the national headquarters if they accept the principles of the party and are willing to subscribe a shilling a year to its funds. The officers of a branch are the president, secretary and treasurer, who are elected annually.

The Scottish National party is likewise composed of individual members enrolled in branches or groups; persons not desirous of joining a branch or group may become members at the national headquarters. A branch consists of not fewer than twenty members, but fewer than twenty members may be formed into a group where it is considered desirable; such groups are not entitled as branches are, to representation at annual or special conferences of the party. Ordinarily membership is limited to persons permanently resident in Scotland, but any person, otherwise eligible for membership, who is resident out of Scotland may become an honorary member of a branch or at headquarters. Persons eligible for membership are those who endorse the party's aims, agree to abide by its policy and direction, accept its constitution and rules, and are not members of any other political party. Each branch is required to appoint a chairman, a secretary and a treasurer, and may appoint other officials. The minimum annual subscription is five shillings, and branches are required to pay to the national headquarters such affiliation fees in respect of each member as may be decided by the annual conference. Two or more branches within a parliamentary constituency may be formed into a constituency association. The officers of a constituency association are a chairman, a vice-chairman, a secretary, a treasurer and an organizer, appointed annually. The expenses of a constituency association are met either by a levy on branches or by such other means as the association may decide.

STRENGTH OF LOCAL ORGANIZATIONS

The size and strength of constituency associations and parties vary greatly. They differ in their area and the size of the electorate, of course, but the zeal and ability of the member or candidate, officers and agent are more important reasons for the variation. Perhaps we can lay it down that every Conservative association or Labour party ought to have an individual membership of at least 1,000. But some have a membership of only a few hundreds while the strongest may have more than 5,000 paying members on their books. The Lanark Labour party in 1950 paid affiliation fees for 2,834 men and 2,684 women, a total of 5,518, while Mr. Herbert Morrison's Labour party in South Lewisham was even better with 4,820 men and 2,200 women —a total of 7,020; in the same year the N.E. Leeds Labour party returned only 156 men and 119 women, a total of 275, and Central Edinburgh 120 men and 120 women, a total of 240. The income of the association or party may vary within corresponding limits—from a few hundred pounds a year to over £5,000 a year. There is no correlation between the size of the association or party and the safety of the seat. The dominant party in many safe divisions has a surprisingly small membership. No Labour member could wish for a safer seat than Aberdare, where the Labour candidate had in 1951 a majority of 27,973 over his Conservative opponent, but in 1950 it paid affiliation fees to the Labour party on only 274 men and 205 women members. Abertillery had a Labour majority in 1951 of 24,917, but the membership of the constituency Labour party was returned in 1950 as 216 men and 408 women, a total of 624. But perhaps it is not surprising, for in such divisions there is little incentive to recruit members. The most active constituency organizations, and very often the largest, are often in marginal divisions where hard work may be rewarded by a parliamentary victory and sloth penalized by the loss of the seat. The figures for Conservative and Liberal membership are not so readily accessible, but as the total membership of the Conservative and Unionist party was announced on 5 November 1951 to be 2,763,968, this means that the *average* membership of a constituency Conservative association must be nearly 5,000. A single ward in South Kensington has over 3,300 members of the local Conservative association, though this is admittedly one of the strongest Conservative areas in the country; and the total membership of the association exceeds 11,000. The Newport Conservative and Unionist Association has also had about 10,000 members in recent years, made up of about 4,500 men and 5,500 women; but this constituency has a larger electorate than the average.

CONSTITUENCY AGENTS

As the electorate has increased and party organization has become more elaborate, the practice of engaging paid officials for the work of constituency organization has become more common. In the Conservative, and in the Labour parties it is considered desirable to have in each constituency a full-time paid certificated agent. A certificated agent is one who has received a certificate from his party headquarters, after tests, guaranteeing knowledge of election law, etc., a constituency official who has not obtained such a certificate may be known as an organizer, and he also may be required to pass certain tests of a less exacting order. A woman may be appointed by the stronger organizations to be a woman's organizer. The Conservative party also has a certain number of 'missioners', especially in marginal or difficult areas. At the general election of 1950 the Labour party had 279 full-time agents and over 340 election agents who were not in the full-time agency service. In September 1952 there were 486 certificated Conservative agents in charge of constituencies in Great Britain, and 64 certificated organizers in charge of constituencies.

It is the agent's duty to be the chief organizer of party activities in the constituency, and to act as secretary to the executive committee. His salary is borne by the constituency association funds. A contribution may be made to these funds for the purpose by the member of Parliament; and a contribution so made is an allowable expense for the purposes of income-tax, though a similar contribution by a prospective candidate would not be allowed as a deductible expense because the prospective candidate has no constitutional position in relation to the constituency nor salary against which an allowance can be set. In order to encourage the engagement of full-time agents the headquarters of the party may also make a contribution to the constituency funds towards the agent's salary. But it is the honorary treasurer of the constituency party who hands him his monthly cheque, normally it is the constituency party which finds all or the bulk of his salary, and he is the servant of the constituency party, and more immediately of its executive committee. An agent has to be always bright and cheerful; he must suffer fools gladly, or at least appear to do so; he must have an unfailing memory for faces and names; he must never be flurried or ruffled; he must accustom himself to long bursts of work with meals at irregular hours; his tact must be inexhaustible; in an election campaign he must inspire his candidate with the confidence of victory, and yet be able to assure him in the hour of defeat that he has pulled out every vote. It may be wondered whether such paragons exist; but candidates and members can name them with gratitude, and they, with their chairmen and other officers, will acknowledge that the agent is the pivot round which the constituency organization turns.[1]

WOMEN'S AND YOUTH ORGANIZATIONS

No one who is familiar with the practical working of a constituency organization can also fail to pay tribute to the activities of the women members. In the Conservative, Liberal and Labour parties it would be universally admitted that the work of the women's branches or women's sections is indispensable. The minor parties are more male parties; or is it that they are minor parties for the same reason that they are male parties? Women are seldom found in the posts of honour, except in those places which have by the rules to be filled by their sex. This work is unobtrusive and often unknown—making tea and cakes, running whist drives, organizing sales of work, addressing envelopes—but it is by such work that the spectacular and well-reported appearances of the candidate or member on the public platform are made possible.

The first Conservative youth organization was the Junior Imperial League, founded in 1906 'with the object of giving scope and direction to the political activities of young persons'. (Organization Series, no. 1, *The Party Organization*, p. 5.) It was only loosely associated with the party, had no formal representation in its councils, and was more social than political. 'Junior Imp' dances were one of its main activities. The Young Britons organization was founded in 1925, 'primarily to counteract the blasphemous and seditious doctrine of the Communists' (Organization Series, no. 11, *The Young Britons Organization*, p. 1). No political teaching was given until 1931, when the constitution of the body was altered for that purpose. Both the League and the Young Britons ceased to function with the outbreak of war in 1939. The League was not revived, but the Young Conservative Organization was created as a formal part of the party structure. The Young Britons organization was revived as 'the juvenile section of the National Union' (*loc. cit.*, p. 4).

The work of the youth organizations is indeed vital, and when a party begins to attract youth it knows that it is on the up-grade. The domin-

[1] The relation of agents to the headquarters and area staffs is considered below, pp. 180–81.

ance of the Labour party at the universities in the thirties was the harbinger of its success in the country in the forties; and the vigorous growth of the Young Conservatives organization after the defeat of 1945 was the sign of the Tory rejuvenation. But youth has always been headstrong, and no doubt always will be. The Labour party between the wars had infinite trouble with its youth organizations, which nearly all came under Communist influences, and it now keeps a very tight hand on the Labour League of Youth. The Conservative party has had better fortune—or is it that the Conservative youths have a greater sense of loyalty and discipline?—but in a few constituencies the Young Conservatives have been known to 'kick over the traces'. It is the way of youth, and if we are wise we shall say 'Bless them', and regard it as an indispensable part of their political education.

Regional, National and International Organization

THE LABOUR PARTY'S model rules make provision for 'central Labour parties' in divided boroughs, that is, boroughs divided into two or more parliamentary constituencies each returning one member to Parliament. The general object is 'to unite the forces of Labour within the borough'. There are three classes of members—affiliated organizations, constituency Labour parties and individual members. The affiliated organizations will often be affiliated to the constituency Labour parties as well, but it is easy to see that there may be cases where an organization, for example a branch of the Fabian Society, is affiliated to the central Labour party but not to any of the constituency Labour parties. The constituency Labour parties are, of course, the parties of the constituencies into which the borough is divided, and although they are not required to affiliate to the central party it is unlikely that any would decline to do so. Individual members can be enrolled only by constituency Labour parties; that is to say, an individual member of a constituency Labour party automatically becomes a member of the central Labour party to which it is affiliated, and the central Labour party will not enrol individual members itself. There are such central Labour parties in Reading, Birkenhead, Stockport, Derby, Plymouth, Gateshead, Sunderland, East Ham, Ilford, Walthamstow, Bristol, Bournemouth, Portsmouth, Southampton, Blackburn, Blackpool, Liverpool, Manchester, Oldham, Salford, Ealing, Harrow, Hendon, Wembley, Norwich, Newcastle-upon-Tyne, Nottingham, Stoke-on-Trent, Wolverhampton, Croydon, Brighton, Birmingham, Coventry, Kingston-upon-Hull, Middlesborough, Bradford, Huddersfield, Leeds Sheffield, Cardiff, Swansea, Aberdeen, Dundee, Glasgow and Edinburgh. The London Labour party may also be regarded as a central Labour party as regards its relationships with the Labour parties of the metropolitan boroughs, but it is recognized in the model rules to be *sui generis*.

The Conservative party provides likewise for central associations in divided boroughs comprising two or more constituencies. Such central organizations are specially valuable when borough elections are contested on party lines or when it is desired to arrange a big party demonstration; but they are, of course, an additional piece of machinery making further demands on the time of busy men and women. There are such central Conservative associations in Gateshead, Sunderland, Middlesbrough, Stockport, Blackburn, Blackpool, Bolton, Liverpool, Manchester, Oldham, Preston, Salford, Bradford, Huddersfield, Kingston-upon-Hull, Leeds Sheffield, Derby, Leicester, Nottingham, Stoke-on-Trent, Birmingham, Coventry, Norwich, Ilford, Croydon, Southampton, Bristol and Dundee.

I. AREA ORGANIZATION

The Conservative, Liberal and Labour parties all agree on the need to have an area or regional organization interposed between the constituency and the national headquarters.

For this purpose the Conservative party divides England and Wales into the following twelve areas:

(1) London (the City of London and all London boroughs)
(2) Northern counties (Cumberland, Durham, Northumberland and Middlesbrough)
(3) Lancashire, Cheshire and Westmorland
(4) Yorkshire (excluding Middlesbrough)
(5) East Midlands (Derbyshire, Leicestershire, Lincolnshire, Nottinghamshire, Northamptonshire, Rutland)
(6) West Midlands (Gloucestershire, Herefordshire, Shropshire, Staffordshire, Warwickshire, Worcestershire)
(7) Eastern (Bedfordshire, Cambridgeshire, Hertfordshire, Huntingdonshire, Norfolk, Suffolk)
(8) Home Counties—North (Essex and Middlesex)
(9) Home Counties—South-east (Kent, Surrey and Sussex)
(10) Wessex (Berkshire, Buckinghamshire, Dorsetshire, Hampshire, Isle of Wight, Oxfordshire, Wiltshire)
(11) Western (Cornwall, Devonshire, Somersetshire, Bristol)
(12) Wales and Monmouthshire.

Each of these 'provincial areas' has an 'area council' on which all constituencies in the area are represented. These area councils are empowered to raise funds for the needs of the area. Each area council has an executive committee, whose primary object is 'to promote, superintend and carry through such work of organization and political education within the provincial area as may be deemed necessary'. It has also a number of advisory committees reporting to the executive committee. The London area organization is known as the London Conservative Union.

The party's Central Office maintains an office in each of these areas, and in charge of it there is an area agent, with a deputy, appointed by the Central Office. The work of the area agent is 'to transact Central Office business in the area, and to act as a channel of communication between the Central Office, the area and the constituencies'. The area agent acts as honorary secretary for the area council.

We here encounter again the duality in organization which has already been noted in the historical section. There is no duality at the constituency level because the constituency agent is the servant of the constituency association. In the area we see the two types of organization meeting—the organization built upwards from constituency units to the national level, and the organization stretching downwards from the national headquarters.

The mid-Yorkshire federation, comprising the constituencies of Barnsley, Dearne Valley, Hemsworth, Normanton and Pontefract, appears to be the only example in the Conservative party of a federation of Conservative associations. This is also an example of building from the constituency upwards. As we shall soon see, federations of constituency organizations are more common in the Labour party.

The Unionist party in Scotland is separately organized from the Conservative and Unionist party in England and Wales. Scottish constituencies are grouped into two divisions—East and West—with a divisional council in each area having offices in Edinburgh and Glasgow respectively. Each constituency association sends five representatives (two men, two women, one Junior Unionist) to its divisional council; Unionist members of Parliament and prospective candidates for constituencies in the area are also members. The chief officers are known as the convener, the convener of the finance panel, the convener of the policy and political education committee, the convener of the women's committee, the honorary treasurer and the convener of the Junior Unionists. The officers are members of the executive committee, which is elected annually by the divisional council.

The constituencies are also grouped into area groups intermediate between the constituency and the division. In the eastern division there are three such groups, consisting of representatives from the constituencies in the north-east, centre and south-east of Scotland.

The Liberal party divides England into the following ten areas:

1. Devon and Cornwall	6. East Midlands
2. Eastern counties	7. West Midlands
3. Home counties	8. Northern area
4. Lancashire, Cheshire and	9. Western counties
North-western	10. Yorkshire
5. London	

The Liberal party constitution lays down that 'for the purpose of developing and improving the organization of the party in the country there shall be a number of area federations, the executives of which shall be elected annually by the affiliated constituency associations, together with representatives appointed by the Women's and Young Liberal area organizations, under regulations to be framed by each federation'. The officers of the federation, elected annually, are a president, chairman and vice-chairman.

Liberals in Wales are organized into the Liberal party of Wales, but the fact that the secretary's address is given as Newtown, Montgomeryshire, which is admittedly one of the most central towns of Wales but also one of the most inaccessible, suggests that the organization is not so distinct from that of England as the title might lead a reader to believe. In the party's executive committee and the Liberal Council Wales takes part on the same footing as the English areas, whereas the Scottish Liberal party is 'represented' on the executive committee and sends 'fraternal delegates' to the council. It would appear, therefore, that despite the name 'the Liberal party of Wales', England and Wales are in practice treated by the Liberals as a unit and Wales and Monmouthshire are regarded as the eleventh area of the unit. The Scottish Liberal party does, however, have an organization distinct from that of Liberals in England.

The National Liberals also have a separate organization in Scotland from that in England and Wales. National Liberal associations in England and Wales are affiliated directly to the National Liberal Council, and in Scotland to the National Liberal Association, without intermediate groupings.

The Labour party treats the whole of Great Britain as an entity for the purposes of organization and does not have in Scotland an organization distinct from that in England and Wales. Constituency parties are encouraged to form county or area federations. With one exception comprising two counties, those that have been formed so far are on a county basis. Such federations hold conferences and generally carry out 'political education' in their area. The following federations were affiliated to the Labour party in 1952.[1]

[1] In the previous year Nottinghamshire and Fifeshire federations were also affiliated.

England

Cumberland and Westmorland
Durham
Buckinghamshire, Hampshire
   and Isle of Wight
Kent
Surrey
Cornwall
Devon
Dorset
Gloucestershire
Somerset
Wiltshire
Essex
Bedfordshire
Hertfordshire
Suffolk

England (cont.)

Derbyshire
Nottinghamshire

Wales

Glamorgan
North Wales

Scotland

Ayrshire
Dumbartonshire
Fifeshire
Lanarkshire
North-cast Scotland
Renfrewshire

It is at this level that we encounter, as in the Conservative and Liberal parties, the duality of organizations—from the bottom upwards and from the top downwards. The federations of constituency parties are an organization from the bottom upwards. In addition the Labour party has a regional organization stretching from its party headquarters downwards. The whole of the United Kingdom is divided for this purpose into the following eleven 'party organizing districts', 'areas', or 'regions'—the terminology is not fixed.

1. Northern	Cumberland, Durham, Northumberland, North Riding except Scarborough and Whitby
2. North-western	Cheshire, Derbyshire, Lancashire, Westmorland
3. Yorkshire	East Riding, West Riding, York, Scarborough and Whitby
4. Southern	Berkshire, Buckinghamshire, Hampshire, Kent, Surrey, East Sussex, West Sussex, Isle of Wight
5. London	Administrative county of London and Middlesex
6. South-western	Cornwall, Devon, Dorset, Gloucestershire, Somerset, Wiltshire
7. Eastern	Bedfordshire, Cambridgeshire, Isle of Ely, Essex, Hertfordshire, Huntingdon, Norfolk, Suffolk
8. Wales	Wales and Monmouthshire
9. Scotland	
10. East Midlands	Derbyshire, Leicestershire, Lincolnshire, Northamptonshire, Nottinghamshire

11. West Midlands   Herefordshire, Oxfordshire, Shropshire, Staffordshire, Warwickshire, Worcestershire

In each of these organizing districts an area agent is maintained. It is his duty to promote the organization of the party and to give all the help he can to constituency parties and federations.

A Scottish regional council of the Labour party had been in existence since 1907 and a Welsh regional council since 1938. In 1940 a regional council was established for Lancashire and Cheshire, and this was the beginning of a policy of covering England with a network of regional councils. A Yorkshire regional council and a Northern regional council were established in 1942, and regional councils for the East Midlands and West Midlands in 1944. Southern and Eastern regional councils were set up in 1947 and a South-western regional council in 1948. The purpose of a London regional council is already fulfilled by the London Labour party. Apart from this exception and the first English council created for Lancashire and Cheshire, the regions are coterminous with the party organizing districts enumerated above. They are a meeting point of the organization stretching from the constituency upwards and the organization stretching from the national headquarters downwards. The affiliated members of the regional council—to take the Yorkshire rules as an example—are (a) constituency parties and borough (or central) parties affiliated to the Labour party nationally, (b) trade unions affiliated to the Labour party and the Trades Union Congress nationally, (c) district councils of trade unions which are affiliated nationally, (d) co-operative societies or organizations, (e) socialist societies affiliated to the Labour party nationally, (f) women's advisory councils, and (g) federations of Leagues of Youth attached to the Labour party. The highest authority of the regional council is the annual meeting, consisting of delegates appointed by affiliated members in proportion to their numbers. Between conferences the highest authority is the regional executive committee, on which a certain number of seats is assigned to each class of affiliated members. The chief officers are a chairman, vice-chairman and treasurer elected by and from the regional executive. This suggests an organization from the constituencies upwards. But it is further laid down in the rules that 'the Yorkshire district organizer of the Labour party shall act as secretary to the regional council'. The national executive committee, moreover, made grants to the regional councils in their formative years, and since 1951 the national executive committee has assumed responsibility for the greater part of the expenses of the regional councils. The annual report of the party for 1951 refers to the change in these words :[1] 'A readjustment has now been made whereby the regional offices become the regional offices of the Labour party, and responsibility is also being accepted for the clerical staff.' This is an organization from the national headquarters downwards, and it will be seen that the regions are now practically identical with the party organizing districts, and the regional councils as much instruments of the national headquarters as associations of the constituency Labour parties and other affiliated bodies.

The co-existence of federations and regional councils may seem cumbrous, and it is certainly the case that the elaborate constitution of the Labour party, involving both affiliated organizations and individual members, requires a great deal of machinery and makes heavy demands upon the time of leading personalities. It may be significant that there is no Yorkshire federation, and the rules of the regional council provide for an East Riding county council committee and a West Riding county council committee 'for the purpose of carrying out the duties of county federations of Labour parties in the counties of East and West Riding in connexion with the county councils'. The main duties are (a) to formulate an electoral programme, to compile a panel of candidates and to endorse candidates after their selection, and (b) to ensure the establishment of Labour groups upon the county councils. In many other areas, however, there are both federations and regional councils. No doubt the reason why the Labour party feels both to be desirable is that the federations are federations of constituency Labour parties, and the constituency Labour parties are notoriously headstrong, whereas the regional councils are more under the influence of the soberminded trade union leaders.

The Co-operative party also treats Great Britain as a whole for the purposes of organization and shows the same duality in organization as the parties already mentioned. The constitution provides that federations of co-operative parties may be formed to co-ordinate the political work of existing co-operative political organizations, to work for the affiliation of non-affiliated societies, and to promote special political campaigns. Federations are required to operate within one or more of the districts of the Co-operative Union Ltd. Societies, parties and branches are urged to constitute such federations and to pay an 'adequate' affiliation fee to them, but they are left very much to their own initiative in so doing. This is the area organization as built from the bottom upwards. Like the other parties, Co-operators also have an

[1] p. 15.

organization stretching from the national headquarters downwards. For this purpose the country is divided into the following 'sections':

1. Midland
2. Northen
3. North-eastern
4. North-western
5. Southern
6. South-western
7. Western (including Wales)
8. Scottish

In each of these districts an organizer is maintained by the national headquarters.

The Communist party likewise does not distinguish Scotland from England and Wales for the purposes of organization. The branches of the Communist party are organized under 'district committees'; the United Kingdom is divided into the following twenty districts:

1. Devon and Cornwall
2. East Anglia
3. Hampshire and Dorset
4. Kent
5. Lancashire and Cheshire
6. London
7. Midlands
8. Midlands, East
9. Midlands, South
10. Midlands, South-east
11. North-east coast
12. North-west
13. Scotland
14. Surrey
15. Sussex
16. Tees-side
17. Wales
18. West of England
19. West Middlesex
20. Yorkshire

In some places there are borough, city or area committees interposed between the branches and the district committee. Districts, as already stated, are constituted by the (national) executive committee. A district congress has to be held every two years, the delegates being sent from branches in accordance with their numerical strength. The district committee is elected by the district congress. It constitutes area, city or borough committees in agreement with the executive committee.

The branches of the Welsh Nationalist party are organized in districts, of which there are 12 in existence. A *pwyllgor rhanbarth* (district committee) is established with the sanction of the (national) executive committee. It consists of representatives of the branches (*canghennau*) with not more than twenty co-opted members. Its officials are a president, vice-president, secretary and treasurer elected annually.

The constitution and rules of the Scottish National party provide that 'area councils may be established for the purpose of co-ordinating the work of branches and constituency associations in a particular area'. The constitution of such area councils is subject to the approval of the party's national council. A chairman, vice-chairman, and secretary are elected annually, and an area organizer is appointed by the national council, to whom he is primarily responsible.

II. NATIONAL ORGANIZATION

NATIONAL UNION OF CONSERVATIVE ASSOCIATIONS

We come now to the national stage in party organization. The National Union of Conservative and Unionist Associations, which we have already met in the historical section, and which is generally known as 'the National Union', is a federation to which constituency associations and central associations in England, Wales and Northern Ireland are affiliated. All such associations have the right to be affiliated on payment of an annual fee of not less than two guineas. At first sight it may appear strange that constituency associations in Northern Ireland should be affiliated whereas those in Scotland are not; the reason is probably that Scotland is large enough to have a completely independent organization, whereas the Northern Ireland associations have greater need of the contacts with a national organization. The rules of the National Union define its functions as being:

'(1) To promote the formation and development of Conservative and Unionist associations in every constituency in England, Wales and Northern Ireland, and to foster thought and effort in furtherance of the principles and aims of the party.

'(2) To form a centre of united action, and to act as a link between the leader and all organizations of the party in England, Wales and Northern Ireland.

'(3) To maintain close relationship with the Conservative and Unionist Central Office.

'(4) To work in close co-operation with the Scottish Unionist Association and the Ulster Unionist Council.'

In order to carry out these functions the National Union works through the provincial area councils already described and through a central executive committee, a central council and a conference.

The central council consists of fifteen different categories of members. Each constituency association is entitled to send four representatives, and there is provision for representatives of central associations, each provincial area, university graduate associations, and various party bodies. Conservative peers, members of the House of Commons and prospective parliamentary candidates are entitled to membership. Various party officials and the Central Office agents in provincial areas have the right to attend its meetings. Provision is also made for representatives of the Scottish Unionist Association (though Scottish associations are not affiliated) and of the Ulster Unionist Council. The central council is thus a large body. It holds an annual meeting and such other meetings as are deemed necessary by the executive committee. At the annual meeting there are elected a president, a chairman and three vice-chairmen who are known as the officers of the National Union and are *ex officio* members of its executive committee.

The executive committee of the National Union is constituted annually and is composed of the leader of the party and other party officers and officials, the chairman of each central advisory committee, five representatives appointed by each provincial area, one representative of the Conservative peers, four representatives of the executive committee of the Conservative and Unionist Members' Committee in the House of Commons, representatives of various party bodies, and representatives of the Scottish Unionist Association and the Ulster Unionist Council.

The following advisory committees of the National Union have been set up: Central Women's Advisory Committee, Young Conservative and Unionist Central Committee, Advisory Committee on Policy, Trade Union Advisory Committee, Local Government Advisory Committee. There are area advisory committees with similar names and objects.

CONSERVATIVE CONFERENCE

The most important task of the National Union is to organize an annual conference, to be held at such time and place as the previous annual conference shall appoint. All the members of the central council are entitled to attend the conference, and each constituency association is entitled to send three other representatives (one of either sex and a Young Conservative), including the honorary treasurer. Each constituency association is thus entitled to send to the annual conference seven representatives—the chairman of the association, the treasurer, the chairman of the Young Conservative divisional committee and one other Young Conservative, the chairman of the Conservative labour advisory committee, one lady, and one other (man or woman). In addition the member of Parliament or prospective parliamentary candidate and the certificated agent and certificated organizer may attend, which makes a possible ten from each constituency. Not all constituencies employ an agent, and few employ both an agent and an organizer, but as there are 554 constituencies in England, Wales and Northern Ireland about 5,000 persons are entitled to attend the conference from constituencies alone. When we allow for other members of the central council and for certain other additional representatives, we see that about 5,600 persons may have the right to attend the conference; and there are usually about 1,000 visitors. Not all the persons entitled to attend do so, but the numbers attending the post-war conferences have been: 1946, Blackpool, 2,900; 1947, Brighton, 3,360; 1948, Llandudno, 3600; 1949, London, 3,992.

A committee on party organization under the chairmanship of Sir David Maxwell Fyfe, which reported in 1949, discussed a reduction of the constituency representation from seven to two, and produced a scheme which would have given the conference a theoretical member-ship of 2,820, and a membership in practice of not more than 2,300; but when this was considered by the conference few representatives were prepared to vote against their chance of attending another year, and it was left in abeyance.

Motions may be put to the conference after proper notice if they have first received the endorsement of a provincial area, a constituency association or a central association for a divided borough; and motions may also be submitted by the executive committee and other com-mittees of the National Union. It is unusual at Conservative con-ferences for divisions to be necessary, but if they are a vote is normally taken by a show of hands, each representative having one vote; very occasionally a ballot has been required.

CONSERVATIVE CENTRAL OFFICE

The National Union is the apex of the organization constructed from the constituencies upwards. In the last resort it is responsible to the constituency associations. Its officers are elected, they are unpaid, and they change from year to year. We must now consider the other side of the organization, that which emanates from the leader of the party downwards. This is the Conservative and Unionist Central Office, which is officially described as the headquarters of the party organiza-tion. Its officers and salaried staff are appointed and they do not change from year to year.

An official description of the Central Office says: 'It is charged by the leader of the party with the responsibility of seeing that the organiza-tion throughout the country is efficient, making known the policy of the party, and conveying to him from time to time the feeling in the con-stituencies. It works in close co-operation with the National Union, with which there is a constant interchange of information'.

The officers of the Central Office are appointed by the leader of the party, and are the chairman of the party, the vice-chairmen and the treasurers. It is the task of one vice-chairman to interview men and women who desire to offer themselves as parliamentary candidates, and particulars of such men and women can be given by him to constituency associations seeking a candidate; and for this reason one of the vice-chairmen is generally a member of Parliament. The other vice-chairman advises on the general policy of political organization and political education. It is usual to have two vice-chairmen of different sexes. The chairman appoints as the principal official in charge of the Central Office a general director, who is at present Sir S. H. Pierssené. The general director is responsible to the chairman for the general organization of the party. Under his control there are departments of the Central Office dealing with constituency organization and finance, publicity and propaganda, information, political education, labour problems, local government, registration and election law, research, speakers, women's committees and the Young Conservative organization.

As already explained, England and Wales are divided into twelve areas in each of which the Central Office maintains an area agent with a deputy. Since 1930 these have been identical with the provincial areas of the National Union. Until that year constituency associations were organized in some places on a county basis. It was then decided to create provincial areas in those parts of the country which had only county organizations, and to make the provincial areas and the Central Office areas coincide. In recent years the Central Office has tended to devolve much of its work on the area offices. Though constituency associations have the right of direct access to the Central Office, they are encouraged to deal with the area office. The Central Office no longer makes grants of money direct to the poorer constituencies; it is considered that this can best be done by the area offices with the local knowledge at their disposal.

It will be apparent that there is reason in the dual organization of the National Union and the Central Office. They correspond to different needs. But it is, of course, desirable to avoid overlapping. In order to achieve this result the Central Office and the headquarters of the National Union have long been housed in the same building, which is at present Abbey House, 2–8 Victoria Street, London, S.W.1, near to the Houses of Parliament. The general director of the Central Office is usually appointed honorary secretary of the National Union, and the area agents of the Central Office are normally made honorary secretaries of the provincial area councils and committees. The dual machinery, thanks to this interlocking, has successfully avoided the friction that might have arisen.

SCOTTISH UNIONIST ASSOCIATION

The Unionist organization in Scotland is quite separate from that in England and Wales, and is financially autonomous, though linked at the highest level by representation on the central council of the National Union and acknowledging the same leader. It has the same dual aspect as the English and Welsh organization. The body corresponding to the National Union is the Scottish Unionist Association. It is a federation of all Unionist associations in Scotland. Its objects are officially defined as being 'to promote Unionist principles and policy, and to further Unionist representation in Parliament.' Its main organ is a central council, which is composed of the eastern and western divisional councils already described in the section on area organization. The officers of the central council are a president, two honorary secretaries, two honorary treasurers, five trustees, two honorary auditors, and a secretary of council.

The Scottish Unionist whip in the House of Commons retained his organizational responsibilities in Scotland long after the chief Conservative whip, in 1911, handed over his corresponding duties in England to the newly created post of chairman of the party organization. He had an office in Edinburgh under the charge of his political secretary. But in November 1950 Mr. Churchill, as leader of the party, appointed a Scottish Unionist member to fulfil the duties, other than those of whip in the House of Commons, previously carried out by the Scottish Unionist whip, with the designation of 'chairman of the Unionist party in Scotland'. It was a measure of separation of powers similar to that carried out nearly twenty years earlier in England. That is to say, the chairman of the party organization in Scotland has been made responsible to the leader of the party for guiding and co-ordinating the work of the party organization in Scotland, for making known the policy of the party and for conveying to the leader feeling in the constituencies. The chairman is appointed by the leader of the party, has direct access to him, and is the channel of communication between the party organization in Scotland and the leader. The political secretary is the chairman's representative in Scotland. By these arrangements the Scottish Unionist whip is enabled to give all his attention to parliamentary affairs.

LIBERAL ORGANIZATION

The Liberal Party organization is defined as consisting of '(i) the Assembly; (ii) the Council; (iii) the Liberal Party Committee; (iv) the area federations; (v) the constituency associations; and (vi) other recognized units'. The constituency organizations and area federations have already been described; and of the 'recognized units' it is sufficient to say that the Union of University Liberal Societies and the Association of Liberal Trade Unionists have this status.

The Liberal Assembly corresponds to the Conservative conference with the difference that it is regarded as a body kept in being between meetings. The Assembly is composed mainly of delegates from constituency associations on the basis of two delegates for 50–150 members, three delegates for 159–200 members, four delegates for 201–250 members, and an extra delegate for every additional 100 paid-up members to a maximum of twenty delegates. All Liberal members of either House of Parliament and all prospective parliamentary candidates and candidates at the last preceding election are members of the Assembly, as are all certificated agents and organizers. The officers and members of the executive committees of the area federations, the women's and Young Liberal area organizations, the Scottish Liberal Party, the Scottish Women's Council, the Scottish League of Young Liberals, and the executive committee of the National Union of Liberal Clubs can claim membership, and there is provision for representatives of university Liberal societies.

There is required to be at least one meeting of the Assembly every year, and special meetings may be summoned by the Council or the executive committee. The annual meeting elects the officers of the party organization, who are a president, a president-elect, not more than four vice-presidents and not more than three treasurers. Apart from these elections, and the elections of certain members of the Council, the functions of the Assembly are 'to receive from the Council, and to consider, reviews of the progress and work of the party, and to receive and deal with an annual statement of accounts', and 'to consider resolutions on public policy'. One such resolution may be proposed at any one meeting by a constituency association; and resolutions may also be proposed by the Council, and certain other bodies.

The Liberal Council roughly corresponds to the central council of the National Union. It is composed of all members of the executive committee, six members of the House of Lords, six members of the House of Commons, all members of the Liberal Party Committee, representatives of the affiliated constituency associations, representatives of the Scottish Liberal Party, thirty representatives of the party as a whole to be elected by the Assembly, and certain smaller categories of members. Included in the general task of doing 'everything in its power to

stimulate militant Liberalism in every part of the country' is the duty
of securing 'that candidates are adopted in as many constituencies as
possible', and for this purpose it has a prospective candidates' committee presided over by the chief whip. The Council has to appoint
annually an executive committee, which includes the officers, the chief
whip, representatives of area federations and representatives of the
Scottish Liberal Party.

The Liberal Party Committee has no exact counterpart in the Conservative organization. It consists of eighteen members presided over
by the leader of the parliamentary party; some of them serve *ex officio*,
and others are 'appointed annually by the leader of the parliamentary
party in agreement with the president of the party organization'. It is
officially stated that 'the prime purpose of the committee is to express
the Liberal attitude on questions of immediate urgency as well as to act
on matters of long-term policy'.

The other aspect of Liberal organization is the Whips' Office, corresponding to the Conservative Central Office. It will be recalled that
the control of the Conservative Central Office lay with the chief whip
until 1911 and that the Scottish Unionist whip controlled the headquarters in Edinburgh for even longer. The Liberals have kept the old
tradition, but in the present attenuated state of the Liberal party the
Whips' Office does not have its old influence.

The head offices of the Liberal Party are close to the Houses of
Parliament—in Victoria Street, Westminster, London, S.W.1.

LABOUR ORGANIZATION

We have already noticed that at the area level the Labour organization manifests the same duality as the Conservative. There are
federations of constituency Labour parties and regional councils along-
side area agents maintained by the national headquarters. At the
national level the duality in organization in the Labour party can still
be discerned, but not so obviously owing to certain differences from the
Conservative and Liberal parties. They may be expressed in this way.

It is rather hard to say precisely what the Conservative party is. We
can say with some precision what the Oxbridge Conservative and
Unionist Association is, or the Mercia Provincial Area Council or the
National Union of Conservative and Unionist Associations or the
Central Office. But 'The Conservative Party'; what entity is this in
law? It is not a federation of constituency and central Conservative
associations, for that is what the National Union is, and the Con-

G

servative party is more than the National Union. It covers both the
Conservatives in Parliament and Conservatives in the country; but
what body can do this? We know that it has a leader, and we know
how the leader is selected, but what exactly he leads is more difficult to
say. Perhaps the Conservative party may be defined as the assemblage
of Conservative organizations in Parliament and throughout the
country; and yet it is difficult to avoid the feeling that there are Conservative organizations—for example, clubs—which are linked with the
Conservative party but are not part of it. Perhaps there is one Conservative party in Parliament and one in the country, and perhaps the
two, though possessing a common name and a common leader, are not
part of any one single entity. The best test is perhaps what would
happen if a person should leave a legacy to 'the Conservative party'; it
may be hazarded that such a bequest would be void by reason of uncer-
tainty, and if anyone is thinking of so doing he would be advised to
consult the treasurers of the Conservative party first.

Similar arguments could be used about the Liberal party. It would
be easier to say what the Conservative party and the Liberal party are
if they had written constitutions, but they do not. The National Union
has a written constitution and so has the Liberal Party Organization,
but not the Conservative party or the Liberal party. But we can say
more precisely what 'the Labour party' is because it has a written
constitution re-published every year in the report of the annual conference. We have several times quoted it already; let us now see what
it has to say about the national organization of the party.

It tells us, in the first place, how the Labour party is built up at the
national level. The national Labour party is a macrocosm of the constituency Labour party. Clause II, 1, of the constitution is similar in
wording to the constituency rules already quoted, but as there is a slight
difference to allow for the affiliation of constituency parties the words
had better be cited exactly:

> 'There shall be two classes of members, namely:—
>   (a) Affiliated members.
>   (b) Individual members.'

Let us look at each of these categories in turn. Clause II, 2, states
that:

> 'Affiliated members shall consist of:
> (a) Trade unions affiliated to the Trades Union Congress or recog-
> nized by the general council of the Trades Union Congress as *bona
> fide* trade unions.
> (b) Co-operative societies.

(c) Socialist societies.

(d) Professional organizations which, in the opinion of the national executive committee, have interests consistent with those of other affiliated organizations.

(e) Constituency Labour parties and central Labour parties in divided boroughs.

(f) County or area federations of constituency Labour parties, hereinafter referred to as federations.'

On a strict interpretation of this clause the affiliated members of the Labour party are the organizations affiliated, each counting as one, and constituency parties being reckoned along with trade unions as affiliated organizations. A member of a trade union affiliated to the Labour party, even though he pays his political levy, is not thereby on a strict interpretation made a member of the Labour party; his trade union is a member, but technically he is not. On this strict interpretation there were 774 affiliated members of the Labour party in 1950 (namely, 83 trade unions, 1 co-operative society, 4 socialist societies, 661 constituency and central Labour parties and 23 federations): and when the Labour party announces that in the same year it had a nationally affiliated membership of 5,920,172 this is not strictly correct. On a strict interpretation, again, the only individual members of the national Labour party are those members enrolled direct by the head office under provisions to be mentioned soon; the individual members of constituency Labour parties should not be reckoned in this way, their parties having already been counted as affiliated members. When the Labour party announces that at the end of 1950 it had an individual membership of 908,161, the meaning is clear, but it is not strictly in accord with its own constitution. This is, however, only a verbal matter and need not be pressed. According to the annual report of the national executive committee to the 1952 conference the membership of the Labour party at 31 December 1951 was 5,849,002, made up of 4,937,427 members in affiliated trade unions, 876,275 individual members, and 35,300 members of affiliated co-operative and socialist societies.

AFFILIATED LABOUR MEMBERSHIP

The trade unions affiliated to the Labour party vary greatly in strength and influence. The best method of reckoning that influence is the number of members on whom affiliation fees are paid to the Labour party. This is not identical with the total membership of the trade union, for those members who contract out of paying the political levy must be omitted. Nor is it always identical with the number of members paying the political levy, for many trade unions pay affiliation fees on a round number of members; this may be greater than the membership paying the political levy, giving the trade union a greater voting power in the Labour party, but is more commonly less, giving the trade union a reserve of funds and votes for an emergency.

The largest trade union affiliated to the Labour party is the Transport and General Workers' Union, which in 1950 paid affiliation fees on 835,000 members—larger than the whole individual membership of the constituency Labour parties. Other big unions are the National Union of Mineworkers, paying affiliation fees on 646,465 members, the Amalgamated Engineering Union (580,612), the National Union of General and Municipal Workers (400,000—a very round figure), the National Union of Railwaymen (338,763), the Union of Shop, Distributive and Allied Workers (317,000), the Union of Post Office Workers (145,520), the United Textile Factory Workers' Association (143,798), and the Amalgamated Society of Woodworkers (134,500). The smallest affiliated union is the Enginemen and Firemen's Union, paying affiliation fees on 60 members.

The four Socialist societies affiliated to the Labour party are the Fabian Society, which paid affiliation fees in 1950 on 3,200 members, the Jewish Socialist Labour party, or Poale Zion (2,200), the Socialist Medical Association (1,600), and the National Association of Labour Teachers (300). These figures are negligible in comparison with most of the trade unions, but the Fabian Society has had an influence in the party out of all proportion to its numbers, and the influence of Poale Zion and the Socialist Medical Association has been far from negligible.

There is only one co-operative society affiliated nationally to the Labour party, namely, the Royal Arsenal Co-operative Society through its political purposes committee. As we have seen, the co-operative movement as a whole has preferred to set up its own party working in close relationship with the Labour party, and in view of the tensions which have from time to time developed we shall need to return to this subject.

The list is completed by the twenty-three federations of Labour parties and the 661 constituency and central Labour parties which in 1950 were affiliated.

Let us return to what the Labour party constitution lays down about affiliated organizations. Clause II, 3, stipulates:

'Political organizations not affiliated to or associated under a national agreement with the party on 1 January 1946, having their own programme, principles and policy for distinctive and separate propaganda, or possessing branches in the constituencies or engaged in the promotion of parliamentary or local government candidatures, or owing allegiance to any political organization situated abroad, shall be ineligible for affiliation to the party.'

This is a way of stating in general language that the Co-operative party is eligible for affiliation but the Communist party and the Independent Labour party are not. The Labour party would probably prefer in its present strength not to have any provisions for affiliated parties, but the door has to be kept open for the continued affiliation of the Co-operative party, which gave valuable support to the Labour party in lean years.

Clause III, 1, lays down that:

'Each affiliated organization must
  (a) accept the programme, principles and policy of the party;
  (b) agree to conform to the constitution and standing orders of the party;
  (c) Submit its political rules to the National Executive Committee.'

In addition each constituency Labour party, central Labour party or federation, by Clause III, 2, already cited, is required to adopt the rules laid down by the party conference. It will be seen that a fairly tight rein is kept on affiliated organizations, but many of them nevertheless contrive to be very fractious.

Clause II, 4, prescribes:

'Individual members shall be persons of not less than sixteen years of age who subscribe to the conditions of membership, provided they are not members of political parties or organizations ancillary or subsidiary thereto declared by the annual conference of the Labour party . . . or by the national executive committee in pursuance of conference decisions to be ineligible for affiliation to the party.'

This is aimed mainly at the Communist party and the network of organizations which have been fostered under innocent-sounding names to win the support of Labour party members for Communist policy. The list of 'proscribed organizations' includes bodies with such admirable names as the League for Democracy in Greece and the British Peace Committee.[1] To other parties it may seem an unwarrantable interference with the freedom of the individual to lay down such a list, but the Labour party has been sorely tried by the loving overtures of the Communists, and some indulgence must be given.

---

[1] See below, p. 219.

The conditions of membership are laid down in Clause III, 3:

'Each individual member must
(a) accept and conform to the constitution, programme, principles, and policy of the party.
(b) if eligible, be a member of a trade union affiliated to the trades union congress or recognized by the General Council of the Trades Union Congress as a *bona fide* trade union.
(c) unless temporarily resident abroad, be a member of a constituency Labour party either (i) where he or she resides or (ii) where he or she is registered as a parliamentary or local government elector.'

Of those conditions, (a) is fair enough and in view of the close relations between the Labour party and the trade unions (b) cannot be cavilled at; it is a case of 'Scratch my back and I'll scratch yours'. The next sub-clause (c) requires explanation. In the lean years between the wars the party managers became conscious that there were men and women who were prepared to join the Labour party centrally, and to contribute handsomely to its funds, but who were loth to join their constituency Labour party. In 1939 the national executive committee attempted to introduce into the party constitution a provision for 'associate members' to meet their needs, justifying the proposal by the argument that such persons might be prejudiced in their careers if they were known to be members of a constituency Labour party. The rank and file of the Labour conference, however, suspected that such reluctance to associate with the local Labour party was snobbishness, and that the applicants wished to be 'associate members' of the Labour party only for their personal advancement. In the end the National Executive Committee was given power to enrol centrally only persons temporarily resident abroad. A similar problem does not seem to rise in any other party, but if anyone should ask for central enrolment it is unlikely that any headquarters would refuse.

LABOUR CONFERENCE

The highest authority envisaged in the Labour party is the party conference. It is described in Clause VI of the party constitution, of which the first sub-clause reads:

'The work of the party shall be under the direction and control of the party conference, which shall itself be subject to the constitution and standing orders of the party. The party conference shall meet regularly once in every year and also at such other times as it may be convened by the National Executive Committee.'

As the conference itself frames and amends the constitution and standing orders, it is the ultimate authority in all party matters. The conference is constituted by delegates appointed by affiliated organizations normally in the proportion of one for every 5,000 members or part thereof and *ex officio* members (mainly members of the parliamentary Labour party and prospective candidates). Under this arrangement a constituency party usually sends one delegate to the conference; the trade unions send delegations in proportion to their size, the Transport and General Workers' Union being entitled to 167, though it contented itself with 40, at the 1950 conference.

As far as voting goes, a single delegate would suffice. Voting in the conference is by the card or block system, that is to say each delegation is given a card bearing the number of votes to which the delegation is entitled, and when a vote is taken one member of the delegation holds up the card for the tellers to see. The basis of voting is laid down in standing order 3, which reads:

'Voting at the annual party conference shall be by cards on the following basis:—

(a) National and constituency organizations: One voting card for each 1,000 members or part thereof on whom affiliation fees were paid for the year ending 31 December preceding the conference.

(b) Federations and central Labour parties: One voting card each.

Voting at any special party conference shall be on the same bases as those upon which voting took place at the preceding annual party conference.'

After a keen debate there are an exciting few minutes while a card vote is being taken. Hundreds of cards bearing the figure 1, 2 or 3 are quickly put into the air, and then delegates look round to see what the transport workers or the miners or the railwaymen are doing. They may have made up their minds already, or may even have been instructed how to vote before the conference opened, but it is possible that there may be a last whispered consultation on the benches. Then there is a little gasp from one side or the other as a card bearing the figure 835 or 647 or 339 or whatever it may be is held aloft. The argument is over. Delegates may be eloquent at the rostrum, but the final word lies with the men who can pull the biggest cards from their pockets.

NATIONAL EXECUTIVE COMMITTEE OF LABOUR PARTY

Voting on resolutions is by the whole conference, so that the low cards of the constituency parties are mingled with the high cards of the trade unions. But for one important purpose the conference is divided into sections, and each votes separately. This is the election of the national executive committee. The rules are contained in standing order 4, which reads:

'For the purpose of nomination and election the national executive committee shall be divided into four divisions:
'Division I shall consist of twelve members, to be nominated by trade unions and elected by their delegations at the annual party conference.
'Division II shall consist of one member, to be nominated by socialist, co-operative and professional organizations, and elected by their delegations at the annual party conference.
'Division III shall consist of seven members, to be nominated by federations, constituency Labour parties, and central Labour parties, and elected by their delegations at the annual party conference.
'Division IV shall consist of five women members, to be nominated by any affiliated organization, and elected by the annual party conference as a whole.'

This accounts for twenty-five members. The leader of the party and the treasurer are *ex officio* members of the executive, bringing the total number to twenty-seven. The leader of the parliamentary party is accepted by the conference as the leader of the party and is not voted upon. The treasurer is elected by the conference, but there is usually only one nomination.

Out of the twenty-seven members, twelve are trade unionists nominated by the trade union delegations from their own members. As the trade unions can nominate candidates in the women's section, and by their predominance in the conference can ensure their election if they act together, the trade unions can always obtain a majority of trade unionists in the national executive committee if they so desire.

There is nothing to prevent women from standing in the first three divisions if they can secure nomination, but their chances of election are small and it is only occasionally that a woman is successfully nominated. The creation of the fourth division ensures that there are always five women on the executive, but attempts to find some way of electing them other than by a vote of the whole conference have not succeeded.

The constituency section is the one that rouses most interest, for the candidates are the best-known figures on the political side of the Labour movement, and the figures indicate whose star is in the ascendant. For some years Mr. Aneurin Bevan has headed the poll. Although they number only seven out of twenty-seven, the constituency members are the most active in the national executive committee, though the last word can always lie with the trade unionists if they choose to have it. Until 1937 the constituency representatives, like the women members to-day, were elected by the whole conference, but in that year the constituency delegations won the right to elect their own representatives. A speech by Ernest Bevin was decisive in persuading the trade unionists to grant this concession.

The national executive committee is defined as being 'subject to the control and direction of the party conference . . . the administrative authority of the party.' The new executive always elects each year as its chairman the person who has been longest a member of the committee and has not previously held the post. This custom has sometimes given the committee a chairman embarrassing to the leader of the party at a critical time. Some of the late Harold J. Laski's pronouncements in 1945 and those of Mr. Shinwell in 1948 when they were respectively chairman seemed to many people to conflict with those of Mr. Attlee as leader, and led them to ask where the real seat of authority in the party stood.

LABOUR PARTY HEADQUARTERS

The two main duties of the national executive committee are

'to ensure the establishment of, and to keep in active operation, a constituency Labour party in every constituency, a central Labour party in every divided borough, and a federation in every suitable area',

and

'to enforce the constitution, standing orders, and rules of the party and to take any action it deems necessary for such purpose, whether by way of disaffiliation of an organization, or expulsion of an individual, or otherwise.'

In order to achieve the former object the national executive committee is responsible for the running of the party headquarters, commonly called 'Transport House' from the building in Smith Square near the Houses of Parliament which it shares with the Transport and General Workers' Union and the Trades Union Congress. The party headquarters corresponds with the Central Office in the Conservative party. Its chief official is described as the 'secretary of the Labour party', and he is selected by the national executive committee for the approval of the party conference. Other leading officials are the national agent, who has the duty of looking after constituency organization, the secretary of the international department, the secretary of the press and publicity department, the secretary of the research department, and the chief woman officer. The regional officers of the party come under the control of the headquarters as already explained.

CO-OPERATIVE PARTY

The constitution of the Co-operative party lays down:

'That there be maintained a national committee, whose objects shall be to secure direct Co-operative representation in Parliament and on local and other administrative bodies in accordance with the decisions of the Co-operative Congress; and to undertake, in furtherance of those objects, such propaganda or other work, either alone or in co-operation with other committees or organizations, as may be deemed desirable with a view to the establishment of a Co-operative commonwealth.'

'The national committee shall be a committee of the Co-operative Union, responsible to the central board of the Union, and through it to Congress.'

The committee consists of thirty-five members, of whom eight are appointed by the central board on a sectional basis (one from each section), eight are elected by societies contributing to the Co-operative party fund (one from each section), and eight are elected by the local co-operative parties (one from each section); three members are appointed by the central executive committee of the Co-operative Union, two by the Co-operative Wholesale Society, one by the Scottish Co-operative Wholesale Society, one by the Co-operative Production Federation, one by the Co-operative Press Ltd., one by the Women's Co-operative Guild, one by the Scottish Co-operative Women's Guild, and one by the National Co-operative Men's Guild. Two representatives of the parliamentary group attend the meetings but do not have the right to vote.

The national committee is required to meet quarterly, and at the first meeting after the Co-operative Union congress, called the annual meeting, it elects a chairman and eight other members to constitute an executive committee; a vice-chairman is elected at the next meeting.

The headquarters of the Co-operative Union are in Manchester, but the Co-operative party naturally maintains headquarters in London near Parliament—at 56 Victoria Street, S.W.1.

The constitution lays down that there is to be a Co-operative party fund, and one of the duties of the national committee is to administer this fund. The constitution adds that 'retail societies participating in the scheme for securing political representation shall contribute at the rate of a halfpenny per year, or such other rate as may be approved by Congress'. (The rate has, in fact, been maintained at a halfpenny for some time.) This is what is meant by saying that a society is affiliated to the Co-operative party, though in the strict sense there is no provision for affiliation, and the national Co-operative party does not consist of a number of affiliated bodies and individual members. In fact, in the strict sense there is no national Co-operative party—only a national committee to co-ordinate local Co-operative parties. One consequence of this system of organization is that the nominal membership of the Co-operative party is far greater than the number of convinced adherents. A decision to participate 'in the scheme for securing political representation' is taken by a majority vote of the members of the retail society, and, once an affirmative vote is given all the members of the society are regarded as members of the society, and a contribution is paid for them, even though 49 per cent may have voted against participation. It is not usual for provision to be made in a society's rules for 'contracting out', and a person may therefore be reckoned a member of the Co-operative party, and have a contribution paid in his name to its funds, even though he voted against 'affiliation'. There are over 1,000 Co-operative societies with a membership of about 10,392,600. On 31 December 1949 there were 672 societies with a membership of 8,679,591 affiliated to the party; on 31 December 1950 there were 665 affiliated societies with a membership of 8,833,704; on 31 December 1951 the 662 affiliated societies had a membership of 9,083,359. This last figure was 85 per cent of the membership of Co-operative societies, which indicates that the unaffiliated societies are mainly the smaller ones. There are, however, some notable exceptions. The Leeds Co-operative Society has not been affiliated since 1925, and in November 1951 the Huddersfield Co-operative Society decided to withdraw after a vigorous debate in which strong protests were made by some members against the support given to the Labour candidate in the general election.[1]

The constitution of the Co-operative party lays down that the national committee shall 'convene an annual conference, which shall

---

[1] See the *Huddersfield Daily Examiner* of 30 November 1951, in which the seconder of the resolution to disaffiliate, Mr. Douglas Graham, is quoted as saying: 'Little more than seventeen years ago, when the society decided to affiliate to the Co-operative party, two things were understood. First, that the Co-operative party was an independent political party free from a link-up with other political parties, and, second, that the then Government in office were thought to be treating the Co-operative movement unfairly by taxation proposals. That night it had been made abundantly clear that the Co-operative party was not a separate political identity—that it was, in fact, so closely linked with the Labour party as to be indistinguishable from it.'

be held at such times and places as the national committee shall determine, and such other conferences as the committee may deem necessary
to the success of its work'. There are indications in other parts of the
constitution that the conference is to be regarded as the highest authority in the party. The decisions are, however, subject to the approval of
the annual congress of the Co-operative Union and are not regarded
as binding Co-operative members of Parliament, who have to consider
their relationship with the Labour party. The conference consists of
'representatives of societies subscribing to the national funds of the
Co-operative party, society Co-operative parties, voluntary parties and
party federations'. Each distributive society subscribing to the national
funds of the party has one vote for every £2 or part thereof subscribed;
each society or organization other than a distributive society is given
the number of votes to which it would be entitled as a distributive
society on the subscription paid; each federation of Co-operative
parties, each society Co-operative party, and each voluntary Co-
operative party has one vote.

COMMUNIST PARTY

According to the rules of the Communist party 'the national congress
shall be the supreme authority of the party, and be responsible for
the adoption of general policy and for the laying down of the general
lines of the work of the party'. It may be suspected however, that
most Communists recognize a far higher authority than the congress,
or, shall we say, regard it as a main duty of the congress to act as a
sounding board for that higher authority. The congress must be
convened every two years and is composed of delegates from district
committees and from branches elected in accordance with their numerical strength. At the twenty-second national congress held in 1952
there were 520 delegates, of whom 448 were men and 72 women. At
the conference an executive committee of forty members is chosen,
and this is given 'full responsibility for the direction and control of the
party's work'. The executive committee is, however, too large a body
and its members are too scattered for it to carry out the administrative
work of the party, and the effective control of the party's work is in
the hands of a political committee of eleven members chosen from its
own members by the executive committee. The political committee is
also known as the *Politbureau* and sometimes, more mischievously as
the *Pollittbureau* from its leading member. The officials of the party
are appointed by the executive committee and are a chairman, a vice-

chairman, a secretary, and the chairman of the party's economic, organization, women's and international departments. The effective leadership of the party is in the hands of its secretary—at present Mr. Harry Pollitt. The headquarters are at 16 King Street, Covent Garden, London, W.C.2. At 31 March 1952 there were 35,600 members of the Communist party organized in 1,200 area and factory branches. The Young Communist League, which is open to persons between the ages of 14 and 30, had a membership of about 3,500 at the same date.

NATIONALIST PARTIES

The Welsh party's constitution lays down that 'the conference (*cynhadledd*) is the highest authority of the *blaid* (party)'. The constitution may not be changed except by a vote of at least two-thirds of the members present at a conference. The conference is constituted of delegates from all party branches (two from every branch of not more than fifty members with one additional delegate for every additional fifty members or part thereof); one delegate from each district committee; the members of the executive committee; and any one who is a *blaid* member of Parliament. (As there has not yet been a Welsh party member of Parliament, this last provision has not yet come into operation.) It is laid down that the conference is to be summoned annually, with special conferences if necessary. The party president is elected every two years by the conference, and the vice-president and treasurer annually.

When the conference is not in session, the government and organization of the party is in the hands of the executive committee (*pwyllgor gwaith*). This is composed of two representatives from each district committee, the party officers, four members elected by the conference (two elected each year for two years), past presidents of the party, the editors of the party organs, and co-opted members not numbering more than one-third of the others. The executive committee appoints the secretary of the party.

The constitution of the Scottish National party likewise lays down that 'the annual national conference of the National party shall be the supreme governing body of the National party'. It consists of representatives or delegates (both terms are used) from branches (two delegates from each branch whose membership does not exceed fifty and one additional delegate for every additional fifty members or part thereof), together with the party officers and members of the national council. This national council is the governing body of the party between conferences, and its decisions are binding upon all members unless rescinded by a conference. It consists of the national office-bearers, twenty ordinary members elected by the annual conference, and one representative from each area council. The national office-bearers (president, chairman, two vice-chairmen, secretary and treasurer) are elected by the annual conference.

MINOR PARTIES

The highest authority in the Independent Labour Party is the annual conference, and the direction of the party between conferences is in the hands of a national council. The party's main activities are now in Scotland, but the offices of the national council are in London—at 318 Regent's Park Road, N.3.

The other minor parties are seldom able to organize national conferences, and their national organization calls for no description. It is usually little more than an address and a telephone number.

PARTY INCOME AND EXPENDITURE

The income of the national Labour party is mainly provided by affiliation fees. As already explained, constituency Labour parties pay 6d. a year to Transport House for every individual member on their books, and each central Labour party pays £6 a year, and each federation a sum ranging from £1 to £4 10s. a year according to the number of constituency parties; under these headings Transport House received £22,456 for 1950. Affiliation fees from socialist societies amounted to £182 and from the one co-operative society (Royal Arsenal) £770. But the great bulk of the income is derived from the affiliation fees of trade unions. These are at the rate of 6d. a member a year, and for 1950 amounted to £124,297. The biggest contributors paid the following sums: Transport and General Workers' Union, £20,875; National Union of Mineworkers, £16,161; Amalgamated Engineering Union, £14,515; National Union of Railwaymen, £8,469; Union of Shop, Distributive and Allied Workers, £7,925; Union of Post Office Workers, £3,638; United Textile Factory Workers' Association, £3,595; Amalgamated Society of Woodworkers, £3,362. These are annual contributions to the work of the Labour party; additional special contributions are voted for general elections. None of the other parties to-day is able to tap such an easy, regular and substantial flow of income. In former days, when the low rate of tax left large monies in private hands, and there were positions of dignity and influence with which large contributors to party funds could be rewarded, and when moreover reasonable contributions to party funds were allowed as business expenses, the older parties were able to command much larger sources of income than the rising Labour party; but to-day it is the Labour party which is in the envious position, and all other parties are sustained out of the heavily taxed income of individuals.

The Labour party has, of course, been greatly helped by the substitution of 'contracting out' for 'contracting in'; and it may be surmised that the financial aspect, rather than any strong democratic principles, has caused this question to engender so much heat. Until 1927 it was the usual practice for trade unions to collect the political levy along with the customary trade union dues unless the member 'contracted out', that is, signed a paper declining to pay the political levy. By the Trade Disputes and Trade Unions Act, 1927, which followed the general strike of 1926, 'contracting in' was substituted for 'contracting out', that is, henceforth the political levy could be collected only from those who signed a declaration that they wished it to be collected. Human nature being what it is, and inertia a big element in it, the political funds of trade unions dropped markedly. The membership of trade unions affiliated to the Labour party dropped from 3,238,939 in 1927 to 2,025,139 in 1928. In 1946, after the Labour, victory at the polls, the Trade Disputes and Trade Unions Act, 1927 was repealed, and 'contracting out' was again substituted for 'contracting in'. The political funds of trade unions felt the benefit at once. According to a parliamentary answer, the percentage of members of all trade unions having political funds who were liable to contribute to those funds rose from forty-five at the end of 1945 to ninety-one at the end of 1947; and the total affiliation fees paid to the Labour party by trade unions rose in the same period from £51,261 to £91,930. By 1950, as already stated, the figure had risen to £124,297.

The Labour party's income in 1950, excluding the balance brought forward at the beginning of the year and the income of special funds such as the fund for insuring against the loss of candidates' deposits, the general election fund and the party development fund was £232,314. Expenditure was £240,273. If the items excluded above are brought in, the total income was £689,615. The total expenditure was £349,193, leaving the following balances in hand: General fund, £52,737; Bequests fund, £4,228; By-election insurance fund, £38,307; Deposit insurance fund, £12,552; Development fund, £80,649; General election fund, £149,281; grants in aid of agents' salaries fund, £2,664.

Most other parties do not publish accounts of their headquarters expenditure in the same way, and this has often been made a reproach against the Conservative party by socialists. The reproaches were taken into the House of Commons on 15 December 1949 when a Labour member, Mr. Geoffrey Bing, moved 'that in the opinion of this House, political parties and all other organizations having political action as one of their arms should publish annually full and adequate statements of their accounts.' A Conservative member, Mr. Quintin Hogg (now Lord Hailsham) moved to add the words, 'but only if the submission of such accounts can be regulated by legislation designed to secure the fulness and accuracy of such accounts, their submission by all such organizations and the inclusion therein of entries in respect of services rendered to each organization concerned by other organizations or individuals or the servants of such organizations or individuals.'[1]

The amendment was defeated by 216 votes to 212 and the original motion carried. Conservative members opposed the motion on the ground that it would be 'highly misleading'; and although the Maxwell Fyfe Committee on Party Organization had recommended in its interim report in 1948 that the treasurer of the party should publish an annual financial statement, as being 'the only effective basis from which to explain to Conservative supporters the main facts about party finance', the Conservative party has so far refused to gratify what the general director of its Central Office, writing in *Parliamentary Affairs* for the autumn number of 1948, called 'the instinctive curiosity about other people's affairs which we all share.'

Although the Labour party publishes annual accounts, the party conference always takes care to go into private session when they are debated, nor can it be blamed for so doing; there is nothing to hide, but a certain reticence in money matters is as natural in the life of parties as of individuals. The full facts of party finance are certainly not provided by the accounts of the headquarters alone. Those of the Labour party have here been summarized as being issued in convenient form and as giving an indication of the scale of expenditure; but they represent only a small part of the total expenditure on Labour party organization and

---

[1] Mr. Hilaire Belloc attempted in the 1906–10 Parliament to secure the passage of a similar motion, and comments thus in the book which he later wrote with Cecil Chesterton: 'When one of the joint authors of this book brought in his motion for the auditing of the secret party funds, the front benches put up an amendment which turned the debate into a discussion upon the abstract economic merits of free trade, and to this day no one knows the opinion of any member of the House of Commons, as expressed by vote, upon this most corrupt feature of all the corrupt features of Parliamentary life.' (*The Party System*, p. 85 n.) This was strong language even for 1911.

propaganda. The expenditure of the constituency Labour parties must be a substantial element in the total, but as each constituency party is financially autonomous, and the cases in which their accounts are published must be very rare, it is not possible to do more than guess at the total. It is hardly possible to run a constituency organization efficiently for less than £1,000 a year, and if we assume the expenditure of the constituency parties to be not less than £500,000 a year we shall probably not err. Allowance must also be made for expenditure by the trade unions and co-operative movement to further the cause of socialism though not incurred through the Labour party. A Conservative handbook states: 'In 1948 the combined income of the political funds of the trade unions amounted roughly to £399,000 of which £113,000 went to the Socialist party in affiliation fees. The whole of the balance of £286,000 was also available for the propagation of socialism.'[1] The handbook also points out that the subscriptions of retail co-operative societies to the Co-operative Union amounted to over £100,000, of which a 'substantial part', it is alleged, was applied to the furtherance of socialist principles; in addition, £370,000 a year is spent by the retail societies themselves on 'education', and it is claimed that this 'cannot be anything but a powerful auxiliary of the Socialist propaganda machine.' The handbook infers that 'the Socialist movement has at its disposal an income of little less than £1,000,000 a year, quite apart from what is raised and spent by the constituency Labour parties.'[2] It would not be surprising if this were so; nor, indeed, is such a figure disproportionate to the issues involved.

Though the Conservative party does not publish an annual statement of its accounts, there is no mystery about how it is financed. As in the Labour party, each constituency organization is financially autonomous, and its income is derived from the subscriptions of members and the proceeds of social activities such as whist drives, sales of work and fêtes. The central work of the party was in the past mainly derived from the subscriptions of firms and individuals supporting the Conservative cause. In the past it was able to secure sufficient support from a relatively small number of people, but penal taxation and the great

---

[1] *General Election 1950: The Campaign Guide Supplement*, p. 94.

[2] In addition, it is necessary to take into account the fact that trade union officials are paid from the general funds of their union, and not the political funds, although much of their time is spent on political work; and that the cost of trade union journals is borne by the general funds, though they further the cause of socialism generally. In a full examination it would also be necessary to take into account bodies not connected with a political party (as the trade unions and the Co-operative movement are), but which propagate ideas favourable to the party. This would carry us very far afield.

increase in the central work of all parties have made it necessary to cast the net wider. In 1947 Lord Woolton, as chairman of the party organization, made an appeal for a £1,000,000 fighting fund in these words: 'It is a new thing for the Conservative party to make a public appeal for money. . . . In the past the party has been shy of asking for money, and it has collected for its central fund from a few hundred people.' The annual conference of the party in that year passed the following resolution: 'That this conference considers that constituency associations should be asked to accept some responsibility for contributing towards the central funds of the party.' It is rather remarkable that previously the constituency associations had not been under such an obligation; they paid, and continue to pay, a minimum affiliation of two guineas a year to the National Union, but had not helped to finance the work of the Central Office. The Maxwell Fyfe Committee on Party Organization found in its interim report in 1948 that there was a gap of £200,000 a year between the party's annual income at the centre and the sum needed to carry out the work properly, and it proposed a voluntary quota scheme based on the number of votes obtained by the Conservative candidate at the last general election. For example, where the Conservative candidate was successful and the ratio of the Conservative vote to that of the runner up was below 7 to 6, the suggested levy was 3d. for every Conservative vote; where the ratio exceeded 12 to 6, the suggested levy was 6d. In cases where the Conservative candidate was defeated, a levy ranging from $\frac{1}{2}$d. to $2\frac{1}{2}$d. a Conservative vote was suggested. This ingenious scheme, designed to take account of capacity to pay, was put forward only as a suggestion to constituencies, and no sanctions were proposed for failure to comply, but it has been adopted by a large number of constituencies, and the quota scheme must now be regarded as an important element in the financing of the central work of the Conservative party.

The Liberal party is now obliged to work on a much more modest budget than either the Conservative or the Labour party. Its annual income is approximately £50,000. It is laid down in the Liberal constitution that each constituency association shall pay to the party treasurers an annual affiliation fee of an amount to be determined by regulation of the Liberal Council. It is at present fixed at five guineas a year; on this half is paid to the headquarters and half to the area federation in which the association is situated. The central work is also financed by donations and subscriptions from individuals. In 1946 the Liberal Foundation Fund was opened to commemorate the founding of the Liberal Federation in 1877. As in the parties already described,

Liberal constituency associations are financially autonomous, and raise their money by membership subscriptions and social activities.

The Co-operative party fund, which finances the work of the national Co-operative party, is replenished in four ways. As already mentioned, affiliated retail societies contribute at the rate of a halfpenny a member annually; wholesale societies, productive societies and other special societies contribute annually such amounts as may be agreed upon by them and the national committee; the Co-operative Union contributes such amounts as may be approved by the central board; and special donations and subscriptions may be received from individuals and organizations. In addition, the Co-operative Union pays the rent, salaries and administrative expenses of the party; the Co-operative party fund is therefore available in its entirety, after payment of expenses, for propaganda and grants to local co-operative parties towards the expenses of parliamentary candidates. The Co-operative Union is itself financed by a levy of 3d. a member annually on all affiliated societies, and as the membership of affiliated societies is now over 10,000,000 this gives the Union an income of at least £125,000 a year. The accounts of the co-operative party are published with the party's annual report, and show for the year ended 31 December 1951 an income of £26,920, of which £19,971 was derived from affiliation fees; expenditure was £31,206, leaving a deficit of £4,286. The deficit was met from the general fund, which at the end of the year was left with a balance of £74,749. In addition there is shown an M.P.s' contingency fund with a balance of £6,980.

It is improbable that the Communist party of Great Britain, despite close ideological links, receives any financial help from Moscow. Apart from other considerations, the difficulties in a world of exchange controls would be too great. The subscriptions and gifts of its members are its main source of income. As already stated, members of the Communist party pay the high minimum subscription of 26s. a year, of which 9s. goes to the executive committee and 2s. to a central election fund. A special feature of Communist finance is the appeal made at meetings where quite large sums are often handed (or thrown) to the person making the appeal; the technique of putting in £5, £10 or even £30 as a 'starter' for such collections is probably not unused. The income of the national headquarters for the year ended 30 September 1951 was £98,413 and the expenditure £94,655. Membership cards and dues stamps produced £23,812, weekly quotas to the centre raised by districts and branches £15,106, donations and contributions to a 'fighting fund' £32,175, and the sale of literature £26,893. But the published accounts of the Communist party are not the place in which a student would expect to find anything specially exciting.

The chief items of expenditure of the Welsh Nationalist party in 1951 amounted to £3,853 and the chief items of income to £5,400. The general election cost the party £1,620, towards which an election fund raised £1,020. The net result of the year's work was that the party was able to reduce its debt from £2,623 to £1,821.[1]

PARTY STAFFS

The headquarters staff of a party together with the area officials and the constituency agents, organizers and missioners constitute the civil service of the party. The constituency agents and organizers (and occasionally the missioners) are maintained by the constituency associations, whose servants they are, even if the headquarters makes a grant for the purpose, but the whole constitutes a corps. The central employment of agents has from time to time been considered, but the gain in efficiency that might result would be more than offset by the loss of local enthusiasm, and in all parties the agent is chosen by the constituency organization, though the headquarters are prepared to give advice if desired. There is, however, considerable interchange between the constituency agents and the area and headquarters staff. An agent may be promoted to be an area official, and an area official may be promoted to a post in the head office, or an official at headquarters may be made an area official. The main parties arrange courses of training for prospective agents and organizers with practical work in constituencies, and, as already indicated, a certificate is given to those who successfully pass an examination. In the Conservative party there is a Conservative and Unionist Agents' Examination Board, and the Labour party has similar arrangements. The head offices require minimum salaries to be paid to agents and organizers. The Conservative scale is: Woman organizer, £400 a year; certificated agent, £500 a year on first appointment and £600 a year after experience of a general election and not less than two years in charge of a constituency rising by annual increments of £25 to £800 a year. Under recent arrangements new male entrants are no longer recognized as organizers. The main parties have superannuation schemes for agents and organizers.

A point of interest in the national organization of parties is the part played by the party officials in relation to the political chiefs. In the Conservative and Liberal parties the tradition of the civil service

[1] See *The Welsh Nation*, August 1952.

has been followed. The officials regard themselves as being the advisers and executants of their political chiefs, and more particularly of the party leader, but as having no responsibility for policy themselves. They carry out their work as unobtrusively—and it must be added as efficiently—as the civil service, and it is very rarely that they come into the public notice. It may be doubted whether the names of even the higher officials of the Conservative and Liberal parties are known to the general public.

At the other extreme the general secretary of the Communist party is the effective leader of the party, and his name—Mr. Harry Pollitt—is the first that leaps to the mind when the Communist party is mentioned. This is in keeping with precedent. Until the outbreak of the last war Mr. Stalin held no post in the Soviet Union except that of general secretary of the Communist party, but he was the real master of the country from 1924 onwards.

The Labour party holds an intermediate position. In theory the secretary is the servant of the conference, and more immediately of its executive committee. But in practice he frequently makes statements on policy hardly distinguishable in character from those of his political chiefs. The secretary of the international department of the Labour party is also by nature of his international contacts frequently brought into the limelight as the Conservative and Liberal officials are not.

III. WIDER ASSOCIATIONS

The Labour party and the Co-operative party differ from the other British parties in being elements in more comprehensive movements.

The Co-operative party is the political element in the Co-operative Union, which is an association of trading societies. The national committee of the Co-operative party is declared in its constitution to be 'a committee of the Co-operative Union, responsible to the central board of the Union, and through it to congress.' The Labour party and the Co-operative Union, together with the Trades Union Congress, make up the 'Labour movement.' The only organ of the Labour movement as a whole is the National Council of Labour. This body had its origin in the National Joint Council set up in 1920. At this time the Trades Union Congress set up its general council to take the place of the old parliamentary committee, and as part of the reorganization the Labour party and the Trades Union Congress drew up a plan for a National Joint Council, to take the place of an old joint board, and to consist in equal numbers of representatives of the general council of the

T.U.C., the national executive committee of the Labour party and the parliamentary Labour party. The National Joint Council was reconstituted in 1931 so as to consist of the chairman and six members of the general council of the T.U.C., the chairman and two members of the national executive committee of the Labour party, and the chairman and two members of the executive committee of the parliamentary Labour party. From the outbreak of war in 1939 leading representatives of the Co-operative movement were informally invited to attend meetings of the National Council of Labour, and this informal arrangement was put on to a formal basis within the next few years when the National Council was reconstituted so as to consist of equal representatives of the Trades Union Congress, the Labour party (including the parliamentary Labour party) and the Co-operative Union. It has a written constitution in which the membership is thus defined:

Representing the Trades Union Congress.—The chairman and six members of the general council.

Representing the Labour party.—The chairman and two members of the national executive committee, together with the chairman and three members of the executive committee of the parliamentary Labour party.

Representing the Co-operative Union, Ltd.—The chairman and six persons nominated by the executive committee.

It is provided that the secretaries of the three bodies shall be joint secretaries of the National Council, and that the chairmen of the three constituent bodies shall be chairmen of the National Council, and shall preside at meetings in rotation as circumstances allow.

It is laid down that the duties of the National Council are to 'consider all questions affecting the Labour and Co-operative movements as a whole and make provision for taking immediate and united action on all questions of national emergency,' and to 'endeavour to secure a common policy and joint action, whether by legislation or otherwise, on all questions affecting the workers as producers, consumers and citizens.' But the National Council cannot override the constituent bodies. The National Council may 'only make pronouncements on matters of national policy after agreement thereto has been signified by the bodies members of the Council, but this shall not prevent the Council in matters of urgency and where the members are unanimous from so doing. Such pronouncements on emergency matters shall not, however, be binding on the respective constituent bodies unless and until such bodies have ratified them.'

In practice the main purpose of the National Council of Labour is to make declarations of policy on great questions of the day in the name of the Labour movement as a whole; but it can do so safely only when there is not likely to be substantial opposition in any one of the three constituent bodies.

IV. INTERNATIONAL AFFILIATIONS

In this study of the organization of British parties we come finally to their international affiliations. The Communist party is admittedly part of an international movement, and its policy and even tactics are dictated from abroad. The Conservative party has no international connexions, though individual Conservatives may have their preferences abroad, and naturally the Welsh, Scottish and Irish nationalist parties have no international links. Between these extremes other parties have varying degrees of international affiliation.

The international links of the Communist party are shown by its full official name—the Communist party of Great Britain. The implication is that the Communist party of Great Britain is part of a wider organization including the Communist party of France, the Communist party of Italy, and above all the Communist party of the Soviet Union. Until the dissolution of the Communist International in May 1943 this was officially recognized, for the Communist party of Great Britain was the British section of the International. The Communist International or Comintern has now given way to the Cominform. The Communist party of Great Britain does not appear to count for much in the counsels of the Cominform or in the eyes of official Moscow. The fact that after thirty years of ceaseless endeavour it has not a single member in the House of Commons seems to have discredited it in the eyes of Moscow. But of its loyalty to the Cominform, as to its predecessor the Comintern, there cannot be any doubt. This was well shown at the outbreak of the war when the general secretary of the Communist party of Great Britain assumed, as he was entitled to do, that it was his duty to support the fight against the Nazis,[1] only to be obliged to recant a week or so later when Moscow explained that it was really a war of rival imperialisms; but after 21 June 1941, when the Soviet Union was attacked by Hitler, it became permissible once more for Mr. Pollitt to support the war against the Nazis. The episode is typical of the unswerving way in which the Communist headquarters in King Street, Covent Garden, follow the party line. There is no 'Titoism' in the Communist party of Great Britain.

[1] See his pamphlet *How to Win the War*, which was withdrawn soon after its publication on 14 September 1939.

A belief in the 'international solidarity of the workers' was one of the strongest articles of faith in the early days of the war, but 1914 showed that nationalism and patriotism were much deeper and stronger forces. The Labour party constitution still makes provision for co-operation with socialists abroad by including among its objects:

'To co-operate with the Labour and socialist organizations in the dominions and the dependencies with a view to promoting the purposes of the party, and to take common action for the promotion of a higher standard of social and economic life for the working population of the respective countries.

'To co-operate with the Labour and socialist organizations in other countries and to assist in organizing a federation of nations for the maintenance of freedom and peace, for the establishment of suitable machinery for the adjustment and settlement of international disputes by conciliation or judicial arbitration, and for such international legislation as may be practicable.'

In pursuance of the former of these objects the Labour party has maintained friendly relations with the Labour parties of Australia and New Zealand. It has regarded their triumphs as its triumphs, their defeats as its defeats. It has also maintained cordial relations with the less powerful Co-operative Commonwealth Federation in Canada. But no formal links exist, and each party is free to formulate its policy and does, without reference to the others.

In pursuance of the latter object the Labour party was a member of the Second International—the Communist International being the Third—until its demise. But as a body for organized action across frontiers the Second International was shattered by the first world war. Out of the various attempts after the second world war to re-create international socialist unity there was eventually set up the International Socialist Conference. In 1952 this comprised thirty-four democratic Socialist parties with a total membership at the latest available date of 9,773,736, towards which the British Labour party contributed 5,907,037; the figures are misleading because all the other parties except the British are built upon individual membership, but the British Labour party has undoubtedly been the biggest element in the conference. The chief organ of this body has been the Committee of the International Socialist Conference, commonly called Comisco. This has met about three times a year, and has passed resolutions on matters of current interest to socialists throughout the world. As the name indicates, the purpose of the International Socialist Conference has been to confer, and there has never been any question of requiring the member-parties to follow a common line laid down by the conference or the committee. The British Labour party and the French Socialist party openly disagreed in their attitudes to the Schuman plan.

The International Socialist Conference in a session at Frankfurt on 30 June 1951 moved towards its predestined goal, or at any rate the goal secretly cherished by its promoters, when it decided, on the proposition of British and Belgian parties, to re-constitute the Socialist International. (This is the 'Fourth International', though it is not so called officially.) By 1951 there had been about five years of cautious co-operation between democratic socialist parties, and the party leaders felt that the time was ripe for trying to re-create the International. The statute or constitution of the new Socialist International[1] conforms closely to that of the International Socialist Conference. Its organs are a congress, to meet at least once every two years, which is declared to be the supreme body of the International; a council; a bureau; and the secretariat. The bureau is what we in Great Britain would call the executive committee. It consists of ten members from the Socialist parties of Great Britain, Scandinavia, France, Germany, Italy, Belgium, the Netherlands, Austria, Canada and Japan; and Mr. Morgan Phillips, secretary of the British Labour party, was elected as its first chairman. The first act of the International was to adopt a 'Declaration of aims and tasks of democratic socialism'.[2] It is further stated that 'the purpose of the Socialist International is to strengthen relations between the affiliated parties and to co-ordinate their political attitudes by consent'. This is a fair statement of the purpose. The member-parties attempt to reach a common policy in the face of common problems, but there is no means of compelling a member-party to follow a line against its own judgement, and no sanctions—except the possibility of expulsion, for what that is worth—against a party that pursues a course of its own against the advice of its fellows. Though the British Labour party may be induced to follow courses that otherwise it would not adopt, its membership of the Socialist International leaves it in the last resort free to follow its own ideas.

Even in the days of the Second International the Labour party was in the habit of addressing and receiving messages and fraternal greetings from socialist parties abroad, and this practice continues. It may be doubted, however, whether its policy is greatly affected by international contacts of this character, or the policy of other parties abroad by their contacts with it.

[1] It is published as Appendix I of the *Report of the fiftieth annual conference of the Labour party, Scarborough, 1951*, pp. 136–7.
[2] It is published as Appendix II of the *Report of the fiftieth annual conference of the Labour Party, Scarborough, 1951*, pp. 138–41.

The Co-operative party, as already noted, differs from all other parties in being an element in a non-political body, namely, the Co-operative Union. The Co-operative Union is itself affiliated to the International Co-operative Alliance, which has 100,000,000 members in its affiliated societies, and an international conference is held. But the political views of world co-operators are very diverse, and there is no question of the Co-operative party in Great Britain taking directions from an oversea body.

The Social Credit party naturally has affinities with similar parties abroad, and especially with the Social Credit party in Canada, where the Social Credit movement has achieved its only striking political successes. But there does not seem to be anything in common except the name and the idea. If the Social Credit party in Great Britain receives any oversea support, it has not produced any notable results.

A Liberal International was founded in 1947, and it has national groups, including a British group. The Liberal International is declared to be non-political in that it is not confined to political parties, the word 'liberal' being used in the literal Latin meaning, 'pertaining to a free man'. But in practice the leading figures both in the International and in the British group are political Liberals. The Liberal International holds an annual congress, which is attended by leading British Liberals in their individual capacity. The Liberal party as such is not officially connected with the International or the congress. The Liberal parties of the world stand to-day for very diverse views, and in some cases have little in common except the name. It would hardly be practicable for the Liberal International to reach conclusions binding on all participants, but there is no doubt value in the exchange of ideas with persons of other countries.

The Liberal and Conservative parties are the heirs of men who in turn governed the country for three centuries, and they know that a Government in office frequently has to work harmoniously with Governments of a very different complexion abroad. For this reason they, and more especially the Conservative party, eschew formal relationships with parties oversea which might prove embarrassing. It could not fail to be embarrassing if her Majesty's Government in the United Kingdom maintained more cordial relations with the Opposition in a friendly country than with the Government of that country; and although a distinction can be made in theory between a Government and the party from which that Government is drawn, not everyone has an intelligence sufficiently subtle to appreciate it. The Labour party developed its international contacts at a time when it hardly expected to shoulder the duty of government; and there can be little doubt that the policy of developing a 'socialist foreign policy' and 'being friendly with socialists everywhere', which misguided members of the party would have thrust upon it, has been embarrassing to it in office. In the maintenance of international peace socialist and 'capitalist' Governments are obliged to work together, and although the Labour party's international contacts have been cautious the Conservative party is wiser in refraining from all oversea alliances.

───── XIV ─────

Parliament and Outside Bodies

IN THE TWO PRECEDING CHAPTERS there has been described first the organization of the parties in Parliament and secondly the organization of parties in the country. The relation between the two is a matter of some delicacy, and the points of interaction now need to be examined a little more closely in the next few chapters.

Two theories are at work. According to one theory, the duty of electors is to choose the man whom they consider best qualified by character, experience and abilities to represent them and the duty of the member, when elected, is to speak and vote as questions come before him according to his lights and conscience in the unfettered exercise of his free judgement. This, as we have seen, is the doctrine expressed in classic form by Burke and it is still the doctrine underlying the Representation of the People Acts, British electoral practice and the procedure of Parliament. It does not mean that a constituency may be saddled till death with a member whom it comes to dislike, for there is a natural term to the life of Parliament and when an election again comes round the electors are free to renew their confidence in their member or to choose someone else in his place. According to this theory, and present constitutional practice, a constituency is married to a member for better or for worse, but only till the next general election do them part. After the dissolution there are for the time being no members of Parliament, and the person who was the member, if he decides to stand again, stands on the same footing as other candidates. But so long as Parliament subsists, according to this view the member is answerable only to his own conscience for his actions. There is no outside tribunal that can call him to account. The other members with whom he chooses to associate in the course of his parliamentary duties are his own concern, and if in the exercise of his unfettered judgement he leaves one set of associates and joins another, as Burke himself did when he saw the fires of revolution glowing across the Channel, that is a matter for him, and for him alone.

This is a theory of Parliament than can work, and it has done so. But it has not been possible to hold the theory in its entirety since the passage of the Reform Act, 1832. The enlargement of the electorate which followed that measure made it necessary, as we have seen, for candidates to state their policy to the voters, and for the leaders of parties to issue manifestoes to which their followers gave general assent. Statements of policy were soon interpreted as pledges, and in the course of time a new constitutional theory of a member's position has been developed.

This is the theory that electors do not vote for candidates but for parties, and that a candidate who deviates from his party's line in Parliament thereby loses his title to his seat and, although he cannot be unseated by any constitutional process, ought in conscience to apply for the Chiltern Hundreds and give the electors a chance of selecting someone else. The party, moreover, is bound just as rigidly by the statement of policy which it put before the country at the general election. It is bound in conscience to carry out every item of policy in the manifesto during the lifetime of that Parliament and should not carry out any other major item of policy without a fresh authorization from the electors.

The former theory may be described as that of 'confidence in the member'; the latter that of the 'mandate to the member'. According to the former, the member of Parliament is the representative of the electors in his constituency, according to the latter he is their delegate. On the one view the electors choose a man, on the other a party programme. The former theory magnifies the office of a member, the latter reduces him to the executant of his party's instructions.

The former, as we have seen, is the theory enshrined in the British constitution, but British practice has gone a long way towards accepting the latter. In the next chapter we shall need to question whether the tendency to vote for parties rather than for candidates has not now gone too far, but in this chapter we are concerned only with the question of organization, namely the relation of the parties in Parliament to the parties in the country.

THE PARTY LEADER

A specially important point of interaction is the leader of the party. As we have seen, the leader of the party in the House of Commons is accepted as the leader of the party in the country. So long as this remains the practice, there is an effective guarantee that the supremacy of Parliament as the focus of our national political life will be maintained. The electoral college in the Conservative party now includes persons from outside Parliament as well as peers and members of the House of Commons, which helps to ensure the acceptability of the chosen leader.[1] I do not know whether it could in theory be open to a member of this electoral college to propose as leader a person not sitting in either House, but in practice this is inconceivable, and it is not necessary to guard against it. The leader of the Liberal party is chosen only by members of the House of Commons and is automatically accepted by the party in the country. The leader of the Labour party is chosen by Labour members in the two Houses, and, like the Liberal, is accepted by the party in the country. Mr. Pollitt, the effective leader of the Communist party, has never been in Parliament, but with this exception the minor parties have tended to follow the traditions of the older parties. James Maxton was not only the leader of the Independent Labour party members in the House of Commons, but of the I.L.P. in the country also; and when Sir Richard Acland was leading his little band of three Common Wealth members in Parliament, he was unquestionably leader of Common Wealth in the country, even though he possessed no formal title to that effect.

The chosen leader of the party at once steps into positions of great influence in his party organization. The leader of the Conservative party becomes, in form at any rate, a member of the central council of the National Union and of its executive committee, and the Central Office comes under his authority. The leader of the Liberal party is permanent chairman of the Liberal Party Committee. The leader of the Labour party becomes automatically a member of the party's national executive committee and is saved the embarrassment of standing for an an election in which, though he might not be defeated, he might easily fail to head the poll.

THE CHIEF WHIP

The post of chief whip used to be in the Conservative party and in the Scottish Unionist party, and still is in the Liberal party, another point of interaction. The Conservative Central Office, as we have seen, was under the direct control of the chief whip (under the authority of the party leader) until 1911, and the Scottish Unionist whip was in charge of the corresponding office in Edinburgh until the post of chairman of the Unionist party in Scotland was created in 1950. The corresponding office in the Liberal party is still run by the chief whip. This is another means of ensuring close and harmonious relations between the party in Parliament and the party in the country. The fact that in the Con-

---

[1] It has been argued above, however, that this practice has grown up without deliberate intent, and that the Conservative party would be truer to its traditions and to its respect for the constitution if the elections were confined, as formerly, to members of the House of Commons. See above, pp. 115–16.

servative party the chief whip no longer has any responsibility for the Central Office does not mean any weakening of the position of the parliamentary party for the chairman of the party organization, who has taken over the chief whip's responsibilities at the Central Office, is appointed by the leader of the party; and, in fact, the leader has always appointed to the post a member of one House or the other.

PARLIAMENTARY SECRETARIAT

Another point of interaction, as we have seen, is that the party headquarters supply the parliamentary parties with their secretariats. The officials so supplied have no responsibility for policy, but they help to ensure that the head offices and the parliamentary parties are informed of what each is doing.

NATIONAL EXECUTIVE COMMITTEE OF LABOUR PARTY

The position of the Labour party needs a little closer examination on account of the peculiar position of the national executive committee vis-à-vis the parliamentary party.

In June 1945 Mr. Churchill invited Mr. Attlee, as the leader of the Labour party, to accompany him to Berlin for discussions with Roosevelt and Mr. Stalin. On 15 June Harold Laski, being at the time chairman of the national executive committee of the Labour party, made a statement in which he said: 'It is essential that if Mr. Attlee attends this gathering he shall do so in the rôle of an observer only.' Mr. Churchill, in a letter of 16 June, drew attention to this statement, and said it was his idea that Mr. Attlee should go as a 'friend and counsellor'. Mr. Attlee, in accepting, said there had never been any suggestion that he should attend 'as a mere observer'.

The matter did not end at this point. In his election broadcast on 30 June Mr. Churchill said:

'It was a revelation to me when I, in all good will, invited Mr. Attlee to come with me to Berlin in July in order to keep the flag of unity flying, that this hitherto almost unknown person, Professor Laski, who has never sought to face the electors and sits at the head of what is called the national executive committee, of which the larger part are not even members of Parliament, should have the right to lay down the law to the leader of the Labour party and tell him that he could only go to the conference in the capacity of an observer and that no continuity in our foreign policy could be undertaken. Many days have passed since this happened. Mr. Laski has in no way withdrawn his instructions to the Labour party. On the contrary he has shown himself the master of forces too strong for Mr. Attlee to challenge. Mr. Laski still remains chairman of the Socialist executive. No vote of suspension, censure, or even deprecation has been passed upon him.

'It appears that this Socialist executive possesses power over Socialist ministers of a most far-reaching character; that it would decide the action a socialist Government could take in particular questions; and that it could require the submission of ministers to its will. This means, for instance, that in foreign affairs, when there had to be discussion on some difficult question, secrets might have to be divulged to this committee of twenty-seven members, very few of whom are privy councillors; and in military matters, though I am sure all care would be taken, this difficulty might arise. The demonstration of power residing in the executive committee also means that Socialist ministers filling high offices of state would not be primarily responsible to the Crown and Parliament, but would have to refer back to an utterly unconstitutional and undemocratic body lying in the background, whose names until the recent trouble have not been known to the public. Such arrangements are abhorrent to the methods hitherto pursued in British public life. They strike at the root of our parliamentary institutions, and, if they continue unabated, will be one of the gravest changes in the constitutional history of England.'

Mr. Attlee in a speech at Peckham on 1 July strongly resented any suggestion that state secrets would be revealed by Labour ministers to the national executive, and there was an exchange of letters between Mr. Churchill and Mr. Attlee on 2 July. The essence of Mr. Attlee's reply is contained in the following sentences:

'Neither by decision of the conference nor by any provision in the party constitution is the parliamentary Labour party answerable to or under the direction of the national executive committee. Within the programme adopted by the party conference, the parliamentary Labour party has complete discretion in its conduct of parliamentary business and in the attitude it should adopt to legislation tabled by other parties. The standing orders which govern its activities are drawn up and determined by the parliamentary Labour party itself.

Polling put an end to these exchanges, but the same issue came up on 13 June 1950 in an even more serious form—for the Labour party was then in office—when the national executive committee issued a document entitled *European Unity* which seemed to pre-judge the attitude of the Government to the Schuman plan. As matters turned out, it is probable that Labour ministers would in any case have adopted a policy similar to that contained in the document, but it is generally agreed that the timing of the document—just before the Government were due to announce their policy—was unfortunate. The timing does not, however, appear to have been done of set purpose.

In the light of these exchanges what are we to think of the relationships between the national executive committee and the parliamentary Labour party? Their formal relationships are defined in one of the standing orders and in a sub-clause of the constitution.

The standing orders, as they were at the time of the Churchill-Attlee correspondence, though then suspended, stated:

> 'The parliamentary party have the authority to withdraw the whip on account of things said or done by members of the party in the House, such decision to be reported to the national executive committee.
> 'Outside activities, whether in writing or speech, which are contrary to the discipline or constitution of the party shall be dealt with by the national executive committee.

> .   .   .   .   .

> 'Where there is persistent refusal to observe the decisions of the parliamentary party it shall be the duty of the liaison committee[1] to bring a recommendation to the party meeting to report the member to the national executive committee, who shall consider the matter in its constituency and other aspects with which the national executive committee is concerned. The member concerned shall have the right to be heard both by the parliamentary party and the national executive committee.'

This is a fair enough attempt to keep parliamentary discipline within the hands of the parliamentary party and discipline in the country within the hands of the national executive committee. On the assumption that discipline is desirable, this procedure seems unexceptional. The business of reporting an unruly member to the national executive committee is rather like handing over a heretic to the secular arm for punishment. The only course open to the national executive committee is to make the member's life uncomfortable in his constituency, and in particular to try and prevent his nomination as prospective Labour candidate for the next election. It would be idle to deny that similar action has been taken from time to time by the headquarters of other parties when M.P.'s have embarked on courses that have brought them into conflict with their leader. It is a risk that members knowingly take when they embark on such independent action, and in such circumstances their constituency organization will as often as not stand by them. Since the Churchill-Attlee correspondence, as we have already

---

[1] Now the parliamentary committee.

H

seen,[1] the standing orders have again been brought into force and revised. The statement that 'outside activities . . . shall be dealt with by the national executive committee' is omitted and, as we have noticed, there is a possibility that the parliamentary committee could take cognisance of a member's activities outside the House. This is a change, but it is not a change giving the national executive committee power over members of Parliament in the course of their parliamentary duties; on the contrary, it is, in theory at any rate, an extension of the powers of the Parliamentary Labour party. The principle of reporting a member to the national executive remains as before, even though the implied threat that the national executive committee shall consider the matter in its constituency and other aspects is omitted.

The constitution has this to say about the relationships of the national executive committee and the parliamentary Labour party:

> 'To confer with the parliamentary Labour party at the opening of each parliamentary session, and at any other time when it or the parliamentary party may desire a conference on any matters relating to the work and progress of the party.'

In pursuance of this provision representatives of the national executive committee and the secretary of the party customarily attend the meeting of the parliamentary Labour party held immediately after the speech from the Throne to consider its contents. This ought to be looked upon as an agreeable custom rather than the intrusion of an outside body into the affairs of a parliamentary party. In the nature of things there cannot be serious debate at such a time when there has been little opportunity to study the Gracious Speech.

It is more disturbing that conferences can be held at any other time, and that the national executive committee can take the initiative in calling such conferences. I feel bound in fairness, however, to say that I cannot remember any such joint conference being called in the six years during which I was a member of the parliamentary Labour party; and on the few occasions when members of the national executive have been invited to be present, they have usually been silent observers rather than participants in the debate. No doubt the leader of the parliamentary Labour party thinks it desirable from time to time to get the reaction of the national executive committee to a proposed course of action—indeed, Mr. Attlee reminded Mr Churchill that he had done so in 1940 when invited to join the coalition. If this were done frequently, it could mean the subordination of the leader and the parliamentary party to the national executive committee; but if it is done

[1] See above, pp. 126–27.

rarely and only on issues of great moment, no exception can be taken. A leader is entitled to seek counsel wherever he pleases; the responsibility remains his.

On the whole the Labour party seems to have done its best, within the framework of its constitution, to avoid intrusion by the national executive committee into the affairs of the parliamentary Labour party and the work of Labour ministers. The 'Laski incident' in 1945 is to be explained by the personality of Harold Laski as much as by anything else. If there had been a different chairman at the time, no attempt would have been made to tell Mr. Attlee that he should go to Berlin only as an observer. It is equally true that another party head might have sought, as Mr. Churchill suggested, to have Laski suspended or censured, but that is not Mr. Attlee's type of leadership.

═══ XV ═══

Party Conferences

THOUGH THE 'LASKI INCIDENT' may not have had the constitutional significance attributed to it at the time, it served to bring out the real constitutional issues. In his last exchange with Mr. Attlee on 3 July 1945, two days before polling, Mr. Churchill wrote:

> 'It is clear that the conference, working through its executive committee, is the controlling body, so far as the work and policy of the Labour party is concerned, whether in office or not.'

This is, in my view, the heart of the matter. The parliamentary Labour party is not controlled by the national executive committee, but both are controlled by the party conference. It is in the supreme authority attributed to the party conference that the main constitutional difference between the Labour party and the older parties lies. Mr. Attlee would not deny it, and it is indeed implicit in his exchanges; and it is something that Mr. Churchill, who has known the innermost workings of the Liberal and Conservative parties but who has not been in the Labour party, may be pardoned for finding strange. We have already studied the structure of the various party conferences; let us now look at their constitutional significance.

Two conceptions of the party conference are interwoven in British practice. The first is that a conference is a party demonstration, the second that it is a deliberative body determining party policy; and they are not compatible.

As mass demonstrations the great party conferences are admirable. They are occasions on which the rank and file can see and hear and even meet the Olympians of the party. Men whose names have hitherto been read only in the newspapers now mingle with their followers from all over the country. These leaders do not face hostile and critical benches as in the House of Commons but a tumultuous and cheering throng of supporters. They stand in the glare of the footlights but see even brighter lights in the eyes of the serried ranks before, around and above them. Thousands hang on their words. The atmosphere is seductive, intoxicating. Platitudes are greeted as revelations. The slightest sally brings forth roars of laughter. Any reference to the opposing party unites the conference as one man behind the speaker.

This is no occasion to suggest that there are two sides to a question or that the party should conceive it possible that it may be mistaken. There are only two colours in the conference artist's palette—black for opponents and white for friends.

For the purposes of demonstration the larger the conference the more successful it is. The sophisticated inhabitants of the conference towns may not be impressed but the faithful go away heartened. For most of them it is a holiday week; they take their families with them and are determined that things shall go with a swing. At a Conservative conference, as we have seen, there may be 4,000 representatives and with visitors the number present may rise to 5,000. At a Labour conference there may be 1,500 delegates, *ex officio* members and agents, and visitors may be equal in number. Even a Liberal or Co-operative conference may run into four figures.

Policy cannot be adequately deliberated by such numbers nor in such an atmosphere. The facts that make for a successful demonstration militate against the cool, balanced probing of a question and against that careful weighing of the *pros* and *cons* which is necessary to the lasting solution of any political problem. It is difficult enough to find the right answer to a question in a committee of twenty; it is unlikely that it will emerge from an audience of cheering thousands.

Yet conferences have claimed, and do claim, to control the policies of their parties. This is particularly embarrassing to a party which is in office, for it cuts at the roots of Cabinet responsibility; but it is only one degree less embarrassing to a party in opposition, for the party in opposition to-day may be the party in office to-morrow. The problem has been made acute by the rise of the Labour party, but it was recognized as far back as 1891 before the birth of the Labour party. The Liberal party conference in Newcastle that year enthusiastically adopted a programme which seriously embarrassed Mr. Gladstone and his colleagues when they took office a year later.

A distinguished political theorist, A. Lawrence Lowell, was led by this experience to say—and he was writing before the Labour party became a force in the land:

> 'So long, therefore, as government by a ministry responsible to the Commons endures, it is obvious that policy must be formulated by the Cabinet alone, and that this is inconsistent with any serious attempt to formulate it by means of a party organization.'

This is the standpoint adopted by the Conservative party.[1] The

[1] Balfour is alleged to have said that he would as soon consult his valet as the Conservative conference about policy.

formulation and announcement of Conservative policy is the prerogative of the leader of the party. This is an attitude that is sometimes represented by opponents as being undemocratic, but, of course, the leader does not formulate policy without advice, nor could he long retain the post unless his formulation of policy met with general approval in his party. The Conservative leader has received particularly valuable advice in recent years from the National Union's advisory committee on policy. This began in 1941 as the post-war problems committee, and the reports of the various sub-committees were submitted to the party leader when he came to prepare his statement of policy for the general election of 1945. In November 1945 the committee was re-constituted as the advisory committee on policy and political education, and under Mr. R. A. Butler's chairmanship it produced a number of 'charters' and other documents that gave a new orientation to Conservative thought. The committee on party organization in 1949 recommended that it be reconstituted as the advisory committee on policy and should cease to deal with political education. It now consists of a chairman and deputy chairman appointed by the leader, five members of Parliament, two peers and seven persons selected by the executive committee of the National Union from its own members. But the leader may seek advice from any quarters that he thinks may be helpful, and the feeling of the rank and file as expressed at a party conference is a valuable element, though for the reasons given it cannot be decisive. This insistence that the formulation of policy is the prerogative of the leader alone is a safeguard against the Conservative party being committed to decisions taken at mass meetings on inadequate information and in an uncritical atmosphere. It is not a complete safeguard, for the pressure from the conference might be so great that the leader would feel, despite his better judgement, that he could not ignore it. It is alleged in many quarters that this happened at the Conservative conference of 1949, when the representatives insisted on writing into the housing aims of the party a figure of 300,000 houses a year. 'This is magnificent', the chairman of the party organization said to the enthusiastic representatives, and then, *sotto voce*—so it was alleged in a witty contemporary account—'this is deuced awkward.' It is certainly better for a party assuming the administration at a difficult time to enter office with as few specific commitments as possible, but the figure of 300,000 houses a year was accepted, and strenuous efforts are being made to attain it.

Though the reservation of the announcement of policy to the leader may save a party from being rushed into ill-considered policies, it brings

dangers of its own, and in particular that a leader may commit his party
to a policy before it has been adequately prepared. The outstanding
case is Gladstone's conversion to home rule for Ireland in 1886.
He had himself given ceaseless consideration to the problem, but few
of his colleagues had been privileged to share his thoughts, and the
public announcement of his adoption of the policy left the Liberal party
bewildered. The party was split and defeated at the polls, and the fulfilment of the policy was long deferred. His action was angrily dismissed by some of his dissident followers as that of an 'old man in a
hurry'. This is, indeed, a danger, but there is no system that will safeguard a party against all dangers, and the vesting in the leader of the
prerogative of announcing policy seems in practice to be the system
most conducive to its considered and democratic formulation.

The Liberal party constitution does not explicitly define the rights of
the assembly in the formulation of policy, but the modern Liberal
attitude is broadly that a policy is not binding on the party until it has
been approved by the assembly.

The Labour party constitution is emphatic that the conference is
responsible for the formulation of the party's policy and programme.
Clause V runs:

'1. The party conference shall decide from time to time what
specific proposals of legislative, financial or administrative reform
shall be included in the party programme.

'No proposal shall be included in the party programme unless it
has been adopted by the party conference by a majority of not less
than two-thirds of the votes recorded on a card vote.

'2. The national executive committee and the executive committee
of the parliamentary Labour party shall decide which items from the
party programme shall be included in the manifesto which shall be
issued by the national executive committee prior to every general
election. The joint meeting of the two executives shall also define the
attitude of the party to the principal issues raised by the election
which are not covered by the manifesto.'

There is some difference in terminology between the parties, and what
the Labour party here calls the programme would probably be called by
Conservatives the policy of the party, and Conservatives would regard
the manifesto as containing the programme.[1] These differences are not
material. The essential point is that in the Labour party the policy, or

[1] The difference between a party's principles, policy, programme and manifesto
are thus expressed in the final report of the Conservative committee on party
organization, 1949, p. 36: 'It will be agreed that the three phases in the evolution
of a party's intentions are principles, policy and programme. Party principles are
stable; the Disraelian principles are as valid to-day as when they were first pro-
pounded. The party programme contains the party's specific proposals whereby
its policy can be given practical effect. The preparation of the programme must

programme, is determined by the conference, and from it the national executive committee, aided by the executive committee of the parliamentary party, extracts the items which go into the election manifesto.

This is often represented by the Labour party as the vindication of democratic principles. But is this what we mean by democracy? Democracy is government in accordance with the will of the governed. But it is one of the truisms of political science, or at any rate has been since Rousseau, that this will is the stable will of the people, and is not to be identified with the momentary will of some mass gathering. Decisions taken in haste are often repented at leisure; and decisions taken in a mass are often regretted individually. Leaders cannot find out the will of a people by asking them to pass resolutions on policy. It is the duty of leaders to give a lead, and only experience will show whether their lead correctly interprets the will of the people. Democracy, as it has been traditionally understood, means that the people choose the persons whom they think best fitted to govern them—and turn them out if they do not like the way they govern. It does not mean that the people themselves tell their governors in detail how they are to govern.

Quite apart from the unsuitability of the atmosphere of a mass conference for the formulation of a party's policy or programme, there is another reason why the Labour conference in particular is unsuited for the task. The members of the conference are not representatives but delegates; and instead of being free to make up their minds on the basis of the information laid before them in debate, they are frequently instructed before the conference opens by the bodies nominating them how they shall vote. In the meantime circumstances may have radically changed—and may change again before the decisions of the conference can be given effect. Moreover the bodies instructing the delegates are often ill-informed, and would possibly have come to a different conclusion if they had even the information made known by the national leaders at the party conference. How can the constituency Labour party of Little Wisdom correctly instruct its delegates on the attitude to be taken over compensation for land betterment or a revision of the Anglo-Egyptian treaty? Such bodies are at the mercy of any local

be a continuing process, but, as the final document has to be related directly to circumstances existing immediately before a general election, the final proposals are normally presented in a party manifesto by the leader on the eve of a general election, and are his responsibility. Policy is the basis upon which practice and programme are founded. It relates Conservative principles to the national and international problems of the day, usually in general terms.'

pundit with the little knowledge that is a dangerous thing, and become the victims of organized pressures. Far from this method leading to the democratic formulation of policy, in practice it may lead to the party machine being captured by propagandist bodies having no real basis in public opinion.

If this objection to the theoretical basis of the Labour party constitution is conceded, we may admit at once that in practice the worst dangers have been avoided. The Labour leaders have themselves been aware of these dangers, and have done their best to safeguard themselves. In the first place they have endeavoured to ensure by the system of voting that the control of the conference always remains in their hands; and in the last resort they are prepared to ignore the decisions of the conference.

The mechanics of the card vote have already been explained, and now we can see its significance. The system, we may recall, is that national and constituency organizations have one voting card for each 1,000 members or a part thereof on whom affiliation fees were paid for the year ending 31 December preceding the conference; while federations and central Labour parties have one voting card each. In theory this can lead to some absurdities. A trade union which has decided by a vote of 51 per cent of its membership to 49 per cent in favour of a certain policy will have a vote cast in favour of that policy in the name of the whole membership. A man may have votes given in his name in several different ways at the conference—as a member of his constituency Labour party, as a member of a central Labour party or federation, as a member of the Fabian society, as a member of a professional organization, as a member of the Royal Arsenal Co-operative Society, and as a member of his trade union. It is possible for him to have eight or even ten votes cast in his name, and quite likely that he will have two or three; and not only may he never have been asked how his votes shall be used, but they may be cast on opposite sides of a question. The system is therefore thoroughly artificial, but its value is that is keeps the control of party policy firmly in the hands of the big trade unions. This can easily be seen from the following figures of the voting power of the several sections of the 1951 conference:

Section	Number	Delegates	Votes
Trade unions	72	572	4,987,000
Labour parties	588	611	1,147,000
Federations	17	17	17,000
Socialist societies	4	4	10,000
Co-operative societies	1	6	31,000

The trade union dominance has been much enhanced by the substitution of 'contracting out' for 'contracting in', for this single measure as we have seen, doubled the number of those paying the political levy of their unions. It may be assumed that a man who has taken the trouble to join his constituency Labour party or who has 'contracted in' to pay the political levy of his trade union is keen on the work of the Labour party, but can we make any such assumption about a man who pays the political levy only because he is too lazy or too afraid to 'contract out'. Nevertheless the trade union vote at the Labour conference is greatly swelled by such persons.

It is not always, or even usually, the case that the trade unions at the Labour conference take one view of a question and the constituency parties the opposite view. Normally both the constituency parties and the trade unions are divided. But if the big trade unions agree they can always make their views prevail; and there have been issues, more particularly the question of co-operation with the Communists, on which a section of the constituency parties fought for years a dogged losing battle with the trade unions.

Trade union voting at the Labour conference has often been likened to a steam roller; and those who have been flattened thereby have from time to time suggested that the trade unions should be affiliated only to the constituency Labour parties, and not to the national Labour party. They are, as we have seen, affiliated in both ways, and the paradox arises that trade union delegates to the general meeting of a constituency Labour party may vote in favour of instructing their delegate differently from the way their own trade union delegation to the national conference wil be instructed. Dispersed in constituency Labour parties throughout the country, trade union members are a weaker force than when organized nationally, and often yield to influences and pressures that make no effect on their national headquarters. But the very reasons that make the malcontents propose this change make the trade union leaders more firmly resolved to keep the control of the Labour conference in their hands.

As a piece of machinery, the system can easily be picked to pieces, but as a practical contribution to the preservation of our democratic way of life it has served the Labour party and the country well. Time and time again sections of the constituency parties have urged the Labour party to courses of action that would have brought it and the country to disaster, and time and time again the Labour party has been saved by the good sense of the trade union leaders and the fact that in concert they can dominate the Labour conference.

The system of voting is therefore one way in which the Labour party avoids the worst consequences of its own theories;[1] and if the voting nevertheless goes against the judgement of the Labour leaders, in the last resort they are prepared to ignore it and to act on their own responsibility. For years the Labour party passed resolutions advocating the setting up of a Jewish state in Palestine, but when the Labour took office in 1945 it ignored these resolutions and worked for a unitary state embracing both Jews and Arabs. When a Jewish state was eventually set up in part of Palestine, it was by the force of arms and not by the decisions of the Labour conference. Year by year the Labour conference passed resolutions demanding the abolition of the 'tied cottage', but when Labour ministers were in office they took no action. It became almost a custom when Mr. Aneurin Bevan was Minister of Health for him to be returned at the head of the poll in the constituency section and then to be obliged to explain to delegates that the abolition of the 'tied cottage' was far more difficult than they supposed.

A big difference in form between the party conferences is that the leader takes an active part in the Labour conference but does not attend the Conservative conference, though by custom he addresses a mass meeting after the close of the conference if invited. This last qualification is sedulously observed.

Though the Conservative and Labour theories of the functions of a party conference are therefore very different, in practice the differences are not so great as might be supposed. They are not, indeed, unimportant. In 1948 Labour ministers were irresolute about proceeding with the nationalization of the steel industry, and might have found some way of avoiding it if they had not held themselves to be bound by decisions taken some years before in very different circumstances. The Conservative attitude is preferable—that votes taken at a party conference are a useful guide to the leader in formulating policy, though not binding upon him. But in practice Labour leaders will either successfully control the voting at their conference or may decide to ignore it, while Conservative leaders may decide that the advice of a Conservative conference is so compelling that it must be accepted even though it goes against their judgement.

[1] Another way in which the conference decisions could be theoretically manipulated is through the choice of resolutions. The affiliated organizations send in far more resolutions than can possibly be debated. Many are rejected, and others are welded into 'composite resolutions' for debate. But the delegates are watchful, and in practice the composite resolutions always bring out the main subjects of controversy.

XVI

Selection of Candidates

WE COME NOW to the final point of interaction between the parliamentary party and the organization in the country, namely, the selection of parliamentary candidates—for the successful candidate of to-day becomes the member of to-morrow.

In the main parties the responsibility for the choice of a parliamentary candidate lies with the constituency organization. In several places we have had occasion to draw attention to the autonomous nature of those constituency bodies. They run their own finances, they appoint their own agents and other staff, they conduct their own business. But in no respect is their autonomy so pronounced as in the choice of a parliamentary candidate. Let us look at the machinery for so doing; and let us first observe that until a general election opens the selected person is only a 'prospective parliamentary candidate'. When an election campaign is opened, the prospective candidate is formally adopted as the candidate, but until that point it is always open to the constituency association, in theory at any rate, to change its mind. If the sitting member wishes to stand again he is normally accepted without question as the prospective candidate of the party to which he belongs. But all candidatures are reopened by the dissolution of Parliament, and the old member has to be adopted as a candidate like anyone else. If a party does not hold the seat, it normally proceeds to choose a prospective candidate at a fairly early date after the last general election. If a by-election occurs through the death or retirement of the sitting member or his elevation to the peerage, the party to which he belongs will need to find a new candidate at once, but the other party or parties contesting the seat will probably have a prospective candidate or candidates in the field already.

When a candidate or prospective candidate has to be found by a Conservative association, the executive council appoints a selection committee. The chairman of the association is normally chairman of the selection committee. There are usually about half a dozen members and it is generally considered desirable to have on it one lady, one Young Conservative and one trade unionist; these are normally the chairmen of the appropriate committees of the association, and may

204

also be vice-chairmen of the association. The selection committee generally receives intimations from a number of ladies and gentlemen that they would like their names to be considered, and the members are free to invite anyone else to allow his or her name to be considered. The selection committee probably asks the National Union's standing advisory committee on candidates to suggest the names of persons who ought to be considered. As already pointed out, one of the two vice-chairmen of the party organization deals with parliamentary candidates and he will know the names of several suitable applicants. Any local applicants would make their wishes known to the committee directly, but the names of former members of the House of Commons and other national figures may be drawn to the selectors' attention by the standing advisory committee. The selection committee is absolutely free to consider any names it pleases, and no preference is conferred on a candidate whose name is on the standing advisory committee's list. By these processes the committee at its first meeting will have a number of names before it. Even for a 'hopeless' seat there are usually a fair number of applicants, and for a 'safe' seat the number may run into hundreds. The committee reviews the names, rejects some, and produces a list of applicants to be interviewed. It would be reasonable to ask a dozen persons to come for interview in the association's rooms, and so important is the part played by a candidate's wife in a modern election campaign that it is becoming increasingly common to ask married applicants to bring their wives at the same time.[1] At such interviews questions are put by the committee, not only to find out the attitude of the applicant to questions of the day but to get a better appreciation of his personality than is possible from a paper record. When the interviews are completed the committee makes a 'short list' of say three persons who are asked to attend a meeting of the executive council and to make a brief political speech.[2] The applicants do not hear each other, but speak in turn, and at the end answer any questions put to them. By this process the executive council, which may be a body of sixty to one hundred members, is able to see how the applicants would shape before a public meeting. When the speaking is concluded, the executive council deliberates, and finally decides to recommend one name to a general meeting of the association for adoption as pros-

[1] I have not known a local association interview the husband of a woman applicant; in such cases the husband usually takes a stroll outside while the interview is in progress.
[2] The story of the applicant who ended his speech by saying, 'Well, gentlemen, those are my principles but I am quite willing to change them if you don't like them' is probably *ben trovato* rather than *vero*.

pective candidate. He makes a general political speech by way of introducing himself to the meeting. It would be open to the general meeting to reject the name recommended,[1] but as the association may be presumed to have confidence in the executive council it has elected this is unlikely to be done, and the recommended person is usually adopted unanimously and with enthusiasm.

The Liberal party procedure is similar. A selection committee may be set up to produce a short list for the executive committee of a Liberal association, and the executive normally recommends one applicant to a general meeting of members. The National Liberals follow the same type of procedure.

The Labour party method is different, and is more tightly controlled. Applicants do not simply intimate that they would like to be considered but must secure nomination in a prescribed manner. When a vacancy occurs, a circular inviting nominations in terms laid down by the national executive committee is sent to affiliated and party organizations entitled to appoint delegates to the general committee. Each of these affiliated and party organizations and the executive committee of the constituency party may nominate an individual member of the Labour party or a member of an affiliated organization, provided that he is not disqualified under the constitution of the party or by a decision of the party conference, for example, by being a member of a party of which membership is incompatible with membership of the Labour party. (This is designed to prevent Communists from securing nomination.) If the person nominated is on the panel of available parliamentary candidates of an affiliated organization the consent in writing of its executive committee must be obtained, in addition to that of the candidate. (This is because the organization will contribute to his election expenses and the revenues of the constituency party.) The national executive committee may also send names from its list of available parliamentary candidates to be considered along with those of the locally nominated candidates, and usually it sends a list of from two to six. The executive committee usually interviews all the persons whose names have been sent down by the national executive committee and from them and the locally-nominated names it produces a 'short list' to go before the general committee. The applicants on the 'short list' all make brief political speeches before the general committee and answer questions. (In the Labour party the process, which is similar

---

[1] This happened when a Conservative candidate had to be selected at Southport in January 1952, and the person chosen was the seconder of the person recommended. (*News Chronicle*, 15 January 1952.)

to that in the Liberal and Conservative parties, is often known as the 'singing competition'.) The delegates—selected, it will be recalled, in accordance with the number of members in their organizations on whom affiliation fees have been paid—then vote upon the applicants. They do so by a system of successive ballots, each delegate having one vote. If there are six applicants on the short list, and no one gets a clear majority of the votes cast, any one who fails to get one-sixth of the votes cast is eliminated. Suppose that four are left. Any one who fails to get one-fourth of the votes cast in the next ballot is then eliminated; and so on until finally one is chosen by a clear majority. His election is then usually made unanimous. In such contests it is generally known how delegations will vote on the first round, and the interest lies in how they will vote when their own man is knocked out.

In all parties the selection of a parliamentary candidate is treated with the conscientiousness it deserves, but it may be doubted whether the national interest always prevails, and in too many cases a local worthy or a party hack or a friend of the chairman or a 'thruster' is preferred before men or women whom the country as a whole, and even the party headquarters, would like to see in Parliament. The final stage of speech-making is a tense occasion for the applicants, and if one or more of them is a national figure it is not without its wider significance. There is not infrequently an element of drama when the applicants are all summoned into the room together to hear the final decision, and the chairman says: 'We should like to have had every one of you as our candidate, but unfortunately we can choose only one, and our choice has fallen on ——'.

From the description given it will be appreciated that the responsibility for the selection lies entirely in the hands of the constituency organization. The formal rights of the national organization are limited to ensuring that the person selected is a fit and proper person to represent the party. In the Conservative party it is expected that a selection committee will not recommend any applicant who has not been approved by the National Union's standing advisory committee on candidates; in the Labour party the executive committee must consult with the national executive committee to determine the validity of the nominations received; the meeting of the general committee to select a candidate may be, and always is, attended by an officer of the national executive committee; and the candidate selected must not be introduced to the public until his candidature has been endorsed by the national executive committee. (It will be endorsed only when he has signed a financial agreement and an undertaking to abide, if elected, by the standing orders of the parliamentary Labour party.) The Communist party probably goes farthest in the direction of central control over candidatures, but its executive committee does not formally claim more than the right to reject the nomination put forward by the local organization and to ask for a new name to be substituted.

This is the formal position, and so jealously do constituency organizations cling to their rights that the several party headquarters have very few means of inducing them to choose particular applicants whom it is desirable to get into Parliament. It often happens that the party headquarters desire to find a seat for a certain person because he would be a valuable addition to the party work in the House, or because he is a useful member who has lost his seat at the general election, but they have to be very careful in making suggestions to constituency organizations or they will have the opposite effect. The Labour party headquarters can probably do more for such applicants than the Liberal or Conservative, but the national executive committee never sends fewer than two names for the consideration of a constituency party; if it specially wants one person to be selected, it will send his along with that of a nonentity to preserve an appearance of indifference.

In former days the amount that an applicant was prepared to pay towards his election expenses and annually towards the funds of the constituency organization was a big element in his selection. This severely restricted the field of candidates, and in modern days may rule out some of the ablest men and women. The Conservative party now requires that the entire expenses of a Conservative candidate in fighting an election shall be the responsibility of the constituency association (including, in suitable cases, the candidate's personal expenses during the period of the election up to a limit of £100), and that no subscription shall be made directly or indirectly by the candidate to the fund for statutory election expenses; each constituency association is required to make annual appropriations to an election fighting fund; any contribution made to the party funds is not to exceed £25 a year in the case of a candidate and £50 a year in the case of a member, and in no circumstances may the question of an annual subscription be mentioned by a selection committee to any applicant before he has been selected as candidate. The Labour party also requires constituency parties to make themselves responsible for the election expenses, but the candidate or any organization sponsoring him, more particularly a trade union, is permitted to contribute up to eighty per cent of the election expenses, provided that these do not amount to more than eighty per cent of sixty per cent of the maximum expenses allowed by law; if the expenses allowed by law are £700, the candidate or his organization may therefore contribute up to £336. The Labour party rules also provide that an individual or an organization may not contribute to the funds of a constituency Labour party for organization and registration purposes more than £200 a year in a parliamentary borough or £250 a year in a county division. These are, of course, substantial sums, and while a trade union may not have difficulty in finding them they are beyond the means of most individuals to-day. They are, indeed, limits and applicants are under no obligation to pay these large sums. But when faced with the opposition of trade union applicants backed by all the resources of their unions unsponsored individuals often feel obliged to offer more than they can really afford. At present we have therefore the situation, which would have been considered paradoxical a generation ago, that a poor man can stand as a Conservative candidate without difficulty whereas only a fairly well-to-do man can stand as a Labour candidate unless sponsored by a trade union. The situation is made more difficult for unsponsored candidates because the trade unions nearly always choose the safer divisions in which to place their candidates. In the charming words of *The Times House of Commons 1950*, 'trade union candidates nearly always contest the safer seats because the sponsoring unions feel that they would not be justified in using their members' contributions to support candidates in constituencies where the prospects of success are doubtful'. In consequence, the proportion of members of the parliamentary Labour party sponsored by trade unions is high. In 1945 out of 125 Labour candidates sponsored by trade unions 120 were returned, and they formed 30 per cent of the parliamentary Labour party; in 1950 out of 140 candidates sponsored by trade unions 111 were returned, and they formed 30 per cent of the the parliamentary Labour party.

The Liberals and minor parties do not have any rules with regard to candidates' contributions.

Another important question which may be put at a selection conference is, 'Are you prepared to live in the constituency. Most applicants hesitate to say 'No';—though one is reported, perhaps apocryphally, to have gained favour in a northern industrial town by saying, 'If you could see my house in Surrey you wouldn't ask such a foolish question!' Yet it may not be practicable for many a good candidate to maintain a home both in London and in the constituency. Some countries, such as the United States, require members of the legislative body to be residents in their constituencies, but this is generally recognized as a defect. Not only does it seriously limit the choice of candidates, but it is very difficult for a defeated member to get back into the legislative body, and impossible for him to get back quickly; and this may impose an undesirable caution on his speaking and voting. There are advantages and disadvantages in having a local resident as the member. His local knowledge may be effectively used on behalf of the constituency, but familiarity may breed contempt. Constituency parties must be allowed their own wishes in such a matter; but 'carpet-bagging', as the practice is known whereby a candidate packs up his bag and seeks the suffrages of some constituency other than his own, is one of the foundations of the British constitution. From Gladstone to Mr. Churchill, nearly all the great statesmen of modern England have been obliged to pack their carpet bags from time to time.

The selection of candidates is the point at which the British constitution displays its greatest strength and its greatest weakness. The strength lies in the firm assertion by constituency organizations of their right to have the candidates of their own choice, and not one foisted upon them by some central body. The weakness lies in the fact that candidates are chosen by relatively small bodies of men liable to all the foibles and failings of mortal human beings, and that the great mass of the electorate have no say in the matter. In the 'safe' division the member is in fact chosen by a small private conclave of the major party, though he may have to go through the formality and expense of a contested election. There is no subject that would so repay the political student as a close analysis of the reasons that lead men to wish to become parliamentary candidates and the means by which they achieve their ambition. It is undoubtedly an advantage at a Labour selection conference to be able to draw from one's pocket a fully paid-up membership card of a powerful trade union, and it is no less advantageous to be able to walk into a Conservative selection conference wearing a black tie with a light-blue diagonal stripe. But beyond a few well-known facts of this character the material would not be easy to collect, and here we have space only to consider the machinery of selection.

Part IV

The Fringe of Parties

CHAPTERS XVII–XX

XVII

Ancillary Organizations

THE ANCILLARY ORGANIZATIONS of a party are those bodies that exist to promote its aims but are not part of the party's formal structure. They have an independent life, they may have other non-political aspects, and they could in theory withdraw their support from the party; but such ancillary organizations have had no small share in creating support for the party and its leaders. They differ from the non-party political bodies to be discussed in the next chapter in that these exist to promote a political policy and do not usually care by what party it is carried out; whereas the ancillary organizations do not attempt to create policy but only to sustain the party with which they are associated. It is hardly an exaggeration to put the difference in these words: the non-party political organization says, 'My policy, right or wrong', whereas the ancillary party organization says, 'My party, right or wrong'.

If we leave out of account the houses of the great Whig and Tory families, which fulfilled the same rôle at an earlier date and continued to play it throughout the nineteenth century, the first ancillary party organizations are the London political clubs. White's, founded in 1698, became a chief resort of the Tories, and Brooks's, founded in 1764, fulfilled the same function for the Whigs. They still confront each other in St. James's St., but both have long since become purely social. The reform movement culminating in the act of 1832 gave a great impetus to political clubs. The importance of the Carlton club, founded in 1832, and the Reform club, founded in 1836[1], has already been noticed[2], and, indeed, for a long time they fulfilled functions that have since been carried out

[1] As the date is incorrectly given in various books of reference as 1832 or 1837, it may be useful to set out the following facts, which I owe to the courtesy of the secretary of the club, Mr. H. C. Bell: In 1834 a Liberal club, known first as 'The Westminster' and afterwards as 'The Westminster Reform Club', was founded with its club-house at 34 Great George St., Westminster. The founder of the Reform Club was the Rt. Hon. Edward Ellice M.P., in whose residence, 14 Carlton House Terrace, the preliminary discussions were held early in 1836. The first formal committee meeting of the Reform club was held at 104 Pall Mall, on 5 May 1836. On 18 May 1836, it was resolved 'that Tuesday, 24 May 1836, be the day for opening the club, to be advertised in the *Chronicle, Globe, Courier, Morning Advertiser, Sun, True Sun, Spectator, Observer,* and *Examiner* papers'.

[2] *V. supra*, pp. 18, 213–14.

by the head offices of the Conservative and Liberal parties respectively. Only the width of Carlton Gardens at its narrowest separated their club-houses,[1] and a definite stage was reached in Gladstone's political journey when a group of young Tory bloods dining in the Carlton one evening conceived the idea of throwing him into the Reform!

The Carlton is still confined exclusively to Conservatives, and normally only members are admitted within its portals. Many Conservative peers and members of the House of Commons are members of the Carlton club and a recent Conservative chief whip, Captain David Margesson (now Viscount Margesson) occupied rooms there during the session. In this atmosphere it is natural for political conversations of great delicacy to be held, and the Carlton remains one of the most influential bodies associated with the Conservative party.   As already noted,[2] it was there that Conservative peers and members of the House of Commons met in 1922—those who are not also members of the club being admitted for such meetings—when the decision to end the coalition was taken; and many lesser decisions of great political consequence are still taken there among groups of members year by year.   The Carlton, being limited in membership, quickly established a long waiting list, and in 1840 the Conservative club was founded to combine social and political purposes.   The demand for such clubs being still unsated, the Junior Carlton was founded in 1864, the City Carlton in 1868, the St. Stephen's in 1870, the Constitutional in 1883, and the Ladies' Carlton in 1906. Despite its name the Junior Carlton is autonomous, and members do not normally pass from one to the other.   The St. Stephen's club-house in Bridge Street, Westminster, has the advantage of being within reach of the division bell in the House of Commons, an advantage much appreciated in the late sittings of recent years.   In the younger Conservative clubs the social side is as marked as the political, and the political activities of the club are generally managed by a political committee; they include periodic meetings addressed by leading figures in the party.

The demand for clubs was not so great among the Liberals as among the Conservatives.   Social influences at all levels played a smaller part among the Liberals, and Brooks's and the Reform remained the only London Liberal clubs until 1882.   By that time there was a considerable

---

[1] A German bomb destroyed the club-house of the Carlton in Pall Mall during the evening of 14 October 1940, when about two hundred and fifty Conservative peers and members of the House of Commons were there. Not one of them was killed, though many suffered injury; Lord Hailsham was carried from the ruin by his son, the present peer, as Anchises had been carried from the blazing ruins of Troy by *pius Aeneas*. The Carlton has since found a temporary home in St. James's St.
[2] *V. supra*, p. 47.

pent-up demand, and the National Liberal club with a much larger membership was founded under Gladstone's own patronage. A few years later the Irish question rent the party in twain, and as neither Liberals nor Liberal Unionists were able to secure control of Brooks's or the Reform, and both sections continued to be admitted to membership, from 1886 onwards these two clubs ceased to exert a political influence and became increasingly social. The National Liberal club continued to represent Gladstonian Liberalism, but with the further rifts in the party, and the decline in the party's membership, this club also ceased to demand adherence to any political tenets. Many members of the Labour party are, in fact, members of the Reform and National Liberal clubs to-day. Members of the Labour Party have not attempted to set up a great political club of their own: there is a National Trade Union club in London, but it is of a less ambitious order.

These great London clubs drew their members from all over the country, but many less famous political clubs of a similar nature were formed in provincial towns, and not a few of them survive to-day. In Birmingham, for example, there is a Conservative, founded in 1882, a Liberal founded in 1877, and a Midland Conservative founded in 1882; in Edinburgh there is the Scottish Conservative, founded in 1877, and the Scottish Liberal, founded in 1879. These clubs served as rallying points for the local Conservatives and Liberals and provided them with a wide range of social amenities also.

The movement to form political clubs was not confined to the wealthier persons. The British are a 'clubbable' people, in Dr. Johnson's phrase, and great efforts have been made to establish political clubs for working men and their families. Working men's clubs and institutes were founded in many towns in the first half of the nineteenth century, and in 1862 the Working Men's Club and Institute Union was founded to co-ordinate such clubs and to promote others. After the extension of the franchise in 1867 the Conservatives quickly recognized the need to establish Conservative or Constitutional clubs, in which working men could be brought into association with the Conservative party; and a large number of such clubs were founded.

The Liberals were slow to adopt this form of activity, but a number of Liberal clubs were set up. The explanation for this difference in enthusiasm lies partly in the question of liquid refreshment. It was soon found that to be successful, socially or financially, a club must be in a position to supply its members with beer, wines and spirits, more particularly beer. The sale of 'intoxicating liquor' was abhorrent to many Liberals, and even those to whom it was not abhorrent were afraid of losing in the chapels the votes they picked up in the clubs. The sale of such refreshments did not impinge on similar inhibitions among the Conservatives, and not only were working men's Conservative clubs encouraged, but they have been formed into an Association of Conservative Clubs and given representation in the councils of the party, both locally and nationally. The party's model rules suggest that the executive committee of each Conservative and Unionist association shall include one representative from each subscribing Conservative club in the constituency, and the suggestion is normally followed. The provincial area councils of the Conservative party are to include, under their constitution, 'not more than two representatives of each subscribing organization and club within the provincial area'. The Central Council of the National Union must likewise include the chairman, secretary and three other representatives appointed by the governing body of the Association of Conservative Clubs. These arrangements may suggest that the clubs should be regarded as part of the formal structure of the Conservative party, but as in all other respects they are independent of the party it seems best to treat them as ancillary organizations and to regard these arrangements as means of liaison.

When the Labour party came on the scene it inherited some of the prejudices of the teetotallers, but the great mass of the party felt no such inhibitions and were not disposed to see the Conservatives sweep the field in the provision of working men's clubs. It is true that the Labour party has not directly set out to found working men's clubs, unite them into an association, and give them a formal place in the party's councils, as the Conservatives have done; this would have needlessly aroused the antagonism of the prohibitionist section of the party. But many working men's clubs and institutes were already in existence when the Labour party was formed, and such clubs and institutes have come in practice to be regarded as centres of Labour activity. Many are trade union clubs, and in others the local Labour leaders often figure on the committee.

These working men's clubs are cultivated assiduously by Conservative and Labour members and candidates, and the agents of either party would be deeply grieved if candidates did not make a round of visits at election time. But it is open to doubt whether the advantages to the party for this courting are proportionate to the efforts put into it. When arrangements are made for the M.P. or candidate to address members, a time is chosen when the largest number of members is likely to be in the club, and by means of a microphone and amplifying system his remarks are usually made audible, not only to members sitting at their tables before him, but in other rooms. The members usually give the speaker 'a good hearing', and possibly reflect on his words afterwards; but when he mingles with them afterwards their talk is usually of personal grievances rather than the big questions of the day, and there is little evidence that public opinion is moulded in the clubs to any considerable extent. Complaints are frequent in both the Labour and the Conservative party that on polling day, when canvassers are urgently needed, the club members are not to be found or prefer to sit over their drinks. The Conservative party has had to take vigilant action 'to prevent the infiltration of individuals hostile to the aims and principles of Conservatism'[1]; quite a number of Communists or fellow-travellers have had to be expelled from membership. Labour clubs have from time to time had to exercise similar vigilance. This infiltration need not all be regarded as an attempt to glean information by members of a hostile party—for usually there is little information to be gleaned. The clubs are primarily social, and the members are mainly attracted by the facilities they offer. It has been a great advantage to the members of the club to enjoy rather more favourable licensing laws than the public houses. This is particularly marked in Wales, where drinks can be obtained on Sunday in the clubs but not in the 'pubs'. In assessing the political importance of the clubs these factors must be borne in mind. That importance can easily be exaggerated. The club members normally gather together, not for politics, but to meet their friends, to drink and smoke in comfort, to play billiards, and to escape from the cares or drabness of their homes. Perhaps they are none the less valuable members of society for not putting politics in the first place.[2]

Another type of club is that founded to provide speakers for party

---

[1] *Final report of the committee on party organization* (Maxwell-Fyfe committee), p. 58.

[2] If some personal reminiscences may be allowed, I think they will illustrate the fundamental good nature to be found in the working men's clubs. On 29 October 1948 I was due in my native village of Cwmbran, Monmouthshire, to make a presentation to another native of the village, Mr. Tom Richards, who had that year finished second in the Olympic marathon race. The area is strongly Labour, and when I was invited I was a Labour member of Parliament. Three days before the presentation I had resigned from the Labour party and two days before the presentation I had made a widely reported speech strongly criticizing the party. When the presentation had been made, I was taken to a working men's club at Cwmbran, and after partaking of the hospitality offered I was about to leave when I was told the members would like me to say a few words before I withdrew. In the course of my remarks I observed that they no doubt had much in their minds my recent action, and I asked them, even if they could not share my views, to believe that I had acted sincerely. When I sat down they spontaneously broke into 'For he's a jolly good fellow'. And this although probably every man in the hall had voted Labour at the last election and intended to do so at the next!

occasions. The Eighty club was formed in 1880 'with the object of promoting Liberal education, and of stimulating Liberal organization, especially with reference to the election which was then shortly to take place'.[1] At a meeting in the House of Commons in 1881 it was decided to put the club on a permanent basis with a view to supplying the needs of local associations in the matter of speakers and lecturers. The United and the Cecil clubs were later founded by Conservatives with similar objects, and have since amalgamated as the United and Cecil club. After the Liberal defeat of 1895 the '95 club was founded to supply speakers in a large area around Manchester.

The origin of the Primrose League in 1883 has already been described,[2] and it remains one of the most influential ancillary organizations of the Conservative party. It could be hoped that the objects for which it was founded—'the maintenance of religion, of the estates of the realm, and of the imperial ascendancy of the British Empire'— might be above party, but in practice the Primrose League has always been closely associated with the Conservative party. The nomenclature of the League is unusual, and bears witness to the knight-errant character of the principal founder. The members are classified as knights, dames and associates. They are organized in local habitations. The management of the league is in the hands of a grand council. The chief officer is the grand master, who is normally the leader of the Conservative party, as is the case at present; and its executive head is called the chancellor. In the days when rank, title and position in society counted for more than they do to-day, the league was a major instrument in Conservative electioneering tactics; to-day it is rather a means of sustaining the enthusiasm of Conservatives, and one of its main activities is the organization of large demonstrations addressed by the leader of the party or some other chief Conservative. The league is given formal representation in the National Union of Conservative and Unionist Associations; it is laid down that the chancellor, secretary and four other representatives appointed by the headquarters of the league are to be members of the central council of the National Union. Nevertheless it seems best, as in the case of the clubs, to treat the Primrose League as an ancillary organization rather than a formal element in the party's structure, for it has a life of its own quite independent of the party.

Swinton Conservative College was opened in 1948 in Lord Swinton's home in the village from which he takes his title near Masham, Yorkshire. It is controlled by a board of governors, and is therefore to

---

[1] *The Liberal Year Book for 1939*, p. 14.   [2] *V. supra*, p. 35.

be regarded as an ancillary organization rather than a section of the party machinery. Courses of varying lengths are held throughout the year, attended by Conservatives from constituencies throughout the country and addressed by Conservative authorities in the subjects under discussion. About 1,800 students a year attend the college.[1]

The Fabian Society, whose origins have already been described,[2] has many of the characteristics of an ancillary body, but as it is affiliated nationally to the Labour party, which it helped to create, and its branches are also affiliated to local Labour parties, it is best regarded as an element in the party structure. The Haldane Society and the Association of Labour Lawyers—the latter created owing to a difference of opinion within the former—are true ancillary organizations of the Labour party.

The Labour party has been much troubled by organizations on its fringe claiming to advance its objectives but in fact undermining them for the benefit of the Communist party. Many of these organizations have attractive names calculated to deceive even the very elect. For this reason the annual conference of the Labour party has empowered the national executive to inquire into the activities of such bodies and to declare them to be organizations ineligible for affiliation to the Labour party. Such bodies are known as 'proscribed organizations'. Most of them are, in fact, Communist in their sympathies, but the list includes some that are ineligible for affiliation on other grounds. The present list of 'proscribed organizations' is:

British Soviet Society
British Soviet Friendship Houses Ltd.
Common Wealth
Communist party of Great Britain
Independent Socialist party
Labour Research department
Marx House
Militant Labour League
Scottish U.S.S.R. Society
Women's Parliament
Student Labour Federation
International Youth Council in Britain
World Federation of Democratic Youth
Women's International Democratic Federation
League for Democracy in Greece
British Peace Committee
Socialist Fellowship
Welsh Peace Council

Members of these organizations are not eligible for membership of the Labour party; and members of the Labour party and affiliated organiza-

---

[1] The Bonar Law Memorial College at Ashridge was founded with a similar intent, but this phase came to an end, and for a considerable time Ashridge, under its own board of governors, has followed a strictly non-party policy of political education.
[2] V. supra, p. 40.

tions are expected not to co-operate with 'proscribed organizations' or to be associated with any conferences they organize.

The existence of this convenient list, even though it includes some bodies that are not Communist controlled, will suffice also for the ancillary organizations of the Communist party. In the rank atmosphere of the Communist underworld such bodies pullulate in extraordinary profusion, and many are disbanded, or change their names, when their parentage is revealed.

——— XVIII ———

Non-party Political Organizations

THE COURSE OF PARTIES in Great Britain since the middle of the eighteenth century has been much affected by the existence of organizations created to achieve a political purpose but standing deliberately outside the party structure. Such organizations do not wish to obtain control of the government, nor to act as an independent party in Parliament. They do not express views on the whole range of policy, but confine themselves to one or a few objects. They may promote the candidatures of men pledged to further their principles, but they would generally prefer to have their candidates distributed among the different parties. If one party accepts their views and another opposes them, they may find themselves compelled by circumstance to throw their influence behind one party, but fundamentally they are neutral in the party struggle. As A. Lawrence Lowell notes,[1] such a group of persons often comes nearer than the great parties of the present day to Burke's definition of a party as 'a body of men united for promoting by their joint endeavours the national interest upon some particular principle in which they are all agreed'. For each of the parties covers a wide range of opinions and includes men who are not wholly united in their principles; 'a party in modern parliamentary government would be more accurately defined as a body of men united by their intent of sustaining a common ministry'.[2]

The first such organization of any importance is identified by Lowell as the Society for Supporting the Bill of Rights. This was founded in 1769 with the object of extending the popular element in the constitution and more particularly to support Wilkes in his fight with the House of Commons. When it became clear that the society was being used to further the personal ambitions of Wilkes, some of the leading members resigned from it and founded the Constitutional Society with the same object. County associations with the same end were founded ten years later, and conventions of county delegates met in London in 1780 and 1781 to petition for the redress of grievances. About this time Lord

---

[1] *The Government of England*, 1912, vol. i, p. 474. For the account of non-party organizations up to his time I am much indebted to this author's work.
[2] *Ibid.*, p. 474.

George Gordon founded another non-party organization of a very different character, the Protestant Association. This was created to maintain the disabilities of Roman Catholics, and stirred up the riots of June 1780.

The outbreak of the French Revolution stimulated the formation of political organizations on this side of the channel. In 1791 the London Corresponding Society was founded to agitate for extreme reforms and in 1792 the Society of the Friends of the People was set up to advocate more moderate reforms. Pitt's Government, determined that what had happened in France should not happen here, persuaded Parliament to pass several repressive measures directed at them, and in an act of 1799 the London Corresponding Society was suppressed by name. The last of the repressive statutes expired in 1825, and the Catholic Association, which had already been organized in Ireland by Daniel O'Connell to agitate for the removal of Roman Catholic disabilities, was free to work in England. Its importance in setting a model both for the organizations of a parliamentary group and for the organization of a party in the country has already been noticed.[1] But it was itself a non-party organization, and when its aim was achieved in the act of 1829 it was disbanded.

About that time the growing demand for reform led to the formation of many political societies. Thomas Attwood founded at Birmingham in 1829 the Political Union for the Protection of Public Rights, and after the passage of the Reform Bill in 1832 similar unions were set up in other parts of the country; an attempt to weld them into a national organization was declared illegal by the Government and abandoned. In 1831 the National Union of the Working Classes had been founded in London with socialist objectives by disciples of Robert Owen: the members were often known as the 'Rotundanists' from the hall where they met. Francis Place rightly suspected that the reform of the franchise would be jeopardized by linking it with socialism, and he founded the National Political Union to back in London the single cause of reform. When the Reform Bill was passed, the societies that had been founded to promote it came to a natural end. About the same time another great and beneficent change was brought to completion largely as a result of the ceaseless pressure maintained on the Government by non-party organizations. The Committee for the Abolition of the Slave Trade had been formed in 1787, and succeeded in obtaining the suppression of the trade in slaves by acts of 1806 and 1807. But slaves continued to exist, and in 1823 the Anti-Slavery Society was founded, with

[1] *V. supra*, p. 30.

William Wilberforce and Thomas Clarkson as vice-presidents, to sweep away the last vestiges of the evil system in the British Empire. This was accomplished by a bill passed in 1837 only a month before Wilberforce's death.

The Reform Act of 1832 gave political power to the middle classes, and when the industrial workers realized that they had not benefited they began to form associations to demand further concessions. The London Working Men's Association published in 1838 a People's Charter of six points. This was enthusiastically adopted by similar associations throughout the country and gave rise to the movement known as Chartism. In 1839 delegates were sent from the local bodies to a People's Parliament in London. Processions of miners and others which converged on Newport from the Monmouthshire valleys in 1839 came into conflict with the authorities, and sentences of death, commuted to transportation, were passed on the leaders. The violence of the language used by the Chartists, and not least by their principal leader, Feargus O'Connor, led the Government to apprehend the danger of an armed rising. It is uncertain how far the Chartists were in fact prepared to resort to violence, but their apparent readiness to do so distinguishes the Chartist movement from other political movements after 1832. With the extension of the franchise it was natural that such bodies should rely more upon peaceful persuasion than upon a display of physical force. The Chartist movement was put on a new basis in 1840 by the creation at Manchester of the National Charter Association, to which four hundred societies were soon affiliated. In 1848, at a time of great hardship among the working classes, and under the influence of the revolution in Paris, the Chartists organized a monster petition said to have been signed by six million persons. Plans were made for a great demonstration on Kennington Common, from which the demonstrators were to march to Parliament with their petition. The military were called out, the Chartist leaders took fright, and when the petition was examined most of the names were found to be fictitious. Thereafter the Chartist movement fizzled out, but its agitation was not without influence on the course of British political history. All of its six points, with the single exception of annual Parliaments, has now been granted— manhood suffrage, secret ballot, the abolition of a property qualification for members of Parliament, payment of members, and equal electoral districts.[1]

[1] It is the intention of recent Representation of the People Acts, and the duty of the Boundary Commissioners, to see that constituencies are approximately equal in the number of their electors, but, of course, there have to be some modifications of the principle for sparsely populated areas.

The Anti-Corn Law League, with which Feargus O'Connor had come into controversy at one time, did not have to wait so long for the acceptance of its ideas, and it is perhaps the most brilliantly successful of all the bodies created to win support for a political object. Its success was partly due to the fidelity with which it pursued the single object of securing the repeal of the laws imposing a duty on foreign corn, and partly to the genius of Richard Cobden and John Bright who directed its agitation. An Anti-Corn Law Association was founded at Manchester in 1838, and similar associations were founded in the other towns soon afterwards. Delegates from these local associations met in 1839, and, at Cobden's suggestion, they transformed these local associations into an Anti-Corn Law League with branches throughout the country. A plaque in Fleet Street commemorates the London offices from which it conducted its memorable campaign. Speakers and lecturers were sent throughout the land, information and guidance was given to the press, pamphlets were circulated in huge quantities, and free-trade candidates for Parliament were supported. Peel was gradually converted, and the failure of the Irish potato crop led Parliament to agree in 1846 to the repeal of the corn laws. The League, having done its work, was dissolved. In looking back at the processes that led to the abrogation of the corn laws Peel used words which describe the methods of all non-party political bodies at their best: 'The name which ought to be, and will be, associated with the success of these measures is not mine, or that of the noble lord (Lord John Russell), but the name of one who, acting I believe from pure and disinterested motives, has, with untiring energy, made appeals to our reason, and has enforced those appeals with an eloquence the more to be admired because it was unaffected and unadorned; the name which ought to be chiefly associated with the success of these measures is the name of Richard Cobden.'

In the second half of the nineteenth century a large number of societies were formed to promote specific political aims, and although some were dissolved with the passage of the circumstances that brought them into being, and others became defunct through lack of support or the death of the organizer, not a few survive to this day. The Howard League for Penal Reform, founded in 1866, is still active. So are the National Anti-Vivisection Society (1875), the London and Provincial Anti-Vivisection Society (1876), the British Union for the Abolition of Vivisection (1898) and the Scottish Anti-Vivisection Society. The National Anti-Vaccination League (1896) is still active, but the Imperial Vaccination League, founded to win support for vaccination, appears to have died. The Marriage Law Reform Association and the Marriage Law Defence Association are another pair of societies founded to win support for opposing views on a great question; and a Marriage Society 'for promoting greater harmony and stability in marriage' has since been founded. The Liberation Society[1] (1844), formed to urge the disestablishment of the Church of England, and the Committee for Church Defence, formed to maintain the establishment, were another pair of opposed societies; as the Conservatives frowned on disestablishment and the Liberals were more prepared to countenance it, in practice the Liberation Society supported the Liberals and the Committee for Church Defence supported the Conservatives, but in essence they were non-party bodies. The Fabian Society, when it was founded in 1884, was a non-party political organization, inasmuch as it sought to 'permeate' all parties and to work through any party willing to accept its ideas; but since the formation of the Labour party, which it helped to bring about in 1900, it cannot be so regarded. The Eastern Question Association was formed in 1876 to oppose Disraeli's Turkish policy, and at the beginning of the present century the Balkan Committee campaigned actively to promote the same ideas. The Industrial Co-partnership Associated was established in 1884, and is now obtaining more support for its views in the political parties than at any previous time. The Proportional Representation Society was also founded in 1884 and is still actively trying to persuade all parties to accept its views, but has been successful only with the Liberals in decline. The temperance societies, of which there are no fewer than thirty-three in existence, have had greater success; but penal taxation and lower gravity have probably played a greater part than their arguments. The National Trade Defence Association was the reply of the brewers to these societies. The Navy League is still actively pursuing the aim, with which it was founded in 1899, of seeing that a strong Navy is maintained; and a similar Air League of the British Empire was founded in 1909, almost as soon as Englishmen took to the air.

The cumulative effect of such bodies on the British parties has been far from negligible, but the one that most invites comparison with the Anti-Corn Law League is the Tariff Reform League. This was founded in 1903 to further the ideas on fiscal reform which Joseph Chamberlain had by that date reached. It is doubtful whether it ought to be noticed here or as an ancillary party organization, for it devoted itself to converting the Conservative party to the idea of a preferential tariff; but

---

[1] In full, the Society for the Liberation of Religion from State Patronage and Control.

I

as it sought to bring about a great reversal of national policy, and worked through the party most likely to accept its ideas, it may conveniently be mentioned at this point. The league organized meetings, supplied members of Parliament and the press with information, distributed vast quantities of literature, and in the end had the satisfaction of seeing the Conservative party adopt its policy as its own; though it had ceased to be in existence when Joseph Chamberlain's son in 1933 made it the national policy also.

The years between the great wars saw the rise of several national organizations with a notable impact upon the party system. The League of Nations Union was founded soon after the first world war, and under its royal charter its first object was: 'To secure the wholehearted acceptance by the British people of the League of Nations as the guardian of international right, the organ of international co-operation, the final arbiter in international differences, and the supreme instrument for removing injustices which may threaten the peace of the world.' This was an aim shared by all the main parties, as was shown by the acceptance of office in the union by the party leaders. But as the years passed, and international friction increased, the union came to advocate policies and methods of international action that were in dispute between the parties. It was, in particular, accused of trying to bring about a wide measure of disarmament while simultaneously requiring the British Government to intervene in international situations in a manner that might involve us in war. It is not now necessary to inquire into the truth of these charges, and it is sufficient to observe that the union, with branches all over the country and a large membership, came to bring considerable pressure upon the parties. This pressure was welcomed by the Opposition of those days and resented by the Government, and resented all the more because they felt obliged to shape their policy in accordance with this pressure against their better judgement. The methods of the union are exemplified by the so-called 'peace-ballot'—a question-begging title—in 1934. The public were asked to vote on the following questions:

'1. Should Great Britain remain a member of the League of Nations?

'2. Are you in favour of an all-round reduction in armaments by international agreement?

'3. Should the manufacture and sale of armaments for private profit be prohibited by international agreement?

'4. Do you consider that, if a nation insists on attacking another, the other nations should compel it to stop by

(a) Economic and non-military measures?

(b) If necessary, military measures?'

The total votes cast were 11,559,165. Over 11,000,000 affirmative answers were given to the first question, over 10,000,000 to Nos. 2, 4 and 4(a), and nearly 10,000,000 for No. 3. The affirmative answers to 4(b) numbered 6,784,368 against 2,351,981 negative answers. There were many complaints that the questions were unfairly framed, and in particular that it was not honest to invite people to vote for 4(a) without telling them that they should also vote for 4(b); but the Government of the day, rightly or wrongly, did not feel that it could ignore the public opinion shown by the large figures, and framed its policy accordingly. The episode illustrates the methods of the non-party political body in all their strength and weakness.

When the League of Nations gave way to the United Nations, the League of Nations Union also gave way to the United Nations Association, founded in 1945. This follows the organizational pattern of its predecessor. It has a national headquarters with branches throughout the country, and includes leaders of all the main parties among its officers. It distributes periodical and occasional literature, and employs speakers and lecturers. It exists to sustain interest in, and to canvass support for, the United Nations. If it has not fallen into the same controversy as its predecessor, one reason is that, owing to the division in the United Nations between the Soviet Union and the Western World, it has seldom been possible to speak of a United Nations policy, and therefore the occasion has not arisen for the United Nations Association to press a particular policy upon the parties.[1]

A group of organizations formed between the wars has been particularly concerned to advance the claims of certain categories of pensions. The British Legion was founded in 1921 and all ex-Servicemen are eligible for membership. It now has a membership of about 1,250,000 in over 5,000 branches in England and Wales. Its main purpose is to act as a benevolent society for needy members and their dependents, and in particular to arrange the annual poppy day appeal and to distribute the proceeds. But it is naturally bound to take an interest in such matters as the pensions and allowances of disabled Servicemen, and has frequently made representations to the Government of the day. It so happens that its president is now a Conservative member of Parliament, the highly respected Sir Ian Fraser, blinded in the first world war; but it has always kept itself strictly neutral between the parties—so much so that in 1952 its annual conference even rejected a motion to make Communists ineligible for membership—and its representations are always heard with sympathy by all parties. Its

---

[1] There has been danger that it might happen in the case of South-west Africa and colonial policy generally.

structure provides for an Officers' Association. There is also an Officers' Pension Society which was in 1952 accepted by the Government as an appropriate body to make representations on behalf of officers' pensions.

Old-age pensions were first granted by the state in Great Britain in 1908 and put on a tripartite contributory basis in 1926. One of the features of recent decades has been the large increase in the number of elderly persons, and their claims to pensions have been correspondingly pressed. A number of old-age pensioners' associations were formed in various parts of the country, and in due course were welded into a National Federation of Old Age Pensions Associations. The head office of the federation issues a paper *The Old Age Pensioner*, promotes the formation of branches, provides speakers and literature, organizes an annual delegate conference, formulates policy, and takes parliamentary action to secure acceptance for its demands. As it is open not only to pensioners but to 'prospective pensioners', there is no limit except the whole population to its potential membership. Among its aims are: the old-age pension to be raised to a minimum of £2 a week each for men and women; the value of the pension not to fall by reason of any rise in the cost of living; the age of qualification to be lowered to 60; the pension to be paid to the wife at the same time as to the husband; the stamp qualification to be removed, homes to be provided at rents that pensioners can afford to pay. These are formidable demands, and have been pressed with a virulence unknown since the Chartists. The local branches have specialized in getting the candidates at parliamentary elections to address them from the same platform, and they make matters as uncomfortable as they can for any candidate not prepared to pledge himself immediately to full acceptance of their demands.

Thanks to the indomitable energy of Miss Florence White, of Bradford, the spinsters have not been behind the old-age pensioners in pressing their claims. This lady formed the National Spinsters' Pensions Association in 1935 with the object of securing pensions for spinsters at the age of 55. It promotes branches, issues literature, provides speakers, holds an annual delegate conference, brings pressure to bear on candidates and takes parliamentary action. Miss White herself stood at a by-election at Preston in 1935, but lost her deposit; and on 27 July 1937 a petition said to bear 11,000,000 signatures was presented to the House of Commons in furtherance of the association's object.

One of the big social revolutions that came with the second world war was the provision of family allowances. This owed as much to the labours of an individual member of Parliament, the late Miss Eleanor Rathbone, as to anybody, but a valuable part in converting public opinion was played by the Family Endowment Association, for which the late Mrs. Eva Hubback worked indefatigably. It was not an easy task as the trade unions were at first very suspicious of the idea lest it should upset wage-rates, but in the end the measure was carried through Parliament with general approval. It differs from the pensions cases just considered, as it was not a matter of individuals banding themselves together to improve their own interests. The children, of course, had no power to do so and had no votes with which to intimidate politicians; and parents, as such, never attempted to combine. It was the latest, and one of the happiest, attempts to secure a purely altruistic object by methods of education and persuasion directed at public opinion and the parties.

Another group of non-party political organizations exists to promote certain aims in industry. One is specifically called Aims for Industry, and endeavours to create a climate of opinion favourable to the continuance of private enterprise. For this reason it has incurred the hostility of the Labour party, and Labour members of Parliament have described it as an organ of the Conservative party. As the Labour party looks with more favour on nationalized industries than on private enterprise, it so happens that the policy desired by Aims for Industry is more likely to be achieved through the Conservative party. But Aims for Industry ought to be classified among the non-party organizations rather than among the ancillary organizations because it pursues the policy of free enterprise for its own sake, and not because it happens to be the policy of the Conservative party[1].

The Empire Industries Association and British Empire League is a body that requires to be similarly distinguished. It issues literature and holds public meetings with the object of promoting trade within the Empire, and in particular to win support for Empire preference in tariffs. As this is also the policy of the Conservative party, it is usual for its speakers and their platform supporters to be prominent figures in the Conservative party of this country or similar parties in the Commonwealth. But the association is structurally and financially independent of the Conservative party, and would be free to align itself with any

---

[1] I can myself bear witness to the scrupulous care with which it tries to create a climate of opinion without identifying itself with a party. When I was sitting in the House of Commons as an Independent Member, I was often asked to speak by Aims of Industry—though in fact I was never able to accept—but after I took the Conservative whip it was intimated to me that I should no longer be an acceptable speaker.

party that adopted its policy. The Empire Economic Union is a similar body which provides speakers on imperial trading matters and produces pamphlets.

These are the main bodies that exist to promote a specific policy through Parliament. There are many others, formed primarily for other purposes, whose work from time to time requires parliamentary action. Among such bodies are the chambers of commerce and the various employers' organizations. Some of these bodies maintain parliamentary committees to study the proceedings of Parliament and advise when action is needed. It would take us too far afield to consider in detail these bodies, whose work impinges on the parties only occasionally. In the nineteenth century the trade unions would have had to be reckoned among the most important of such bodies. They were formed primarily to improve the remuneration and working conditions of their members, and this was mainly achieved by direct negotiations with employers. But as the years passed it became increasingly common to rely on parliamentary action to further these ends, and many unions set up parliamentary commmittees. In due course, as already related,[1] the Trades Union Congress took a major part in creating the Labour party. Those trade unions that are affiliated to the Labour party have ceased to be 'non-party political bodies', and cannot even be regarded as 'ancillary organizations', of the Labour party; they are structurally an element in that party, and have been treated accordingly.

[1] *V. supra*, pp. 40–41.

——— XIX ———

Parties and the Press

NEWSPAPERS HAVE PLAYED an extremely important part in the formation of political opinion in Great Britain ever since the birth of the party system. The British press and the British party system arose together in the reign of Charles II, and have been closely intertwined in the succeeding years. It is only in recent times that any parties have come to exercise a direct control over newspapers through ownership or part ownership, and even to-day this is true only of the Labour, Co-operative and Communist parties. But it has always been a major concern with the parties to ensure that their case is adequately stated in newspapers with a sufficiently wide or influential circulation, and this art used to be known as 'managing the press'. In the early days of newspapers, before industry and commerce had grown to such an extent as to make commercial advertising a major source of revenue, the Government of the day kept control over its favoured newspapers by disbursements from the secret funds, by the placing of official advertisements and by the distribution of 'Government intelligence'. The Opposition was not in so strong a position to influence the press, but used its party chest in the same way that Government funds were distributed; and there was always the possibility that the Opposition of to-day would become the Government of to-morrow. The connexion between the parties and the press was bluntly stated by Dr. Johnson in the prospectus of the *London Chronicle* issued on 1 January 1797:

'Of those writers who have taken upon themselves the task of intelligence, some have given, and others have sold their abilities, whether small or great, to one or others of the parties that divide us; and without a wish for truth, or thought for decency, without care of any other reputation than that of a stubborn adherence to their abettors, carry on the same tenor of representation through all the vicissitudes of right and wrong, neither depressed by detection, nor abashed by confutation; proud of the hourly increase of infamy, and ready to boast of all the contumelies that falsehood and slander may bring upon them, as new proofs of their zeal and fidelity.'

When Johnson wrote these words, the press was still suffering from the evil effects of Sir Robert Walpole. The corruption of journalists had, indeed, been practised before his time, but he carried it to depths previously unknown. The secret committee of the House of Commons appointed to inquire into his activities found that in the years 1731–41 he had spent more than £50,000 upon 'pension papers', as the sub-sidized organs were known. It was a long time before these evil habits could be shaken off. *The Times* claims to have given a lead, from 1803 onwards, in making itself independent of subventions. According to the official history of that newspaper:[1]

> 'Acceptance by the press of payments from the Treasury, or of funds supplied by subscriptions to the Opposition party chest, knew one great exception from 1803, *The Times*. The determination of its later editor, Thomas Barnes, to "thunder for reform" and ignore parties and politicians in the service of public opinion, brought the paper in 1821–41 an unprecedented influence. John Walter I accepted subsidies; John Walter II ignored them; Thomas Barnes took it upon himself to destroy the system.'

It required more than determination, however, to achieve this result. What made it possible was the growth of industry and com-merce, the rise of the middle classes accompanying this phenomenon, and the removal of the tax on advertisements. The independence then achieved became the most cherished quality of newspapers, and in most cases still is to-day. Algernon Borthwick, the great editor of the *Morning Post*, made it the first of his principles, and in a leading article on the hundredth anniversary of the newspaper's birth, 2 November 1872, he wrote:[2]

> 'Independence is the first condition of influence, and a journal to be listened to must speak in its own name alone, and with the weight which years of experience in public affairs free from the ties and trammels of mere party can alone give to its utterance.'

This great change in the standing of newspapers did not mean that the parties ceased to have any connexion with newspapers, only that the connexion took a new and healthier form. The parties were no less interested in trying to ensure, by persuasion and influence, that their views were adequately supported in the press; and we enter a period of intimate relationships between statesmen and editors. It was a natural consequence of this new phase that newspapers tended to be identified with the views of the statesmen they supported rather than with a party organization. A particularly close relationship grew up in the time of the Borthwicks between the *Morning Post* and Palmerston, described in the history of that journal as 'of all the skilled manipulators of the

---

[1] *The History of the Times*, vol. i, *The Thunderer in the Making*, p. 18.
[2] *The Morning Post 1772–1937*, by Wilfrid Hindle, p. 217.

press in the nineteenth century . . . perhaps the most skilful'.[1] Another
such close relationship from 1880 onwards was that between the *Pall
Mall Gazette* and Gladstone; in 1886 he took John Morley, who had
been its editor, into his Cabinet, and Morley became one of the three
intimate friends of his old age. At a later date another such intimate
relationship grew up between Asquith and J. A. Spender, appointed
editor of the *Westminster Gazette* in 1895; and Spender lived to become
Asquith's co-biographer.

These were great days both at Westminster and in Fleet Street, and one
of the reasons for the high standards of journalism was the general
acceptance of editorial responsibility. Proprietors were in general
content to remain in the background, leaving both the policy and the
day-to-day direction of the newspapers in the hands of the editor. But
towards the end of the nineteenth century proprietors began to assert
their influence again, and the practice of acquiring newspapers in order
to give expressions to political views opened another era in the relationship between parties and the press. It had not, indeed, been unknown
in earlier days for a newspaper to change its allegiance completely with
a change of proprietorship. The *Pall Mall Gazette* was intended at its
foundation in 1865 to be independent in its political attitude but under
its first editor, Frederick Greenwood, it gave strong support to the
Conservative party and especially to Beaconsfield's foreign policy.
But in 1880, when the proprietor, George Smith, made it over to his
son-in-law, Henry Yates Thompson, it was converted into a Liberal
organ; Greenwood resigned and Morley took his place.[2] But this was
still removed from the practice which sprang up at the turn of the
century of acquiring newspapers with the object of using them to express
a particular point of view. The *Daily News* had been a consistent supporter of the Liberal party since its foundation in 1846, but the Liberal
party became split over the Boer war. Under the editorship of E. T.
Cook, the *Daily News* supported the Liberal imperialism of Rosebery,
but in 1901 George Cadbury acquired the chief interest in the journal,
and made it the organ of the anti-imperialist section of the Liberal
party. Cook retired, and A. G. Gardiner became editor. The leading exponent of the 'pro-Boer' element was Lloyd George, and throughout his
political life he took great care in his relationships with the newspapers;
in 1918 he acquired a main interest in the *Daily Chronicle*, which had
long shared his views and then became the mouthpiece of them.

[1] *Loc. cit.*, pp. 188–89.

[2] After 1892, when Yates Thompson sold the paper, the *Pall Mall Gazette* again
became a supporter of Conservative policy.

It so happened that about the turn of the century the proprietor tended to become a more active force in some newspaper offices for reasons not directly connected with politics, but rather with the perception of such men as George Newnes, Arthur Pearson and Alfred Harmsworth (later Viscount Northcliffe) that a new reading public created by elementary education was waiting to be exploited. In those cases, generally in the provinces, where the proprietor actually edited the paper, no change in journalistic conceptions was involved. But the new type of London proprietor was apt to intervene in the editing of the paper spasmodically and capriciously, and it became impossible for the editorial staff to follow a consistent political attitude. The new age was typified by Lord Beaverbrook, owner of the *Daily Express*, and the first Lord Rothermere, brother of Lord Northcliffe and proprietor of the *Daily Mail*, which newspapers were denounced by Baldwin as 'engines of propaganda for the constantly changing policies, desires, personal wishes, personal likes and personal dislikes of two men'.[1]

We have come finally in our own time to another stage in journalistic history in which some newspapers are owned by parties, or by movements of which parties are the expression. There is, indeed, nothing reprehensible in this practice. It is not to be compared with the secret suborning of the press in the nineteenth century. It is open and well understood, and there are some advantages in being able to ascertain from the party organ what the views of the party on a particular question are, or are likely to be. But it is the negation of that principle of editorial independence and responsibility won in the second quarter of the nineteenth century. It makes for dull journalism, in that the party newspaper has to be cautious in expressing a view lest it should conflict with the more deliberately canvassed views of the party. It is not always convenient to the party, for it is better for a party to have the general support of a newspaper without being committed to every expression of opinion therein. It is bad for democracy, in that the party newspaper abdicates from the function of helping to mould the views of the party and becomes only an instrument for expressing them.

To follow in detail the changing allegiances of newspapers to parties, political personalities, and policies would be to re-write the history of England from the reign of Charles II; and even to do so for the present century would require a substantial volume. It must suffice to add a few notes about the political attitude of the leading British newspapers at the present time.

[1] In a speech on 17 March 1931.

PARTY ALLEGIANCE OF NEWSPAPERS

As far as the London national newspapers are concerned, this task is made much easier by their present fewness. Many newspapers that have played a famous rôle in the history of party are now defunct or absorbed in others. But among those that remain we can still find exemplified all of the different phases of journalistic history specified above, save happily the methods of Walpole and his contemporaries.

The Times, founded in 1785 and now having a circulation of about 200,000 zealously maintains the principle of independence, and the editorial responsibility for all that appears in its editorial columns is untrammelled. It is often regarded by foreign readers as expressing the views of the Government of the day, but though close relationship has long been maintained with the Government of the day it remains free to express its own views, and has not infrequently embarrassed a Government with whose members the editor has been on terms of personal friendship. It has defined its own aim in the lofty words 'to help the Government of the day to find a national policy', which formula, indeed, expresses the aim of all high-class newspapers. In some handbooks the policy of *The Times* is decribed as 'independent Conservative', but although the description seemed reasonable enough in the long period of Conservative rule between the wars when Geoffrey Dawson was editor, it was not strictly accurate even then, and would not do at all for subsequent years. Under his successor, R. M. Barrington-Ward, *The Times* was taunted in some Conservative circles as 'the threepenny edition of the *Daily Worker*', largely on account of the favour shown to the revolutionary Communist movement in Greece; and even to-day *The Times* opens its columns hospitably to a wide variety of views.

The term 'independent Conservative' is, however, correctly applied to the *Daily Telegraph and Morning Post*. The amalgamation between the *Morning Post*, founded in 1772, and the *Daily Telegraph*, founded in 1855, was affected in 1937, and the newspaper to-day has a circulation of nearly 1,000,000. The *Morning Post* had become the champion of Conservatism, imperialism and protectionism in the middle of the last century, and immediately before the amalgamation had followed a 'high Tory' policy under the distinguished editorship of H. A. Gwynne. The *Daily Telegraph* supported the Liberal party until 1878, but it disagreed with the opinions expressed by Gladstone in his Midlothian campaign, and from 1886 embraced the Unionist cause. Since the amalgamation the *Daily Telegraph and Morning Post* has been the outstanding exponent of Conservative policy, but it is quite independent of the Conservative party, and on many occasions has not hesitated to differ from official Conservative policy if it considers that the interests of the country so require; on such occasions it has not infrequently been responsible for giving a new orientation to Conservative policy. Its revolt against the policy of 'appeasing' the dictators was, for example, a significant stage in the abandonment of that policy. In days nearer to our own the *Daily Telegraph and Morning Post* has severely criticized the Excess Profits Levy of a Conservative Chancellor of the Exchequer and certain features in the Transport Bill of another Conservative minister. The managing editor, in whose hands the day-to-day production of the newspaper rests, is a former Liberal member of Parliament, Mr. Colin R. Coote, who has expressed under his own name his personal conviction that Liberals should now throw in their lot with the Conservatives. Viscount Camrose, the chief proprietor, is the editor-in-chief, but the daily work of producing the newspaper is delegated to the managing editor. The Berry brothers acquired the *Daily Telegraph* in 1927, and in 1937, when the amalgamation with the *Morning Post* took place, there was a division of the Berry interests as a result of which Lord Camrose retained the *Daily Telegraph and Morning Post* together with the *Financial Times*, and his brother, Viscount Kemsley, took the other newspapers of the group. The rise in the circulation of the *Daily Telegraph* from under 100,000 before these events to nearly 1,000,000 is one of the outstanding chapters in the history of Fleet Street.

The *Daily Mail* was founded in 1896 by Alfred Harmsworth (later Viscount Northcliffe), and its foundation is usually taken as the beginning of the era of modern, popular journalism. It is now owned by a limited liability company, Associated Newspapers Ltd., of which the second Lord Rothermere, a nephew of Lord Northcliffe, is chairman. In politics the *Daily Mail* is often described as 'independent Conservative', but before the last war the independence was more pronounced than the Conservatism. It was the first newspaper in the world to achieve a circulation of over 2,000,000 copies a day.

The *Daily Express* was founded in 1900 by Arthur Pearson as a rival to the *Daily Mail*, and in 1915 was acquired by Lord Beaverbrook, who is still the chief proprietor. It has now a circulation of over 4,000,000 copies a day—much the largest circulation of any daily newspaper in the world, and truly amazing by whatever standard it is judged. Since he acquired the newspaper Lord Beaverbrook has always used it as a means of expressing his personal views on political questions. He was a minister in the two war-time coalitions, and has not been a member of any other party except the Conservative; but a few years ago he resigned his membership of the Epsom Conservative and Unionist Association, and the *Daily Express* has always borne the impress of his puckish, individualistic personality. It is best classified as 'independent' without any further attempt to gain precision.

The name of the *News Chronicle* came into being in 1930 as a result of the amalgamation of the *Daily Chronicle*, founded in 1877[1] with the *Daily News*, founded in 1846. The *Daily News* had previously absorbed the *Morning Star*, the *Morning Leader*, founded in 1892, and the *Westminster Gazette*, founded in 1893, The *Daily Chronicle* had a varying political allegiance in its early days, but became consistently Liberal from 1893; the *Daily News* had championed the Liberal cause steadily from its foundation. The *News Chronicle* is mainly owned by the Cadbury family, and its circulation is about 1,400,000. In the years immediately following the amalgamation it would have been correctly described as 'independent Liberal'. But the divisions in the Liberal party, and the conversion of so many Liberals either to the Conservative or to the Labour cause changed the character of its own readership; and the description which it would probably be most ready to accept is 'independent progressive'.

The *News Chronicle* is read, not only by Liberals and by persons of no fixed political allegiance, but by many Labour readers who prefer the vigour, and even the vagaries, of its columns to the official orthodoxy of the *Daily Herald*. This newspaper was founded as an independent militant Labour weekly and was converted into a daily in 1912. It became a weekly again in the first world war, but was re-issued as a daily in 1919. As an independent Labour newspaper it failed to attract many readers, and was in danger of failing financially. In 1929 Odhams Press Ltd. and the Trades Union Congress made arrangements for converting the newspaper into an official Labour organ and putting it on a sounder financial basis. Since that date fifty-one per cent of the shares have been held by Odhams Press Ltd. and forty-nine per cent by the Trades Union Congress. Odhams is a highly successful publishing firm with no special political views and with a wide variety of newspapers under its control. Opponents of socialism take some pleasure in pointing to it as a very successful example of capitalism in practice. The majority financial holding of Odhams ensures that the business arrangements of the newspaper are kept on sound lines. But the agreement reached in 1929 lays down that in political matters the policy of the *Daily Herald*

---

[1] By the conversion of the existing *Clerkenwell News*.

shall be that of the annual conference of the Labour party and in industrial matters that of the general council of the Trades Union Congress. Effect is given to this agreement through the board of directors. There are five directors appointed by Odhams and four by the Trades Union Congress, and where no official policy for the party has been laid down in the last resort the four T.U.C. directors decide. In many matters it is obvious what line the newspaper should take in the light of this agreement, but there are a large number where the indications are far from obvious. In these cases there has to be hurried consultations with political or industrial leaders, or the newspaper is compelled to 'hedge' until the party line has become clear. As a result of the arrangements made in 1929 the circulation was rapidly increased to over 2,000,000 a day, and it is still in the neighbourhood of that figure.

The *Financial Times* may be included in the list of national morning newspapers inasmuch as it includes much general political news. Like the *Daily Telegraph*, as already indicated, it is owned by Lord Camrose, and although its pages are mainly occupied with financial intelligence it also expresses in its leading articles an independent Conservatism.

The *Daily Worker* is published by the Daily Worker Co-operative Society Ltd., and is the official organ of the Communist party of Great Britain. Shares in the Daily Worker Co-operative Society Ltd. are held by readers, and the *Daily Worker* is claimed to be 'the only daily newspaper owned by its readers'.[1] It had its origin in the *Sunday Worker*, founded in 1925, which was converted into a daily in 1930 as a protest against the 'betrayal' of the *Daily Herald* to a capitalist group. Its circulation has never been large, and it is obliged to appeal to its readers from time to time for subscriptions to keep itself in existence.

An interesting national newspaper published in London daily is the *Morning Advertiser*. This journal was founded as far back as 1794 and is owned by the Incorporated Society of Licensed Victuallers. It is described as 'independent and anti-prohibitionist', and it would use its influence against any party that tried to restrict unduly facilities for drinking; but as this is not a live issue, and as it does not normally take a partisan attitude to other political questions, and as moreover its circulation is not large, it is unnecessary to particularize further.

This list of national morning newspapers published in London is completed by two illustrated journals.

---

[1] This is perhaps not quite fair to *Reynolds News*, which is owned by the Co-operative movement and, being mainly read by co-operators, may be looked upon as a newspaper owned by its readers.

The *Daily Sketch* was founded in 1909, but was bought by the Berry brothers in 1926 and merged with the *Daily Graphic*. In the division of the Berry interests in 1937, Lord Kemsley took the *Daily Graphic and Daily Sketch*. In 1952 it was acquired by Associated Newspapers Ltd., and early in 1953 it was announced that the *News of the World* would be linked with it, and that it would be known in future again as the *Daily Sketch*. Its politics remain to be seen.

The *Daily Mirror* was founded in 1903 by the Harmsworths, but is now owned by a limited company, Daily Mirror Newspapers Ltd. The ultimate financial control and the policy of the newspaper have been the subject of much unnecessary speculation in recent years. The policy has always been in recent years 'anti-Tory', but of a far more virulent character than that of the official Labour party or the *Daily Herald*. It is perhaps best classed as 'independent anti-Conservative'.

There are several morning newspapers published in the provinces that have a national influence. Among them the *Manchester Guardian* and the *Yorkshire Post* are pre-eminent. The *Manchester Guardian* has long been the most thoughtful exponent of radical Liberalism, but it has no official connexions with the Liberal party; its policy has been reached by its staff under a succession of able editors, and may best be described as 'independent radicalism'. The *Yorkshire Post* is owned by a company known as Yorkshire Conservative Newspapers Ltd., and as the name suggests it gives general support to Conservative policy; but it has no official connexions with the party. The *Scotsman* and the *Glasgow Herald* have a national influence in that important part of the kingdom that lies north of the border. Neither has official party connexions, but the *Scotsman* is commonly classified as Unionist; and the *Glasgow Herald*, though commonly listed as independent, is generally in harmony with the views of the Conservative and Unionist party.

A strong local influence is exercised in many regions of Great Britain by newspapers published in provincial towns. Many of these belong to groups of newspapers, of which the Berry, the Starmer and the Harmsworth are the most important from the point of view of party politics. In these groups the editors have varying degrees of freedom to express their views and present the news in their own way, but it is natural for them, when dealing with national as opposed to local issues, to rely on the views formed in their London offices by colleagues who have better opportunities of reaching a sound judgement. When the Berry interests were divided in 1937, the provincial newspapers fell to Lord Kemsley, and are in the main owned by or through a limited liability company known as Allied Newspapers Ltd. The newspapers of this group support the Conservative party. The Starmer group is so called after a former managing director, the late Sir Charles Starmer, and the name of the owning company is Westminster Press Provincial Newspapers Ltd. The Cowdray (Pearson[1]) family has financial control, the Rowntrees have also been represented on the board, and the antecedents of the group are Liberal. It once included a Liberal daily the *Westminster Gazette*, and when this was amalgamated with the *Daily News* in 1927 the group retained an interest in that paper and later in the *News Chronicle* until 1936. The London editor of the group is a former Liberal candidate for Parliament, Mr. Norman Robson.[2] But the group has no official connexions with the Liberal party and no longer attempts to pursue a common Liberal policy. The local editors are left free to follow their own views of what national policy should be, and this is also the aim of any guidance given from London. The provincial newspapers of the Harmsworth group are mainly owned by Associated Newspapers Ltd., and their political stand is perhaps best regarded as 'independent'.

The evening newspapers are nearly all 'stable companions' of morning newspapers, but political partisanship is even less marked in the evening newspapers than in the morning. Not infrequently an evening newspaper, making a substantial profit from sporting news, is used by the the proprietors to finance a more serious morning newspaper. Owing to problems of distribution, none of the evening newspapers can have a national influence. The London evening newspapers, now reduced to three, come nearest to having such an influence; and they also have more political news and views than their provincial sisters. The *Evening Standard*, founded in 1827 and now owned by Lord Beaverbrook, may be classified, like the *Daily Express*, as 'independent', but on the whole has been a more consistent supporter of Conservative policy; the *Evening News*, founded in 1881, and now the evening counterpart of the *Daily Mail*, may be regarded as 'independent Conservative', and the *Star*, founded in 1888 and issued from the same presses as the *News Chronicle*, is 'independent progressive'. The evening papers in the provincial groups present even less of a party

---

[1] There is no connexion with Sir Arthur Pearson, founder of the *Daily Express*.
[2] It may introduce some readers to the more agreeable side of party politics, and help to explain why the party system works, if I state that Mr. Robson was my Liberal opponent in the contest at Keighley in the General Election of 1945 when I was the successful Labour candidate. In 1949, when Mr. Robson had become the London editor of this group, and I had joined the Conservative party, he invited me to write leading articles on foreign affairs in which he knew that I had interested myself. I was touched by this stretching of the hand across party barriers, and readily did so for the next few years.

aspect than the morning papers, and in most other provincial papers it is hard to detect a party bias.

Except for the two high-class Sunday newspapers, the *Sunday Times* and the *Observer*, politics play a subordinate part in the Sunday press. The *Sunday Times* is owned by Lord Kemsley, and like the other newspapers in his ownership gives its distinguished support to Conservative policy. The *Sunday Graphic* and several provincial Sunday papers are also owned by Lord Kemsley. The *Observer* is owned in the family of Viscount Astor, but it has not been possible in recent years to discern any consistent political attitude in it, and it is best described as 'independent'. *Reynolds News* is owned by the Co-operative Press Ltd. an organ of the Co-operative movement, and expresses the views of the Labour and Co-operative parties; the main political feature is a weekly commentary by the Labour member of Parliament, Mr. Thomas Driberg. The *Sunday Pictorial*, which is the Sunday companion of the *Daily Mirror*, shares the 'independent anti-Conservative' outlook of that journal, and has a weekly political commentary by a Labour member, Mr. Richard Crossman. The *People* is published by Odhams, but no such arrangements have been made with the Trades Union Congress as for the *Daily Herald*, and the politics of the *People* are not aggressive. The main political feature of the *Sunday Express*, the Sunday companion of the *Daily Express*, is a political commentary by a member of the staff using the *nom-de-guerre* 'Crossbencher'; it deals more with personalities than with policies, and members of all parties have borne the searchlight directed on them with such composure as they may. The *News of the World*, which has a circulation of over 7,000,000 copies —incredible if it were not fully authenticated—keeps strictly aloof from any party allegiances; nor do the politics of any other Sunday newspaper, London or provincial, call for comment. With the exception of the high-class papers mentioned, and a few others, the Sunday press in general serves out the recipe prescribed by Kennedy Jones for a high circulation—crime, women and sport.

There are five weekly organs of opinion that make a contribution to the formation of party opinion. The *Economist*, founded in 1843, is a carefully written journal, ranging far beyond purely economic matters; it is closely studied in all parties and forms the basis of not a few of the best speeches in Parliament. It is owned by a limited liability company, the Economist Newspaper Ltd., of which the chairman is the well-known Liberal peer, Lord Layton. But the responsibility of the editor, at present Mr. Geoffrey Crowther, is unfettered, and the *Economist* is in every sense of the word independent. The *Spectator* is also in the fullest sense of the word independent, and is, indeed, at present edited by Mr. Wilson Harris, who was an independent member of Parliament for Cambridge University until his seat was abolished. *Time and Tide* used to described itself as 'Independent Non-party', but on 6 October 1951 it dropped the words 'non-party' and adopted the description 'The Independent Weekly'. It still remains unattached to any party, the chief proprietor being Viscountess Rhondda, and it is as independent as the *Economist* or the *Spectator*; but the term 'non-party' was dropped because it did not appear that the objectives of the paper could be obtained by neutrality in the struggle between the parties. *Time and Tide* has, in fact, come to the conclusion that its objectives cannot be obtained through the Labour party, but it still remains free to criticize any party.[1] The *New Statesman and Nation* differs from the three organs already mentioned in being a professedly socialist newspaper. But it has no organic connexion with the Labour party or the Trades Union Congress, being owned by a limited liability company in which a number of socialist individuals have shares; and the socialism which it professes under the editorship of Mr. Kingsley Martin has often been more embarrassing to the Labour party leaders than the *Economist*, the *Spectator* or *Time and Tide* has ever been. *Tribune* is an independent socialist organ founded more recently, at first published weekly, then fortnightly, and since 26 September 1952 weekly once more. It is owned by a limited liability company, Tribune Publications Ltd., in which individual socialists hold shares, and its editorial board consists of four 'Bevanite' members of Parliament. It exists to win support within the Labour party for the distinctive views of Mr. Aneurin Bevan and his associates.

BOOKS AND PAMPHLETS

The political influence of books and pamphlets over the centuries has been immense, and may exist long after the death of the author. The Labour Government's work from 1945 to 1950 was the practical achievement of *Fabian Essays* published in 1884, and the *Communist Manifesto* published by Marx and Engels in 1847 is still creating tides of human emotion among people who have never read a line of it. All parties regard the production of political pamphlets as a main activity. The output of such pamphlets every year is considerable, and they are often published below their cost price. Few are of perma-

---

[1] 'We are tied to no party, but we are committed to oppose any party that believes in nationalization and controls.' (*Time and Tide*, 6 October 1951.)

nent or even lasting significance, but their cumulative effect is far from negligible. In contrast, the parties have seldom commissioned, subsidized or lent any support to the production of books—though the longer pamphlets may be regarded as booklets; and such books as have been helped are usually historical. The production of books is still the most individualistic and the most competitive of all forms of private enterprise. We can say of books only that the wind bloweth where it listeth; but naturally when a good book supporting the party aim appears on the stalls there is rejoicing in the party headquarters and it may be commended for reading.

BROADCASTING AND TELEVISION

Owing to the monopoly of broadcasting enjoyed by the British Broadcasting Corporation, this medium for reaching the public has not presented the same problem as the press to the parties. In this case the problem is to ensure that the B.B.C. as such preserves an attitude of strict impartiality between the parties and that the time allotted to political broadcasting is fairly distributed between the parties. The corporation is deeply conscious of the responsibility and is keenly watched by the parties. A distinction is made between 'party political broadcasts', whether during general elections or at other times, and ordinary talks bearing on politics.

In the case of 'party political broadcasts' the scripts are not seen in advance by the corporation, and no responsibility is assumed by the B.B.C. either for the choice of speakers or for the content of their talks. The only problem for the corporation is to ensure that the total time set aside for such broadcasts bears a fair relation to the total time available for broadcasting, bearing in mind that certain hours are more popular with listeners than others; and to ensure that the time given is fairly distributed between the parties. In view of the fairly even division of opinion between the Conservative and Labour parties, it is easy to decide that these two parties must be given the same number of hours on the air, and when there is thought to be any advantage in a choice of date, as in winding up an election series, no one will contest that the party forming the Government of the day is entitled to this position; in fact, the Prime Minister of the day always concludes the series of election broadcasts. The only difficulty that arises is in allocating time to the minor parties. In the series of general election broadcasts the rough-and-ready rule is adopted that a party putting a certain number of candidates into the field is entitled to a certain time on the air. The

Liberal party has always qualified, and the Communist party occasionally. These arrangements have given general satisfaction, though there has naturally been some criticism from the minor parties.

The corporation's problem is greater in the case of other political talks, or broadcasts that may have a bearing on politics, and in particular the presentation of the news. This last matter is of special importance, because the preparation of the news bulletins is the direct and sole responsibility of the corporation, and because they are listened to more than any other feature. The work has often to be done at great speed—not infrequently a fresh item of news is placed in front of the reader after he has started broadcasting—and an inflexion of the voice could be more partisan than the most brazen headline in a party newspaper. No doubt errors of judgement occur from time to time, but the strict impartiality of the corporation and its readers is not seriously questioned. Though the corporation's responsibility in the matter of talks other than party political broadcasts is not quite so direct, the fact that the speakers are chosen by the B.B.C., that it insists on seeing the scripts in advance, and that it not infrequently suggests changes in the scripts implies that the B.B.C. assumes responsibility. In the case of the Saturday talks entitled 'The Week in Westminster' given during the session by members of Parliament, the corporation gives equal representation to Conservatives and Labour, with appropriate representation to Liberals; and in the past the Independents have also had a fair share of representation. To forestall criticism, the B.B.C. has normally relied on the party whips to suggest speakers, and the only criticism that can be made is that this has sometimes given the listening public the most faithful members of the parties instead of the best broadcasters. In the case of other political talks, the corporation seems rather nervous of inviting members of Parliament or candidates lest it should provoke criticism, and tends to look outside the ranks of the parties. It would be too much to say that the choice of speakers and their subject matter have escaped criticism. The parties and the newspapers are ever vigilant, and the B.B.C. has sometimes erred; but its errors have been committed through inadvertence rather than through intent. The wish of the corporation to preserve neutrality between the parties is not seriously questioned. The anxieties of the B.B.C. do not end with the news and the talks, for there is hardly any feature that could not in some circumstances give rise to criticisms of partisanship. Plays have not infrequently been a subject of contention, and *Party Manners* in particular was withdrawn after strong criticism in the *Daily Herald*. Unscripted 'gags' by comedians have to be specially watched, and have given rise to trouble. It is recognized, however, that in such cases the B.B.C. is not to blame and that it has always done its best to rectify any damage.

What has been written about broadcasting may be applied also to the medium of television. This was employed for the first time in the party battle during the general election of 1951. It had no small effect on that occasion, not only among the direct viewers but through newspaper reproductions, and it is likely to become increasingly important. On that occasion Conservative, Labour and Liberal speakers were shown on the screen, and effective use was made of graphs of the cost of living. It may be taken for granted that the B.B.C. will adopt the same canons of impartiality between the parties as those that have been worked out for broadcasting.

PARTY LITERATURE

Though the main impact of the parties on the nation is exerted through the independent newspapers and the B.B.C., most parties issue their own literature, occasional and periodical, with a view to maintaining the enthusiasm of members, winning converts and supplying information to the press. Not only do the party headquarters issue periodical literature, but many Conservative associations and local Labour parties, and some Liberal associations, have their own magazines. The National Union of Conservative and Unionist Associations has an advisory committee on political education and an advisory committee on publicity and speakers. The Conservative Central Office has a group of departments concerned with these matters under a chief publicity officer. An important development has been the establishment by the Central Office in 1945 of the Conservative Political Centre, with bookshops in London, Leeds, Newcastle and Cardiff. Among the periodical literature issued by the Conservative party are the *Weekly News Letter*, *Notes on Current Politics* (fortnightly), *Tory Challenge* (incorporating *The Onlooker*, monthly), the *Monthly Survey of Foreign Affairs*, *The Councillor Advance* (the magazine of the Young Conservative and Unionist Organization, every two months), and *Objective*, the journal of the Conservative Political Centre. The Labour Party maintains at Transport House a press and publicity department under the control of a secretary. The following periodicals are issued: *Labour Press Service* (monthly), *Fact* (monthly), *The Labour Woman* (monthly), *Labour Organizer* (monthly), *Advance* (the League of Youth journal, monthly), and *Talking Points* (twice monthly). The Liberal party maintains a press publicity department and a publications department; the only periodical publication now is *The Liberal News*. The Liberal International publishes a quarterly magazine, *World Liberalism*, with supplements, which is read by many individual Liberals in Great Britain. Apart from the *Daily Worker*, the Communist party line can be obtained every week in *World News and Views*, containing articles on international affairs and every month in *Communist Review*, and young Communists are provided weekly with a paper entitled *Challenge*. The Welsh Nationalist party issues two monthly papers, *Y Ddraig Goch* ('The Red Dragon') in Welsh and *The Welsh Nation* in English.

In leaving this subject we may observe that neither the number of newspapers supporting a party nor their total circulation bears in modern times any ascertainable relationship to its hold upon public opinion as measured by its success at the polls. According to Kennedy Jones,[1] in 1906 eighty per cent of the London press and the majority of the provincial daily newspapers were in favour of tariff reform, but Joseph Chamberlain's proposals were overwhelmingly rejected at that time by the nation. The Labour party came to office though it could count on the consistent support of only its one official newspaper, and it achieved its greatest triumph in 1945 when supported by only two national daily newspapers. From 1918 onwards Northcliffe turned the full blast of his newspapers against Lloyd George, but the Prime Minister was able to hold his position until the Conservative party withdrew its support in 1922. Lord Beaverbrook and Lord Rothermere in 1930–31 campaigned in their widely read newspapers in favour of Empire free trade and against Baldwin's leadership of the Conservative party. Baldwin with his hands firmly on the party machine won a complete victory. To consider all the implications of these facts would take us too far afield into a study of the so-called power of the press[2]; but it should be borne in mind that the number of leading articles written in support of a party is no reliable index to its prospects at the polls.

[1] *Fleet Street and Downing Street*, p. 3.
[2] This is the theme of Kennedy Jones's book; and although the tone of that work may be deprecated, his cynically low estimate of the influence of the mass-circulation newspapers that he did so much to create may be accepted. The high-class newspapers, and especially *The Times*, the *Daily Telegraph*, the *Manchester Guardian* and the *Yorkshire Post*, have, however, all shown in recent years that they have power to influence the course of events.

XX

Parties and Religion

IN HIS ROMANES LECTURE at Oxford in 1926[1] Dr. G. M. Trevelyan set before himself the task of discussing 'how far and in what sense there was a continuity of life linking the party of Shaftesbury and Somers to that of Fox and Grey, the party of Danby and Bolingbroke to that of the younger Pitt and Canning'.[2] His conclusion is that 'the continuity was to be found mainly in the unbroken connexion of the Tories with the Church interest, and of the Whig aristocrats with the Protestant Noncomformist voters'.[3]

This identification of the Tory cause with the Church and the Whig cause with the Noncomformists persisted throughout the nineteenth century when the Tories became Conservatives and the Whigs gave way to the Liberals. There were paradoxes in this situation, not the least in that the churchman Gladstone[4] became the venerated leader of the Liberals and the Jew Disraeli the leader of the Conservatives. It could hardly have been forecast from their early manhood that Gladstone would have introduced the measure to disestablish the Irish Church or Disraeli the Public Worship Regulation Act. But the paradox is always in the persons; the attachment of the Conservatives to the Church and the Liberals to the Protestant Noncomformists was almost unbroken. Towards the end of the century, when Nonconformists began to espouse the teetotal cause, the Liberal party became increasingly identified also with 'prohibition' or 'local option'[5]; and conversely the Conservatives became identified, at any rate in the minds of their opponents, with 'the trade'. It was no doubt in this period that the Church of England was mockingly described as 'the Conservative party at prayer'.

There are a few pockets in the country where the identification of

---

[1] *An Autobiography and other Essays*, pp. 183–99. [2] *Ibid.*, p. 185.
[3] *Ibid.*, p. 197.
[4] I grew up in a Baptist Liberal home in Monmouthshire under the impression that Gladstone was a Welshman and a Nonconformist. It was with no little surprise that I later learnt that he was a high churchman and was 'of unmixed Scottish origins' (Morley, *Life*, chap. I, ii). His residence at Hawarden no doubt helped to account for the belief that he was a Welshman.
[5] When Gladstone's son Herbert (later Viscount Gladstone) was elected M.P. for Leeds he became—perhaps it would be true to say he felt it necessary to become—a teetotaller.

the Conservatives with the Church (together with freedom in the matter of liquid refreshment) and the Liberals with the Protestant Nonconformists (together with the curtailment of freedom in this matter) still persists. I have already mentioned[1] the remark with which I was greeted at my first election in Spen Valley: 'Call yourself a Socialist! Why, you drink and go to church; you're nothing but a Tory!' But this division of the parties on religious grounds practically died with the first world war. Its last great manifestation was the Welsh Church Disestablishment Act, introduced by the Liberals and so strongly opposed by the Conservatives that it was placed on the statute book in 1914 only with the help of the new Parliament Act. There were the familiar paradoxes which the Victorian examples already cited would lead us to expect. The measure was denounced by the Conservative F. E. Smith (later Lord Birkenhead), whose support for the Church was, like Melbourne's, in the nature of a buttress rather than of a pillar,[2] as 'a bill which has shocked the conscience of every Christian community in Europe'; and Smith was in turn denounced in a poem of blistering invective by the doughty churchman, G. K. Chesterton.[3] But the paradoxes were again in the persons; the parties remained true to their history.

This division of the parties along religious lines was shattered after the first world war. The main reasons were the marked decline in religious observance that followed the war; the collapse of the Liberal party, with which the Protestant Nonconformists had been so closely identified; the rise of the Labour party, which had no historical religious adherence; changes in the social background and the political allegiance of the clergy and to some extent of the laity of the Church of England; the social and economic advancement of the Protestant Nonconformists; and the rise of the Roman Catholics from the position of a small minority to that of a relatively substantial fraction of the worshipping population. As a result of the decline in the hold of religion upon the mass of the people, the great national parties began to feel that religion was not a question upon which they could properly align themselves— that religion was a matter to which, in the original sense of the word, they should be indifferent. It has now become the invariable practice in Parliament to permit a free vote on questions affecting the doctrine,

---

[1] *V. supra,* p. vi *n.*

[2] Lord Melbourne is, I believe, the first, though not the last, statesman who is reputed to have said that his support for the Church was more of the nature of a buttress than of a pillar—he supported it from the outside.

[3] *Antichrist, or the Reunion of Christendom: an Ode,* by G. K. Chesterton, *Poems,* pp. 87–89.

ceremonial and discipline of a religious body, even when that body is the established Church of the land. This was notably shown in 1927 and 1928 in the parliamentary debates on the revision of the Book of Common Prayer. These debates indicated that, despite the decline in religious attendance, there was an immense latent interest in religious questions, but the interest cut right across party lines. Supporters and opponents of the revision were to be found in all parliamentary parties. The collapse of the Liberal party made Nonconformists, themselves a declining force, reluctant to identify themselves inestricably with its fortunes; and the fact that so many Nonconformists had risen to positions of affluence and influence, especially in the world of commerce, had already led many of them within the fold of the Conservative party. The great majority of Conservative peers and members of Parliament continued to regard themselves as members of the Church of England, but no surprise was felt when Neville Chamberlain, a Unitarian, and Kingsley Wood, a Methodist, rose to dominating positions in the party and eventually occupied Numbers 10 and 11 Downing Street. The Church of England had been going through a transformation no less profound. In the nineteenth century its bishops and priests had been drawn almost without exception from the upper and middle classes, and their family associations inclined most of them to the Conservative party: the hierarchy and the 'squirearchy' were allied by social interest and consanguinity. But in the present century the clergymen of the Church of England have been drawn from all social strata. Such institutions as the College of Resurrection at Mirfield and the House of the Sacred Mission at Kelham were founded to ensure that all young men who had a genuine sense of vocation should be enabled to proceed to ordination whatever their means. In the course of half a century this process has filled the benefices of the Church of England with men who do not by their early upbringing feel an instinctive attachment to the Conservative party; and many of those who had received the traditional upbringing were led to different political views either by academic reflexion or by work in the slums and industrial towns, where the new socialist philosophy was making rapid headway. It was a sign of the times when William Temple, a former member of the Labour Party was appointed to the see of Canterbury on the recommendation of a Conservative Prime Minister. There had been two much criticized appointments of Socialist dignitaries on the recommendation of MacDonald—Dr. E. W. Barnes to the see of Birmingham in 1924—and Dr. Hewlett Johnson to two successive deaneries—but these appointments were widely resented in the Church. Temple's appointment on the recommendation of Mr. Churchill was of a different order, for it was inconceivable that anyone else should have been appointed; and although he had resigned from the Labour party in 1938 on a question of foreign policy, it was the only party to which he had ever belonged and his appointment showed how far the Church of England had travelled since it was first dubbed 'the Conservative party at prayer'. The Labour party in the meantime had also travelled far. In the words of its secretary, Mr. Morgan Phillips, to the international socialist conference at Copenhagen on 2 June 1950, British socialism was 'Methodist, not Marxist'; but perhaps he would more accurately have said that the Labour party contains both Marxist and Methodist elements. The Marxist element accounts for the fact that many of the early members of the Labour party were identified in the popular mind with atheism or agnosticism. The Methodist element was typified by Arthur Henderson. In the light of these opposing tendencies the Labour party adopted a strict neutrality in religious matters. As the years passed, the Labour party began to attract men who were neither Marxists nor Methodists, and several of its leaders in recent years have acknowledged a religious allegiance to the Church of England. Mr. Attlee himself is a member of the Church of England who had a brother in holy orders; the late Sir Stafford Cripps was the son of a great churchman, and the Christian religion as practised in the Church of England was the inspiration of his life, and especially his later years; nor are these all. The agnostic or frankly atheistic element remains in the Labour party, but it is recognized that such opinions are purely private.

It is probable that the great majority of Roman Catholics in Great Britain vote Labour, but this is a social and economic rather than a religious phenomenon. It arises from the fact that the great majority of Roman Catholics in Great Britain are of Irish origin, and the Irish immigrants have naturally belonged to the poorer strata of the population and have tended to vote Labour. The Irish immigrants are largely concentrated in Liverpool, Glasgow and Cardiff, and in those cities have helped to send many Labour members to Parliament. But there is no necessary connexion between the Roman Catholic Church in Great Britain and the Labour party. It is, indeed, rather paradoxical, in the light of so many papal pronouncements on the incompatibility of Christianity and socialism, that the vast majority of Roman Catholics in this country vote Labour; it is explained, by those who have the duty of explaining, that British socialism is very different from the socialism of the continent, which the popes have had in mind. It is also the case that, apart from the Irish immigration, Roman Catholics in

Great Britain do not tend to vote Labour, and some of their best-known apologists express views that may be regarded as ultra-Tory. There are a few converts, such as Lord Pakenham, who have adhered to the political views that they held before their change of religious allegiance, but most members of old Roman Catholic families and Roman Catholics of foreign extraction tend on the whole to be anti-Labour.

A glance at the House of Commons in recent years would suggest that Jews have a closer connexion with the Labour party than with any other. There has certainly been a strong preponderance of Jews on the Labour benches, but in this respect the House of Commons is not entirely representative of the country. As with Roman Catholics, the political views of Jews in Great Britain are largely correlated with social and economic differences. Jews are, in fact, to be found in all parties; and if there are more Labour or Communist voters in British Jewry than Conservative or Liberal this signifies only that British Jews on the whole are to be found among those social and economic groups where the Labour and Communist parties draw their strongest support.

At the present time it is therefore true that religious divisions cut across parties and party divisions cut across religion. A member of a British political party may have any religious views or none, nor can we even say that there is a probability that a member of any given party will hold a particular set of religious views. His religious beliefs have become, like the colour of his hair, a personal question in regard to which the party is neutral. But this does not mean that the parties regard religion as a matter of no consequence. All parties except possibly the Communist would frown upon an attempt to identify them with materialistic or atheistic views, and even the Communist party would regard opposition to religion as inopportune and tactless. The main parties have gone even farther along the way of showing their benevolence towards religion. The annual conference of the Labour party at Margate in 1947 was preceded by a service in the parish church at which the Archbishop of Canterbury preached, and the next conference of the Conservative party, at Llandudno in 1948, was also opened with a religious service.[1]

As religious differences cut across parties, and the parties cut across religious beliefs, it would be impossible in Great Britain at the present time to create a party founded on religious beliefs. The religious dif-

[1] Some commentators saw a political significance in the choice of the hymn, 'Lead, kindly light, Amid th' encircling gloom', and others in the line 'Remember not past years', which shows the pitfalls that the organizers of such services must avoid.

ferences are in any case too great to hope for the creation of a single Christian party, but even the idea of a Church party, a Free Church party or a Roman Catholic party would find little support owing to the differing political allegiances within these religious groups. The idea of a party based on religion has been mooted from time to time, and a Christian Democratic candidate has even appeared at the general election of 1950, but existing political allegiances are too strong. On the continent parties that are openly or in fact composed of adherents of the Roman Catholic religion, and exist largely to support Roman Catholic aims, are common; under varying names such parties have for several years provided the main elements in the governments of Italy, the Federal Republic of Germany, and Austria, and are powerful in France and the Netherlands. But the conditions that permit their existence do not exist in Great Britain. In Italy and Austria and even in France nearly all Christians are Roman Catholics; and in Germany and the Netherlands there is a sharp division into Catholics and Protestants, unlike the many gradations in Great Britain. Moreover in none of these countries is there a strong two-party system with a long history behind it. The conditions are therefore far more favourable on the continent than in Great Britain for the creation of a Roman Catholic party; and if it were seriously proposed, there can be no doubt that it would meet with the strenuous opposition of leading Roman Catholics in the main parties.

A speech made by Dr. Richard Downey, the Roman Catholic Archbishop of Liverpool in that city on 24 November 1951 was widely interpreted as meaning that he wished to see a Roman Catholic party, but this was denied by him on 13 February 1952. In his original speech he hoped that the equal division of the parties would go on for some time 'because the longer it goes on, the stronger will be our influence as a Catholic body, and I think we may yet get the privilege of holding the balance of power'.[1] It could be argued that a body holding the balance of power between the parties for any length of time would itself be indistinguishable from a party, but Dr. Downey in his second speech pointed out that on first coming to Liverpool a quarter of a century before he had urged the dissolution of the Roman Catholic party in the city council, so that Roman Catholics might be free to work through any party; and it is clear that by 'holding the balance of power' he was referring only to occasional decisive interventions in questions in which Roman Catholics are specially interested. This is an attitude that no doubt commends itself to those Roman Catholics who have no strong

[1] *The Observer*, 25 November 1951.

interest in party politics, but can hardly commend itself to those who are playing an active rôle in one party or the other.

THE SCHOOLS QUESTION

The main question over which a conflict of allegiance might arise for a Christian member of a political party is that of the schools. A system of elementary education was provided by Church and other voluntary schools long before the State took the task in hand, and in these days of advancing educational standards the financial problems of bringing these schools into line with the requirements of the educational authorities are substantial. The solution of handing the schools over to the state is not one that many Christians care to contemplate, holding that they have done a duty to bring up their children in their own beliefs and not being satisfied that this duty would be adequately discharged by State schools. In point of numbers of schools the problem is largest for the Church of England, but the solution reached in the Education Act, 1944 has commended itself to most Anglicans, and for them the schools are ceasing to be a political problem; some Church schools will pass into the ownership of local education authorities, others will be brought up to the required standards and retained as Church schools, while the act of worship and religious instruction in the State schools, though not fulfilling all that an Anglican parent might wish, are recognized as a genuine attempt to meet a real difficulty. Though the number of Roman Catholic schools is much smaller, the danger of political conflict is greater, inasmuch as Roman Catholics will not be content with anything short of a full Roman Catholic education for all their children. They would be willing to see the dual system abolished if Roman Catholic instruction in a Roman Catholic atmosphere were given for all Roman Catholic children in State schools; but as this proposal has not found favour, in practice Roman Catholics concentrate on securing sufficient public funds to ensure that their schools are brought up to the required standards. For this purpose at all recent elections a deputation of Roman Catholic laymen has sought an interview with each candidate. In church on the Sunday before the poll it has become customary for the priest to advise his flock that they should not vote for candidates whose answers are regarded as unsatisfactory, but may without sin vote for any candidate whose answers are regarded as satisfactory.

This practice can be justified but has obvious dangers. Any elector is entitled to inquire what are the views of a candidate, and the practice of sending a deputation for that purpose is well established. Provided that a priest does not transgress the law by threatening spiritual penalties, he is entitled to advise all those in his spiritual care who seek his advice. But if candidates commit themselves in advance of election to specific policies involving large sums of public money, without hearing the arguments fully put and chiefly through fear of losing votes, it will be the end of parliamentary democracy. There is no reason why this practice, which in its cruder forms can hardly be distinguished from blackmail, should be confined to the single question of the schools; the same technique could be applied by all interested bodies to all questions.[1] The chief safeguard so far against its misuse has been that the two main parties, which co-operated in the passage of the Education Act, 1944, have adopted a basically identical attitude towards its revision. Any candidate who commits himself to a radical alteration in the basis of aid for provided schools has been made aware that he may get into difficulties in the House if elected.[2] Most candidates of the major parties give a cautious answer when approached by such deputations, possibly referring the questioners to official party statements. If the main candidates give the same broad answer to the deputation, the technique breaks down; and this is what has tended to happen. The existence of this practice nevertheless deserves close study, and the first requirement is to find out what happens in as many constituencies as possible.[3] It may perhaps be suggested to the Roman Catholic hierarchy that the advantages gained from it in the shape of pledges from a certain number of members are outweighed by the resentment of those who have the responsibility for shaping policy in their various parties.

RELIGIOUS VIEWS OF CANDIDATES

The last question that needs to be asked is whether a person's religious views are a help or a hindrance when he seeks to become a candidate or a member. There are some constituencies where religious views are

[1] Indeed, it has been employed on many occasions in the matter of old-age pensions, and occasionally in the matter of service pensions.

[2] *V. infra*, p. 264, for the Labour party's attitude.

[3] As a contribution to such a study I may mention that in one election in which I have taken part there were three candidates interviewed by a deputation of Roman Catholic laymen. In the Roman Catholic churches on the Sunday before polling the congregations were informed that the answers of the Conservative and Liberal candidates had been satisfactory and that of the Labour candidate unsatisfactory. There was consternation in the Labour camp, for there was a large Roman Catholic population that in the main voted Labour; and the Labour candidate explained by advertisements in the press and in other ways that there had been a misunderstanding. It was then made known that his answer was now satisfactory, and he won by a large majority.

a factor. In particular, there are a number of divisions of Liverpool and Glasgow, peopled largely by Irish immigrants or their descendents, where it is an advantage to profess the Roman Catholic faith. But it is by no means a decisive factor, and there is abundant evidence that political allegiances are stronger than religious affinities. The classic case is the success of Mrs. E. M. Braddock, who makes no religious profession, in the Exchange division of Liverpool, where it is admitted that the Roman Catholic vote is preponderant. Standing as the Labour candidate in 1945, she wrested the seat from Sir John Shute, a leading Roman Catholic of the city who had held it since 1933. At the general election of 1950 she repeated her success against another Roman Catholic, Sir John Reynolds, and confirmed it in 1951 with a third victory against another Roman Catholic opponent, Mr. J. O. Tiernan.

In other parts of the country it is probable that the local associations would prefer, other things being equal, that their candidate should not be a Roman Catholic. But the words 'other things being equal' must be borne in mind, for if a Roman Catholic candidate has superior qualifications there are few associations that would regard his religious allegiance as an impediment. In the present House of Commons there are twenty-one Roman Catholic members, of whom fifteen are Labour, four Conservative, and two Irish Nationalists. In a House of 625 members, this does not over-represent the Roman Catholic element in the population. It is 3·4 per cent of the whole membership. The Roman Catholic population of England and Wales was estimated in *The Catholic Directory* for 1951 at 2,837,700 which is 6·6 per cent of the total population.

In contrast, the proportion of Jews elected to Parliament is considerably higher than the proportion of Jews in the whole population. The number of Jewish members in the present House of Commons is seventeen—all of them Labour members. This is 2·7 per cent of the whole membership, whereas the 450,000 Jews in Great Britain are just about 1 per cent of the total population. A curious fact is that the only constituency where the Jewish electors are sufficiently numerous to determine the issue—Mile End—has not had a Jewish member since 1945. (Mr. Dan Frankel, a Jew, represented the constituency from 1935 to 1945.) It seems clear that Jewish electors do not necessarily seek a Jewish candidate, and that many constituencies where Jews are in a small minority are content to be represented by Jewish members. The question of religion is not regarded as so important as the candidate's personal qualifications and attitude to political questions.

Part V

Some Current Problems

CHAPTERS XXI–XXIII

K

XXI

Parties and Individuals

SINCE 1832 there has been an elaboration and strengthening of party organization until it seems to many people at the present time that the party is all-important and that the individual, whether candidate or member, counts for nothing.

An extreme view was expressed eight days before the poll in the general election of 1950 by Mr. Elton Halliley, Conservative agent for Bury St. Edmunds, who wrote an article in the *Sunday Dispatch* of 12 February 1950 answering the question, 'What is the secret of winning an election?' His answer was:

> 'I learned it 35 years ago from the lips of the greatest electioneering agent this country ever knew the late Sir Leigh MacLachlan, one-time chief organizer and principal agent to the Conservative Party, who said: "It's the machine that puts them in, my boy—the party machine can win any election if it is good enough. It could even put in a beer-glass."
> 'How right he was. The machine *can* just about put anybody into Parliament.'

Mr. Halliley presumably did not mean to imply that a sufficiently strong party machine could secure the election of a candidate in any constituency—that, for example, a good machine could put a Conservative candidate in for West Rhondda or a Labour candidate in for South Kensington. He conceded that certain constituencies in Wales and Durham might prove 'unbeatable' Labour strongholds, and there are equally unbeatable, though not quite so many, 'Conservative strongholds'. The implication of his remarks is presumably that the party machine could secure the return of any Labour candidate in West Rhondda or any Conservative candidate in South Kensington; that in a marginal division the effectiveness of the party machine may mean the difference between success and failure; and, in general, that a good party machine will pull out all the possible votes for the party's candidate, whoever he may be. To this theory he himself makes one or two qualifications, admitting, for example, that 'foreign and odd-sounding names might baffle the machine.' The private lives of candidates, once they become public property, may also qualify the general law. But

259

Mr. Halliley's principle, in the form in which it has been here re-stated, and with the qualifications mentioned, comes too near to the truth to be very comfortable. The difference between having one candidate and another to carry the party banner in a constituency election can be measured in hundreds of votes rather than in thousands. Most electors at the present time would vote for the adopted candidate of their party whoever he might be. They may dislike doing it; but they will do it nevertheless.

The tendency of modern electors to vote for parties rather than for candidates is borne out by some remarkable comments by Mr. Herbert Morrison in 1949 on advertisements by industries threatened with nationalization. Now that the dust of that conflict has settled, it may be worth recalling the circumstances on account of the constitutional principles involved. The national executive committee of the Labour party had issued a policy statement 'Labour believes in Britain' which asked for the nationalization of the cement, sugar and meat industries and the business of industrial assurance as well as the steel industry, to which the party was already committed; this document was subsequently endorsed by the party conference at Blackpool. The directors of the industries concerned had no wish to see them nationalized, and began to issue advertisements pointing out the services which those industries were rendering to the public under private enterprise. It was then that 'Mr. Cube' and 'Sir Loin' began to make their appearance on the hoardings and the public became aware that 'under private enterprise British cement is the cheapest in the world.' There was no mention at any point of any political party or any candidate for Parliament, but Mr. Herbert Morrison, speaking on 26 November 1949, said:

'For several months past enormous sums of money have been spent on covering the hoardings, putting advertisements in the newspapers, and so on, with propaganda which our opponents hope will help to procure the election of anti-Labour candidates when the time comes. I am not afraid of it. All the same this campaign, partly conducted by parties and partly in relation to predicted election issues by industrial and commercial concerns, does raise some very serious political and legal issues. Nobody objects to these concerns putting forward a reasoned statement of their views on nationalization or other matters affecting them. But when vested interests throw the full weight of their financial resources into political controversies, not by reasoned and objective statements of facts to M.P.s and candidates, or by speeches, etc., but by expensively publicized vote-catching slogans and wholly tendentious propaganda, grave questions arise, not simply from the point of view of individual shareholders whose money may be used for what in effect is party politics without their consent, but from that of the public, many of whom do business with the companies and pay for their goods or services.

'It would be a very dangerous thing if it were allowed to become a feature of our political life that big business could intervene in elections both by secret subscriptions to political funds and by direct large-scale propaganda campaigns calculated to influence the result. It must not be thought that the law as to permitted expenditure relates only to a period after the issue of the writs for an election. When the time comes for the returns of election expenses to be rendered, we must see whether all this vast expenditure is included and how these matters are dealt with.'

The law on the subject, now and at the time when Mr. Morrison made his speech, is contained in section 63 of the Representation of the People Act, 1949, and is as follows:

'63.—(1) No expenses shall, with a view to promoting or procuring the election of a candidate at a parliamentary or local government election, be incurred by any person other than the candidate, his election agent and persons authorized in writing by the election agent on account
(a) of holding public meetings or organizing any public display; or
(b) of issuing advertisements, circulars or publications; or
(c) of otherwise presenting to the electors the candidate or his views or the extent or nature of his backing or disparaging another candidate.'

This act was a consolidating measure and reproduced the language of the Representation of the People Act, 1948; but even this measure did not in these respects alter the law contained in earlier statutes. The natural interpretation of this section is that it prohibits unauthorized expenditure designed to secure the return of a particular candidate for a particular constituency. Any body of persons is, and always has been, free to express any views it pleases on political matters without being obliged to have them included in election expenses provided that they are not designed to secure the return of a particular candidate for a particular constituency. It would be intolerable, to give one example, if the cost of an anti-vivisection campaign had to be included in the expenses of those candidates who expressed their determination, if elected, to seek an end to that practice. This clear distinction between general political propaganda and support for a particular candidate is the reason behind the practice, already noted, whereby local party associations disband themselves when the date of an election is announced and they choose definite candidates to contest it. When the Attorney-General of the day, Sir Hartley Shawcross, was questioned in

the House of Commons on 5 December 1950 about the issues raised by
Mr. Morrison he replied :[1]

> 'I think it right to add, however, that whilst I can lay down no
> binding rule in the matter, which is one to be considered on the facts
> of each particular case, it is my view that the prohibition of certain
> expenditure on propaganda calculated to influence an election is not
> necessarily restricted to propaganda in which any particular can-
> didate is expressly referred to.'

As an abstract proposition this may readily be granted; propaganda
may be so cunningly worded as to say 'Vote for Bloggs' without men-
tioning Bloggs. But what Sir Hartley Shawcross did not say, and could
hardly have said without derogating from the legal standing of his
office, is that industries are precluded from opposing nationalization
because a political party happens to have included it in its programme.
Proof of this is contained in the fact that, despite the statements of Mr.
Morrison and Sir Hartley Shawcross, the steel, cement, sugar and meat
industries and the insurance business continued to oppose nationalization, but no action was taken against them although Sir Hartley
Shawcross 'gave instructions to the Director of Public Prosecutions
that, should occasion arise, he should institute such proceedings as he
thought proper without asking for the consent of the Attorney-
General.'[2]

Since these words were spoken, the law has, however, been tested
and the interpretation given above is confirmed in a far more authoritative quarter. On 19 November 1951—that is, six days before the general
election—an advertisement by the Tronoh-Malayan tin group of
companies was published in *The Times*. Among other passages the
advertisement included these:

> 'The nation, let alone your valuable companies in Malaya, cannot
> survive if the worm of socialism is permitted to continue to eat into
> the very core of its economic life. . . . The coming general election
> will give us all the opportunity of saving the country from being
> reduced, through the policies of the Socialist Government, to a
> bankrupt "Welfare State".'

In due course *The Times* Publishing Company Limited, along with
Tronoh Mines Limited and the secretary of the company were charged
on indictment with unlawfully incurring expense on account of this
advertisement with a view to promoting or procuring the election of a
candidate at the general election, namely, the election of a candidate

---

[1] 470 H. C. Deb. 5s., col. 1515.
[2] House of Commons, 7 December 1949, 470 H. C. Deb. 5s., col. 1890.

other than the Socialist candidate in the constituency of the cities of London and Westminster. Mr. Christmas Humphreys, opening the case for the Crown at the Central Criminal Court on 14 February 1952,[1] said the Crown alleged that the advertisement in *The Times* was inserted with a view to promoting the election of an anti-Socialist candidate. As *The Times* might be taken to circulate in all constituencies, the Crown could have put before the jury indictments containing some 600 counts. That would have been absurd. Therefore one particular constituency had been chosen for a case which he would admit frankly was a test case on the meaning of an Act of Parliament. In his closing speech on 18 February 1952[2], Mr. Humphreys introduced the idea of voting for a party. The offence in this case, he said on behalf of the Crown, was not in what was said, or even where it was said, but that space in a newspaper was bought on behalf at least of a party if not on behalf of a candidate in any particular election. The purpose of the section was to stop rich partisans, as distant from a candidate, buying space for such advertisements and to prevent outsiders from spending money to the advantage of their candidate and to the disadvantage of the candidate of another party which had not so much money.

Mr. Justice McNair, before whom the case was tried, said that on the view he took of the construction of section 63 of the Act he did not think there was a case he could properly leave to the jury. Notwithstanding that the Interpretation Act, 1889, provided that, unless the contrary intention appeared, words in the singular should include the plural, he thought that the reference to the election of a candidate at an election meant a candidate at a particular election, not elections generally. He had reached the conclusion that no reasonable jury on the evidence could find that the advertisement in question was an advertisement presenting to the electors of any constituency any particular candidate, still less presenting to the electors of the constituency of the cities of London and Westminster the Conservative candidate, or any anti-Socialist candidate, or his views. The fact that the section provided no mode by which an advertisement in a national newspaper, circulating generally throughout the country, supporting the views of a particular party and not the views of a particular candidate, could be authorized lent strong support to the view that this particular form of advertisement was not prohibited.

On the judge's direction the jury brought in a formal verdict of *Not Guilty* against each of the defendants and they were discharged.

In the light of this decision it will be readily appreciated that the

[1] See *The Times* of 15 February 1952.   [2] Ibid., 19 February 1952.

industries threatened with nationalization in 1949 were entirely within their rights in putting before the public by well-designed advertisements their case for remaining under private enterprise; and candidates who took the same view had no obligation to return in their election expenses any portion of the expenditure incurred on these advertisements. As a matter of law this could never be seriously controverted, and now is beyond dispute. The law is still based on the premise that electors vote for candidates in particular constituencies. But the assumption behind Mr. Morrison's speech quoted above, that in modern times electors do not vote for candidates but for party programmes, is almost equally incontrovertible. The law and the reality have been diverging for some time. Mr. Morrison did not even think it necessary to argue that electors vote for parties, not for candidates; it is implicit in his whole attitude.

Piquancy is given to Mr. Morrison's attitude by a letter sent by the National Executive Committee of the Labour party in October 1948 to all Labour members and candidates urging them not to give pledges on matters of public policy.

'As those experienced in these matters will know, organizations of one sort or another seek to involve members of Parliament and candidates with specific commitments on particular issues which are liable to become embarrassing. By the time a parliamentary debate and division occurs the facts may have changed, or the Government for good reason may advise the House against the policy implied in the pledges. If and when that situation arises the members who have given specific undertakings are liable to be faced with an embarrassing situation which may involve the Government in difficulties as well.'

The letter gave three illustrations—specific commitments to payments to particular classes from public funds, pledges to support stated reductions in taxation, and the ending of partition in Ireland—and continued:

'These, however, are only examples, and generally speaking, members of Parliament and candidates should not commit themselves outside the field of declared Government policy in the election manifesto of the Labour party. Otherwise members of Parliament are liable to find themselves in the position of instructed delegates rather than public representatives who have a duty to give their vote in Parliament after they have heard the *pros* and *cons* of debate.'

The advice is sound enough for candidates in all parties; a party candidate who goes beyond the declared policy of his party will almost certainly run into trouble. But all we are now concerned with is the assumption that the electors vote for parties, not for candidates. It is not explained why it is right for parties to bind themselves by specific undertakings but wrong for candidates. Above all, it is not explained why a successful candidate who gives a personal pledge becomes thereby an 'instructed delegate', whereas if he endorses a pledge by his party he becomes a 'public representative'. Are Labour members free 'to give their vote in Parliament after they have heard the *pros* and *cons* of debate?' It may be suspected that the author of this piece of pure Burke must have had his tongue in his cheek for he could hardly be ignorant of the standing orders of the parliamentary Labour party. Do parties never find their election pledges embarrassing because 'the facts may have changed', or do facts change only for individuals? The advice in the letter is sound, but the reasons given are wrong. The true reasons are much simpler and less metaphysical; they are that members of Parliament can effect reforms only if they work with others, and it is therefore unwise to go beyond what has been agreed with those with whom they will normally associate.

The careers of Lloyd George in the Liberal party, Ramsay Mac-Donald in the Labour party and Mr. Winston Churchill in the Conservative party show that a powerful personality in a high position can still exercise a dominating influence on his party's fortunes. But the words 'in a high position' must not be overlooked. Lloyd George and MacDonald were able, and Mr. Churchill has been able, to sway their parties' fortunes because the British constitution, as it has developed over the course of centuries, invests ministers, and especially the Prime Minister, with immense powers; and so great is the respect of the British people for ancient constitutional usages that the parties have not sought to derogate from these constitutional rights of ministers. At his desk 'the Minister' or 'the Secretary of State' is supreme; he is responsible for every detail, alike in policy and in administration, within his department, and his authority is unquestioned. In the Cabinet room at No. 10, Downing Street the Prime Minister is clothed with the whole panoply of power; he is in theory only the first among equals, but he recommends whom he pleases to be his equals and he can get rid of them at a moment's notice. With such power in his hands it is small wonder that a Prime Minister, a Chancellor of the Exchequer or a Foreign Secretary is still able by the force of his personality to alter his party's course. But once out of office his powers drop away—'there is nothing so *ex* as being an *ex*-minister' as one of them said a little ruefully—and if he should also lose his seat in Parliament he becomes a nobody. For the two years 1922 to 1924 Mr. Churchill, who had held a glittering succession of high offices and had moulded the fortunes of his country, was unable to find a seat in Parliament. When he eventually returned to the House, and had again ceased to hold office, his robust personality battled in vain for eight years against the leaders of his party. It was only when the outbreak of war brought him back into office that he was able to have a dominating influence in his party; and when counsellors who were not entirely disinterested besought him as the leader of a coalition not to become the leader of a party he was wise enough to give no heed to them. In the Labour party Sir Stafford Cripps, another markedly individual personality, campaigned ceaselessly but ineffectively from 1932 to 1939 against his party leadership; he was then expelled and was out of the Labour party until 1945; it was only when in high office, and re-admitted to the party, that he was able to have any real influence on its course.

The cases cited should not therefore mislead us. They are the exceptions that test the rule. They do not show that there is great scope in current party politics for individual action. A long time ago Walter Bagehot said that any well-trained poodle could do most of the duties of the average member of Parliament. Not quite so long ago John Morley defined the duties of a private member as being to support his leaders in the House by his vote and in the country by his voice. What is the position to-day?

In the first place, the Independents have been completely eliminated from the House of Commons, and it is unlikely that we shall ever again see an Independent elected, at least until the university seats are restored. If an Independent were elected, it would almost certainly be with the support of one or the major parties, as Mr. W. J. Brown might have been elected (though in fact he was not) for West Fulham in 1951 with Conservative support.

The position of an Independent member is ideal in many ways from his personal point of view. His time is his own; he can, if he chooses, absent himself from the House for weeks at a time, without being answerable to anybody except his own conscience; he is not obliged to serve on the many party committees that consume so much of a party member's time; he can vote in whichever lobby he pleases, or not at all, without being called in question by anyone; he is heard with respect because each of the major parties likes to have his support; in view of the healthy tradition that gives minorities in the House more than their share of the available time he probably has more chance of being called in debate than a party member; he can take up subjects that a party member could not espouse, and outside organizations, anxious not to compromise themselves with any one party, are only too ready to supply him with ideas and material; he must, of course, renounce the highest ambitions, which can be achieved only through parties, but it is not impossible for him to be given office; in his constituency he is obliged to keep some kind of organization of his own in being, at any rate if he wishes to be re-elected, but he is free from the call of committees and social engagements that exhaust the party member. From his point of view, the position of an Independent member has many attractions; but is it a matter for national regret that Independents should now be eliminated from the House?

The answer generally given, even in the major parties, is 'Yes'. The value of Independent members has sometimes been overstated, not least because it has generally been stated by Independent members themselves, who are often persuasive writers and speakers. But they have in the past carried out work of great importance that would not be practicable for a party member, especially pioneer work in social progress. The name of the late Miss Eleanor Rathbone will be the one that occurs most readily to her former colleagues in the House, and it is to her more than to any other single person that we owe the institution of a national system of family allowances. It would have been difficult for a party member to have done this pioneer work because he would have been restrained by the desire not to embarrass his party.

The case should not be exaggerated. Some of the Independents in the House were independent only in the sense that they did not belong to a party organization and accept its whip; but they tended to vote with one major party or the other. They were really Independent Conservatives or Labour Independents as the case might be. Others tended to vote now with the Conservatives, now with Labour, on a basis of rough justice to them rather than on the strict merits of the case. Independent members were responsible for initiating some major social legislation, but time will be needed to evaluate its full consequences. In any case their work could be done only against the background of an extensive party organization. If by some electoral miracle 625 Independent members were returned to Parliament, the House of Commons just would not function. No business would be transacted, because the machinery for the allocation of time and the priority of tasks would not exist. The House of Commons would become a talking-shop and nothing more. A Parliament of Independents would be both impracticable and undesirable; but a dozen Independents in a House of 625 members can be the leaven that leaveneth the lump.

It is on these lines that the disappearance of the Independents is to be regretted, but there has come about a parliamentary change far more important than the disappearance of the Independents, and that is the loss of independence of mind within a party.

Parliamentary parties are good, and if they did not exist they would have to be invented. But a parliamentary party should be a body of men who associate together because they hold the same general views. They should not hold the same views because they belong to the same party.[1] A party should not crush the individuality of its members, but should give form and expression to it.

This was the case in the greatest days of parliamentary government. There were no Independent members in our sense of the word in the Victorian Parliaments, and there was no need of them because there was far greater independence within parties. It is true that members occasionally described themselves as Independent, and sometimes spoke as if the Independents were a recognizable class of members. In a speech on 20 April 1877, E. Whalley, for example, said: 'I may be permitted to speak on behalf of an unfortunate, and it may perhaps be a small number of members of this House—I mean the Independent members . . .'[2] But it appears that what he meant, and others who used similar expressions, was that he conceived it to be his duty to act as a check upon the executive. He did not, in fact, stand as an Independent, and in Parliament he usually voted with his party. It is a remarkable fact that from 1832 to 1914 there was never in the House of Commons a single member who had stood for election as an Independent. In 1862 an Independent stood at Wycombe and received one vote, possibly cast by himself. In each of the 1885 and 1892 elections there were six Independent candidates, but none was elected. It was not till 1906 that the Independent candidates began to be separately listed in the parliamentary handbooks, and the first Independent member in the modern sense of the words was E. Pemberton-Billing, who was returned at a by-election in 1915. It is not easy to catalogue the Independent members

---

[1] 'In order to throw an odium on political connexion, these politicians suppose it a necessary incident to it, that you are blindly to follow the opinions of your party, when in direct opposition to your own clear ideas; a degree of servitude that no worthy man could bear the thought of submitting to; and such as, I believe, no connexions (except some Court factions) ever could be so senselessly tyrannical as to impose. Men thinking freely will, in particular instances, think differently. But still, as the greater part of the measures which arise in the course of public business are related to, or dependent on, some leading general principles in government, a man must be peculiarly unfortunate in the choice of his political company if he does not agree with them at least nine times in ten.' E. Burke, *Thoughts on the Cause of the Present Discontents*, ed. Payne, vol. i, p. 89.

[2] I owe the illustration, and much of the information that follows to a valuable essay by Commander Stephen King-Hall, himself a former Independent member, entitled 'The Independents in Politics' in *Parliamentary Affairs*, winter 1951, pp. 103–15. (*The British Party System*, pp. 101–13.)

who have been subsequently elected, as their Independence was very
often only a stage in their transition from one party to another—or
back into the same party. Commander King-Hall[1] reckons that the
general election of 1918 returned seven Independents 'and another
thirteen who were described as Independents plus this or that'. In 1922
and again in 1923 there were three; in 1924 and in 1929 there were four;
in 1931 there were three; and in 1935 there were two. By the dissolution in 1945 the number of Independents had risen for a variety of
reasons to twenty, and at the general election eleven were returned. As
already noted, none was returned in 1950, but at the dissolution in 1951
Mr. Raymond Blackburn, who had resigned from the Labour party,
was sitting as an Independent; no Independent was elected in 1951.

The Independents of recent years have been classified by Sir Harold
Nicolson[2] as 'the fortuitously Independent', elected during a period of
party truce; the 'academic Independents' returned for university seats;
the 'temperamental Independents'; the 'forlorn Independents', the
survivors of a dead party; and the 'true Independents', those who fight
an election without a party machine and do not take a party whip in
the House. But until the first world war none of these categories would
have had any reason for a separate existence. The party system could
not have worked, of course, if all members had been like the scion of a
noble house who is said never to have spoken and always to have voted
with the opposite party; or, at least, it would have worked in a peculiar
way like a traffic system in which drivers always turn the opposite way
from that in which their indicators are pointing. But even though
members did not usually distinguish themselves in this bizarre way, they
manifested considerable latitude of opinion and action within their
parties. Whereas *Dod's Parliamentary Companion* now considers it
sufficient to list a member as Conservative, Liberal or Labour, in its
earliest days, from 1832 onwards, it went to considerable trouble to
particularize the shades of opinion among members. In the bio-
graphical section each member's attitude to the great questions of the
day, such as the Reform Act, the Church and Ireland, was specified so
far as it was known, and any pledges that he had given were particularly
noted; the editors of *Dod* in those days did not consider it sufficient to
label members as Whig or Tory. These deviations from the normal
attitude in the party were reflected in the division lobby. It has been
calculated that in the years round about 1850 at least ten per cent of a
party's membership always voted against their own leaders.

[1] *Loc. cit.*, pp. 111–12. (*The British Party System*, pp. 109–11.)
[2] *The Independent Member of Parliament*, in the Hansard Society's *Papers on
Parliament*.

What is the position of the member of a parliamentary party to-day? In the Liberal party there has been for a long time a liberty of opinion amounting to licence. The difficulty in their case is to decide whether the Liberal party can now be looked upon as a parliamentary party in any customary sense of those words. It ought perhaps to be looked upon as a collection of individuals rather than as a party. This state of affairs was acknowledged by seventeen Liberal candidates who wrote a letter on 27 November 1951 to the *Liberal News* arguing that the first duty for Liberals was 'to agree upon some measure of discipline in our party' and continuing:

> 'The case for discipline seems to us to be unanswerable. If we band ourselves together as a political party it can only be in order to work together to achieve common aims. If we claim, in the name of liberty, the right to work and speak in public against each other we are no longer a party and we can never achieve anything.'

As indicated in earlier pages, the formal position of a member of the parliamentary Labour party is rigorous. He is expected never in any circumstances to speak or vote against his party; the utmost liberty allowed to him is to abstain from voting on a matter of conscience, such as religion or temperance. He is expected to consult the officers of his party before tabling any motion, amendment or prayer, and the only action he can take without seeking prior approval is to put down questions or raise a matter in the debate on the adjournment. If these rules were rigorously observed, the life of a Labour member of Parliament would indeed be little better than Bagehot's poodle. But in practice they do not seem to trouble the more individualistic members of the party. From time to time members have been expelled by an exasperated party meeting, others have narrowly escaped expulsion, and two have resigned their membership, but much provocaton is endured before matters come to this pass; and although the more individualistic members of the Labour party have often spoken, and spoken violently, in a sense contrary to party decisions, they have generally refrained from carrying their convictions to the division lobby as this would mean 'voting with the Tories'. Not the way men speak, but the way they vote, is regarded in all parties as the important thing; speeches can be explained away, but votes cannot. In brief, members of the parliamentary Labour party are in theory allowed virtually no liberty of action in the House, but in practice they take a great deal.

In the Conservative party there are no such rigid rules, and it may be that they are not so necessary. By upbringing and by education Conservative members have acquired a strong sense of loyalty to each other, and they do not need rigid standing orders to support each other by speech and vote. A similar sense of corporate loyalty can be seen among the trade union members of the parliamentary Labour party, but it is not so marked among the so-called 'intellectual' wing. This sense of corporate loyalty can be trusted to bring Conservative members into the same lobby when any question involving the fate of the Government or party is under discussion; but there is a wide range of questions over which considerable liberty of speaking and voting is tolerated. There is, indeed, one respected Conservative member of the House who has so often differed from his colleagues that he has acquired in his generation a reputation akin to that of the noble lord already mentioned, and far from being expelled from the party, he and his actions are regarded with affection and indulgence.

What is here said about the several parties applies to their attitude on the floor of the House of Commons. In the committee rooms upstairs party feeling and discipline are far less rigid. These standing committees in which the committee stage of bills is normally taken, are constituted in accordance with party strength in the House, but as they consist of only sixty members and the atmosphere is more intimate, there is a good deal of mutual 'give and take'. The questions to be decided are not the merits of bills as a whole but particular points in them that do not lend themselves so readily to decisions on party lines. Members who dislike the whole principle of a bill, but have been defeated in their efforts to get it rejected on second reading, may nevertheless co-operate with its promoters to improve it as much as possible in committee. This more complaisant attitude is helped by the way the votes are taken. Members do not go into one or other of two lobbies, as in the chamber, but answer 'Aye' or 'No' as their names are called out in alphabetical order. In the absence of rigid party discipline the first members to be called often given an answer different from the one their party expects, but they can correct their vote at the end, and the procedure always gives rise to some good-humoured chaffing.

The Conservative party has preserved more than the Labour party the parliamentary ideal, but it cannot be denied that in all parties the individual member to-day has less scope than in the past, and if this tendency continues fewer men and women of ability will be attracted into political life and the prestige and vitality of Parliament will suffer. The re-introduction of Independents into Parliament can be only a partial remedy. The true remedy lies in restoring the dignity and independence of members within their own parties. A time when parliamentary majorities are so small, and every vote counts, may not seem propitious for making this suggestion, and yet it points to the first needed reform. This is that Governments should not feel obliged to resign if defeated in the House of Commons unless the question of censure or confidence is specifically put. This is already the practice with regard to the standing committees, and is an additional reason why the party atmosphere is not so pronounced upstairs as on the floor of the House. Governments with a large majority in the House have often been defeated in committee, but do not feel put in any great difficulty thereby. Sometimes the decision of the committee is accepted, sometimes the Government seeks to reverse it on the floor of the House at the report stage, putting on the whips for the purpose, but no thought of resignation occurs over a defeat in committee. On the floor of the House, however, in recent years every vote has become in effect a vote of confidence. The underlying issue is never simply the one on the paper, but the question whether the Government should carry on or go out. In a close House this imposes an intolerable strain on members, especially ministers, and it means that the merits of the question on the paper are seldom discussed adequately. If the Government of the day were prepared to bow to the will of the House in all minor matters, and resign only if the question of confidence were specially put, this would not only enhance the prestige of Parliament but would enable members to vote more freely according to their conscience and lights. It would enable many more 'free votes 'to be taken, that is votes for which the whips are not 'put on'; and it is generally agreed that some of the most effective debates in the House have taken place before a free vote. In this way the loyalty of a member to his party and his desire to vote after hearing the *pros* and *cons* of debate could be reconciled; and when the question of confidence is specially put, and members would be expected to vote with their parties or get out of them, the significance of the occasion would be correspondingly heightened.

This change would go a long way towards restoring the status of members, but it would need to be matched by a corresponding tolerance in the constituency organizations. An executive committee should not take it amiss, any more than the parliamentary leaders, if its member occasionally shows divagations in speech and vote. Provided that the question of confidence is not involved, they should regard such divagations within limits as being a healthy sign that their member has a mind and will of his own. An executive committee which is always brooding over the member's speeches, passing resolutions of censure on his votes, and threatening him with the withdrawal of support at the next election is doing a great disservice to representative government.

Such incidents may not be common, but that they take place will not be denied by anyone with a knowledge of the facts. The most recent example was the action of the excutive committee of the South Dorset Conservative and Unionist Association in October 1952 in deciding not to recommend their sitting member, Lord Hinchingbrooke, for adoption as their future candidate on account of certain lines of policy he had adopted; and the principles of parliamentary government were vindicated on 30 October 1952 when a motion of "no confidence" in the executive was carried by 836 votes to 468. The executive committee thereupon resigned and a new one was elected. It should always be borne in mind that a British member of Parliament is a representative, not an instructed delegate; and a representative must have some latitude.

——— XXII ———

Parties and Local Government

ON SEVERAL OCCASIONS we have noticed how a development in party organization has been acknowledged by a new entry in the various constitutional handbooks. One of the most important has just found recognition in *Whitaker's Almanack* for 1952. It is thus introduced: 'In view of the fact that municipal elections are increasingly conducted on "party lines", an addition has been made to the municipal directory showing for the first time the party representation in English boroughs.'

The table mentioned gives a list of the party affiliations in 337 English boroughs, and in only 27 of them are there no members with party labels. The following are the first entries under each letter of the alphabet in the table; they give a fair indication, by sample, of the extent to which borough elections are now conducted on party lines.

Abingdon: *Ind.* 15, *Lab.* 1.

Bacup: *Lib.* 9, *C.* 8, *Lab.* 7.
Calne: *Ind.* 14, *C.* 1, *Lab.* 1.
Dagenham: *Lab.* 28, *Ind.* 3, *C.* 1.
Ealing: *C.* 41, *Lab.* 18, *Ind.* 1.
Falmouth: *Ind.* 11, *Lab.* 5.
Gateshead: *Lab.* 26, *Ind.* 14.
Halesowen: *Ind.* 8, *C.* 6, *Lab.* 3, *Lib.* 3.
Jarrow: *Lab.* 22, *C.* 6.
Keighley: *C.* 18, *Lab.* 12, *Lib.* 6, *Ind.* 4.

Lancaster: *C.* 12, *Ind.* 12, *Lab.* 5, *Lib.* 3.
Macclesfield: *C.* 33, *Lab.* 14, *Lib.* 1.
Nelson: *Lab.* 26, *C.* 4, *Ind.* 2.
Oldbury: *Lab.* 20, *C.* 6, *Ind.* 2.
Penryn: *Ind.* 14, *Lab.* 2.
Queensborough: *C.* 7, *Lab.* 6, *Ind.* 3.
Radcliffe: *C.* 26, *Lab.* 9, *Ind.* 1.
Saffron Walden: *Ind.* 9, *C.* 7.
Tamworth: *Lab.* 15, *C.* 5, *Ind.* 2, *Lib.* 2.
Wakefield: *Lab.* 24, *C.* 20.

C.=Conservative, *Lab.*=Labour, *Lib.*=Liberal, *Ind.*=Independent.

Similar tables could be produced for the Welsh boroughs and Scottish burghs, and for the county councils. A very large number of urban district elections are also contested on party lines, and even a fair number of rural district elections. It is only in the parish councils that the party system is virtually unknown. Mr. J. H. Warren[1] estimates that the party system is to be found in about nine-tenths of the counties and larger towns, in about half of the 572 urban districts and in about a

[1] *Parliamentary Affairs*, vol. v, no. 1, winter 1951, p. 180. (*The British Party System*, p. 178.)

quarter of the 475 rural districts; he also notes that the party system in local government is more pronounced in the north than in the south.

One reason why the party system has been slower in taking root in local than in parliamentary government is that our modern system of borough, county and urban district councils is much younger than Parliament. For practical purposes the modern system of elected borough councils began with the Municipal Corporations Act, 1835. From 1873 onwards, as we have seen, the Liberals were successfully fighting the Birmingham municipal elections on party lines, and later the Conservatives obtained a similar hold over municipal elections in Liverpool, but at the end of the century there were still relatively few councils divided on party lines. In Manchester the councillors were divided into Conservative and Liberal groups, but neither made a markedly party approach to the council's business and did not use its majority, when it had a majority, for party ends; and this is typical of what happened in many other cities and towns. The present system of county councils was established in 1888, and almost immediately two organized groups appeared in the London County Council: the Moderates, later called Municipal Reformers, were mainly Conservatives and the Progressives were mainly Liberals. From the outset their approach to the council's business was on strictly party lines, but this must be correlated with the immense size of the business to be considered—larger than that of many sovereign states—and the parties were specifically related to the needs of London, and not a mere copying of the parliamentary system. The party system gradually took possession of the other county councils, but until 1914 the party system was the exception rather than the rule in local government.

It was the rise of the Labour party which led to a big increase in the number of council elections fought on party lines. The Labour party has never doubted that the party system is just as applicable to local government as to Parliament. It was predisposed to this attitude by the 'gas and water socialism' and the doctrine of 'permeation' held by the Fabians, who sought to gain control of local government councils as the most effective means of securing acceptance for their views. It was also predisposed by its ability to furnish more numerous, and more suitable, candidates for local government than for Parliament, particularly in the days when members of Parliament were unpaid. In those days it seemed a remote possibility that the Labour party could secure a majority in Parliament, but control of many councils was well within the bounds of practicability. The Labour party also perceived at an early date that many changes it might carry through in Parliament, when it did obtain a majority, would need the co-operation of local authorities in carrying them out, and might be frustrated if these local authorities did not share its views. For these and other reasons the Labour party has always laid great emphasis on local government, and far more Labour than Conservative or Liberal leaders have gone to Westminster by way of service on a local authority; Mr. Attlee, for example, has recalled with pride that his public life began as mayor of Stepney. When the Labour party began the practice of contesting local elections on party lines, the other parties had perforce to follow, or they would soon have found the councils dominated by their political opponents.

The Labour party has justified its entry into local government by alleging that the members of councils described as Independents were not true Independents but Conservatives or Liberals 'in disguise'. It is true that many of the Independents, now as then, are members of the Conservative or Liberal parties, and in the deliberations of the councils they no doubt speak and vote as Conservatives or Liberals might be expected to speak and vote. But this is not what is meant by the party system in local government.

The introduction of party politics into local government means two things. It means in the first place that the party organization is used to support and possibly to finance the party's candidates at the election; and it means in the second place that the party's successful candidates take concerted action in the council.

The ward is the territorial unit for borough council elections, and the polling district is the unit for county urban district and rural district council elections. As we have seen, these are also the units of party organization. When a party decides to contest local elections, it has first of all to choose its candidates. The Conservative booklet on *Local government and the party organization* says: 'Whenever it may be necessary to select for support a local government candidate for the ward or electoral division, the branch Committee concerned shall recommend a candidate to the executive council, and if he (she) is approved by the executive council, shall present him (her) to a general meeting of the branch for adoption.' The Labour model rules for a borough provide for the executive committee to invite nominations for a list of available candidates from affiliated and party organizations and to submit the list for endorsement by the general committee; the candidates to contest particular wards are chosen from the list at joint meetings of the executive committee and the respective ward committees. The expenses of contesting a local government election may vary from a few shillings in a rural area up to a hundred pounds or so in the metropolis. Constituency Labour parties (or the ward and polling district committees) now usually meet the expenses of their candidates, and Conservative associations (or the ward and polling district branches) are doing so to an increasing extent; the general principle in both cases is that no desirable candidate should be debarred solely for financial reasons. When an election campaign opens, the whole constituency party organization is thrown into it. The work is supervised by the agent, an election address is printed and sent to each elector, generally on behalf of all the party candidates, a canvass of the voters is taken, cars are registered to take voters to the poll, party members take down the number of voters as they leave the polling stations, and the registers are marked at the committee rooms as for a parliamentary election.

The successful candidates of a party act as a group within the council. The leader of the majority party is regarded as, and is often called, the leader of the council; the leader of the chief minority party is looked on as the leader of the opposition. Before a sitting of the council the members of a party hold a meeting among themselves to decide their attitude; and, having taken a decision, they normally vote in accordance with the decision in the council.

In the early days of the Labour movement Labour members on a local authority were often expected to report on the business transacted to the constituency Labour party or to the local trades and labour council, and were frequently instructed in advance by those bodies how they should vote. There are obvious objections to such a course, and the Labour party's model standing orders now provide that representatives from the party may sit with the Labour group in its private meetings but may not vote;[1] and it is laid down that although the election programme is to be formulated by the party organization, the council group is to be responsible for the conduct of council business. In the early days of the Labour party it was also customary for constituency Labour parties to review with their representatives on the council the business coming before the committees, that is to say, before the issues had been clarified and before the permanent staff had an opportunity to give their expert advice. The party's model standing orders now provide that the group meeting shall be held at a con-

[1] For the purpose of maintaining contact between the group and the central Labour party, constituency Labour party or local Labour party, as the case may be, three representatives of the latter may attend group meetings in a consultative capacity and without voting power, provided that the number of such representatives shall not exceed one-third of the membership of the group.

venient time between the issue of the council agenda and the meeting of the council, that is, between the committee stage and the full council. These changes minimize the grave objections formerly taken to Labour party procedure on local authorities, but the Conservative party shows greater constitutional propriety in leaving its representatives on a council answerable only to the electorate for their conduct in the council.

The greater part of a council's work is done through its standing committees, which are constituted roughly in accordance with party strength in the full council; and the agenda of the full council consists very largely of reports from the committees. The chairman of each standing committee acts as the spokesman of the committee in the council; and is often consulted by the officials when it is necessary to take action in the name of the whole committee in virtue of powers delegated to the committee. In some places it is felt that the chairmanships should be distributed between the majority and minority parties, but where the party system is fully developed the majority party takes all the chairmanships and the minority party would decline to hold any even if invited. There are obvious difficulties in a minority chairman acting as the spokesman for a committee in which his own point of view has suffered defeat; and it is difficult for a chairman to act in the name of a committee, unless he is sure that he will have the backing of a majority at its next meeting.

The chairman of a committee, when uncertain what course he should pursue, will usually consult the leader of his party, and in this way the leader of the majority party comes to have a general oversight over the whole of the council's business. In a sense the chairmen of committees are the 'departmental ministers' of the council and the leader of the council is the 'prime minister' and just as at an early date it was found desirable to draw the ministry from one party, so there are advantages in giving one party all the chairmanships.

Most councils run on party lines have developed conventions whereby the mayoralty or chairmanship of the council is held by each of the parties in turn, the Independents being given their place in the rota along with the parties; and there are usually conventions regulating the distribution of the aldermanic seats among the parties and Independents. From time to time friction is caused by one party or another refusing to abide by these conventions when it suits its purpose not to do so, and sometimes situations arise when it is difficult to know how the conventions should be applied; but on the whole these conventions lead to the filling of the vacant offices with less friction and more expedition than in purely Independent councils unregulated by such conventions.[1]

It will be recognized that the position of Independents, even though they happen to be members of political parties in their area, is quite different from that just described.

When a candidate stands as an Independent, even though he may be a member of the Conservative, Liberal or Labour party, he normally does so without the backing of the party organization, though there are cases where the help of the party organization may be offered to and accepted by an Independent candidate. He issues his own election address, makes his own arrangements for addressing meetings and persuading electors to vote for him, and pays his own expenses. If he is successful, he is under no obligation to consult with anyone about how he shall speak and vote in the council chamber. It is, however, an indication of the strength of the tendencies making for the party system that in many places the Independents, even though not members of parties, issue a joint election address and meet to concert their attitude in the council. They become 'the non-party party'.

Many people regret the introduction of party politics into local government and there are undoubtedly many questions in local government that do not lend themselves to settlement on party lines, and will be settled worse if they are decided on party lines. There is no Conservative way of repairing roads, nor a Liberal way of filtering water, nor a Labour way of maintaining the drains. Far more than in national politics, local government is the art of applying the best techniques to the life of the community. Even when strong bodies of opinion develop on certain questions, and therefore parties begin to arise, there is no reason why in all cases these should be the same parties as those into which the Parliament at Westminster is divided; the precedent set in London by the division into Moderates and Progressives may have some value. Moreover personalities are bound to play a far greater part in local politics than in national. The candidates are generally well known to the electors among whom they live and work, and there is less occasion for a party organization to make their merits known— and useless to ascribe to them merits that they do not possess.

The party system in local government therefore has all the disadvantages of the party system in national politics and some additional ones of its own. Nevertheless its introduction into the larger councils

---

[1] 'The Conventions of Local Government' is the subject of an article by Professor W. J. M. Mackenzie in *Public Administration*, vol. xxix, winter, 1951, pp. 345–56.

has been inevitable, and in retrospect need not be regretted. The same reasons that lead men to act in parties in Parliament lead them to act in groups on councils; thereby they exert far more influence than they could possibly have as individuals. Although there are some questions over which the division into groups need not be on the same lines as the division into national parties, some of the more important issues, especially housing and education, tend to divide councils in the same way as Parliament; and although the administration of the poor law has now been taken out of the hands of the local authorities this also was a big national issue dividing councils in the same way as Parliament when the party system first began to be applied to local government.

On the whole we need not therefore regret overmuch the introduction of the party system into local politics provided that it is not pushed to extremes. The general opinion in the Conservative party has been against the introduction, and for a long time it was justified only as the necessary answer to the Labour challenge; but the Conservative party now recognizes certain positive merits in the system. The official booklet on *Local government and the party organization* says:

> 'Whilst it can be argued that the aim of democratic government should be to attract the very best men and women regardless of party considerations and that much of the business to be decided by local authorities is more commercial than political, yet it must be recognized that huge sums of public money are being spent on providing services for the public. How these services are to be used is becoming more and more a matter of politics. . . . Another aspect of the question is that the party system tends to bring more defined policy into the management of affairs. The establishment of a majority party clearly gives the power to make decisions more quickly than where there is no such organization. The leader of the majority party, or even of the minority party for that matter, can speak with authority knowing that he has the backing of his party. This can be very important in the conduct of business, particularly in cases where negotiations are involved about wages, schemes involving purchases of land, collaboration with neighbouring authorities involving highly confidential business and where it is necessary to have some authoritative opinion. . . . This aspect is emphasized by the increasing tendency to form associations of local authorities with elected executive officers who are authorized to speak for the whole body of authorities in negotiation with some higher authority, say the county council or maybe a government department.'

This view is confirmed by an independent observer already cited,

Mr. J. H. Warren, who writes thus of the party system in local government:[1]

' We may say that in the sphere of policy it has on the whole a beneficial effect because, like the party system in national politics, it arouses electoral interest, segregates issues of a genuinely political kind for popular judgement and, at the same time, tends to produce an integrated policy for the locality as a whole; and that in doing all this it renders responsibility for the general level of council achievement visible to the public, facilitates judgment at the polls, and through the ups and downs of party fortunes at successive elections, brings shifts in public feeling forcibly to the council's notice. While the system may confer rôles of prominence and influence upon leading personalities, either as "leaders of the council" or chairmen of committees, it does so by democratic group vote and on lines which are at any rate capable of securing the necessary restraint over purely personal dominance; whereas in independent councils dominating personalities can attain to a personal rule which owns no kind of responsibility to others.'

To sum up, we should not seek to introduce the party system into those local authorities, especially the smaller ones, for which it is unsuited, but where it comes as a national growth we need to regret it overmuch but should rather aim at curbing its shortcomings. In particular, the electors should always be prepared to vote for an outstanding candidate to whatever party he may belong; constituency organizations which have helped to secure the election of a candidate should not try to bind his actions in the council but should leave him answerable to the electorate; party groups should remember that there are many questions of a technical or commercial character into which it is undesirable to intrude party politics; and the member should at all times bear in mind that he is in a party solely as a means of improving the life of the men and women among whom he lives and works.

It may also be permissible to express a note of regret that party affiliations should be allowed to enter into the appointment of justices of the peace—one of the oldest and most honourable forms of local government. In the light of history, especially of such matters as the administration of the poor law and the execution of the game laws, it is easy to understand why parties have wished in the past to be fairly represented on the bench. But party organizations are concerned with the making of laws, not with their administration, and at the present time there is really no reason why a man's party affiliations should

[1] *Parliamentary Affairs*, vol. v, no. 1, winter 1951, p. 193. (*The British Party System*.)

carry any weight when his fitness for the bench is being considered. It is rare for a justice of the peace to allow his party sympathies to interfere with his judgement of the case before him; but the danger is latent, and it would be better for magistrates to be chosen simply for their presumed fitness for work on the bench.

——— XXIII ———

Future of the Parties

THE BRITISH PARTY SYSTEM has gone through great changes in the past and we need not doubt that it will do so in the future. It would be rash to assume the mantle of prophecy, but we can profitably consider in turn some of the problems that the various parties have to face.

THE LIBERAL PARTY

The problem of the Liberal party is nothing less than whether it should exist. This may seem a cruel saying to many Liberals; but it can be argued that the Liberal party must die in order that liberalism may live.

Liberalism in England has now ceased to be the creed of a political party. One of the fundamental tenets of the historic Liberal party, free trade, has ceased to be regarded as practical politics by any responsible person in Great Britain, including Liberals, whatever may be thought about its merits in the abstract. The remaining tenets of liberalism have become part of the common mental stock of all British parties. For both reasons, there is no longer need of a Liberal party in Great Britain. 'The price of liberty is eternal vigilance,' but we need not assume that the Liberal party is the only possible watchdog of liberalism.

The future of liberalism is assured. It has taken its place in our national make-up as surely as the constitutional monarchy and representative government. The rôle which the Liberal party has played in this achievement will never be forgotten. Fox, Grey, Melbourne, Russell, Palmerston, Gladstone, Cobden, Bright, Forster, Asquith, Lloyd George and Beveridge have made an imperishable contribution to British life. Not only their names, but their work, lives for evermore. But nothing can be added to this achievement by the Liberal party to-day. It is only *magni nominis umbra*—the shadow of a mighty name. If it had not been for the rise of the Labour party, the story might have been different, but if the analysis in these pages is correct the fate of the Liberal party was sealed once the Labour party decided that its candidates must sever other political connexions. The country as a whole has already decided that it wants to be ruled by a Government drawn

283

either from the Conservative or from the Labour party; and the Liberal party as a parliamentary force can be kept in existence only by an alteration in our electoral system which would not only keep the Liberal party alive but would cause other minor parties to pullulate and would for ever confuse that simplicity of British party politics which is one of its great virtues. The price is too high to pay even for the sake of keeping alive the great name of the Liberal party. Mr. Arthur Greenwood was quite right in 1934 when he told Liberals that they should come under one umbrella or the other, either the Conservative or the Labour, and in fact most Liberals have already done so. The National Liberals made their choice in 1931. They showed that in association with the Conservatives it was possible to preserve both the name and the substance of the Liberal party as they understood it. In more recent years those Liberals who have felt that they could no longer vote Liberal have tended to go either to the Conservative or to the Labour side in the proportion of about two to one. In the next few years others will follow their example until there is left only a rigid, unyielding cohort of Casabiancas. It would surely be better from the point of view of preserving liberalism to join one of the major parties and work inside it for liberal ideals. Gladstone's grandson, Asquith's daughter and Lloyd George's son have decided that these ideals will best be preserved in association with the Conservatives; Lloyd George's daughter thinks that they will be safest in Labour keeping; and perhaps Liberals will break up between the major parties in these proportions. What is hardly defensible is to go on fighting in the nineteen-fifties the battles of 1905.

The Liberal party is not, however, a party of old men and women reluctant to change their allegiance. An analysis made by the British Institute of Public Opinion and published by the *News Chronicle* in the booklet *Behind the Gallup Poll*[1] shows that out of a typical 100 Liberal voters 13 are in the age group 21–29; 42 are in the age group 30–49; 32 are in the age group 50–64; and only 13 are aged 65 or more. Of this typical 100 voters, 54 are men and 46 women. Out of the same 100 voters only 5 per cent are described as 'well-to-do', 27 as enjoying a middle income, 57 as 'working class', and 11 as 'very poor'. No fewer than 25 out of the 100 are trade unionists. The Liberal party has therefore continued to attract young persons in all walks of life— perhaps the children of Liberals, but new recruits nevertheless—and one of the saddest aspects of the decline of the Liberal party is that

---

[1] I am grateful to the *News Chronicle* for allowing me to make use of the information in this booklet.

so many brilliant men now in the prime of life are condemned to political futility because they belong to a party that has no hope of office. It is not only a personal misfortune but a national loss.

THE LABOUR PARTY

The Gallup Poll published by the *News Chronicle* shows that a typical 100 Labour voters are made up of 54 men and 46 women. Of this 100 voters 22 are in the age group 21–29; 41 are in the age group 30–49; 26 are in the age group 50–65; and 11 are 65 or over. None of the 100 is classed as 'well-to-do' in respect of income, 9 are 'middle class', 65 are 'working class' and 26 are 'very poor.' The 100 includes 35 trade unionists. An interesting discovery of the poll is that in the Labour party, as in the Liberal, there is a big preponderance of men over women; and it is rather surprising that out of each 100 only 35 are trade unionists. Even if we rule out the women—and many women are, in fact, members of trade unions, it is still surprising that out of 54 male Labour voters not more than 35 are trade unionists. The conclusion is inescapable that there are many male workers who are not trade unionists, or that many trade unionists do not vote Labour.

THE TRADE UNIONS

Both conclusions are true, and this points to the biggest question mark before the Labour party. We have seen how the Labour party differs from the Conservative and Liberal parties—and indeed from all other British parties except the Co-operative—in mainly consisting, not of individual members but of affiliated bodies, of which the trade unions are the chief. The advantages of this system from the point of view of the Labour party are obvious. It gives the party a large automatic membership and a large steady income. But is it in the interests of the trade unions themselves?

The trade union movement in the country has roots going back to the middle ages. It has a continuous history from the year 1823 when the legal right to workmen's combination was first recognized, only to be quickly taken away and later restored. The trade union movement is far older than the Labour party and it would go on if the Labour party were dissolved.

The objects of trade unions are to secure by collective bargaining with employers the best possible wages and working conditions for their members. It can be argued—and personally I think the argument is sound—that in order to achieve these objects trade unions should hold themselves aloof from all political parties. In this way they will best be able to negotiate with the Government of the day, from whatever party it may be drawn. If the trade unions are affiliated to one party, and to one party alone, inevitably there is bound to be a certain degree of suspicion between the trade unions and other parties. If the trade union movement keeps itself free from all party connexions, all parties will tend to court it, and its bargaining power will be correspondingly enhanced. The 'floating voters' have long been recognized as the most important element in a two-party system. The main efforts of the parties are put into attracting these floating voters. If the trade unions keep themselves free from party ties, theirs will be the most vital of all the floating votes.

For a long time the trade unions held this point of view, and the American trade unions, very much to their advantage, hold it to-day. The trade unions were induced to join in the creation of the Labour party because they realized that negotiations between employers and employed were dependent upon the general economic policy of the country. The ability of South Wales mineowners to grant an extra shilling a shift or of Lancashire mill-owners to knock half an hour off the day might depend on the rate of exchange between the pound and the dollar or the imposition of a tariff on Japanese textiles. For these reasons many trade unionists came to think it would be desirable to influence Government policy directly by having their own party based on trade union membership and pledged to the advancement of trade union interests. After the passage of more than half a century it may be doubted whether this expectation was soundly based. There is a fallacy in the argument for three reasons. In the first place, as already noted, trade unions cannot have their own party without thereby in some measure antagonizing other parties; in the second place, though the ability of employers to grant concessions is admittedly dependent on Government policy, in its turn Government policy is dependent upon world conditions, and these cannot be influenced by a trade union party or by any other party; and in the third place, as also noted, trade unions can in any case exert more influence upon Government policy by holding themselves free to bargain with all parties than by forming their own party.

The position of the trade union movement becomes most difficult when its own party is called upon to form a Government. When the party is in opposition, the trade union leaders and the party leaders can concert a policy acceptable to their members without undue regard for economic facts. But when the party leaders find themselves in places of less freedom and greater responsibility, their policy is limited by world causes. The trade union leaders must then choose between acquiescing in the decisions of the political leaders and losing their hold over their own members, or retaining their hold over their own members at the cost of a rupture with their political friends. In the six years of Labour rule from 1945 to 1951 the trade union leaders took the course of acquiescing in the decisions of their political friends; they tended to lose the confidence of their own members, and these years were marked by waves of unofficial strikes in defiance of the trade union leaders' advice.

Particular difficulties arise in the connexion between the trade unions and the Labour party because the Labour party has proclaimed itself to be 'a socialist party, and proud of it.' Under socialism the employer becomes the state, and a strike borders on a mutiny. In the Soviet Union this problem was early recognized, and the trade unions soon found that their rôle in a socialist state was not to work for the raising of their members' wages and the shortening of the working week— these were 'bourgeois' ideas—but to obtain workers for needed jobs and to win acceptance for Government policy, in short, to act as recruiting agents and public relations officers for the Government.[1] These are special difficulties because the Labour party is pledged to socialism, but most of the difficulties mentioned above would arise even if the trade unions tied themselves to a non-socialist party. The wisest course for a trade union is to have no party ties and to hold itself free to negotiate with all parties.

There are many trade unions that recognize this course and are not affiliated to the Labour party, and even among the trade unions that are affiliated to the Labour party a large number of members are not socialists; many of them are members of the Conservative and Liberal parties. We have already seen how the system of 'contracting out' works, and many trade unionists are reckoned as affiliated members of the Labour party only because they are too lazy or too timid to contract out. We have also seen how the 'block vote' works at the Labour party conference, and many votes are cast in the name of members who may at the last election have voted Conservative or Liberal. This fact is well known in the Labour party. Ernest Bevin once warned the party, without exaggeration, that 'millions of trade unionists voted Conservative', and statistical evidence is now available from the Gallup

[1] See *Soviet Communism: A New Civilization*, by Sidney and Beatrice Webb, pp. 169–72.

poll published by the *News Chronicle*. This shows that out of a typical 100 Conservative voters, no fewer than 15 are trade unionists.

THE CONSERVATIVE PARTY

The poll further shows that the 100 typical Conservative voters is made up of 47 men and 53 women. This is also a rather remarkable fact. 'Votes for women' was no more palatable to the Conservative party before 1914 than it was to the Liberal, but in fact it has been to the advantage of the Conservative party. The extension of the franchise to women over 30 in 1918 was followed by eleven years of Conservative or predominantly Conservative rule, broken only by nine months of minority Labour government, and there can now be little doubt that the Conservative majorities were swelled by the new women voters. Baldwin's further extension of the franchise in 1929 to cover all adult women was followed by an immediate Conservative defeat, but in the long run it has been to the party's advantage. This is not really surprising, for woman is a more conservative creature than man, and wherever the franchise has been given to women—notably in Italy in 1948—their votes have nearly always been used in a conservative sense.

The Gallup poll further shows that the 100 typical Conservative voters are made up of 18 persons in the age-group 21–29; 41 persons in the age group 30–49; 31 persons in the age group 50–64; and 10 persons aged 65 and over. Of the 100 typical Conservatives, 9 are described as 'well-to-do', 31 as 'middle', 48 as 'working class', and 12 as 'very poor'.

As the number of Conservative and Labour voters in the country is now almost equal, it may be helpful to set out the analysis side by side for these two parties.

Classification	Division	Conservatives	Labour
Sex	Men	47	54
	Women	53	46
Age	21–29	18	22
	30–49	41	41
	50–64	31	26
	65 and over	10	11
Income	Well-to-do	9	—
	Middle	31	9
	Working class	48	65
	Very poor	12	26
Trade union membership	Trade unionists	15	35
	Not trade unionists	85	65

The differences are just what might have been expected. There are more Labour voters than Conservative in the age group 21–29, and more Conservative voters than Labour in the age group 50–64, and there are exactly equal numbers in the age group 30–49. An old saying is, 'The man who is not a socialist at 20 has no heart, the man who is still a socialist at 40 has no head.' Be that as it may, the table certainly shows a correlation between Conservatism and age up to 65. After that age the number of Conservative and Labour voters is almost equal; the tendency to become more Conservative as one grows older is countered by the fall in income on retirement from work. The table shows that there is a rough relationship between income and party, but it is not nearly as marked as might be expected. In view of so many well-known examples to the contrary it is rather surprising that there is not one 'well-to-do' Labour voter in the typical 100, as opposed to 9 'well-to-do' Conservatives. The table indicates that the 'middle class' is pre-dominantly Conservative, and the 'working class' and 'very poor' pre-dominantly Labour, but each party draws considerable support from these three sections; no one of those sections can be regarded as the preserve of any one party. It is noteworthy that the Conservative party gets far more support from the 'very poor' than the Labour does from the 'well-to-do'.

An analysis of the social and educational background and the occupations of members of Parliament shows that party representation in the House of Commons does not, in these respects, correspond with party membership in the country. This is a subject which Mr. J. F. S. Ross has made peculiarly his own.[1] He has ascertained that six out of every seven Conservative members have been educated at public schools, and one in every four at Eton, whereas only one in forty received his early education at an elementary school. Half the Conservative members were at Oxford or Cambridge, and more than half the rest were at some other university, or at a service college, or at one of the inns of court. One third of the Conservative members are regular officers of the fighting services or practising barristers, in about equal numbers. Another third, Mr. Ross finds, is composed of farmers, journalists, manufacturers, former civil servants or members of the diplomatic service, solicitors, stockbrokers and merchants; while a

[1] See his book *Parliamentary Representation*, 2nd ed. 1948, and his article in *Parliamentary Affairs*, vol. v, no. 1, winter 1951, pp. 170–78 (*The British Party System*, pp. 168–76), from which the information given here is drawn. The same article contains a useful analysis of the electorate which may be used to support the deductions from the Gallup poll given above. Though Mr. Ross's analysis is of the Parliament elected in 1950, it would be substantially true of that elected in 1951 also.

L

typical thirty-six Conservative members would include eleven employers and twenty-two professional men, it would contain only one former wage-earner. One in every four is a lawyer (barrister or solicitor, practising or non-practising), and three in every eight are company directors. Nearly a third of the members have a close connexion with families possessing hereditary titles; and fewer than one in twenty of such members in the House of Commons belong to a party other than the Conservative. One in every four Conservative members has served on a local council.

Of Labour members of Parliament rather more than half were educated at elementary schools and received no further education; of the remainder, rather fewer than half attended public schools and rather more than half attended secondary schools. Only one in six had been to Oxford or Cambridge, but about four in every eleven had received some kind of university education.[1] About a quarter of the Labour members consist in nearly equal numbers of ex-miners, and ex-teachers, and another two-fifths is made up of barristers, journalists, clerks, metal workers, solicitors and railwaymen. There are about fifteen Labour members of professional status to every fourteen former wage-earners, but only about three employers and managers for every fourteen former wage-earners. One in every seven Labour members is a lawyer (practising or non-practising). One in eleven is a company director, and one in three a past or present trade union official. Very few have connexions with families bearing hereditary titles.[2] Four out of every seven Labour members have served in local government.

Mr. Ross's summing up is:

'It will be seen that, whereas by far the greater part of the Conservative parliamentary party is fairly homogeneous in its composition and outlook, there is no such uniformity in the Labour party. Here we can clearly distinguish two main streams. The first is that of the rank-and-file workers, mostly of elementary education and manual occupation, who have risen to prominence through their trade union activities. The second is that of the "intelligentsia", typically (though not invariably) men and women of lower middle-class or working-class origin, who have climbed up by means of school and university scholarships, have graduated (often in economics or allied subjects), and have become school-teachers, adult education tutors,

[1] Mr. Ross very properly notes that 'no account of the educational background of Labour members would be complete, however, without a reference to the efforts that many have made to remedy early educational deficiencies by attendance, mostly part-time, at technical and commercial colleges, Workers' Educational Association classes, and other comparable institutions'. (*The British Party System*, p. 172.)
[2] *The British Party System*, pp. 172–73.

journalists, civil servants and lawyers. Though these streams differ widely in experience and outlook, neither has much in common with the typical Conservative M.P.'

The Liberal members of Parliament are too few to provide material for a similar analysis, but an analysis of Liberal candidates shows them to lie, as might be expected, between Conservative and Labour members in respect of social, educational and occupational characteristics.

There is a disparity between the Labour electorate in the country and the Labour representation in Parliament, but it is not so marked as the disparity between the Conservative electorate and the Conservative representation.[1] There is, of course, no obvious reason why the representation of a party in Parliament should have the same characteristics as its voters in the country. We should expect members of Parliament to be men of education who hold, or have held, responsible posts in a variety of fields. A Parliament that faithfully reflected the social, educational and occupational characteristics of the people would be in no position to give the people the leadership they need. It would probably be to the advantage of the party system and of the nation if the disparity between Conservative members and their electors was smaller than it is to-day and the disparity between Labour members and their electors rather greater. In particular, if there were fewer trade union officials on the Labour benches and rather more on the Conservative benches it would be a healthy change. Lawyers are found in considerable numbers on either side—and rightly so, for a sufficient number of competent lawyers is essential in any parliamentary party— and it is desirable that social background, educational attainments and occupational experiences should be rather more evenly distributed among the parties than they are.

ATTRACTING NEW VOTERS

Both the major parties can, however, in all truth claim to draw their supporters from every stratum in society, and in this sense each of them is a truly national party. In each representative 100 the biggest element is necessarily drawn from the 'working classes' because the 'working classes' are so much more numerous than any other section of the community. No party can hope to become a national party unless it attracts a large 'working class' element. In view of the present virtual

[1] Mr. Ross notes: 'Disparity there is (in the Labour party), but in the main it is between those who have risen above their initial environment and circumstances and those who have remained there; whereas in the Conservative party it is between people who are, and have been from birth, of different social classes'.

equality of votes between the Conservative and Labour parties, the problem before each of them is to find enough new voters to break the deadlock. The first thought in either camp is that these new voters may come from the Liberals. Even if the Liberal party should decide to ally itself as a whole with either the Conservative or the Labour party this would probably not be decisive; for in 1951 there were 13,948,385 votes for Labour and Co-operative candidates, 13,724,418 votes for Conservatives and associates, and only 730,551 votes for Liberals. The Liberal vote is therefore hardly sufficient to turn the scale.

We cannot reach a different conclusion by considering the 2,621,489 Liberal votes in 1950, when there were far more Liberal candidates, for in 1951 most of these votes must have been distributed among Conservative or Labour candidates, and therefore the only Liberal votes left to turn the scale are the 730,551, and they are not sufficient. But by now it should be clear that the Liberal party will not, and cannot, associate itself as a body either with the Conservative or with the Labour party. It may be expected that in the course of the next few years some of these Liberal voters of 1951 will turn Conservative, others will turn Labour, and a hard core will say 'A plague on both your houses' and will abstain from voting. On recent indications, and as a very rough estimate, perhaps 220,000 will abstain from voting, 340,000 will vote Conservative, and 170,000 will vote Labour. These transfers cannot be decisive. If the deadlock is to be broken it must therefore be by the Conservative party attracting voters who have hitherto voted Labour, or by the Labour party attracting voters who have hitherto voted Conservative, or by either party attracting into its fold a big majority of the new voters coming on to the register every year.

There seems to be more scope at the present time for the Conservative party to attract Labour voters than for the Labour party to attract Conservative. The reaction after the first and second world wars, and the economic depression between the two wars, gave the Labour party organizers opportunities that were exploited to the full. There is not now the same scope. Many of Labour's proposals that attracted voters are now written indelibly on the statute book, and furthermore six years of 'office with power' have removed from the Labour party its virgin purity in the eyes of many voters. It now takes its place as one of the great traditional parties of the state to be judged by its performance as well as by its promises. The Conservative party, in contrast, has a great potential source of recruits in those trade unionists who have hitherto voted Labour out of a sense of 'working-class solidarity' but without any strong convictions. It has organized itself effectively for that purpose from the national headquarters down to the association level, and as we have seen it secures a larger measure of trade unionist support than is commonly realized. In some quarters it is argued that what is needed to clinch these efforts is to give a few 'safe' seats to Conservative trade unionists. If there were only half a dozen trade unionists sitting on the Conservative benches along with the scions of noble houses and the captains of industry, the argument runs, it would do more to break the Labour hold on the trade unions than any other single measure.

Another way in which the present deadlock may be broken is by a dissolution of the alliance between the Co-operative and Labour parties, and even by a dissolution of the Co-operative party itself. The argument is analogous with that for the trade union movement. The Co-operative movement sprang from the desire of people to trade among themselves and so eliminate the element of profit from their purchases. It far antedates the rise of the Labour party or the formation of the Co-operative party, and fundamentally it has nothing to do with party politics. Co-operators were led to form their own political party for much the same reason as trade unionists; they realized that successful trading was dependent on Government policy, and by forming a party of their own they hoped to be able to influence Government policy more directly. But there is the same kind of fallacy as in the trade union argument. By forming their own party, and associating it with the Labour party, they inevitably tend to lose the sympathy of other parties. They would really be in a stronger position to influence Government policy by keeping free of all party affiliations. This is widely realized among Co-operators, a very large number of whom vote Conservative or Liberal in their private capacities. The existence of the Co-operative party is disapproved by many Co-operators, and the close association with the Labour party is even more widely disapproved. From time to time this association has been very embarrassing as the Co-operative movement broadly represents the consuming interest and the Labour movement the producing interest, and the two often clash. There was, as we have noticed, no little friction over the introduction of the purchase tax, and Co-operators also dislike the ideas of municipal and State trading. The decision of the big Huddersfield Co-operative Society in November 1951 to disaffiliate from the Co-operative party may be a sign of the times.[1]

If the above notes suggest that the Labour party and its associates are more likely to experience disruption than the Conservative, this

[1] See above, p. 171.

should not be dismissed as wishful thinking on the part of the author. It is in the nature of parties on the left to be fissiparous and parties on the right—to use terms that are convenient though not strictly applicable to British politics—to remain united. For those who wish in general to conserve the existing state of affairs find ready points of agreement but those who wish to innovate can innovate in a score of different ways, and the likelihood of disagreement increases. This has been the experience of conserving and innovating parties in all countries at all times. The general principle is complicated only by the fact that in a changing world it is often necessary for a party to change in order to remain the same.

THE COMMUNIST PARTY

The future of the Communist party will be mainly dependent on that of the Labour party. If the Labour party maintains its integrity, it is unlikely that the Communist party will meet with any more success than it has done in the past thirty years. But if the Labour party should split up into right and left wings, this will give the Communist party the opportunity for which it has waited so many weary years. The Labour party is by no means homogeneous in outlook. It is really a coalition of 'socialists' and 'Labourites'. But the knowledge that the Communist party is waiting round the corner will probably keep the coalition in existence for a long time. The Labour party is

> *Like one that on a lonesome road*
> *Doth walk in fear and dread . . .*
> *Because he knows a frightful fiend*
> *Doth close behind him tread.*

But if the Communist party really wishes to become a major force in the land, it would be well advised to drop the Stalinist and adopt the Titoist form of communism. Nothing has done it more harm than the belief—the well-founded belief—that it is the puppet of a foreign power. One thing that unites all British subjects in the major parties is love of their country.

THE NATIONALIST PARTIES

It is love of country that has given rise to the nationalist parties that have sprung up in Wales and Scotland; but in their case it is love of the part rather than of the whole. What is to be their future? Most of us regard their patriotism as genuine but particularist and misguided. We do not think we are any the worse Welshmen ar Scotsmen for being good Britons. On the contrary, we who are Welsh or Scottish think we serve Wales or Scotland best by maintaining the integrity of the United Kingdom. The dissolution of that unity would not be to the advantage of Wales or Scotland. It would mean an immediate and severe financial loss—for there can be little doubt that Wales and Scotland receive far more from the revenues of the United Kingdom than they contribute—and it would deny to Welshmen and Scotsmen openings that they have filled with personal distinction and to the general advantage. There is every reason to develop to the fullest extent the independent cultural life of Wales and Scotland, but a political separation from England would be folly. As this is generally realized in Wales and Scotland, it is unlikely that the nationalist parties will get much support; and the great majority of those in the principality and north of the border who seek to advance Welsh and Scottish interests will prefer to do so through one or other of the great United Kingdom parties.

Epilogue

For long after the party system had taken firm root in England, the very idea of party was regarded with horror by many public-spirited people. Pope put the common feeling into one of his unforgettable couplets—

> *The names of party I detest*
> *Badges of slavery at best.*

It was commonly supposed that a man seeking to advance the interests of his party could not at the same time be pursuing the good of his country. Macaulay's lines at a later date—

> *Then none was for a party;*
> *Then all were for the state—*

—expressed the antithesis that was usually felt. Parties were generally termed factions; and Halifax was not alone in thinking that they were conspiracies against the general public. Even after the precedent in the reign of William and Mary for selecting the ministry from the dominant party—which we now regard as one of the great constitutional advances in the history of Great Britain—Queen Anne wrote with abhorrence of the idea of party and prayed that she might never be delivered into the hands of any one set of men.[1] According to Cobbett, similar sentiments were uttered in a parliamentary speech by Lord Shelburne on 10 July 1782.[2]

---

[1] 'Besides, I must own freely to you, I am of the opinion, that making a party man secretary of state, when there are so many of their friends in employment of all kinds already, is throwing myself into the hands of a party, which is a thing I have been desirous to avoid. . . . All I desire is, my liberty in encouraging and employing all those that concur faithfully in my service, whether they are called Whigs or Tories, not to be tied to one, nor the other; for if I should be so unfortunate as to fall into the hands of either, I shall not imagine myself, though I have the name of Queen, to be in reality but their slave, which as it will be my personal ruin, so it will be the destroying of all government; for instead of putting an end to faction, it will lay a lasting foundation for it. . . . Why, for God's sake, must I, who have no interest, no end, no thought, but for the good of my country, be made so miserable, as to be brought into the power of one set of men?' (Queen Anne to Godolphin, quoted in W. C. Costin and J. Steven Watson, *The Law and Working of the Constitution: Documents 1660–1914*, vol. i, pp. 359–60.)

[2] 'And it would have been very singular, indeed, if he should have given up to them all those constitutional ideas, which for seventeen years he had imbibed from his master in politics, the late earl of Chatham; that noble earl had always declared,

It appears to have been Burke who first gave a justification of party in the closing pages of his *Thoughts on the Cause of the Present Discontents*, published in 1770, nearly a hundred years after the party system had been working in practice. For him a party was 'a body of men united, for promoting by their joint endeavours the national interest, upon some particular principle in which they are all agreed'; and provided we bear in mind that political principles are not immutable but must be adapted to changing circumstances, the definition will serve.[1] The reasoning by which he justified the development of parties may still be read with equal pleasure and profit to-day.

'Where men are not acquainted with each other's principles, nor experienced in each other's talents, nor at all practised in their mutual habitudes and dispositions by joint efforts in business; no personal confidence, no friendship, no common interest, subsisting among them; it is evidently impossible that they can act a public part with uniformity, perseverance or efficacy. In a connexion, the most inconsiderable man, by adding to the weight of the whole, has his value and his use; out of it, the greatest talents are wholly unserviceable to the public. No man, who is not influenced by vain glory into enthusiasm, can flatter himself that his single, unsupported, desultory, unsystematic endeavours are of power to defeat the subtle designs and united cabals of ambitious citizens. When bad men combine, the good must associate; else they will fall, one by one, an unpitied sacrifice in a contemptible struggle'.

---

that this country ought not be governed by any party or faction; that if it was so governed, the constitution must necessarily expire . . . their Lordships might recollect a particular expression that he had used some time ago, when speaking of party, he declared that he would never consent that the "King of England should be a king of the Mahrattas", among whom it was a custom for a certain number of great lords to elect a peshaw, who was the creature of an aristocracy, and was vested with the plenitude of power, while the king was, in fact, nothing more than a royal pageant or puppet. These being his principles, it was natural for him to stand up for the Crown, and insist upon the King's right to appoint his own servants.' (Cobbett's *Parliamentary History*, vol. xxiii, p. 192, quoted by Costin and Watson, vol. i, pp. 240–41.) A year later, however, on 6 March 1783 as related by the same authority, Fox put the argument that has ever since been accepted: 'It had been argued again and again, that the King had a right to choose his own ministers. In that particular, he rested on the spirit of the constitution and not on the letter of it; and grounding his opinion on the spirit of the constitution, he ever had, and ever would maintain, that his Majesty, in this choice of ministers, ought not to be influenced by his personal favour alone, but by the public voice, by the sense of his Parliament, and the sense of his people. An administration in whom the House did not place confidence, was such an administration as it was unsafe to lodge the government of this country in at their crisis. It was no argument to say, "I am a minister, because his Majesty has made me one."' (Cobbett's, *Parliamentary History*, vol. xxiii, p. 596, quoted by Costin and Watson, vol. i, p. 241.)

[1] The definition is criticized on this ground by Mr. John Plamenatz in *Parliamentary Affairs*, vol. v, no. 1, winter 1951, p. 213.

It was by such reasoning that Burke justified 'connexions in politics', which he regarded as 'essentially necessary for the full performance of our public duty, accidentally liable to degenerate into faction'. Madison writing a little later in distant America,[1] held to the older view that parties were factions, and for him faction was a 'number of citizens . . . united and actuated by some common impulse of action, or of interest, adverse to the rights of other citizens, or to the permanent and aggregate interests of the community'. Faction, or party, was therefore evil, but it was a necessary evil. It was the price paid for free discussion. His remedy was to have many parties in order that none might gain decisive control.

The debate has gone on until the present day, and is not likely to be closed, for the party system is itself continually changing; and a man writing on the subject at the present time can only offer his own contribution towards it without any expectation of finality.

The system described in the above pages may seem an elaborate and precarious method of determining the set of men who shall govern a country and the principles on which they shall rule. No doubt simpler and more expeditious forms of government have existed, but in a country that encourages free discussion some kind of party system is bound to emerge. For parties are an inevitable consequence of the fact that men form different judgements about the manner in which any given problem should be resolved. Men who take similar views of a problem naturally tend to associate with each other, recognizing that they have far more likelihood of achieving their aim if they work together than if they work separately. 'Party', said Disraeli in the briefest and best definition yet offered, 'is organized opinion'. When men find themselves acting together on repeated occasions, a party is born.

The growth of parties is therefore inevitable and natural. It is out of strife, said an ancient Greek, that truth is born; and the strife of parties does much to make representative government a reality and to convert what would otherwise be a Babel of voices into an instrument of action. 'I believe', said Disraeli again, 'that without party parliamentary government is impossible.' The party system sustains the interest of the country in personalities and policies. It ensures that the issues are placed before the electors and before the legislature in clear and concrete form. It guarantees that men who speak for a considerable body of opinion receive the attention that their following deserves. It enables the executive, by being drawn from the same party, to be col-

[1] In *The Federalist Papers*, no. 10.

lectively responsible for policy, and it ensures that if the executive should fail or weary there is always a fresh body of men ready to carry on the government. It causes the administrative actions of the executive to be brought under a searching scrutiny. It establishes that measures are carefully prepared before they are published and minutely examined before they become law.

These are great merits and should not lightly be cast aside even though the party system, like all human arrangements, has the defects of its qualities. In order that men may act together 'in a connexion' at all, parties are often forced to compromise and to rely on makeshifts and expedients. Individual judgement must frequently be subordinated to the requirements of party. The strife of parties leads men to criticize for the sake of criticizing and to see only partial aspects of truth.

Each successive enlargement of the electorate has brought new problems and exposed the party system to new dangers. The simplicity of the original alignment of parties in Parliament has given way to an elaborate network of organizations covering the whole country. The processes of democracy have necessarily become slower and more cumbrous. The individual can do little except as a member of a hierarchy of time-consuming committees, and original contributions get lost in a maze of resolutions and reports. The professional politician becomes a necessity and men 'think in battalions'.

It has seemed to some observers that in the process the parties have ceased to be instruments of democracy and have become devices whereby an oligarchy exercises power in the name of the hypnotized masses.[1] That this may happen cannot be denied, but it really rests upon a misconception of the nature of democracy. Only in the smallest communities does democracy mean that the people exercise power directly. As the bounds of the state become enlarged, democracy comes to mean government with the consent of the governed. Democracy, the rule of the *people*, must be distinguished from *laocracy*, the rule of the *multitude*, and *ochlocracy*, the rule of the *mob*. The *people* is a concept presupposing a certain degree of political organization, and in a modern state the party system provides that organization. The party system should be looked upon as a device for ensuring that government is with the consent of the governed. The people may not be able to say without

[1] This is the conclusion of Ostrogorski, writing in 1902, and the theme of Michels, writing in 1915. Circumstances have, of course, greatly changed since they wrote, and the danger to-day is not that the few may manipulate the many, but that the many should push the few into courses against their better judgement. 'I am their leader, I must follow them', said the French revolutionary as he saw from his window the crowds rushing down the street; that is the danger to-day.

guidance what persons they want to see as governors and what policies they wish to see adopted, but when they are presented with a choice of persons and policies, backed with the material necessary to form a judgement, they can say, 'I want these men' or 'I desire these measures.' Though at any given moment it may appear that one or a few men control a party, in fact they can exercise their control only by consent; and if that consent is taken away to any marked degree their authority disappears.

The rise of parties is therefore both inevitable and good in itself, and the organization of parties has enabled the voice of the people to find expression in an indirect manner even in the large states of the modern world. But the party system has its defects even at its best; and when it is misused or abused great evils can flow. When individuals or 'interests' gain control of a party and use it for their own ends, the purposes for which parties came into existence are frustrated. Opinion is manufactured, decisions are manipulated, intrigue takes the place of argument, the 'wirepuller' becomes more important than the statesman, and the power of the purse prevails over the counsels of the wise.

It would be idle to deny that these things have happened and may happen again, but if we would judge the party system aright we must judge it at its best, or at any rate as it is intended to be; and if we take a broad view of history we cannot doubt that the party system as it has developed in Great Britain since 1679 has been to the advantage of the country. Let us consider for a moment what happens when the party system is abandoned.

A common way in the modern world of bringing party strife to an end is to prohibit all parties except one, or at any rate to make the life of other parties impossible. But in the process the party that survives ceases to be a party in any real sense of the word. A one-party state is a contradiction in terms. Parties are parts, and there cannot be fewer than two parts to a whole. What is called 'the party' in such a state may have some of the appearance and organization of a democratic party, but it cannot be a party in any true sense for there is no other party against which it can be set. 'The party' in such a state is, in fact, only an instrument of autocratic or oligarchic rule.

We have never in this country had experience of one-party rule since the time of Cromwell, but there have been several periods in which the normal operation of the party system has been suspended during coalitions of parties; and to some extent the same criticism can be made against coalitions as against the one-party system. In our long history there have been times when coalitions have been necessary, but this is only to say that there have been times when it has been necessary to subordinate the normal processes of democracy to the requirements of national existence. In a coalition the outward form of the parties is preserved, but the spirit is lost, for the spirit is engendered only in their strife with each other. 'England does not love coalitions,' said Disraeli, and the instinct is sound. It was perhaps fortunate that the original coalition between Fox and North in 1783 was so conspicuously devoid of principle as to make Englishmen ever afterwards require the case for coalition to be proved beyond a doubt before they would accept it. Party strife was maintained throughout the Napoleonic wars, and in the first world war it was only when military disaster seemed likely in 1916 that a coalition was formed.[1] It was a war necessity, but the manner in which Asquith was displaced in the formation of the second coalition left a nasty taste in many people's mouths; and the continuance of the coalition for four years after the end of the fighting was accompanied by such a lowering of the tone of British public life that the Conservative decision to bring the coalition to an end in 1922 was greeted with relief. England had found even less reason to love coalitions, and when a world war again descended on the nation in 1939 there was a marked unwillingness to create a coalition until military events made it imperative. The coalition then created under Mr. Churchill's leadership was honourably formed and served the country well. But it was created for the sole purpose of winning the war, and divergences of view began to appear as soon as the problems of peace came under discussion. Perhaps it was as well that this great coalition was dissolved with its memory untarnished on the morrow of the European victory, and the settlement of our domestic problems left to the tried and ancient arbitrament of party conflict.

[1] Lloyd George had attempted in 1910 to secure, not exactly a coalition, but a party truce, and it has often been argued that the bitterness of the party strife in Great Britain was one of the reasons that led the Kaiser to think he could neglect this country in his calculations. The reason why Lloyd George failed throws an interesting light on the working of the party system, though the power of individuals behind the scenes is less great to-day than it was then. The proposals found some favour with Balfour and other Conservative leaders in Parliament, but Balfour said there was one other man he felt he would have to consult, and thought Lloyd George would be surprised when he heard the name. This was the case, for the name was that of Akers-Douglas, who had been the chief Conservative whip but had gone to the House of Lords as Lord Chilston and had ceased to play any public part in political life. The sequel is thus told by Lloyd George: 'Mr. Akers-Douglas, however, turned down the project for co-operation in settling these momentous national issues, and there was an end to it. It very nearly came off. It was not rejected by the real leaders of the party, but by men who, for some obscure reason best known to political organizations, have great influence inside the councils of a party without possessing any of the capabilities that excite general admiration and confidence outside.' (*War Memoirs of David Lloyd George*, vol. i, p. 23.)

The period of national government from 1931 onwards was not a period of coalition in any usual sense of the word. If Ramsay Mac-Donald had been right in his expectation that at least half the Labour party would have followed him, a form of government approaching a coalition would have emerged. As it was, only a small section of the Labour party followed his lead, and after the general election his tenure of office rested upon a large Conservative majority in the House of Commons. It would not be accurate to describe the next few years as a period of Conservative rule, for although Conservatives provided the bulk of the Government's support in Parliament their policy was limited by their obligations to MacDonald as Prime Minister and even after his retirement by the presence of other elements in the Government's majority. Nevertheless it was a period of predominantly Conservative rule, and this points to another way in which the normal operation of the party system in Great Britain has been from time to time partly suspended.

Though we have not in modern times had experience of a one-party system, there have been several periods in our history when the parliamentary triumph of one party has been so complete that in the House of Commons there has been virtually only one party, able to carry any measure that it pleased. Such triumphs may be sweet at the time, but they bring their retribution in future. They tend to make the dominant party too self-confident and too ready to ride rough-shod over the rights of minorities. Such great majorities have been returned to the House of Commons by the general elections of 1832, 1906, 1931 and 1945, and the danger has grown greater with the removal of one check after another on the power of a majority in the House of Commons to do as it pleases. From 1832 to 1835 the fact that members still accepted an individual responsibility for speaking and voting, and that the Irish members would follow their own course, acted as a check on the Whig leaders. From 1906 to 1910 the Liberals in the House of Commons were always conscious that any extreme measures they might propose would come under the veto of the House of Lords. From 1931 to 1935 the Conservative majority in the House of Commons were restrained by the knowledge that they were only the predominant partners in an alliance, whose political head was for several years drawn from another party. From 1945 to 1950 the Labour majority in the House of Commons were limited in their power to do as they pleased only by a power of delay in the House of Lords, which they proceeded to reduce still further. Though anxiety was felt at the time on account of the overloading of the parliamentary machine and the use of timetables and the guillotine to limit discussion, in retrospect we may concede that the powers of the majority were not as misused as they might have been; but the quotation from *Alice in Wonderland*, 'We are the masters now', made by Sir Hartley Shawcross in moving the repeal of the Trade Unions and Trade Disputes Act in 1946, though no doubt intended only as an oratorical embellishment, brought home the dangers that can arise when a party's triumph over its rivals is too complete. So eminent a Conservative statesman as Mr. L. S. Amery has acknowledged that the Conservative triumph in 1935 was not good for the party. Disraeli rightly made one of his characters in *Coningsby* declare 'No Government can be long secure without a formidable Opposition'; and we can lay it down as a general rule that the party system will function effectively only if the dominant party's majority over its rivals is not so large as to produce *hybris*.

But we can also lay it down as a general rule that the party system will function effectively only if the majority party has a sufficient lead over its rivals to provide a strong government and to carry the measures which in the judgement of ministers are required by the state of the country. If the Labour party's majority from 1945 to 1950 was too swollen, its majority from 1950 to 1951 of five over all others was too small for effective government, nor can the Conservative majority of seventeen from 1951 onwards be regarded as adequate. The constant attendance of ministers in the House of Commons required by such small majorities is harmful to their own health and the work of their departments, and often leads them to propose, not what they regard as in the best interests of the country, but what will least offend the Opposition. There will be no agreement on what constitutes the minimum majority needed for good government—my own estimate would be forty—but it will be generally conceded that among the best governments in British history were Peel's Conservative administration formed in 1841 and Gladstone's Liberal administration formed in 1868, and their respective majorities were seventy-nine and one hundred.

As a result of the slender majorities produced by the general elections of 1950 and 1951 a new threat to the effective working of the party system became manifest. This is the tendency of the opposition party to adopt as its policy the undoing of measures carried into law at the instance of the Government of the day. If this became common, it would reduce politics to a game of battledore and shuttlecock, and eventually to chaos. The effective working of the party system hitherto has depended upon the acquiescence, maybe reluctant, of one party in measures carried by the other. In pursuance of this instinct the Conservatives accepted the Reform Act of 1832 and made no attempt to undo it when they returned to power a few years later. The Conservatives in 1846 accepted the repeal of the Corn Laws; and when this was followed by other measures of a similar character virtually bringing about free trade the Conservatives throughout the whole of the century made no attempt to reverse the trend. Once the Parliament Act of 1911 was on the statute book the Conservatives, despite all the vehemence with which they opposed it, never made it part of their programme to repeal it.

The first major break in this tradition occurred in 1927, when the Labour party vowed that at the first opportunity it would repeal the Trade Disputes and Trade Union Act passed in that year. The opportunity did not come until nearly twenty years later, when by a one-clause measure, the Trade Disputes and Trade Unions Act, 1946, the offending enactment was removed from the statute book. In their general election manifesto of 1950 the Conservatives pledged themselves, if returned to power, to repeal the nationalization of iron and steel, as provided for in the Iron and Steel Act, 1949, before that act could come into force; to sell back to free enterprise those sections of the road haulage industry which had been nationalized; to restore as wide a measure as possible to free enterprise in civil aviation; and to give greater local autonomy to regional boards for the coal and railway industries. The resulting Parliament showed that the parties were almost equally strong, and the Conservative proposals were repeated in the general election of 1951. The Conservatives then came into power with a small majority, and proceeded to carry out the measures to which they had pledged themselves. Thereupon the Labour party, fortified by the knowledge that opinion in the country was running in their favour, threatened to renationalize any industries that were denationalized by the Conservatives. It began to be widely felt in the country that great industries could not function successfully if they were liable to be radically changed after every general election. The limit was generally felt to have been reached on 8 May 1952, when Mr. Herbert Morrison, a few hours after the Government's transport policy had been made known, indicated that it would be reversed by the next Labour Government. Thereafter a more restrained mood seemed to develop, for it had become quite clear that a great industrial country could not permit its economy to be made a plaything of party in this way.

The two-party system may occasionally lead to slender majorities, but where there are many parties seeking the suffrages of electors it is unlikely that any of them will ever gain a majority over all others. This fragmentation of parties is another way in which the effectiveness of the party system can be impaired or destroyed. In a multi-party or group system, instead of policy being settled by the open clash of parties it is determined by back-stairs agreements, and ministries are formed without any real community of belief between their members.

We have seen that the British people tend always to revert to a two-party alignment, and that this two-party alignment is in part the product of our electoral arrangements, and in part the result of conscious preference—a preference fostered by the historical accident that our parties used to sit either on the *decani* or on the *cantoris* side of the site of an ancient chapel. This is a system that is hard on the lesser parties, but it normally gives us well-defined and well-organized bodies of opinion, clear issues in debate, strong government in the present and an alternative government for the future.

The two-party system as it has evolved in the Anglo-Saxon countries is probably the best machinery of representative government that has yet been devised. It has obvious superiorities over the one-party system in some countries and the many-party system in others. But it is not automatic in its working.

We have seen in the above pages that even now there are some grounds for anxiety about trends in the British party system. There is cause for anxiety lest the growth of party machines should lead to the suppression of individual judgement; lest the ablest individuals should shrink from entering politics through fear of becoming only a cog in a machine; lest policy should come to be determined at mass meetings on inadequate information and in an atmosphere prejudicial to sound judgement. The party system is continually evolving, and we need to be constantly watching how it adjusts itself to changing circumstances. At the present time its weakest points are perhaps the selection of candidates and the place of the party conference in determining policy.

But at all times the successful working of the British party system has in the last resort depended on the characters and personalities of those engaged in it. It has worked because those who were engaged in it wanted it to work and were determined that it should work.

This fact, which is really the great glory of the British party system, was made the basis of a curious attack upon it in 1911 by Mr. Hilaire Belloc and Cecil Chesterton. Mr. Belloc had been a Liberal member of Parliament from 1906 to 1910, and the chief impression left on his mind was that of a collusion between the two front benches, from which even

Mr. Speaker was not exempt. In *The Party System* these two authors in a series of brilliant paradoxes put forth the view that the party strife was an elaborate sham and that the members of the two front benches, united in many cases by the ties of blood and marriage, were at one in their determination to keep in existence the same type of society, a type of society from which they both benefited.

It is a curious judgement, for in retrospect we can see that party strife in 1911 was more real and more bitter than perhaps it ever has been; and whatever may be thought about the opposition of Liberals and Conservatives in 1911, it will hardly be contended that the division between Conservatives and Labour to-day is an 'organized imposture'. The truth would appear to be that Mr. Belloc, for all his great gifts in other directions, was temperamentally unfitted to be 'a Parliament man'. He has always been an individualist, and he did not take kindly to the system under which the time of the House of Commons is mainly allocated to organized bodies of opinion. Owing to this temperamental disqualification, and to changed circumstances since he and Cecil Chesterton wrote, it might not be worth recalling their views if it were not that the facts on which they relied, when properly understood, are the main reason why the party system works.

Parties, as we have said earlier, are parts, and parts have no meaning except in relation to the whole. In the case of parties the whole is the country, whose interests they each serve in their several ways. It is the duty of the majority party to provide the Government and of the minority party to provide the Opposition, but each has its constitutional function to perform. It is the duty of the Government to govern and the duty of the Opposition to oppose, and out of the resulting clash of views it is most likely that the right policy will emerge. But the Government must not ignore the Opposition, nor the Opposition forget the heavy load of responsibility that lies on those to whom the Queen has entrusted the executive administration. Policy is determined, not solely by the Government of the day, but by the inter-play of Government and Opposition; and a Government must have regard, not only to the men who sit on the other side of the clerk's table, but to the millions in the country for whom they speak.

If ministers form 'Her Majesty's Government', those who oppose them are equally 'Her Majesty's Opposition', a term first used in jest, it is believed, by John Cam Hobhouse before the enactment of the Reform Bill, but expressing a great constitutional truth recognized since 1937 by the provision of a salary out of the public funds for the leader of the Opposition.

An understanding of this fact removes one of the objections often made against the party system, namely, that it results in a great waste of talent that might be employed for the public good. There is, indeed, no system yet devised that has succeeded in employing all the talent available for the service of the state, and where the competition for public honours is so keen and the places of service so limited in number it is inevitable that much talent must be unemployed or under-employed. But the party system, whereby an unwanted minister goes into opposition, is a more kindly method of dealing with this problem of superfluous talent than was the Greek method of ostracism, or the medieval method of banishment; just as ostracism or banishment is in its turn a kindlier solution than assassination which has been the favourite method of dealing with this problem in some countries from earliest days until the present. But the defence of the party system does not rest solely on this negative virtue. It does not rest even on the fact that in opposition members may be recovering from the physical and mental strain of office, thinking out their position anew, and preparing to be the ministers of the future. The real defence is that in the British party system the Opposition has a vital part to play in the working of the constitution and that the front Opposition bench plays a part in the shaping of policy and legislation second only to that of the Treasury bench.

This is the justification for the fact that neither side in the two-party system is usually wholly right in its presentation of the facts. Each side has usually a partial apprehension of the truth, and out of the clash of parties something like the truth emerges. The two-party system is well illustrated by the story of the Irish railway station with two clocks. A waiting passenger pointed out to the stationmaster that the two clocks kept different times. 'And what', said the stationmaster, 'would be the use of two clocks that kept the same time?'

It has often been the case that parties in British history have carried measures that might rather have been expected to come from their opponents. In 1845 Peel was said by Disraeli to have 'caught the Whigs bathing, and walked away with their clothes'; and the theft, if theft it be, has been repeated so often that we have come to expect 'right-wing' measures from 'left-wing' governments and 'left-wing' measures from 'right-wing' governments.

In part this is due to the fact that when ministers take office they often find the facts to be different from what they had supposed them to be when in opposition. This was Peel's dilemma in 1845; and Gladstone was not the only minister to regret things that he had said at a time of 'greater freedom and less responsibility'. When in office ministers have always at hand civil servants to put the country's interests before them without consideration of party; and in considering how the British party system works we must not omit this silent, constant influence of the civil service. By injunction and usually by inclination the higher civil servant carefully refrains from publicly identifying himself with any of the political parties. He may be a member of a political party and may subscribe to its funds. But he may not make a party speech in public, nor may he stand as a candidate for Parliament without resigning from the civil service, and thereby giving up not only his establishment in the service but his pension rights. Rigid adherence to these rules has enabled the civil service to build up a tradition of disinterested advice to ministers that corrects their more exuberant inclinations. It is typified by the civil servant who is related, perhaps apocryphally, to have said to his minister, 'Well, sir, if you are bound to do a deuced silly thing, must you do it in a deuced silly way?' and to have proceeded to advise him how best to carry out a policy of which he cordially disapproved.

The disinterested advice of the civil service is therefore a powerful influence in keeping British policy stable despite the changes in the party complexion of governments. But in the last resort the British party system depends for its successful working on the realization by those engaged in it that parties are only instruments to serve a higher end.

This has led to the acknowledgement that there are some aspects of public policy which should not be brought into the arena of party strife. Our party divisions have arisen in the main over domestic differences, and successive generations of British statesmen have endeavoured to keep foreign and imperial policy out of the party conflict. It is, indeed, difficult to see how it is possible to have a foreign or imperial policy at all unless it is one which foreign countries and our partners in the Commonwealth know will survive the fall of ministers in the United Kingdom. There is no understanding on these matters between the parties, and occasionally differences arise between them on party lines, especially with regard to the conduct of foreign affairs; but on the whole there has been a striking absence of party recrimination in these fields.

From time to time voices have urged that great domestic issues should also be kept out of the arena of party strife. 'Take poverty out of politics' and 'take housing out of politics' have in their turn been favourite cries in some quarters. The nation has been wise in turning a deaf ear to these blandishments. Our domestic matters are our own concern, and we need not be restrained by the thought that other governments will be perplexed if British policy changes from election to election; and these domestic matters such as poverty and housing are matters on which the electors have ample evidence in their own experience and are well capable of reaching an informed judgement. The reasons why it is desirable to keep foreign and imperial policy out of the party conflict are precisely the reasons why domestic issues should be settled by a clash of parties. They will be settled better in that way than by any other.

But they will be settled best in that way, not only because the clash of parties causes the issues to be better presented than in any other, but because the human beings operating the system are public-spirited men who know its limitations and are usually prepared to compromise rather than drive a party advantage home. In the House of Commons they see each other nightly, not only across the floor of the House, but in the more intimate social intercourse that takes place in a hundred nooks and crannies outside the chamber. They get to know and to respect each other, and most of them find themselves forced to concede that there is good in the opponents and that no party has a monopoly of wisdom and good faith. Back in the chamber or in the committee room they will fight the party battle keenly, but always with a consciousness that it is subservient to the welfare of the whole country.

This is not a mentality that can be prefabricated or exported, nor is it easy to explain to one who does not understand it already. The British party system works successfully because those who take part in it have been nurtured in a tradition of 'fair play', a concept which is so distinctively Anglo-Saxon that the words are usually left untranslated in other languages. Though it has become fashionable in some quarters to scoff at organized games, we can hardly exaggerate the influence of the games our children play in youth in moulding their characters for adult life. To most of those who have made the British party system work it has become second nature to play in a team and for a team, to subordinate their individual actions to the common purpose, to pass the ball so that someone better placed may score, to strive with all their might for victory, but not to mind overmuch if victory goes the other way so long as the game is good and clean. The battle of Waterloo may not have been won on the playing fields of Eton; but the battles of Westminster have been rehearsed on a thousand village greens.[1]

---

[1] Other nations often recognize the influence of games upon our national life more easily than we do ourselves. I am reminded of a translator for the League of Nations who told me that only once had he failed to give a rendering into French of any English speech. This occurred when a British delegate observed, with regard to some proposal, 'That's not cricket,' and an Australian added, 'No, it's body-line bowling.'

The British party system cannot be understood simply as a piece of elaborate machinery skilfully devised to ensure government by the consent of the governed. The spirit in which it is worked is of far greater importance than the machinery. This spirit cannot be expressed in written constitutions and rules of procedure. It can be studied only by a close acquaintance with those who are themselves engaged in the party struggle. It may often be witnessed on the floor of the House of Commons by the discerning visitor; but it is seen at its best in a room in the Palace of Westminster where no outsider may ever tread. The committees and councils of the British party system may be imitated with exactness, but unless the spirit that pervades the smoking room of the House of Commons can also be reproduced a vital element will be lacking.

Select Bibliography

General

[TOLAND, J.], *The Art of Governing by Parties*. London: Bernard Lintott, 1701. viii+182 pp.

BURKE, EDMUND. *Thoughts on the Cause of the Present Discontents*. First published 1770. Republished in vol. i, pp. 1–92, of *Burke Select Works*, edited with introduction and notes by E. J. Payne. Oxford: Clarendon Press. Third edition, 1897. 3 vols.

MADISON, JAMES. *The Federalist Papers*, No. 10. First published 1787.

YOUNG, Sir FREDERICK. *Exit Party: An Essay on the Rise and Fall of 'Party' as the Ruling Factor in the Formation of the Governments of Great Britain*. London: Chapman and Hall. 1900. viii+76.

OSTROGORSKI, M. *Democracy and the Organization of Political Parties*. Translated from the French by Frederick Clarke. With a preface by James (later *Lord*) Bryce. London: Macmillan. 1902. 2 vols. (Vol. i, lviii+628 pp., deals with British parties; vol. ii, xliv+794 pp., with American.)

LOWELL, ABBOTT LAWRENCE. *The Influence of Party upon Legislation in England and America*. (Annual report of the American Historical Association for the year 1901). Washington. 1902. 319 pp.

LOWELL, ABBOTT LAWRENCE. *The Government of England*. New York: Macmillan Company. First published 1908. New edition, with additional chapter, 1912. 2 vols. Vol i, xviii+584 pp. Vol. ii, x+564 pp. (Part ii deals with 'The Party System', vol. i, pp. 449–584 and vol. ii, pp. 1–128.)

BELLOC, HILAIRE and CHESTERTON, CECIL. *The Party System*. London: Swift. 1911. 226 pp.

MICHELS, ROBERT. *Political Parties: A Sociological Study of the Oligarchical Tendencies of Modern Democracy*. Translated from the Italian by Eden and Cedar Paul. London: Jarrolds. 1915. xiv+426 pp.

FARBMAN, MICHAEL. *Political Britain: Parties, Policies and Politicians*. London: Europa Publications. 1929. 193 pp.

CAMBRAY, PHILIP GEORGE. The Game of Politics: *A Study of the Principles of British Political Strategy*. London: Murray. 1932. 194 pp.

PIKE, EDGAR ROYSTON. *Political Parties and Policies: A popular explanation of the tenets of the chief political parties and a guide to the*

311

understanding of current politics. London: Pitman. First published 1934. Third edition, 1950. 102 pp.

SAMUEL, HERBERT (*Viscount* Samuel). *The Party System and National Interests.* London: Hansard Society. 1946. 20 pp.

SCHATTSCHNEIDER, E. E. *Party Government.* New York: Farrar and Rinehart. 1942. xvi+220 pp.

DUVERGER, MAURICE. *Les partis politiques.* Paris: Librairie Armand Colin. 1951.

CAMPION, *Lord* (Editor). *Parliament: A Survey.* London: Allen and Unwin. 1952. 296 pp. Chap. viii, 'The British Party System', by Ivor Thomas.

BAILEY, SYDNEY D. (Editor). *The British Party System.* London: Hansard Society. 1952. xii+214 pp.

COSTIN, W. C. and WATSON, J. STEVEN. *The Law and Working of the Constitution: Documents 1660–1914.* London: Black. 1952. 2 vols. Vol. i, 1660–1783, xviii+456 pp. Vol. ii, 1784–1914. xx+532 pp.

Dod's Parliamentary Companion. London: Business Dictionaries Ltd. First published 1832. Published annually.

Whitaker's Almanack. London. 13 Bedford Square, W.C.1. First published 1869. Published annually.

The Constitutional Year Book. London: Harrison and Sons. First published 1885. Published annually until 1939.

Part 1.—Growth of the Parties

General

COOKE, GEORGE WINGROVE. *The History of Party from the Rise of the Whig and Tory Factions in the Reign of Charles II to the Reform Bill.* London: Macrone. 1836–37. 3 vols. Vol. i, 1666–1714, xii+612 pp. Vol. ii, 1719–1762, viii+498 pp. Vol. iii, 1762–1832, viii+628 pp.

ALINGTON, CYRIL ARGENTINE. *Twenty years: Being a Study in the Development of the Party System between 1815–35.* Oxford University Press, 1921. 208 pp.

See also Ostrogorski, M., in 'General' section above. References to developments in the party system will be found in the standard works of history and in the political biographies, autobiographies and memoirs. A list of political biographies is given on pp. 15 and 16 of *Parliament: A Reader's Guide* (published by the Cambridge University Press for the National Book League).

Conservative

KEBBEL, THOMAS EDWARD. *History of Toryism, 1783–1881: From Pitt to Beaconsfield.* London: W. H. Allen. 1885.

KENT, C. B. ROYLANCE. *The Early History of the Tories.* London: Smith Elder. 1908.

WOODS, MAURICE C. *A History of the Tory Party in the Seventeenth and Eighteenth Centuries, with a sketch of its Development in the Nineteenth Century.* London: Hodder and Stoughton. 1924. xii + 460 pp.

FEILING, KEITH GRAHAME. *A History of the Tory Party, 1640–1714.* Oxford: Clarendon Press. 1924. 526 pp.

HAYTER, L. H. *An Outline of the History of the Conservative Party.* Taunton: Phoenix Press. 1925.

ELLIOT, WALTER. *Toryism and the Twentieth Century.* With an introduction by the Rt. Hon. Stanley Baldwin. London: Philip Allan. 1927. xii + 136 pp.

HEARNSHAW, FOSSEY JOHN COBB. *Conservatism in England: An Analytical, Historical and Political Survey.* London: Macmillan. 1933. xii + 322 pp.

FEILING, KEITH GRAHAME. *The Second Tory Party, 1714–1832.* London: Macmillan. First published 1938. Reprinted 1951. vii + 452 pp.

BIRCH, NIGEL. *The Conservative Party.* With 4 plates in colour and 21 illustrations in black and white. London: Collins. 1949. 50 pp. (*Britain in Pictures*).

Liberal

FYFE, HAMILTON. *The British Liberal Party: An Historical Sketch* London: Allen and Unwin. 1928. 272 pp.

SLESSER, *Sir* HENRY. *A History of the Liberal Party.* London: Hutchinson. 1944. 172 pp.

CRUIKSHANK, ROBERT JAMES. *The Liberal Party.* With 4 plates in colour and 19 illustrations in black and white. London: Collins. 50 pp.

Irish National

O'DONNELL, F. H. *A History of the Irish Parliamentary Party.* With portraits and other illustrations. London: Longmans. 1910. 2 vols. Vol. i, xiv + 508 pp. Vol. ii, x + 494 pp.

Radicalism

MACCOBY, S. *English Radicalism, 1832-1852.* London: Allen and Unwin. 1935. 462 pp.

Labour

WEBB, SIDNEY, and WEBB, BEATRICE (later *Lord* and *Lady* Passfield). *History of Trade Unionism.* London: Longmans. First published 1894. Revised edition extended to 1920, 1920. xvi+784 pp.

HOBHOUSE, LEONARD TRELAWNEY. *The Labour Movement.* London: Fisher Unwin. First published 1893. Third edition revised, 1912. 160 pp.

HUMPHREY, A. W. *A History of Labour Representation.* London: Constable. 1912. xvi+199 pp.

PEASE, EDWARD R. *The History of the Fabian Society.* London: Fabian Society. First published 1916. Second edition with a supplementary chapter and 13 illustrations, 1925. 306 pp.

TAWNEY, RICHARD HENRY. *The British Labor Movement.* New Haven: Yale University Press. 1925. 190 pp.

TRACEY, HERBERT (*Editor*). *The Book of the Labour Party: Its History, Growth, Policy and Leaders.* London: Caxton. 1925. 3 vols. Illustrated. Vol. i, xiv+280 pp. Vol. ii, viii+344 pp. Vol. iii, viii+354 pp.

HEARNSHAW, FOSSEY JOHN COBB. *Survey of Socialism: Analytical, Historical and Critical.* London: Macmillan. 1935. 485 pp.

COLE, GEORGE DOUGLAS HOWARD. *British Working-Class Politics, 1832-1914.* Routledge. London: 1941. 320 pp.

TRACEY, HERBERT (*Editor*). *The British Labour Party: its History, Growth, Policy and Leaders.* London: Caxton. 1948. 3 vols. Illustrated. Vol. i, x+248 pp. Vol. ii, viii+302 pp. Vol. iii, x+348 pp.

BEER, MAX. *A History of British Socialism.* London: Allen and Unwin. First published 1919. One volume edition with a new chapter, 1940, reprinted 1949. 452 pp.

COLE, GEORGE DOUGLAS HOWARD, and POSTGATE, RAYMOND WILLIAM. *The Common People, 1746-1946.* London: Methuen. First published 1938. Fourth edition 1949. 752 pp.

COLE, GEORGE DOUGLAS HOWARD. *A History of the Labour Party from 1914.* London: Routledge and Kegan Paul. 1948. viii+516 pp.

COLE, MARGARET. *Makers of the Labour Movement.* With 19 illustrations. London: Longmans. 1948. xv+319 pp.

HALL, WILLIAM GLENVIL. *The Labour Party.* With 4 plates in colour and 22 illustrations in black and white. London: Collins. 1949. 50 pp. (*Britain in Pictures.*)

WILLIAMS, FRANCIS. *Fifty Years' March: The Rise of the Labour Party.* London: Odhams. 1950. xvi+384 pp.

COLE, GEORGE DOUGLAS HOWARD, and FILSON, A. W. *British Working Class Movements: Select Documents. 1789–1875.* London: Macmillan. 1951. xxii+630 pp.

Co-operative

WEBB, BEATRICE (later *Lady* Passfield). *The Co-operative Movement in Great Britain.* London: 1891.

COLE, GEORGE DOUGLAS HOWARD. *A Century of Co-operation.* Manchester: Co-operative Union. 1946. iv+428 pp.

Communist

GOLLAN, JOHN. *Thirty Years of Struggle: the Record of the British Communist Party.* London: Communist Party. 28 pp.

Welsh Nationalist

EVANS, GWYNFOR. *Plaid Cymru and Wales.* Llandebie, Carms: Silurian Books. Undated (?1950). 74 pp.

WADE, A. W., EVANS and others. *Seilian Honesyddol Cenedlaetholdeb Cymru* ('Historical Bases of Welsh Nationalism'). Cardiff: Plaid Cymru. 1950. 144 pp.

Scottish National

GIBSON, T. H. *The Scottish National Party: What it is and what it stands for.* An address by the President of the Scottish National Party. Glasgow: National Headquarters of the Scottish National Party. 1951. 12 pp.

Election Guides

General Election 1950: The Campaign Guide, London: Conservative Central Office. First published 1949. Third impression 1950. 724 pp.

General Election 1950: The Campaign Guide Supplement. London: Conservative Central Office. 1950. 102 pp.

The Campaign Guide 1951: An Encyclopaedia of Politics. London: Conservative Central Office. 1951. 420 pp.

General Election 1951: The Campaign Guide Supplement. London: Conservative Central Office, 1951. 192 pp.

Part II.—The Two-Party System

General

TREVELYAN, GEORGE MACAULAY. *The Two-Party System in English Political History.* Oxford University Press. 1926. 28 pp. Reprinted in *An Autobiography and other Essays,* pp. 183–199. London: Longmans. 1949. 238 pp.

The General Elections of 1945, 1950 and 1951

The Times House of Commons 1945. With a map. London: *The Times Office.* 1945. 170 pp.

The Times House of Commons 1950. With a map and portraits of members. London: *The Times Office.* 1950. 320 pp.

The Times House of Commons 1951. With a map and portraits of members. London: *The Times Office.* 1951. 256 pp.

McCALLUM, RONALD BUCHANAN, and READMAN, ALISON. *The British General Election of 1945.* Oxford University Press. 1947. xvi+312 pp.

NICHOLAS, HERBERT G. *The British General Election of 1950.* With an appendix by D. E. Butler. London: Macmillan. 1951. x+354 pp.

BUTLER, D. E. *The British General Election of 1951.* London: Macmillan. 1952. viii+290 pp. 3 plates.

Demand for Electoral Reform

Report of the Royal Commission on Systems of Election. London: H.M. Stationery Office. 1910. Cmd. 5163. iv+64 pp.

DANIELS, S. R. *The Case for Electoral Reform.* London: 1938.

ROSS, JAMES FREDERICK STANLEY. *Parliamentary Representation.* London: Eyre and Spottiswoode. First published 1943. Second enlarged edition 1948. vi+344 pp.

DUVERGER, MAURICE. *L'Influence des systèmes électoraux sur la vie politique.*

See also the publications of the Proportional Representation Society.

Part III.—Party Organization

Conservative

Interim and Final Reports of the Committee on Party Organization (the Maxwell Fyfe Committee), 1948 and 1949. London: National Union of Conservative and Unionist Associations. 1949. 72 pp.

Organization Series. London: Conservative and Unionist Central Office.

No. 1. *The Party Organization.* 20 pp.
No. 2. *Duties of Officers.* 24 pp.
No. 3. *Model Rules.* 24 pp.
No. 4. *Procedure at Business Meetings.* 16 pp.
No. 5. *The Young Conservative and Unionist Organization.* 24 pp.
No. 6. *Constituency Finance.* 16 pp.
No. 7. *Electoral Registration.* 28 pp.
No. 8. *Organization of Indoor and Outdoor Meetings.* 30 pp.
No. 9. *The Voluntary Worker and the Party Organization.* 36 pp.
No. 10. *Local Government and the Party Organization.* 16 pp.
No. 11. *The Young Britons Organization.* 24 pp.

The Rules of the National Union of Conservative and Unionist Associations. Adopted at the annual meeting of the Central Council, 13 March 1947 and amended 17 March and 15 July 1949. London: Party Headquarters. 12 pp.

Annual Conference of the National Union of Conservative and Unionist Associations. *Verbatim report of the proceedings.* London: National Union of Conservative and Unionist Associations. Published annually.

The East of Scotland Year Book. Edinburgh: Eastern Divisional Council of the Scottish Unionist Association. Published annually.

Liberal

The Constitution of the Liberal Party. Adopted by the Liberal Party Convention June 1936 and amended in 1937, 1945, 1946, 1947, 1948 and 1949. London: Liberal Party Organization. 18 pp.

Report of the Liberal Party Organization to the Assembly. Published annually.

Specimen Constitution and Rules for a Parliamentary Borough Liberal Association. London: Liberal Publications Department. 4 pp.

Labour

CROFT, HAROLD. *Party Organization.* London: Labour Party Head Office. Ninth edition. 1950. 56 pp.

Constitution and Rules for Constituency Labour Parties in Single and Undivided Boroughs. Set A. London: Labour Party Head Office. 32 pp.

Constitution and Rules for Constituency Labour Parties and Local Labour Parties in County Constituencies. Sets B and C. London: Labour Party Head Office. 40 pp.

Constitution and Rules for Central Labour Parties and Constituency Labour Parties in Divided Boroughs. Sets D and E. London: Labour Party Head Office. 44 pp.

Constitution and Rules for Trades and Labour Councils with Industrial and Political Purposes in Undivided Boroughs. Set F. London: Labour Party Head Office. 40 pp.

Labour Groups on Local Authorities. A memorandum with appended Model Standing Orders. (Memorandum based on one approved by the annual conference, 1936; Standing Orders based on the model approved by the annual conference, 1930.) London: Labour Party Head Office. 4 pp.

Report of the Annual Conference of the Labour Party. London: Labour Party Head Office. Published annually. (Includes the constitutions of the Labour Party and the National Council of Labour, and the standing orders of the Parliamentary Labour Party.)

HAMILTON, MARY AGNES. *The Labour Party Today: What it is and How it Works.* London: Labour Book Service. 1939. 95 pp.

ATTLEE, C. R. *The Labour Party in Perspective—and Twelve Years Later.* Being *The Labour Party in Perspective* first published in 1937 and now re-issued with a new short foreword by the Prime Minister and a new long introductory chapter by Francis Williams, showing how the policy outlined in 1937 is being faithfully put into practice. London: Gollancz. 1949. 200 pp.

Co-operative

WEBB, SIDNEY, and WEBB, BEATRICE (later *Lord* and *Lady* Passfield). *The Consumers' Co-operative Movement.* London: Longmans. First published 1921. New impression 1930. xii+504 pp.

Constitution of the Co-operative Party: as approved by the annual Co-operative Union Congress 1951. London: Co-operative Party. Manchester: Co-operative Union Ltd. 16 pp.

The Co-operative Party: Comments upon the New Constitution. London:
Co-operative Party. Manchester: Co-operative Union Ltd. 1951.
12 pp.

*Report of the National Committee of the Co-operative Party to the
Annual Conference.* London: Co-operative Party. Manchester:
Co-operative Union Ltd. Published annually.

Proceedings of the Co-operative Party Annual Conference. London:
Co-operative Party. Manchester: Co-operative Union Ltd. Published annually.

Communist

Rules of the Communist Party. As revised at the 22nd National Congress 1952. London: Communist Party. 8 pp.

*Report of the Executive Committee to the National Congress of the
Communist Party.* London: Communist Party. Published before
each Congress.

Report of the National Congress of the Communist Party. London:
Communist Party. Published after each congress under various
titles.

*Resolutions and Proceedings of the National Congress of the Communist
Party.* London: Communist Party. Published after each congress.

Welsh Nationalist

Constitution and Standing Orders of the Welsh Nationalist Party. Cardiff
and Carnarvon: Gwyddfa Plaid Cymru. 8 pp.

Welsh Republican

Welsh Republican Manifesto. Reproduced in *The Welsh Republic*, by
C. Bere. Cardiff: Welsh Republican Movement. 8 pp.

Scottish Nationalist

Constitution and Rules of the Scottish Nationalist Party. Glasgow:
National Headquarters of the Scottish Nationalist Party. 16 pp.

Part IV.—The Fringe of Parties

Ancillary Organizations and Non-party Political Organizations

Many of the bodies mentioned in the text publish an annual report,
together with other literature.

Parties and the Press

JONES, KENNEDY. *Fleet Street and Downing Street.* London: Hutchinson. 1920. x+364 pp.

WILLIAMS, FRANCIS. *Press, Parliament and People.* London: Heinemann. 1946. 254 pp.

CAMROSE, Lord. *British Newspapers and their Controllers.* London: Cassell. First published 1947. Revised edition 1948. x+178 pp.

Report of the Royal Commission on the Press 1947–1949. Cmd. 7700 London: H.M. Stationery Office. 1950. vi+364 pp.

The Newspaper Press Directory. First published 1852. London: Benn. Published annually.

Willing's Press Guide. First published 1875. London: Willing's Press Service. Published annually.

Further information may be found in the memoirs, reminiscences and biographies of journalists.

Parties and Religion

This subject does not appear to be dealt with in books specifically devoted to the topic, but the background may be sought in such works as the following, and in the ecclesiastical biographies:

TAWNEY, RICHARD HENRY. *Religion and the Rise of Capitalism: A Historical Study* (Holland Memorial Lectures, 1922). With a prefatory note by Dr. Charles Gore. London: John Murray. 1926. xiv+340 pp.

WEARMONTH, ROBERT F. *Methodism and the Working-class Movements of England 1800–1850.* London: Epworth Press. 1937. 290 pp.

WEARMONTH, ROBERT F. *Methodism and the Common People of the Eighteenth Century.* London: Epworth Press. 1945. 276 pp.

DEMANT, VIGO AUGUSTE. *Religion and the Decline of Capitalism* (Holland Lectures, 1949). London: Faber. 1952. 204 pp.

Part V.—Some Current Problems

HOLLIS, CHRISTOPHER. *Can Parliament Survive?* London: Hollis and Carter. 1949. 148 pp.

NICOLSON, HAROLD. *The Independent Member of Parliament.* London: Hansard Society. 1946. 20 pp.

Conservative

CECIL, Lord HUGH (now Lord Quickswood). *Conservatism*. Oxford University Press. First published 1912 and frequently reprinted. 254 pp. (*Home University Library*.)

BRYANT, ARTHUR. *The Spirit of Conservatism*. Ashbridge: Bonar Law College. 1929. 175 pp.

FEILING, KEITH GRAHAME. *What is Conservatism?* London: Faber. 1930. 36 pp.

COOK, E. THOMAS. (*Editor*) *Conservatism and the Future*. London: Heinemann. 1935. 319 pp.

NORTHAM, REGINALD. *Conservatism: The Only Way*. London: Gifford. 1939. xii+276 pp.

AMERY, LEOPOLD STENNETT. *Framework of the Future*. Oxford University Press. 1944. vii+159 pp.

HOGG, QUINTIN (now Lord Hailsham). *The Case for Conservatism*. Harmondsworth: Penguin Books. 1948. 320 pp.

BRAINE, BERNARD. *Tory Democracy*. London: Falcon Press. 1948. 144 pp. (*Forum Series*.)

WALKER SMITH, DEREK. *Coming This Way?* London: Sampson Low. 1948. 142 pp.

BERRY, MICHAEL. *Party Choice: The Real Issue between the Parties*. London: Eyre and Spottiswoode. 1948. 120 pp.

BOYD-CARPENTER, JOHN. *The Conservative Case: Choice for Britain*. London: Wingate. 1950. 64 pp.

Liberal

HOBHOUSE, LEONARD TRELAWNY. *Liberalism*. Oxford University Press. First published 1911 and frequently reprinted. 254 pp. (*Home University Library*.)

BEVERIDGE, Sir WILLIAM HENRY (now Lord Beveridge). *Why I am a Liberal*. London: Jenkins. 1945. 115 pp.

DODDS, GEORGE ELLIOTT. *Let's Try Liberalism*. London: Liberal Publications Department. 1945. 128 pp.

FOOT, ISAAC. *Liberty and the Liberal Heritage*. London: Gollancz. 1948. 34 pp. (*Ramsay Muir Memorial Lecture*, 1947.)

McFADYEAN, Sir ANDREW. *The Liberal Case*. London: Wingate. 1950. 64 pp. (*Choice for Britain series*.)

M

Labour

SHAW, GEORGE BERNARD, and others. *Fabian Essays in Socialism.* First published in 1889 and frequently reprinted. Jubilee edition, 1948. With a postscript by the original editor, Bernard Shaw, 'Sixty Years of Fabianism'. xliv+246 pp.

MACDONALD, J. RAMSAY. *The Socialist Movement.* Oxford University Press. First published 1911 and frequently reprinted. viii+256 pp. (*Home University Library.*)

CATLIN, G. E. C. (*Editor*). With a preface by the Rt. Hon. Arthur Henderson. *New Trends in Socialism.* London: Lovat Dickson. 1935. xiv+294 pp.

DALTON, HUGH. *Practical Socialism for Britain.* London: Routledge. 1937. ix+401 pp.

DURBIN, EVAN FRANK MOTTRAM. *The Politics of Democratic Socialism: An Essay on Social Policy.* London: Routledge. 1940. 384 pp.

MORRISON, HERBERT, and others. *Forward from Victory.* London. Gollancz. 1946. 88 pp.

JAY, DOUGLAS PATRICK THOMAS. *The Socialist Case.* London: Faber. First published 1937. Revised edition with a foreword by the Rt. Hon. Clement Attlee. 1947. xx+298 pp.

MUNRO, DONALD (*Editor*). *Socialism: The British Way.* By Evan F. M. Durbin and others. With a foreword by the Rt. Hon. Herbert Morrison. 1948. 346 pp.

PARKER, JOHN. *Labour Marches On.* Harmondsworth: Penguin Books. 1948. 220 pp.

Trade Unions and Politics

Report of the Annual Conference of the Trades Union Congress. London: Trades Union Congress. Published annually.

BAROU, NOAH. *British Trade Unions.* London. Gollancz. First published 1947. Third edition, 1949. xvi+272 pp.

CITRINE, Sir WALTER (now Lord Citrine). *British Trade Unions.* London: Collins. 1942. 48 pp. (*Britain in Pictures.*)

PEP (Political and Economic Planning). *British Trade Unionism.* Six studies. London: PEP. First published 1948. Second edition 1949. 184 pp.

TURNER-SAMUELS, M. *British Trade Unions.* London: Sampson Low. 1949. xii+212 pp. (*Living in Britain* series.)

LASKI, HAROLD JOSEPH. *Trade Unions in the New Society.* London: Allen and Unwin. 1950. x+182 pp.

Communism

LASKI, HAROLD JOSEPH. *Communism*. Oxford University Press. First published 1927 and frequently reprinted. 256 pp. (*Home University Library*.)

BURNS, EMILE. *What is Marxism?* London: Gollancz. 1943. 68 pp.

LENIN, V. I. *Selected Works*. Moscow. Foreign Languages. Publishing House. 1946. 2 vols. Vol. i, 758 pp. Vol. ii, 856 pp.

STALIN, JOSEPH. *Problems of Leninism* (including *The Foundations of Leninism, On the Problems of Leninism*, and other writings). Moscow: Foreign Languages Publishing House. 1947. 642 pp.

PLAMENATZ, JOHN. *What is Communism?* London: National News Letter. 1947. 120 pp.

GALLACHER, WILLIAM. *The Case for Communism*. Harmondsworth: Penguin Books. 1949. 208 pp.

HUNT, ROBERT NIGEL CAREW. *The Theory and Practice of Communism*. London: Bles. 1950. viii+232 pp.

MARX, KARL, and ENGELS, FREDERICK. *Selected Works*. Moscow: Foreign Languages Publishing House. London: Lawrence and Wishart. 1951. 2 vols.

Welsh Nationalism

Can Wales Afford Self-Government? Cardiff: Plaid Cymru. First published 1939. Revised edition 1947. 108 pp.

Welsh Republicanism

BERE, C. *The Welsh Republic*. Cardiff: Welsh Republican Movement. 8 pp.

Scottish Nationalism

Policy of the Scottish National Party. A statement of the Aim and Policy of the Scottish National Party. Reprinted from *The Scots Independent*, January 1947. 16 pp.

Scottish Self-Government. A statement of policy. Edinburgh: Scottish Liberal Party. 12 pp.

Index

Agents, 144–5, 152, 180–1
Aims for Industry, 229
Asquith, Herbert Henry (later Earl of Oxford and Asquith), 44, 47
Asquithian Liberals, 45, 46, 47, 48
Attlee, Rt Hon C. R., 95, 118, 128, 191–6

Bartlett, Vernon, 85
Belloc, Hilaire, 305–6
Birmingham, 19, 20, 21, 25, 35
British Empire League, 229
Broadcasting, parties and, 243–5
Brown, W. J., 85
Burke, Edmund, 15, 297
Burt, Thomas, 39

Carlton Club, 18, 47, 214
Caucus, Birmingham, 25
Central Office, Conservative, 23–24, 26, 149
Chamberlain, Sir Austen, 47
Chamberlain, Joseph, 20, 21, 25, 26, 36, 37, 71
Chamberlain, Neville, 115, 117
Chartist Movement, 223
Chesterton, Cecil, 305–6
Churchill, Lord Randolph, 22, 23, 35, 57
Churchill, Rt Hon Winston S., 10, 35, 95, 97, 117, 118, 191–6, 210
Clubs, party, 18, 213–14
Common Wealth, origins, 71; electoral fortunes, 72, 86–7
Communist International, 52
Communist Party of Great Britain origins, 52–3; relations with Labour Party, 53–4, 66–7, 165, 294; electoral fortunes, 67–8; local organization, 140–1; regional organization, 154; national organization, 172–3; party finance, 179–80; international affiliations, 183; party newspaper, 238

Conferences, party, 156–7, 166–7, 172, 173
Conservative and Unionist Party, origins, 8–9; first use of nmae Conservative, 9–10; use of name Constitutional, 9–10; Sir Robert Peel's influence on organization, 13–17; first headquarters at Carlton Club, 18; first representative constituency association (Liverpool), 18–19; National Union, 21–23, 155–6; Central Office, 23–4, 157–8; opposition to Liberals in Victorian era, 29; rise of 'Fourth Party', 34–5; alliance of Liberal Unionists, 36–7; success in 1918 General Election, 45–6; Carlton Club meeting and decision to end coalition, 47; success in 1924 general election, 48; defeat in 1929 general election, 48; attitude in 1931 crisis, 61–2; differences between 1931 and 1939 conducted within framework of party organization, 80; fortunes in 1950 general election, 83; fortunes in 1951 general election, 89; effects of system of voting on party fortunes, 95; leadership of party, 115–16, 116–18, 189–90; Conservative Members' Committee, 119–20; parliamentary committees, 129–30; constituency organization, 133–4, 134–6; central associations in divided boroughs, 147–8; area organization, 148–9; national organization, 155–8; Scottish Unionist Association, 159; party finances, 176–8; certification of agents, 180; relation of party officials to political chiefs, 180–181; no oversea affiliations, 186–7; position of whips, 23,

325

Conservative and Unionist Party, *cont'd*—
190–1; selection of candidates, 204–6, 207; Conservative clubs, 213–14, 216–17; Conservative speakers' clubs, 218; other ancillary organizations, 218–19; Conservative newspapers, 233, 235, 239, 240, 241; attitude to individuals, 270–1; attitude to parties in local government, 276, 280; analysis of typical Conservative voters, 288–9; analysis of Conservative members, 289–90; prospects, 292; attitude to trade unions, 292–3; to Co-operative movement, 293.

Constitution, parties and the, 3
Co-operative Party, origins, 50; electoral fortunes, 54, 64–5; relations with Labour Party, 50, 54, 64–6, 293; adopts written constitution, 64–5; parliamentary organization, 132; constituency organization, 139–40; regional organization, 153–4; national organization, 170–2; annual conference, 171–2; party finances, 179; relations with Co-operative Union Ltd., 170 186; prospects, 293
Co-operative Union Ltd., 170, 181–2, 186
Craven-Ellis, W., 85

Daily Herald, 237–8
Daily Telegraph and Morning Post, The, 235–6
Davies, Rt Hon Clement, 69
Devonshire, Georgiana Spencer, Duchess of, 28
Devonshire, Spencer Compton, 8th Duke of (formerly the Marquess of Hartington), 36–7
Disraeli, Benjamin (later Earl of Beaconsfield), 17, 22, 24, 25, 298, 303, 307
Electoral reform, 92–105

Empire Industries Association, 229
Exclusion Bill (1679), 7

Fabian Society, 40, 50, 201, 219
Feiling, Dr Keith Grahame, 7, 8, 313
Finances, party, 174–80
Fourth Party, 34–5

George V, His Majesty King, 59–60
Gilbert, W. S., 29
Gladstone, Herbert (later Viscount Gladstone), 43
Gladstone, William Ewart, 13, 26, 31, 33, 34, 214
Gorst, Sir John E., 23
Granville, Edgar, 93, 94

Hardie, James Keir, 38
Harris, William, 19–20
Headquarters, party, 17–18, 157–158, 161, 169
Henderson, Arthur, 53, 61

Independent Labour Party, origins, 38; helps to found Labour Representation Committee, 40; relations with Labour Party, 49–50, 54–6, 63–4; fortunes in 1950 and 1951 general elections, 88–9; objection to standing orders of parliamentary Labour Party, 126; organization in country, 174
Independents in Parliament, 84–5, 266–9
Irish Nationalists, 29–31

Jews, 164, 251, 255

King-Hall, Cmdr S., 85

Labour Independents, 85–6
Labour Party, origins, 38–43; adoption of name, 43; progress until first world war, 43, 44; split in first world war, 44; new

Labour Party *cont'd*—
constitution, 46; relations with
I.L.P., 49–50, 63–4; with Co-
operative Movement, 50, 64–6,
181–3; with Communist Party,
52–4, 66–8; with Common
Wealth, 71–2; attitude to
socialism, 49–51, 287; fall of
second Labour Government,
58–61; parliamentary party
leadership, 118; parliamentary
party meeting, 119, 120–3, 124–
125; parliamentary party standing orders, 125–9; parliamentary party groups, 130–1; constituency organization, 133,
136–39, 143; youth organizations, 146, 152; central Labour
parties in divided boroughs,
147; county federations, 150-1,
153; regional organization, 151–
153; national organization,
161–3; total membership, 163;
affiliated membership, 163–6;
party conference, 166–7;
national executive committee,
167–9; party headquarters
(Transport House), 169–70;
finance, 174–5; oversea affiliations, 184–5; proscribed organ-
isations, 219; relations with
trade unions, 163–4, 230, 285–7;
attitude to individuals, 260–2,
264, 270; attitude to parties
in local government, 275–6,
277–8; analysis of Labour
voters, 288–9; analysis of
Labour members, 290
Labour peers, 116, 119
Labour Representation Committee, 41, 42, 43
Labour Representation League,
39
League of Nations Union, 226–7
Liberal Association, 18
Liberal Assembly, 160
Liberal International, 186
Liberal Registration Association,
18

Liberal Party, origins, 7; first use
of name, 9–11; effect of rise of
Labour Party, 42–6; eclipse,
47–8; secession of Liberal
Nationals, 57–8; attitude in
1931 crisis, 68–71; cause of
recent defeats, 90–1; electoral
fortunes, 94–7; support for electoral reform, 93, 94; Liberals in
Parliament, 131; constituency
organization, 134, 136; regional
organization, 148, 150; national
organization, 159–61; party
finance, 178; international links,
186; Liberal conference (Assembly) and policy, 199; selection of
candidates, 206; Liberal clubs
and ancillary organizations, 18,
214–16, 218; attitude to individuals, 270; prospects, 283–4;
analysis of typical Liberal voters,
284–5; analysis of Liberal candidates, 291
Liberal Party Organization, 27
Liberal Unionists, 36–7; name
revived, 70–1
'Lib-Labs', 39
Liverpool, 18
Lloyd George, David (later Earl
Lloyd-George), 43, 45, 51, 58,
61, 62
Lloyd-George, the Rt Hon Major
Gwilym, 62, 69, 93
Lloyd-George, Lady Megan, 62
Local Government, parties in,
274–82

MacDonald, Alexander, 39
MacDonald, Malcolm, 68
MacDonald, Ramsay, 41, 48,
68
Maxwell Fyfe Report, 157, 178
Mosley, Sir Oswald, 57, 62, 63,
66
National Council of Labour, 120 *n*,
181–3
National Labour Party, origins,
60, 62; electoral fortunes, 68
National Liberal Federation, 24–7

National Union of Conservative and Unionist Associations, 21–24, 155–6
National Liberal Party (formerly Liberal National Party), origins, 57–8; relations with Liberal Party, 68–71; adoption of present name, 69; electoral fortunes, 69–71; relations with Conservative Party, 70–1; parliamentary organization, 70–1; regional organization, 150
National Liberals (Lloyd George Liberals), 69
New Party, 57, 62, 63
News Chronicle, 237, 284, 285, 288
Newspaper, parties and, 231–46
Nicolson, Sir Harold, 59 *n*, 68, 117 *n*

Owen, Robert, 41

Patronage Secretary, 111
Peel, Sir Robert, 13–14, 15–16, 61, 307
Peelites, 33–4, 38
Pierssené, Sir S. H., 158
Popular Front, 67
Primrose League, 35, 218
Pritt, D. N., 85–6
Proportional Representation, 94, 100–5
Proscribed organizations (Labour Party), 218
Public Opinion polls, 284, 288–9

Reform Act (1832), 9, 12, 13, 223
Reform Act (1867), 19, 21
Registration associations (societies), 13
Representation of the People Acts, 3, 223 *n*
Radicals, 31–3
Roman Catholics, 31, 73, 222, 250–1
Royal Arsenal Co-operative Society, 59 *n*, 174

Samuel, Sir Herbert (later Viscount Samuel), 58, 59 and *n*, 60, 69
Schnadhorst, Francis, 20, 21, 24
Scottish Convention, 78
Scottish Nationalist Party, 76–8, 79, 294
Scottish Unionist Association, 159
Simon, Viscount (formerly Sir John), 57, 58, 69
Sinn Fein, 86, 87
Social Credit Party, 86, 87, 186
Social Democratic Federation, 40, 49
Social Democratic Party, 49
Standing Orders of Parliamentary Labour Party, 125–9
The Times, 253, 262–3
Tory Party, origins of, 7–8; rebirth, 8; revived use of name, 10. See also Conservative and Unionist Party
Trade Disputes and Trade Unions Act (1927), 175
Trades Union Congress, 39, 230
Trade unions and parties, 230
Two-party system, 83–4, 91, 92–8, 105

Ulster Unionist Party, 86, 155
Unionists, Unionist Party; see Conservative and Unionist Party, Liberal Unionists.
United Front, 67

Welsh Liberal Party (Liberal Party of Wales), 150
Welsh Nationalist Party, 72–6, 141–2, 154, 180
Welsh Republican Movement, 74–75
Whigs, 7–10
Whips, 23, 24, 109–14
Wolff, Sir Henry Drummond, 34
Women's organization, 28, 145–6
Woolton, Lord, 178
Woolton-Teviot Agreement, 70